Exploring Kenotic Christology

The Self-Emptying of God

EDITED *by* C. STEPHEN EVANS

REGENT COLLEGE PUBLISHING
Vancouver, British Columbia

This edition published 2010 with special permission by

Regent College Publishing
5800 University Boulevard
Vancouver, BC V6T 2E4 Canada
Web: www.regentpublishing.com
E-mail: info@regentpublishing.com

Views expressed in works published by Regent College Publishing are those of the
author and do not necessarily represent the official position of Regent College.

Library and Archives Canada Cataloguing in Publication

Exploring kenotic Christology : the self-emptying of God /
edited by C. Stephen Evans.

Includes bibliographical references and index.

ISBN 978-1-57383-444-5

1. Jesus Christ—Person and offices. I. Evans, C. Stephen

BT203.E97 2010   232'.8   C2009-904595-8

Acknowledgements

This project was made possible by a generous grant from the Calvin Center for Christian Scholarship at Calvin College, which brought the authors together for a symposium to think through and discuss these issues. All of the authors are grateful to the Center, its director, James Bratt, and capable staff, Donna Romanowski and Amy Bergsma, for their help.

I am personally grateful to all of the authors for making time in their busy schedules to work on this kind of interdisciplinary project. It has been a privilege to work with such an outstanding group of biblical scholars, theologians, and philosophers.

I also would like to thank my graduate assistant at Baylor University, Jay Bruce, for preparing the Bibliography, and Donna Praesel, the Administrative Assistant for the Baylor Philosophy Department, for her vital expertise and help in getting this work ready for the publisher. I am also indebted to James Bouwmeester for preparing the index.

C. Stephen Evans
Baylor University

Contents

Notes on Contributors

Sarah Coakley (Ph.D. in Theology, Cambridge University) taught at Lancaster and Oxford universities before coming to Harvard Divinity School in 1993. She became the Mallinckrodt Professor in 1995. A systematic theologian and philosopher of religion, she also teaches topics in feminist theory and theology, patristic thought, and applied theology. Her most recent books are *Powers and Submissions: Spirituality, Philosophy and Gender* (2002) and *Re-Thinking Gregory of Nyssa* (ed.) (2003). She is currently completing a co-edited volume, *Pain and Its Transformations: The Interface of Biology and Culture* (Harvard University Press, forthcoming), a product of her work in the interdisciplinary 'Mind, Brain, Behavior' group at Harvard; and she is at work on a four-volume systematic theology, the first volume of which will appear as *God, Sexuality and the Self: An Essay 'On the Trinity'* (Cambridge University Press, forthcoming). Previous works include *Christ Without Absolutes: A Study of the Christology of Ernst Troeltsch*, and an edited volume on comparative religion, *Religion and the Body*. She is a recent recipient, with Professor Martin Nowak of Harvard, of a major Templeton Foundation award to study the relation of evolutionary biology and theology.

Stephen T. Davis (M.Div., Princeton Theological Seminary; Ph.D., Claremont Graduate University) is the Russell K. Pitzer Professor of Philosophy at Claremont McKenna College. He is the author or editor of some fourteen books, including *Risen Indeed* (Eerdmans, 1993), *God, Reason, and Theistic Proofs* (Edinburgh University Press, 2000), *Encountering Evil* (Westminister John Knox Press, 2001), and *Christian Philosophical Theology* (Oxford University Press, 2006). Davis is the co-editor of three volumes from Oxford University Press: *The Resurrection*, *The Trinity*, and *The Incarnation*, and has published widely in both the philosophy of religion and Christian theology.

Edwin Chr. van Driel has degrees in theology and philosophy from Utrecht University (the Netherlands) and Yale University. He is currently a doctoral candidate in Yale's Religious Studies Department.

His dissertation project concerns 'supralapsarian Christology', the notion that the Incarnation is not contingent upon sin. Van Driel is also a fellow of the Episcopal Church Foundation.

C. Stephen Evans (Ph.D. in philosophy, Yale University) is currently University Professor of Philosophy and Humanities at Baylor University. His writings include sixteen books, among which are *Kierkegaard's Ethic of Love: Divine Commands and Moral Obligations* (Oxford: Oxford University Press, 2004), *Faith Beyond Reason* (Edinburgh: Edinburgh University Press, 1998), *The Historical Christ and the Jesus of Faith: The Incarnational Narrative as History* (Oxford: Oxford University Press, 1996), and *Passionate Reason: Making Sense of Kierkegaard's* Philosophical Fragments (Bloomington, Indiana: Indiana University Press, 1992). More popular works include *Why Believe?* (Eerdmans) and *Pocket Dictionary of Philosophy of Religion and Apologetics* (Inter-Varsity Press). Evans has published many professional articles and has received two Fellowships from the National Endowment for the Humanities and a major grant from the Pew Charitable Trusts. Prior to coming to Baylor, Evans taught at Wheaton College, St. Olaf College, where he served as Curator of the Howard and Edna Hong Kierkegaard Library as well as a member of the Philosophy Department, and at Calvin College, where, besides teaching philosophy, he served as Dean for Research and Scholarship and was the inaugural holder of the William Spoelhof Teacher-Scholar Chair. He is a past president of the Society of Christian Philosophers and the Søren Kierkegaard Society.

Gordon D. Fee (Ph.D. in New Testament studies, the University of Southern California) is currently Professor Emeritus of New Testament Studies at Regent College, Vancouver, B.C., Canada, having taught at Regent for sixteen years before his recent retirement. Before joining the faculty at Regent he held New Testament posts at Southern California College (now Vanguard University), Wheaton College, and Gordon-Conwell Theological Seminary. He is a member of the TNIV translation committee and is currently editor of the New International Commentary (New Testament) series (Eerdmans). He has also given stated lectures at many colleges and seminaries. Besides scores of articles in his field of specialization (NT textual criticism, exegesis, and theology), his writings include *The First Epistle to the Corinthians*, NICNT (Grand Rapids: Eerdmans); *New Testament*

Exegesis: A Handbook for Students and Pastors, 3rd edn. (Louisville: Westminster John Knox, 2002); *God's Empowering Presence: The Holy Spirit in the Letters of Paul* (Peabody: Hendrickson, 1994); *Paul's Letter to the Philippians*, NICNT (Grand Rapids: Eerdmans, 1995); *To What End Exegesis? Studies Textual, Exegetical and Theological* (Grand Rapids: Eerdmans, 2001). He is also an ordained minister with the Assemblies of God (USA).

Ronald J. Feenstra (Ph.D. in Religious Studies at Yale University) is Heritage Professor of Systematic and Philosophical Theology and Director of Doctoral Studies at Calvin Theological Seminary, where he has taught since 1992. After writing a dissertation on kenotic Christology, he taught for eight years in the Department of Theology at Marquette University in Milwaukee, Wisconsin. With Cornelius Plantinga, Jr., he edited *Trinity, Incarnation, and Atonement: Philosophical and Theological Essays* (Notre Dame: University of Notre Dame Press, 1989). He has published articles in *Modern Theology, Logos: Philosophic Issues in Christian Perspective, Calvin Theological Journal, The Reformed Journal*, and the *Routledge Encyclopedia of Philosophy*, as well as in several collections of essays.

Bruce N. Fisk (Ph.D. in New Testament, Duke University) is currently Associate Professor of New Testament at Westmont College in Santa Barbara, California, where he has taught since 1999. Fisk's revised dissertation, done under the supervision of Richard B. Hays, is now published with Sheffield Academic Press under the title *Do You Not Remember? Scripture, Story and Exegesis in the Rewritten Bible of Pseudo-Philo*. He has also contributed a guide to *First Corinthians* for the Interpretation Bible Studies series published by Geneva Press. His articles have appeared in *New Testament Studies, Catholic Biblical Quarterly, Journal for the Study of the Pseudepigrapha, Trinity Journal* and in several edited collections and encyclopedias. His primary research interest concerns the composition and interpretive conventions of narrative in the Graeco-Roman world. He is currently working on a student's guide to historical Jesus studies.

Ruth Groenhout (Ph.D. in philosophy, Notre Dame) is currently Professor of Philosophy at Calvin College. She previously taught at Southwest Missouri University and Spaulding University. She has recently published *Connected Lives: Human Nature and an Ethic of Care* (Rowman and Littlefield), *Transforming Care: A Christian*

Vision of Nursing Practice, co-authored with Mary Molewyk Doornboss and Kendra Hotz, and *Philosophy, Feminism, Faith*, co-edited with Marya Bower (Indiana University Press). Her research interests and recent journal articles include an analysis of Reformed thinking in bioethics, an ethics of care and the new genetic technologies, and how gender structures accounts of the love of God.

Edward T. Oakes, S.J. (Ph.D. in Systematic Theology, Union Theological Seminary) is Chester & Margaret Paluch Professor of Theology at the University of St. Mary of the Lake in Mundelein, Illinois. He entered the Society of Jesus (Jesuit Order) in 1966 and was ordained a priest in 1979. He is the author of *Pattern of Redemption: The Theology of Hans Urs von Balthasar*, 2nd edn. (Continuum, 1997), editor of *German Essays on Religion* (Continuum, 1995), and, with David Moss, the co-editor of *The Cambridge Companion to Hans Urs von Balthasar* (Cambridge, 2004). His translations of Balthasar's works include *The Theology of Karl Barth: Exposition and Interpretation* (Ignatius Press, 1992) and *Explorations in Theology, Volume IV: Spirit and Institution* (Ignatius Press, 1995). Oakes writes frequently for *First Things*, and has appeared in such periodicals as *The Journal of Religion*.

Cornelius Plantinga, Jr. (Ph.D., Princeton Theological Seminary) is the President of Calvin Theological Seminary. Prior to this he served as Dean of the Chapel at Calvin College. His other books include *Not the Way It's Supposed to Be: A Breviary of Sin* and *Engaging God's World: A Christian Vision of Faith, Learning and Living*, both published by Wm. B. Eerdmans. He is also the co-editor (with Ronald Feenstra) of *Trinity, Incarnation, and Atonement: Philosophical and Theological Essays* (University of Notre Dame Press, 1989).

Thomas R. Thompson (Ph.D., Princeton Theological Seminary) is Professor of Religion at Calvin College. He is the editor of *The One in the Many: Christian Identity in a Multicultural World* (Lanham, MD: University Press of America, 1998), and is currently working on a book project 'Imitatio Trinitatis: The Trinity as Social Model in Contemporary Theology' (contracted with Wm. B. Eerdmans Publishing Co.). He has written several articles and reviews, principally in the area of Trinity and Christology, which is his major long-term research interest.

1

Introduction:
Understanding Jesus the Christ as
Human and Divine

C. Stephen Evans

From the earliest days of the Christian Church, the followers of Jesus of Nazareth have struggled to understand the special status of their founder. That Jesus was genuinely human—that he in fact died after being crucified by Pontius Pilate—was recognized from the beginning. But Jesus seemed to those early followers not to be merely human. Already in the writings of the New Testament this special status is affirmed: the author of the Fourth Gospel acclaims Jesus as the 'Word' who was not only 'with God' in the beginning but simply 'was God'.

The affirmation of Jesus as both human and divine of course achieved its classical formulation at the Council of Chalcedon, which affirmed that Christ is 'truly God and truly man', because he possesses both a divine nature and a human nature. The two natures are distinct and not confused, but nevertheless the Christ who possesses those two natures is only 'one person and subsistence'.[1] This formulation at Chalcedon does not attempt a theoretical understanding of what it means for Jesus of Nazareth to be God Incarnate; it simply lays down some boundaries for what is to count as an orthodox Christian understanding of Jesus' status. Philosophically,

---

[1] Henry Bettenson (ed.), *Documents of the Christian Church* (New York: Oxford University Press, 1960), pp. 72–3.

Chalcedon leaves many questions open: Are the two 'natures' individual entities of some sort, or is a 'nature' here to be taken as an abstract entity, a set of properties? Does having both a divine and human nature imply that Christ has both a human and a divine mind? Does the duality of natures really allow for the unity of the person?

THE VALUE OF CHRISTOLOGY

The task of Christology is to answer such questions, and of course many others, about the person of Jesus. The attempt to understand what it means to say that Christ is both divine and human is regarded by some as a suspicious enterprise. Is not God's action in becoming one with us in Christ a supreme mystery, the absolute paradox, to use Søren Kierkegaard's phrase? We can be sure, I think, that the Incarnation will remain a mystery, at least to some degree, despite the best efforts of theologians and philosophers. Nevertheless, there are at least two reasons why the attempt to understand the identity of Jesus is valuable.

The first reason is that such an understanding may allow Christians to give an answer to criticisms that what the Church asks them to believe is impossible and/or unintelligible. To some critics of the Christian view that Jesus was God Incarnate the questions raised by the doctrine seem unanswerable. John Hick, for example, at one period of his career affirmed that 'orthodoxy has never been able to give this idea [that Jesus is both human and divine] any content. . . . For to say, without explanation, that the historical Jesus of Nazareth was also God is as devoid of meaning as to say that this circle drawn with a pencil on paper is also a square.'[2] Christian believers may well think that the Incarnation is mysterious, but they must not think that it is unintelligible.

---

[2] John Hick, 'Jesus and the World Religions', in Hick (ed.), *The Myth of God Incarnate* (London: SCM Press, 1977), p. 178. Hick has since retreated somewhat from this claim.

The second reason why attempts to understand Christ's status have value is that theological understanding of Jesus is by no means a purely theoretical affair with no implications for the practical life of Christians and the Church. Those whose understanding of Jesus does not allow for true divinity cannot really understand him as a divine saviour who offers a solution to the problem of sin and guilt; the practical implication of this is that Jesus is invariably reduced to a wonderful moral exemplar and ethical teacher. However, such a moral example and teacher may increase our sense of moral failure, rather than provide us with an answer, and the practical consequence will be that practices such as the Eucharist and Baptism must be understood differently from the way they have been traditionally, if they are continued at all.

From the other side of the theological fence, many conservative or 'evangelical' Christians, who ardently affirm the divinity of Jesus, are not fully comfortable with Jesus' full humanity.[3] Much popular piety in this branch of Christendom tilts, at least practically and implicitly, towards what might be called a mild form of 'docetism', to recall the ancient heresy that refused to accept the full humanity of Christ.[4] Such a Christology makes it difficult for Christians to think of Jesus as fully identifying with the human condition (and thus their own situation). This also makes it hard for such Christians to accept the often very human portrait of Jesus given in the gospels, despite the fact that many of these Christians profess a high view of Biblical authority.

THE KENOTIC CHRISTOLOGY PROJECT AND TEAM

In the nineteenth and early twentieth centuries, a group of theologians, first in Germany and later in the United Kingdom, attempted to understand the Incarnation by taking seriously the clue offered in

---

[3] See, for example, the anecdotes related by Gordon Fee about contemporary seminary students in Ch. 2, pp. 25–7.

[4] To be precise, the view I have in mind is not strictly a form of docetism, since it does not deny that Jesus had a real body, but in popular usage, the term 'docetism' fits this tendency to fudge the full humanity of Jesus.

Philippians 2:5–11, which says that, though Christ was 'in the form of God', he did not 'consider equality with God something to be grasped' but 'emptied himself', or, as the NIV has it, 'made himself nothing'. The Greek verb employed here, '*kenoo*', meaning to 'empty oneself', inspired these theologians to consider the idea that, in becoming a human being, God the Son in some way limited or temporarily divested himself of some of the properties thought to be divine prerogatives, and this act of self-emptying has become known as a 'kenosis'. It is important to recognize, and Gordon Fee's essay in this volume makes this plain, that, although the term 'kenotic' is suggested by this Philippians passage, kenotic Christology is rooted not in this one Biblical passage, but enjoys widespread support from the New Testament, particularly from Hebrews and the Synoptic Gospels.

The kenotic theology that developed in the nineteenth and early twentieth centuries is very diverse, as is evident from Thomas Thompson's essay in this volume, 'Nineteenth-Century Kenotic Christology: The Waxing, Waning, and Weighing of a Quest for a Coherent Orthodoxy'. Thompson explores the reasons for the development of kenotic Christology as a matter of theologians struggling to reconcile the newer historical picture of Jesus with the claims of orthodoxy. The kenotic movement seemed gradually to die off as it was attacked from both the right and the left: orthodox theologians found it difficult to reconcile the idea that Christ did not have properties such as omnipotence and omniscience during his earthly career with his full divinity. More liberal theologians, on the other hand, rejected the whole idea that a pre-existent Son of God could become human, and thus found kenotic Christology's notion of 'self-emptying' to be too tied to traditional formulations.

A relatively small number of philosophers and theologians have remained interested in kenotic Christology and convinced that its dismissal was hasty and premature. Theologians such as David Brown and Ronald Feenstra and philosophers such as Stephen Davis and myself discovered that they shared a common conviction that kenotic Christology at least deserved to be developed and explored as one way of understanding the humanity and divinity of Christ. The present volume had its roots in a conversation that Stephen Davis and I had at the 'Incarnation Summit' held in Dunwoodie, New York, at Eastertime, 2000. At this meeting, I presented a paper defending a kenotic account of the Incarnation, discussing the work of Davis, Feenstra, and others. Afterwards, Davis and I decided it would be very exciting to assemble an interdisciplinary team of theologians, Biblical scholars, and philosophers to explore the issues raised by kenotic Christology. We recognized from the beginning that such a group should include critics of the project as well as proponents.

A generous grant from the Calvin Center for Christian Scholarship allowed this dream to come to fruition. The members of the team wrote preliminary drafts of papers and then came together to discuss them at Calvin College in May 2002. After three days of intense discussion and criticism, each of us went back to our computers to revise our work in light of the work of the others. The result is the present volume.

Most of the authors can fairly be described as advocates of kenotic Christology, at least in the sense that they are convinced that this approach is a promising one to explore, even if not all of them are convinced of its final adequacy, but at least two of the authors are decidedly critical of the kenotic approach. Many of the essays have a tentative and exploratory tone. All of us recognize that kenotic Christology may not in the end be the final answer to the problems Christians raise about Jesus, but proponents and critics alike are convinced that there are promising ideas raised by kenotic theory that deserve further development and criticism. Even those who opt for a more traditional type of Christological theory recognize the ways in which attention to kenotic views can enrich those traditional theories.

All of the authors are committed Christians, though they come from different theological and ecclesiastical traditions, from Baptist to Presbyterian to Roman Catholic. All of us take seriously the authority of the Christian Scriptures, and none of us would lightly differ with the ancient ecumenical creeds of the Church. We therefore set ourselves the task of seeing if a viable kenotic theory could be developed within the boundaries of Christian orthodoxy, broadly and generously conceived. This question of whether kenosis can be orthodox lies at the centre of Stephen Davis's essay, but all of the authors have worked with the goal of assessing the worth of a kenotic theory in light of its faithfulness to Scripture, Christian tradition, and the experience of faithful Christians. However, faithfulness to the Christian tradition is consistent with seeing Christian theology as a creative intellectual task requiring imagination and new insights, as the tradition is rethought in light of new problems.

STRENGTHS AND WEAKNESSES OF A KENOTIC APPROACH

Before looking in some detail at the individual essays in this volume, it might be worthwhile to reflect briefly on the possible strengths and weaknesses of a kenotic approach to the problems of Christology. The advantages of the approach centre on two issues: (1) the religious power inherent in the idea of God's self-giving love and (2) the ability of a kenotic theory to develop an account of Jesus as divine that does full justice to his humanity and particularly to the very human portrait of Jesus presented in the gospel records. Each of these two themes deserves careful consideration.

Consider the situation of someone who is engaged in a difficult and painful struggle. Take, for example, the Civil Rights Movement in the American South in the 50s and 60s. Those who struggled for justice and equal rights faced intense opposition and danger. In such a struggle, the advocates were no doubt grateful for those who offered support and sympathy. There is, however, a quantum difference between those who offered such support at a distance, and those courageous and committed people who came to the South—only to be denounced as 'outside agitators'—to share in the struggle and participate in the demonstrations. This is particularly true for those who gave up positions of privilege and power to live in poverty and share in the danger.

Although people who sacrifice in this way for their ideals inspire admiration in all of us, it is natural for those who are suffering to feel a special love and gratitude for those who have shown their solidarity by becoming part of their world. In an analogous but even more profound way, a God who is willing fully to share in the human condition, becoming part of our world so as to liberate us from the prison of sin and guilt, moves us to love and gratitude.

Nietzsche, surely an odd thinker for a Christian to appeal to in this context, says that '[t]he gods justified human life by living it themselves—the only satisfactory theodicy ever invented'.[5] Nietzsche of course had in mind the Homeric gods, but his claim is true in a profounder sense for Christians who believe that Jesus of Nazareth was God Incarnate. Despite the assurances of theologians and philosophers, when we humans look honestly at the suffering present in the natural order it is not always easy to believe that the God of heaven and earth is a God who is both all-powerful and all-loving. When theodicies fail to satisfy, most Christians are steadied by faith: a trust and confidence that God is good and has good reasons for creating and governing the world as he has, even if we do not always know those reasons. It is far more credible to believe that God does care about human suffering when he has himself demonstrated his love by sharing in our suffering.

Of course this will be true in some measure for anyone who believes in the truth of the Incarnation, no matter what theoretical account of the Incarnation is adopted, and not just for kenotic theorists. However, this does suggest how very close to the centre of the concept of the Incarnation is the idea of kenosis. Even non-kenotic theories contain what we might call a kenotic dimension or make use of a kenotic motif. The special power of kenotic theories of the Incarnation is that they take the idea that God has fully shared in the human condition in its full force. For on the kenotic view, as we shall see, Jesus has no hidden divine powers in reserve, so to speak, to draw on in a pinch, but has chosen to endure the human situation in the same way that all of us must. A God who is incarnate in such a kenotic form is a God with whom we can identify, since he is a God who can fully empathize with us.

The second major strength of a kenotic theory is that it does full justice to the New Testament picture of Jesus as fully human, a being who shows ignorance, grows in knowledge, struggles with temptations. This theme is of course not unrelated to the first. However, it is important in its own right, because, if a version of a kenotic theory can be developed that is fully consistent with Chalcedon, this implies

[5] *The Birth of Tragedy*, trans. Francis Golffing (Garden City, New York: Doubleday, 1956), p. 30.

that Biblical scholars who wish to be orthodox Christian believers can investigate the historical record without any need to bifurcate the historical Jesus from the Christ of faith. The God who is the Eternal Word is really the person who is born as a helpless infant, and lives a very Jewish life in first-century Palestine.

Critics of kenotic Christology tend to come from two incompatible perspectives, as I have already noted. Some see such a view as too tied to traditional metaphysical doctrines, since a kenotic theory forthrightly sees Jesus of Nazareth as the Incarnation of the pre-existent Son of God. Such critics think that such metaphysical doctrines are no longer credible in the contemporary world. This book does not, for the most part, address this kind of worry, although several of the authors have done so in other contexts. Rather, the authors in this book who are advocates of kenotic Christology have confidence that traditional Christian doctrines are intelligible and defensible. We see the fact that kenotic Christology is committed to the pre-existence of Christ as a strength and not a problem.

A more troubling kind of criticism for the authors of this book stems from the worry that a kenotic account of the Incarnation will compromise or undermine the divinity of Christ. Some kenotic theories may in fact be guilty of this; the view is often carelessly described as the view that, in becoming incarnate, the Son of God gave up divinity or ceased to be God. This kind of error is easily avoided just by stating the view in a careful manner, making it clear that what is given up in the Incarnation is not divinity but some of the divine prerogatives. However, serious questions can be raised about whether God can limit himself or divest himself of some of his attributes without ceasing to be God. The critics rightly press questions about what attributes are essential to divinity and whether a kenotic view is consistent with what we must say about God. The critics also rightly ask whether or not the problems that kenotic theorists try to solve cannot be dealt with adequately within the limits of more traditional theological perspectives. Perhaps there are unnoticed resources within those perspectives that a consideration of kenotic alternatives will recall to our attention. However, advocates of kenotic Christology are convinced that a kenotic understanding of Christ's Incarnation is consistent with his full divinity.

THE CONTOURS OF THIS BOOK

This book begins, as serious Christian theology always must, with some serious wrestling with the Biblical witness. Gordon Fee, in 'The New Testament and Kenosis Christology', gives an overview of the New Testament passages that might seem to suggest or even imply a kenotic view of the Incarnation. Fee begins by describing the seminary students he has taught who have difficulty accepting the full humanity of Jesus, and he sees these teaching experiences as symptomatic of tendencies within the evangelical church towards a 'naive docetism'. Fee urges us to look carefully at the Biblical record as a whole, preserving the ambiguity in the data, refusing to pass over or minimize the extent to which that record attests the full humanity of Jesus.

Fee's treatment of Philippians 2:6–8 well illustrates the ambiguity he speaks about. On the one hand, Fee argues, over against J. D. G. Dunn, that the passage does indeed imply that the pre-existent Son of God became human for our sake. One should not read the passage as simply saying that Jesus, as a 'second Adam', chose the path of humility rather than pride. However, Fee also claims that when Paul says that Christ 'emptied himself' that it does not clearly imply that Christ divested himself of any divine attributes. On this view Christ 'emptied himself' by becoming human, but this emptying does not mean that Christ emptied himself *of* anything. The Philippians passage, then, while consistent with a kenotic account, does not demand it.

Fee actually thinks that more Biblical support for a kenotic view of Christology can be found in such books as Hebrews, and particularly in the Synoptic Gospels. The support for kenotic views of the Incarnation are found not in one text, but in the pervasive portrait of Jesus given as fully human. The writer of Hebrews stresses the 'utter dependence' of Christ on the Father in prayer, and the way in which Christ learned obedience through suffering. Fee concludes that 'an orthodox biblical Christology almost certainly must embrace some form of a "kenotic" understanding of the Incarnation', though he insists that such a theology must continue to affirm the full divinity of Christ as well. There may well be various forms of theology that will satisfy this requirement. Fee can be seen as arguing then that the New Testament does indeed offer significant support for kenotic Christology, even if it does not require us to be kenoticists.

Bruce Fisk, another New Testament scholar, gives a powerful frame for a key New Testament passage in his essay, 'The Odyssey of Christ: A Novel Context for Philippians 2:6–11'. Fisk attempts to help us see how this passage would have sounded to hearers (or readers) in Paul's time by a comparison with Graeco-Roman novels that have plots that echo the structure of the kenosis passage: a 'V-shaped pattern' of initial high status, followed by descent into humiliation and eventual triumph and exaltation. His purpose is not to find literary influence or echoes, but to increase our understanding of the way such a pattern would have been perceived by first-century readers. A look at some novels of the day gives us a better sense of the 'narrative expectations' of a first-century reader by 'helping us to understand the moral and literary sensibilities of Paul's day'.

Although the Philippians passage is highly condensed, it is telling a story, and thus can usefully be compared with other stories of the period. Fisk focuses on three of the earliest examplars of the novel: Chariton's *Chaereas and Callirhoe*, Xenophon's *An Ephesian Tale*, and Achilles Tatius' *Leucippe and Kleitophon*. Fisk looks at five areas in which the novels and Pauline passage can usefully be compared: the plot-structure, narrative beginnings, the place of human choices in the stories, the centrality of death, and the role of divine interventions.

The similarities are striking indeed. The novels contain detailed stories in which high-ranking individuals, described as possessing god-like characteristics, descend to a world of humiliation and slavery, a descent culminating in death or a death-like experience. At the bottom of the V, however, the gods intervene, and the heroes and heroines are vindicated and exalted. We learn, then, that in this literary world 'divine-like beings are *supposed* to fall headlong from the heights. Heroes are *expected* to suffer hardship and humiliation. And the gods *must* respond with deliverance and vindication.'

However, the dissimilarities are also significant. One is especially important from the point of view of kenotic Christology. The familiarity of the V-shaped plot makes one distinctive feature of the Christ story stand out starkly: the voluntary character of Christ's humiliation. 'Very little in the Hellenistic popular culture could have prepared Paul's readers for the self-humiliation of Christ depicted in Philippians 2:6–8. Too much value was attached to honour and status; too many Roman institutions shielded the elite from the masses; too many risks attended disruptions of the status quo, for Christ's voluntary descent into slavery and death to make sense.' That aspect of the Incarnation that kenoticists regard as its centre thus stands out all the more powerfully when we see it against the backdrop of Roman expectations that are embodied in Paul's story.

With Thomas Thompson's essay, 'Nineteenth-Century Kenotic Christology: The Waxing, Waning, and Weighing of a Quest for a Coherent Orthodoxy', our volume turns to the historical origins of kenotic Christology. In turning to Christology, however, we have not completely turned attention away from the New Testament, since a key part of the inspiration for nineteenth-century kenotic Christology was the encounter with modern Biblical criticism. Thompson traces the development of kenotic Christology proper—a phrase he contrasts with what he calls the kenotic gospel motif, which is a fundamental part of the Christian tradition over its entire history—in nineteenth-century Germany and Great Britain.

The story begins with the Lutheran theologian Gottfried Thomasius, who argues that Christ's assumption of human nature must be seen as including a real kenosis, a self-divestiture of the 'divine glory which he had from the beginning with the Father'. This act of self-limitation is necessary if the assumption is to be a genuine Incarnation and Christ's early life is to be fully human. Nevertheless, Thomasius insists that, in so doing, the Logos does not cease to be God and therefore does not lose anything that is essential to divinity. The complexities begin when Thomasius attempts to account for how this act of kenosis can occur without the loss of divinity, though his most well-known proposal involves a distinction between what he called the 'immanent' and the 'relative' attributes of divinity.

The proposal of Thomasius was followed by a flurry of alternative kenotic accounts. Thompson traces out three types, exemplified in the work of J. H. August Ebrard, Wolfgang Friedrich Gess, and the Danish theologian H. L Martensen. Thompson's saga then crosses over to Great Britain to examine the work of Hugh Ross Mackintosh. Thompson proceeds to look at some of the criticisms that led to the waning of kenoticism. His essay, however, is not simply an exercise in historical understanding, valuable as that task may be. Rather, he attempts to argue that the criticisms that led to the diminishing of kenotic Christology are far from decisive. He concludes with a provocative claim that the best way forward may lie in the approach of Gess, the most consistent and in some ways the most radical of the kenotic Christologists.

Stephen T. Davis's essay, 'Is Kenosis Orthodox?' provides a natural follow-up to Thompson's historical essay, since many of the criticisms that led to the waning of kenoticism were rooted in the perception that the theory was unorthodox in some way. Davis, who has in earlier work developed at least two versions of a kenotic theory of the Incarnation, in this essay attempts to show that kenotic Christology is orthodox in the sense that it is a theological claim that is 'acceptable for belief by the people of God'. To do this, Davis sets out to show that a kenotic theory of the Incarnation is consistent with Scripture and the boundaries laid down by Chalcedon.

The heart of his understanding of kenotic Christology lies in the distinction between essential and contingent properties, the distinction between those properties a thing must have to be the kind of thing it is and those properties that it has but might not have had. Davis suggests that a Christ who has become kenotically incarnate is truly human without being merely human, truly divine without being divine *simpliciter*. Whether this is possible hinges on there 'not being any essential divine properties that no human being can have and on there not being any essential human properties that no divine being can have'. If we wish to accept a kenotic account of Christ, Davis argues, following a suggestion from Tom Morris, we must be willing to accept that God's essential properties are not properties such as omnipotence and omniscience, but such properties as 'being-omnipotent-unless-freely-and-temporarily-choosing-to-be-otherwise'.

Having clarified the kind of kenotic theory he wishes to defend, Davis then asks how Christians should decide whether or not a theory is orthodox. This requires that one look at what various Christian traditions accept as authoritative, Scripture alone for

Protestants, Scripture plus tradition for Catholics. Davis gives an interesting account of how each of these two traditions might be understood, and in fact makes a substantive proposal designed to lessen the gap between Protestants and Catholics by giving an interpretation of 'Scripture alone' that is consistent with recognizing an important role for tradition. With these foundational issues dealt with, Davis proceeds to argue that a kenotic theory, while not explicitly taught in Scripture, is a permissible interpretation of the Scriptural evidence. With respect to tradition, Davis argues, drawing on the work of Sarah Coakley, that the formulations of the Councils of Nicaea and Chalcedon leave many key issues undecided, since key terms are undefined. These creedal formulations do not therefore teach a particular theory of the Incarnation, but rather set boundaries so as to help us determine which theories are or are not orthodox. Davis argues that kenotic theories pass this test, and in conclusion tries to show that the kenoticist has good responses to many of the common arguments that try to show the theory is unorthodox.

Ronald Feenstra builds on Davis's argument and extends it to focus explicitly on methodological questions in 'A Kenotic Christological Method for Understanding the Divine Attributes'. Feenstra begins with a discussion of the classical Christian creeds and early debates about Christology, focusing particularly on the doctrine of the 'communication of attributes', the orthodox view that both the divine and human natures of Christ are 'communicated to' the one person, Jesus. This concept appears as early as Tertullian and plays a prominent role in Athanasius' defence of orthodox Christology; it also plays a key role in Cyril of Alexandria's battle with Nestorius.

The difficulty with the doctrine of the communication of attributes is that it appears to lead to predicating incompatible attributes to Christ, given the disparity of the divine and human natures. Feenstra discusses a number of strategies used by theologians to deal with this problem, ranging from Leo through Aquinas to twentieth-century figures. While he does not claim that these strategies cannot possibly work, he does show that there are serious difficulties. These difficulties seem serious enough that figures such as John Hick give up on orthodox Christology altogether, treating the doctrine of Christ as both divine and human as a metaphor. Feenstra then shows how kenotic Christology can resolve these difficulties, reviewing its Biblical support and responding to common criticisms.

It is in dealing with these criticisms that Feenstra raises the methodological question. Philosophical critics such as Thomas Morris and Richard Swinburne argue that kenotic Christology, which claims that the attributes essential to divinity are properties such as 'being-omniscient-unless-kenotically-incarnate', rather than omniscience *simpliciter*, are problematic because they do not square with our philosophical intuitions. Swinburne argues, for example, that the kenotically inspired concept of God is more complex than the classical concept and that a simpler hypothesis is more likely to be true. Morris argues that kenotic Christology leads to a picture of God that is not consistent with his 'Anselmian intuitions', inspired by Anselm's description of God as 'a being than which none greater can be conceived'. Morris thinks that a God who had the kenotic attributes would not be the greatest possible being, and that this implies that such a being would not be God.

Feenstra questions how much weight Christian theologians should ascribe to such a priori philosophical intuitions. Appealing methodologically to figures as diverse as Tertullian, Karl Barth, Alvin Plantinga, and N. T. Wright, Feenstra argues that if the Incarnation is true, then for the Christian the most reliable way of gaining insight into the nature of God is to look at Christ. We should not form our understanding of what God is like independently of the revelation of God in Jesus Christ, but rather be open to correcting our a priori conceptions of the divine in light of God's gracious revelation. If the Biblical record supports a kenotic account of Christ's divine nature, we must be willing to revise our understanding of God accordingly.

If we take seriously the idea that the Incarnation provides us with our best window to understanding the nature of God, then this means that a kenotic understanding of Christ will shape in a profound way much of what we say about God. There is a fairly direct link between Christology and the Christian doctrine of the Trinity. It is only because Christians believe that there is both plurality and unity in God that they can debate how Jesus of Nazareth can be fully divine as well as human. If no one had come to the conviction that Jesus was divine, it seems likely that no one would have thought that God could be three-in-one.

In 'Trinity and Kenosis', Thomas Thompson and Cornelius Plantinga attempt to assess some of the connections between kenotic Christology and what is usually called 'Social Trinitarianism'. To put things as simply as possible, Christian understandings of the Trinity generally follow one of two strategies: either to begin with an understanding of God as one and then attempt to account for God's threeness, or to begin with an understanding of God as Father, Son, and Spirit, and then attempt to account for God's oneness. Social Trinitarianism opts for the second strategy; it develops a well-differentiated account of the Trinitarian persons, an account that takes seriously the idea that Father, Son, and Holy Spirit, while intimately related and unified, form a genuine community. Thompson and Plantinga argue in their essay that a kenotic Christology must embrace a Social Trinitarian perspective.

Critics of Social Trinitarianism will see this as one more difficulty for kenotic Christology, since Social Trinitarians are regularly accused of being tri-theists who undermine the unity of the divine being. Thompson and Plantinga do not claim that such a differentiated conception of the Trinity can only be developed from a kenotic perspective. On the contrary, they argue that such differentiation is already implied by the distinctions between Father, Son, and Spirit. However, on their view the kenotic model 'certainly accentuates these distinctions and is clearly dependent on them'. In the discussion that follows, Thompson and Plantinga clearly exemplify the methodological lesson drawn by Feenstra: Christian theological discussions must be shaped primarily by the narrative history of Father, Son, and Spirit rather than by a philosophical theism that is ruled by a priori intuitions about the divine.

As Thompson and Plantinga see things, there are many lines of thought that converge on Social Trinitarianism. These include a more dynamic and relational conception of God's relation to creation, and a more social understanding of the nature of human persons. Contemporary theologians have drawn on the personal analogies used by the Cappadocian Fathers to make sense of the Trinity so as to liken the Trinity to a family, a community, or a society of persons. If Social Trinitarianism is itself attractive, then the dependence of kenotic Christology upon it can be seen as a strength and not a weakness.

In the last section of their essay, Thompson and Plantinga respond to a number of criticisms of Social Trinitarianism, including the charge that the doctrine involves an invidious ranking of the divine persons and that it really amounts to tri-theism. In responding to these charges, they discuss a number of different ways of viewing the unity of God. In the end, it may well be that no human theological model is completely adequate to describe either the Trinity or the person of Christ. We should not be surprised that the community that is the Trinity is not *completely* like a human family or society, and that the three persons are one in a way that no human community can fully match or even grasp. Nevertheless, these social analogies may be the best model we can develop to understand the God who has acted in Christ to save a fallen humanity.

C. Stephen Evans continues to develop the methodological lesson that Feenstra's essay draws by looking at the relation between kenotic Christology and what is best described as 'kenotic theism'. If the Incarnation is indeed our best window into the nature of God, then it makes sense that a kenotic Christology should lead to a kenotic theism, in which the self-giving love shown in Christ is seen as central to God's very nature. Recently, there has been a surge of interest in such a kenotic understanding of God, and Evans begins by considering a volume of essays dedicated to this theme, *The Work of Love: Creation as Kenosis*, edited by John Polkinghorne.

Evans seconds an observation made about this volume by Sarah Coakley: that most of its contributors think primarily about the significance of kenosis in terms of God's relation to the world, turning to Christological meanings only as paradigmatic or illustrative of this fundamental characteristic. Several of the essays in *The Work of Love*, for example, take as their primary focus the autonomy or independence of the natural, scientific order, as God, out of love, steps back to allow nature to 'do its thing'. Evans attempts to follow Coakley's implication that a genuine kenotic theism should be substantively informed by a kenotic understanding of Christ. In agreement with Feenstra, he tries to see how our philosophical understanding of God might be changed if we take the Biblical narrative, understood kenotically, as providing our primary data for thinking about God.

Evans then proceeds to sketch a kenotic Christology that is broadly similar to that found in Davis, Feenstra, and the essay by Thompson and Plantinga. Such a Christology could be used to explore many issues dealing with the nature of God, but Evans chooses to focus on God's capacity for self-limitation. The question whether or not it is possible for God to limit himself has long been debated in philosophical theology in the debate over the 'paradox of the stone', the question whether God can create a stone that he himself could not cause to rise. When debated in this form, the question appears trivial, but it is not. Whether God can limit himself is central, not only to questions about the relation of God to the natural world, as is shown by the essays in *The Work of Love*, but also to questions about the problem of evil, the reality of human freedom, and even the question, central to the Biblical narrative, whether God can make promises that are binding on himself. If God cannot make such promises, then the key Biblical notion of 'covenant' threatens to fall apart.

If we take the Incarnation as our most basic source of insight about God, and understand the Incarnation as involving a kenosis, then this suggests that self-giving love that limits itself is not only possible for God but central to God's very being. The act of the Logos in divesting himself of such properties as omnipotence and omniscience shows that self-limitation is not only possible for God but is a manifestation of a characteristic that is central to his nature. This in turn suggests that God is indeed capable of binding himself by his commitments in making promises, by 'withdrawing himself' from his creation in such a way that nature has its own relative autonomy, and by endowing his human creatures with the kind of relative autonomy that makes it possible for their relations with God to be genuinely personal relations. If this capacity for self-limitation is central to God's nature, then this also implies that the properties kenoticists attribute to God, attributes such as 'being-omnipotent-unless-choosing-to-limit-himself', are not second-best substitutes for 'real' divine properties. Perhaps genuine omnipotence *includes* a capacity to limit itself, so that a being who lacked this capacity would be less than omnipotent.

In conclusion, Evans addresses another worry of Coakley, that such a concern for freedom and autonomy is the result of a 'gendered' perspective that reflects male bias. Evans argues that seeing

God as a being who allows his creation to have a measure of independence does not mean God is a standoffish, distant God, but just the reverse. God is a God who wants intimate relations with creatures who are capable of real relationships with him.

In a very different way, Edward Oakes also explores the implications of kenotic Christology for our understanding of God's own nature in ' "He descended into hell": The Depths of God's Self-Emptying Love on Holy Saturday in the Thought of Hans Urs von Balthasar'. Oakes therefore connects the discussion of kenotic Christology to a clause in one of the earliest creeds of Christianity, the so-called 'Apostles' Creed'. Oakes begins with a review of the way the doctrine of Christ's descent into hell between his death and resurrection, while pervasive in both the New Testament and in the early Church, has been softened, mitigated, or even eliminated by both Protestants and Catholics alike. The doctrine is evidently one that creates considerable discomfort and even consternation.

Nevertheless, Oakes describes the way this doctrine made a comeback in the twentieth century, referring to the Presbyterian theologian Alan Lewis, but giving an extended treatment of the work of the Swiss Catholic theologian Hans Urs von Balthasar. According to Oakes's account, Balthasar connects the concept of kenosis with two key problems that lie at the very centre of the doctrine of the Incarnation: the 'scandal of particularity', that asks how a particular person within the universe can also be the source of the universe, and the problem how a changeless God can be involved in the drama of salvation. On Balthasar's view, the saving effects of Christ's resurrection must somehow radiate to both past and future, providing a 'ballast, an absolute counterweight' that can outweigh every complaint against God. Only a God whose Incarnation is radical and complete can do this. Echoing the ancient principle that what has not been assumed by the Son cannot be redeemed by the Son, Balthasar holds that Christ's victory over death requires that Christ completely take on the consequences of sin; Christ's complete 'solidarity' with humans even extends to his participation in death.

Balthasar's Christology is thus kenotic in a very radical way indeed, in that he does not merely stress the way the Logos divested himself of heavenly glory to become human, but highlights the fact, as does Philippians 2, that Christ's humiliation included death, 'even death on a cross'. On Oakes's account this need for kenosis is not rooted in some kind of punitive principle, as some have alleged, in which the Logos must experience hell so that God's penalty for sin is fully paid. Rather, the kenosis tells us something profound about the inner being of God, whose love for his fallen humanity requires him to incorporate into the life of the divine Trinity the 'godforsakenness' of his creatures. Only in this way can that which is absolutely singular nevertheless incorporate that which is universal. Christ can be 'the Way, the Truth, and the Life', because the resurrection validates his claim to have plumbed the depths of human experience. Not even death lies outside the power of God's redemptive activity. Once more, as with Evans and Feenstra, a kenotic understanding of Christ-ology transforms our understanding of the very being of God.

Having looked at kenotic proposals and their implications in some detail, it is now time to consider some critical perspectives. Sarah Coakley raises some serious problems for kenotic Christology in 'Does Kenosis Rest on a Mistake? Three Kenotic Models in Patristic Exegesis'. Besides raising critical questions for contemporary kenoti-cists, Coakley shows the richness of classical Christology and the resources that the patristic tradition affords for thinking about the Incarnation. In particular, she suggests that there may be traditional ways of understanding the Incarnation which provide some of the benefits of kenotic Christology without the difficulties.

To this end Coakley looks at three patristic accounts of the 'self-emptying' passage from Philippians. She begins by noting that, for better or worse, none of the Church Fathers even considered the possibility of questioning 'divine impassibility or other cognate char-acteristics in light of the Incarnation'. Contemporary treatments of the issue have failed to notice the sophisticated and complex ways that the patristic figures employed the doctrine of the 'communica-tion of the idioms' to understand the Incarnation of the Logos. Coakley considers the treatments of kenosis found in Cyril and Nestorius first, then concludes with a look at the earlier work of Gregory of Nyssa.

It is clear from Coakley's treatment of Cyril of Alexandria that ancient theologians were acutely aware of the Philippians passage, to the degree that 'Cyril's entire Christological undertaking could be ranged under the heading of an extended exegesis of Philippians 2.'

On Cyril's treatment, the self-emptying of the Logos is an *assumption*, neither a simple addition and certainly not a blending, but not an act in which God the Son literally divests himself of anything either. On this view the kenosis involves a 'transference of divine "energy" into the human nature'. Difficulties arise, however, when Cyril attempts to understand the 'communication' of the divine and human attributes, particularly with respect to the suffering of the very human Jesus. At this point Cyril either has recourse to paradox or else strains the unity of the person of Christ by relegating the suffering to the human nature only.

Nestorius' account is quite different in some respects, according to Coakley, but equally committed to divine impassibility. As Nestorius sees things, Philippians 2 describes an 'additive' view in which there is a 'conjunction' or union of the Logos with a human being. The 'emptying' is seen as both a metaphysical act of Incarnation and as present in Christ's 'human/historical' life in which the effects of Adam's sin are undone by radical obedience. Though acknowledging interpretive difficulties, Coakley suggests that Nestorius may think that the divine and human natures are both to be referred to the person of Christ such that in Christ 'there may be a transformative and salvific exchange without detrimental effects for the integrity of either: neither the divinity is besmirched, nor the humanity magicked into a form which denies its natural and embodied frailty.' However, Coakley claims that it remains somewhat murky how this is managed, and whether the 'communication' is genuinely ontological or merely linguistic.

Having described Cyril's reading of Philippians 2 as one that stresses assumption, and that of Nestorius as centring on conjunction, Coakley describes Gregory of Nyssa's account of Philippians 2 through the metaphor of progressive transfusion. Gregory combines elements from several patristic traditions, accepting 'the "Alexandrian" tradition of the Incarnation involving an actual, ontological transformation of the human in virtue of the Logos's kenosis', but also insisting 'on the integrity of a (particular) human being, Jesus, as being the "tabernacle" where this transformation occurs'. But what is really distinctive about Gregory is that the transformation of the human in Christ is not immediate but involves a process, not one in which sin is removed but one that nevertheless requires a gradual purification, a movement towards maturity and triumph and certitude, none of which are immediately present merely because of the assumption of human nature by the divine Logos.

Coakley sees this as a promising approach, because Gregory's perspective allows us to do justice to some of the Scriptural themes that are important to contemporary kenoticists, particularly those passages that see Christ as growing and suffering. She suggests that if theologians make full use of the doctrine of the 'communication of idioms' employed by such figures as Gregory, then contemporary kenotic approaches, which require controversial modifications of traditional accounts of God, may be unnecessary.

In 'The Logic of Assumption', Edwin Chr. van Driel turns from the patristic period to the medieval period, but his aim in many ways mirrors Coakley's. He also wants to see whether or not there are underutilized resources in traditional Christology which will enable theologians to satisfy the concerns of kenoticists without fundamentally revising traditional theological formulations. Kenotic theologians, says van Driel, see classical Christology as impaled on the horns of a dilemma. Either the classical theologian 'does not take seriously that Christ has two full, complete natures, in which case Christ's human consciousness is too godlike to fit the Gospel narratives', or else the theologian does take both natures seriously, 'in which case you make Christ schizophrenic'.

Van Driel mainly addresses the first horn of the dilemma in this essay, though he makes some remarks about the unity of Christ's consciousness near the end. Van Driel admits that many classical pictures of Christ's human life seem to describe him in ways that do not do full justice to his humanity and which do not seem consistent with the Biblical portrait. In particular, he examines the pictures of Christ given by the medieval thinkers Thomas Aquinas and Duns Scotus. These medieval thinkers do see Christ in his human life as possessing the gifts of 'maximal grace' and the 'beatific vision'. However, van Driel argues that a careful examination of their accounts of the hypostatic union, the union of the divine and human natures in one person, does not in fact require this. It is true that a Christ who possesses maximal grace and the beatific vision is a Christ who cannot easily be seen as a being who must grow and be tested. However, these claims about Christ are not in fact required by the claim that the divine Word has assumed a human nature, whether that ontological fact be understood in accordance with Aquinas' 'part–whole' model or along the lines of Scotus' view, which uses an analogy drawn from the 'substance–accident' relation.

Van Driel argues therefore that the metaphysical claims that the classical theologian wishes to make are in fact consistent with the kind of human portrait of Jesus that kenotic Christologies try to safeguard. Thus, he thinks, some of the concerns of kenotic Christology can be met without giving up traditional views of the divine nature. The key to doing this is to recognize that the classical account is compatible with various views of what the divine and human natures are actually like, and that the relation of ontological dependence that is essential to the hypostatic union does not necessarily have the implications for Christ's psychology that many traditional theologians have thought that it had. Van Driel and Coakley, drawing on two different periods of theological reflection, thus present a spirited defence of the claim that traditional Christological formulations can meet some of the legitimate concerns of kenotic Christologists.

The volume then moves to an essay by Ruth Groenhout, 'Kenosis and Feminist Theory', that examines the practical implications of kenotic Christology. Many of the essays in the volume have stressed the powerful religious meaning packed into the ideal of God's self-sacrificing love. However, there are legitimate concerns that such an ideal may have untoward ethical implications as well. Much feminist theory has claimed that 'women are socialized to be inordinately self-sacrificing, and that this socialization is a bad thing'. A divine saviour whose nature is defined by an act of self-sacrifice might appear to be a poor model for women to emulate, even if the message given is one that many men need to hear.

Groenhout begins by sketching the feminist case against self-sacrifice, drawing on the work of Valerie Saiving and Serene Jones. Groenhout recognizes that the picture these critics paint contains a good deal of truth, but it is problematic when taken as the whole truth. She agrees that 'theology and various Biblical texts have been used to justify and sometimes worsen abuse' of women. She warns, however, that we must not succumb to a simplistic gender-dualism that limits women's experience to oppression. A sound feminist theory must neither uncritically endorse nor reject self-sacrifice, but rather take a more nuanced approach. The questions we must ask concern the meaning and purposes of self-sacrifice. Groenhout, drawing on some earlier work of Sarah Coakley, first canvasses the range of meanings that 'self-sacrifice' might be thought to have, ranging from mere self-limitation to outright self-annihilation. Groenhout argues that both extremes on this continuum are theologically questionable, and she offers a spirited critique of an interpretation of kenosis as a kind of self-sacrifice in which the self (as well as the church) must simply disappear as metaphysical realities. Simone Weil's understanding of self-sacrifice also verges too far in the direction of annihilation. Feminists have good reason to be wary of a kenotic self-sacrifice that is understood in this manner.

However, it would be a grave mistake for feminists to reject the ideal of self-sacrifice altogether. Genuine self-sacrifice is not a pointless or masochistic embrace of suffering, but a willingness to sacrifice personal goals for the purpose of stopping or limiting 'the destruction of other people or of healthy social relations'. This kind of sacrifice is intrinsic to personal agency. No one, and no feminist, can really work for the good and the elimination of injustice, without the assumption that this kind of self-sacrifice is possible. To deny to women the possibility of genuine, healthy self-sacrifice is simply to deny women the status of genuine moral agents. This kind of healthy self-sacrifice does not stem from a diminished sense of the self, but 'always occurs in the context of a robust sense of the worth of the self'. It is because I know who I am and what I believe in that I am willing to sacrifice for what I see as right and just.

This does not mean that self-sacrifice is not real sacrifice. The choices that a person is called upon to make are sometimes painful and even tragic. But such painful acts of self-sacrifice do not have to stem from a self that does not desire its own good. Rather, it is because the self really does desire its own flourishing that the sacrifices are real. Groenhout concludes with some lessons from feminist theorists about how theologians should think about kenotic self-sacrifice. The right balance between self-actualization and self-sacrifice will be struck if we think of God as the one who has created human persons in his image as beautiful gifts to be treasured and enjoyed, but who has also given us in Christ a powerful example of love that gives itself for the good of the other.

The book concludes with a brief essay by Stephen T. Davis and C. Stephen Evans that attempts to draw together some of the main strands made by the proponents of kenotic Christology today. Drawing on the previous essays, Davis and Evans argue that the reasons commonly given to reject kenotic Christology are not strong, and issue a challenge to traditional theories of the Incarnation to account for the way in which the Incarnation must at least involve a relinquishing of the divine glory, as implied in John 17:5. The self-emptying character of God shines through clearly in the 'mini-kenosis' seen in Jesus' action in washing the feet of the disciples (John 13:1–20). Even in John's Gospel, which has the most exalted view of Jesus as divine, there is a strong emphasis on Jesus as the one who lives in continual dependence on the Father and the Spirit. There is thus no contradiction between a divine Jesus who shows supernatural power and a kenotic Christ who manifests self-emptying love.

We hope these essays will inspire more thought about the ways Christ's self-emptying love shown in his Incarnation can inspire Christian reflection and devotion. Perhaps this act of kenosis provides the key to understanding both the identity of Jesus the Christ and the inner meaning of the Trinitarian God who sent the Son for our salvation. Whether this requires a full-fledged kenotic Christology, as most of the authors think, or closer attention to the kenotic motif that can inform classical Christologies, is not a question that one book can settle. However, we hope that we have shown that kenotic Christology deserves serious consideration and elaboration, and that it is a project that can be carried on within the boundaries of orthodox, confessional Christian faith.

2

The New Testament and Kenosis Christology

Gordon D. Fee

Orthodox Christology affirms that Christ in his Incarnation was at once fully God and fully human. To put this my way, the common faith of the historic church is that, in the Jewish Messiah Jesus, God was living out a genuinely human life on planet earth. The theological-philosophical issue resultant from this affirmation is to find a way to hold tenaciously to both sides of the incarnate reality—fully God/fully human—without diminishing one in favour of the other.

1. AT ISSUE: THE AMBIGUITY OF THE BIBLICAL DATA

Historically, holding both realties about Jesus together has not been easy to do, as I discovered during a quarter-century of teaching a Life of Jesus course in two major evangelical theological schools. Over the years, I found that many students had great difficulty coming to terms with the historical Jesus as a *truly* human person. Evangelical students tended regularly to hold a kind of naive docetism, where Jesus appeared as a real person, but who was God in such a way that it superseded anything truly human about him except for the accidents of his humanity—basically his bodily functions: eating, talking, sleeping, and so on.[1]

---

[1] In fact one of the difficulties in writing this chapter was to find a way of speaking about the 'truly human', since there is a kind of latent dualism among many orthodox

The basic perspective of most evangelical students, who of course had not really thought much of this through, was illustrated for me many years ago, when I was channel-surfing for a sporting event and was stopped by a wide-eyed little black girl's shout of 'Jesus'. I had landed on Art Linkletter, whose apparent question had been, 'If you could be anyone on earth when you grow up, who would you like to be?' Her bold answer brought the house down, including Linkletter. So he followed up by asking, 'And why would you like to be Jesus?' Her immediate, non-calculated response was a perfect illustration of many evangelicals' Christology. With right index finger pointing to her left palm, she exclaimed, 'Because whenever I get hungry, I could just go "zap" and there I would have a hamburger right in my hand!'

This accidental, whimsical moment was a kind of paradigm of the way many of the students in my Life of Jesus course understood Jesus. For the course always hit the fan at two points:

(1) Early on, in the lecture on Jesus' baptism and testing in the desert, besides all the necessary things that needed to be said about this two-sided event—his deliberately stepping into the role of Israel and in the desert coming through victorious where Israel had failed—I press hard as to whether the testing was a real one. That is, was Jesus, as Son of God, *really* tempted to turn a stone into bread? And when I suggest that it was indeed a real one, and follow up by suggesting that his Incarnation is more truly meaningful if the choice of the cross was also a real one, not some kind of robotic inevitability—because he was God, after all—the questions simply will not cease. I have discovered that these students do not want a true Incarnation, but an Apollonarian one. Indeed, I suggest at one point in this lecture that I could have beaten Jesus one on one in basketball; and many of the students consider this close to blasphemy (all he would have to do would be to call on his divine powers and slam dunk me!).

(2) The other place where this struggle comes to the fore for the student is in the final lecture on Jesus' messianic self-consciousness, in which I argue that the evidence suggests that this is something

---

at this point. They vigorously affirm the humanity of his bodily functions, but often just as vigorously deny humanity to his thought processes. I intend to include the latter in this language, and thus intentionally exclude from it the view here described.

Jesus actually learned about himself through the work of the Holy Spirit. This, after all, is clearly the perspective of Luke's two-volume work: that he actually grew through the enabling work of the Spirit, and that his whole ministry was the evidence of one fully dependent on the Spirit of God, who went about doing good, not because he was God Incarnate, but because God was *with* him (Acts 10:38).

But part of the tension on the part of the students was my insistence that a 'life of Jesus' had to be told essentially from the perspective of the Synoptic tradition, although with forays into the Gospel of John. They, on the other hand, had always begun with the Jesus presented in the Fourth Gospel and thus found themselves exceedingly uncomfortable with the Synoptic Jesus.

This anecdotal history, however, does not represent something new. Indeed, it fairly well represents the theological tensions that also came to persist in the early Christological controversies, and have continued to this day. It surely should come as no surprise that John's Gospel is cited more often by far than the Synoptics in the preserved Christological writings of the orthodox Fathers.[2] At issue is not the 'truth' of the two Gospel traditions, but the emphatically post-Easter telling of the story that John engages in, as he regularly reminds his readers, that 'only after Jesus was glorified did they realize' what had been going on before their very eyes.

I want to suggest in this essay that the issue of 'kenotic Christology' boils down at its most elementary level to the ongoing struggle among the orthodox—who believe all of Scripture to be equally inspired by the Spirit—over this apparent tension between the Synoptic and Johannine portrayals of Jesus.

At the theological level this tension eventually comes to the fore at one crucial point. Was the earthly Jesus *posse non peccare* (able not to sin) or *non posse peccare* (not able to sin)? And over the years it has become clear to me that this question is always answered on the basis of whether one starts from below, with the actual evidence of the biblical documents themselves, especially the Synoptic Gospels (thus *posse non peccare*) or from above, with our later understanding, based

---

[2] The operative words in this phrase are 'preserved', 'Christological', and 'orthodox'. The preservation of history for the most part goes to the victors; and it is in these writings especially that the Gospel of John plays such a crucial role.

28

Gordon D. Fee

primarily on the Johannine tradition, of who Jesus really was as God Incarnate (thus *non posse peccare*).[3]

This question, of course, is an imponderable, because the documents are clear enough—there was no sin found in him. But I have wondered from time to time (and now I have a chance to wonder these things aloud with some theological and philosophical colleagues) if the answer to this question is very much like the answer to the Incarnation itself: clothed in mystery in such a way that both are in some sense true. Because in any case, this question seems to me to be answered almost invariably on the basis of one's stance: from below (working with the biblical data themselves) or from above (working with larger, ultimate realities).

Let it be said again, then, that the issue itself is the direct result of the tensions inherent in the New Testament (NT) data. For however one finally handles the theological and philosophical issues of the doctrine of the Incarnation, the NT documents themselves are the fundamental starting point for all Christological discussion. And besides the perceived tension described above between the Synoptics and John, our difficulties stem from two other interrelated realities.

First, the overwhelming evidence of all the Gospel accounts is that the Incarnation was real, in the sense that, whatever else, Christ's humanity was the one reality that confronted his contemporaries and to which the Gospel writers bear faithful witness. So much is this so that the evidence from all the accounts, including the Gospel of John, is that during his pre-crucifixion lifetime, Jesus' deity was unrecognized even by those who were closest to him—even though the accounts were all written after the conviction of his deity was a firmly established reality.[4]

Secondly, and on the other hand, given that all the NT documents, including the Gospels, were written post-Easter, post-exaltation, when by way of the Spirit it had become clear to them who Jesus really was (after all, an 'exalted Jesus' understanding of Psalm 110:1 pervades the entire NT), it is equally remarkable that not one of the

---

[3] It is of some interest that in the three evangelical institutions where I have taught there was lingering tension between the systematic theologians and the NT faculty on this point.

[4] Indeed, careful reflection on this reality should have issued in a great deal more caution in the handling of the data on the part of the Jesus Seminar!

NT writers attempts to minimize the first reality: that Jesus was truly human in his Incarnation. In fact, the acknowledged high Christology of the Johannine Gospel and letters seems directed specifically against 'false prophets' who would appear to do this very thing.

This dual reality of our NT writers—their faithfulness to Christ's full/true humanity even after they had come to believe he was the pre-existent, now exalted Lord—is what creates most of the Christological tensions for later articulations of theological Christology.[5] The purpose of this chapter, then, is to set forth once more the primary NT data that call for careful analysis, paying special attention to the way they speak about Christ's humanity, since many of the pertinent texts, apart from the Gospel of John, seem to express *some form of self-limitation of divine prerogatives on the part of the earthly Jesus.*[6] I will look at the data in their supposed chronological sequence (Paul, Hebrews, the Synoptics, John).

In beginning with the Pauline data, I offer a brief exegesis of Philippians 2:6–8—since I assume that subsequent discussion in this volume will have frequent occasion to refer to this text. After all, it is Paul's use of the verb κενόω in this passage that has led, ironically,[7] to the language of *kenosis* as one way of articulating a viable option for orthodox Christology. But I also begin with Paul because, even though—for good reason—there is a paucity of data as to Jesus' human life, nonetheless it is common in some quarters to pin a low Christology on Paul, including a denial that he believed in, or articulated, Christ's pre-existence (the necessary presupposition of the doctrine of the Incarnation).[8]

---

[5] I use the term 'theological Christology' to distinguish discussion about the 'two natures' from the kinds of Christological concerns raised by NT scholars over the data themselves, as to Christ's deity as such and how the earliest believers might have understood that, even when the concept itself is 'allowed'.

[6] I emphasize this because it will be my working definition of what I take 'kenosis' to mean.

[7] 'Ironically' because Paul's usage, as will be pointed out below, is almost surely metaphorical, not literal, so that the suggestion that Christ 'emptied himself' *of* something is quite foreign to Paul's own concern. See the exegesis below.

[8] The point here, of course, is that if they were proved to be right, then the whole discussion of kenotic Christology as a Pauline phenomenon is moot.

2. THE APOSTLE PAUL: PHILIPPIANS 2:6–8

The first issue in Paul is whether he held to the kind of high Christology that all accord to John and the author of Hebrews. This is especially relevant when approaching our primary text: Philippians 2:6–8.[9] To get there, we need to have some sense as to its reason for being at all.

At issue in Philippi is some degree of dissension within the believing community at the very time they are also experiencing a degree of persecution from the local pagan population. These two matters are presented together in the appeal in 1:27–30, while the issue of dissension becomes front and centre in 2:1–16. After a passionate appeal for them to 'have the same mindset', Paul indicates negatively the kind of mindset that destroys unity: 'Do nothing', he says, 'out of selfish ambition (ἐριθεία) and vain conceit (κενοδοξία)', but rather in 'humility' put concern for others before yourselves (vv. 3–4). At which point he then appeals to the 'mindset' of Christ (v. 5).

In the well-known telling of Christ's story that follows, and in direct contrast to the language of verse 3, Paul essentially makes two points: 'As *God*, he ἐκένωσεν himself, by becoming human [vv. 6–7a]; as *a human* he humbled himself, by becoming obedient unto death [vv. 7b –8]'. Thus he demonstrated God-likeness—over against 'selfish ambition'—by 'pouring himself out' in assuming the role of a slave; and he demonstrated true humanness (what it means to be in God's own image)—over against 'vain conceit'—by humbling himself in an obedience that led to the cross. Verses 9–11 then go on to relate his vindication through exaltation, by having bestowed on him *the name* (= LORD).

While all of this seems to be the plain sense of the text, in terms of both its language and grammar, this reading of the text has been challenged from time to time, especially by J. D. G. Dunn, who along with others is enamoured by the possibility of an Adam Christology at work in the text.[10] And in Dunn's case especially this means that

---

[9] For a larger discussion of what follows see G. D. Fee, *Paul's Letter to the Philippians*, NICNT (Grand Rapids, Mich.: Eerdmans, 1995), 191–229.

[10] See *Christology in the Making* (London: SCM, 1980), 114–29, more recently defended with some vigour in his *The Theology of Paul the Apostle* (Grand Rapids, Mich.: Eerdmans, 1998), 283–8.

one should read verses 6–7b not 'from above' but 'from below'. To make this work, he posits the following 'correspondences' with Adam:

2.6a—in the form of God
2.6bc—tempted to grasp equality with God
2.7—took the form of a slave [to corruption and sin]
2.8—obedient to death
2.9–11—exalted and glorified[11]

Thus, the human Christ, who was in God's image, did not follow Adam's example of trying to be equal with God, but rather chose servanthood and death—but was later raised and exalted by God.

But what is striking in Dunn's list is the lack of a single *verbal* correspondence with the Genesis account. While it is true that μορφή ('form') has some verbal overlap with εἰκών[12] ('image'), that is of almost no value here, since the overlap is so slight as to be negligible and especially since 'image' would be the *one essential* pickup word that would catch the reader's attention. Moreover, the Genesis account does not say that Adam and Eve tried to be 'equal with' God; the tempter offered simply that they would be like God in the sense of 'knowing (= determining for themselves?) good and evil'.

---

[11] Each of these is footnoted with references to Genesis or other biblical literature; the second is seen to correspond to the words of the serpent ('you will be like God', Gen. 3:5); the third to Wis. 2:23 ('God created the man in incorruption; and made him in the image [εἰκών] of his own eternity'); the fourth to Gen. 2:17 and 3:22–4; the fifth to Ps. 8:5b–6 (which refers to humanity in general, not Adam in particular). On the alleged echo to Wis. 2:23 see next note, since this is a reference to Adam pure and simple and not to Wisdom!

[12] That there is a 'considerable semantic overlap' between these two words is often asserted in the literature; but assertion falls far short of reality. If each word's semantic field were pictured as a circle, then the overlap does not embrace even a tenth of each word's circle. In fact, the meaning of the passage would carry an altogether different meaning had Paul used εἰκών, and would make nonsense of line 4: 'being found in the *image* of a slave'. The overlap between these two words lies at the point of 'form, likeness'; but Paul's point with the use of μορφή has less to do with 'form' in this case and moves much closer to 'essential nature'. Thus the two words are not true synonyms, in which both words carry much of the freight of the other (as in 'bear' and 'endure'). The analogy between εἰκών and μορφή would be words like 'bear' and 'turn', when the former is used in the idiom 'bear right or left'. See further, David Steenburg, 'The Case Against the Synonymity of *morphe* and *eikon*', *JSNT* 34 (1988), 77–86.

This is not to say that a conceptual echo of Genesis 2–3 might not be heard in this passage, but it is to say that such an echo cannot be the starting point of the discussion in such a way that the plain sense of the words and grammar are bent all out of shape in order to conform to this alleged echo. I briefly list the following lexical and grammatical points:

(1) The reason for Paul's choice of μορφή seems to be that it is the one word available in Greek that would fit the two participial expressions on either side of the main verb (ἐκένωσεν); thus here it does not carry the sense of 'image' (which it never carries, in any case), but refers rather to the essential quality of godlikeness, on the one hand, and of servanthood, on the other. But whatever else it is, it is *not* a synonym of εἴκων.

(2) Grammar should count for something in exegesis as well. And in this case the τό before the infinitive εἶναι (τὸ εἶναι ἴσα θεῷ) is especially damaging to the view from below, since it serves as an anaphora, spelling out what 'being in the form of God' meant to Paul, while at the same time serving as the direct object of the clause. Thus: 'the being equal with God [just mentioned] he did not consider ἁρπαγμόν'.

(3) Making the alternative view work requires a considerable stretch of the phrases ἐν ὁμοιώματι ἀνθρώπων and σχήματι εὑρεθεὶς ὡς ἄνθρωπος (how can a human being created in God's image 'come to be in the likeness of human beings and be found in appearance as a human being'?). Thus this view seems to run roughshod over the plain meaning of words in order to support a merely conceptual echo.

(4) Finally this view seems to make little or no sense at all of the primary verb in the opening sentence, ἐκένωσεν, especially if taken literally (how can Christ as second Adam empty himself by becoming a slave?). One could, however, make some sense of it as a metaphor (as the new Adam, Christ made himself nothing by bearing the very nature of a slave). But then the question must be, Why such a *strong* metaphor, when all the second Adam must do is to *reject/renounce* Adam's grasping after 'god-likeness' in order to show the way of servanthood? The verb κενόω (to empty), taken either literally or metaphorically, is simply too strong to sustain the analogy with Adam.

So in the end, the view from below seems to be a clear case where an agenda outside the text drives the reading of the text, thus causing one to grasp at exegetical straws in order to make it work. But rejecting this view does not make the exegetical task any easier. In my commentary I point out that most of the exegetical difficulties in this passage are concentrated in this opening sentence, and that the reason for it seems plain enough: 'On the basis of *what was known and came to be believed* about Jesus' earthly life, Paul is trying to say something about *what could not be observed,* yet *came to be believed* about Christ's prior existence as God'.[13] That is, it is precisely the difficulty of finding a way to express the otherwise unknowable that has led to most of our difficulties.

That leads us, then, to ask whether the verb ἐκένωσεν is best understood literally or metaphorically, as a way of expressing what Christ did 'as God'. Did he literally 'empty himself *of something*' when he took the form of a slave? Or did he metaphorically 'make himself nothing' by assuming the form of a slave, in becoming human? Part of the answer to this question will depend on how one understands the participial phrases that follow, whether they are temporal/consequential or modal ('emptied himself *when he took* the form of a slave' or 'made himself nothing *by taking* the form of a slave').

While none of these questions can be answered definitively, it is at least arguable, on the basis of the basic parallel structure of the *two* sentences in verses 6–8, that the participles very likely carry the same sense in both instances. And here, it would seem, one can make more sense of both of them when understood as having a modal relationship to the main verb in each case. That is, this is the *way* Christ emptied himself and humbled himself: by 'becoming human' and by 'becoming obedient'. And if this is the case, it would also seem more likely that the verb is an intentional, very powerful *metaphor,* similar to Paul's usage of the verb regarding the cross in 1 Corinthians 1:17. Just as the cross would lose its meaning and power if presented in the guise of the 'wisdom of word', so Christ, fully equal with God as he was, nonetheless made himself nothing by taking the form of a slave.[14]

---

[13] Fee, *Philippians,* 198.

[14] Part of the reason for going this way is that the (much briefer) companion text to this one (2 Cor. 8:9) is so obviously metaphorical in trying to express the same reality: 'For you know the grace of our Lord Jesus Christ, that though he was rich, yet for your sake he became poor, so that you through his poverty might become rich.'

If this is the case, and one cannot have certainty here, then the question is not *what* Christ emptied himself *of*, but how else could Paul possibly have expressed the divine mystery of God Incarnate except by this kind of powerful imagery? And this is indeed where I come out as an exegete, asking the kind of grammatical and contextual questions that must be answered first. The real issue for Paul is the selflessness of God, expressed by the pre-existent divine Christ, whereby in his 'becoming human' he took the μορφή of a slave—one who expressed his humanity in lowly service to others.

In any case, I for one have some difficulty with the language of *kenosis* when applied to Christ in his Incarnation, if by that, on the basis of *this* text, we mean that the Son *'emptied* himself *of* anything' in his becoming human.[15] I find that language hard to reconcile with the affirmation that he was 'fully God'. I prefer rather to speak of the Son as deliberately choosing, by the very nature of his assuming a truly human life, to limit certain divine prerogatives that in the end seem incompatible with his being *truly* human, most notably his omnipresence, omnipotence, and omniscience. Thus, without ever 'setting aside' or 'emptying himself of' anything essential to his being truly God, he chose in becoming incarnate to live out a truly human life on our planet, in which he would be totally dependent on the Father through the work of the Spirit.

But having said that, the question still remains whether Paul gives any indication elsewhere about the nature of Christ's humanity, and especially whether such statements imply some degree of 'self-limitation' regarding divine prerogatives on the part of Christ. And the answer in Paul's case seems to be 'no'. His primary interest in Christ's humanity is threefold: (a) in his being the Davidic 'Son of God',[16] who (b) in his earthly life as 'Son' was also the true bearer of the divine image,[17] and (c) whose death served as God's means of our redemption.[18] Thus what we have in Paul is this one, especially strong,

[15] Hence this is where I strongly part company with the earlier kenotic theorists.

[16] See especially Rom. 1:3 and Col. 1:13; this latter text is full of echoes of the OT story, including deliverance from slavery and the Davidic covenant (cf. 2 Sam. 7:14, 18 in the LXX).

[17] See Rom. 8:29; 2 Cor. 4:4; and Col. 1:15.

[18] See esp. Col. 1:14 and 20; note that all three of these concerns merge in Col. 1:13–20.

metaphor as to what the Incarnation entailed, but very little by way of other information as to how that might further be understood.

3. HUMANITY AND DIVINITY IN HEBREWS

When we turn to Hebrews from Paul,[19] we come to more promising material for assessing how NT writers understood the nature of the Incarnation. Indeed, Hebrews is especially fruitful because both dimensions of what came to be understood as orthodox Christology are so strongly affirmed, and are so because both are absolutely necessary to the writer's exhortation.

On the one hand, at stake for our author is the absolute supremacy of Christ over all things, and as such God's final Word to all. Thus he cannot express Jesus' deity strongly enough. The Son, who is God's ultimate Word, is so because he is both the outshining of God's own glory and the express 'imprint' of God's character, who stands at the origin of all things as Creator and at the end as Heir (1:3). By putting this as the 'foreword' of his 'word of exhortation' (13:22), he certainly intends the whole to be read in light of it, even though he seldom returns to this issue except by way of presupposition.

But equally important to him, on the other hand, is the absolute reality of Christ's Incarnation. And this, because the heart of his appeal is going to rest on the all-sufficiency of Christ's priesthood that makes the whole former system now irrelevant. Thus his present session as heavenly high priest is made effective precisely because of *his truly human life*, so that he could become truly empathetic in our 'hour of need' (4:14–16; cf. 2:17–18). Indeed, so genuine was his humanity that our author declares that 'we have one who was tempted in every way, just as we are—yet he did not sin' (4:15). This, in fact, is why he had to be made 'lower than the angels for a little while' (2:9). All of this is stated boldly and propositionally in chapters 2–4.

---

[19] I have no passion to argue for a date for Hebrews vis-à-vis Paul; I would start this discussion with Paul in any case. Nonetheless, I do think the argumentation in Hebrews 7–10 implies that the temple is still standing in Jerusalem.

This emphasis on the genuineness of Christ's humanity becomes even more emboldened when in chapter 5 the author begins his long exposition of the nature of Christ's priesthood. In order for Christ to be a true and sympathetic priest, he must, as with all priests, share fully in their human lot, including its suffering. The 'climax' of this argument stands at the beginning, and also serves as grist for our theological mill: 'During the days of Jesus' life on earth, he offered up prayers and petitions with fervent cries and tears to the one who could save him from death, and he was heard because of his reverent submission. Son though he was, he learned obedience from what he suffered and, once made perfect, he became the source of eternal salvation for all who obey him' (5:7–9, TNIV). Emphasis on the reality of Christ's humanity can hardly be made more strongly than this. And, whether one uses the language of 'kenosis' or not (a rose by any other name?), this sentence presupposes some form of self-limitation on Christ's part in his human life on earth. He expresses utter dependence on the Father in prayer, and then submits to his will in full obedience—an obedience he *learned* through suffering.

The point is, our author could not possibly have intended to imply that Jesus in his humanity was modelling something for *us*, although it was not an actual reality for *him*. Precisely the opposite; his argument works only if Christ's learning obedience through suffering was intensely real for him, thus making his high priesthood a genuine one, in which the perfect, sinless priest (Jesus) offers the perfect sacrifice (Jesus) on the basis of a new covenant in the perfect (heavenly) sanctuary.

So, as with Paul, what one gets Christologically are strong affirmations of genuine, full humanity lived out by the pre-existent, Incarnate Son of God. These epistolary documents are especially important because they reflect appeals to Christ's Incarnation in the twofold interest of either bolstering faith (Hebrews) or encouraging imitative behaviour (Philippians); they are not Christological in terms of their primary intent. And what is learned from them is that a very high Christology in term of affirmations of deity exists alongside very strong recognitions/affirmations of full humanity.

4. HUMANITY AND DIVINITY IN THE SYNOPTIC TRADITION

When we turn from the Epistles to the Gospels we meet a different kind of phenomenon. The Synoptic tradition reflects a post-Easter, post-Pentecost situation of (probably) some thirty-five plus years after the events, when the theological understanding found in Paul and Hebrews is in full sway. Yet we find here a kind of faithfulness to the historical data that does not yield to presenting Jesus' earthly life in a way that could very easily be dubbed 'the earthly life of God'. To the contrary, and despite their individual interests in telling the story, they bear all of the marks of trying to capture the story as it 'essentially happened'.

Since some of what needs to be said here has already been spoken to in the introduction to this chapter, at this point I am interested only in the data that suggest some form of limitation of divine prerogatives during Jesus' earthly life—besides the obvious limitation on omnipresence that Incarnation itself presupposes.

It should be noted at the outset that one of the features the Synoptic Gospels have in common is their portrayal of Jesus as a prophetic figure, who is never recognized as divine by his fellow human beings; only the demons give him away, and they are silenced—and certainly are not believed by either the disciples or crowds. And when the disciples finally catch on that he is the long-awaited Messiah, their own categories of meaning make it impossible for them to allow that he will be killed by the authorities (Mark 8:27–33). Furthermore, Jesus does nothing to make the crowds or disciples think otherwise. The authority to forgive sin belongs to the 'Son of Man', not to one who is overtly divine (Mark 2:10 and parallels); and when confronted by the One who stills the waters, the disciples ask with amazement, but not with understanding, 'Who, then, is this?' (Mark 4:41).

Thus it comes as no surprise that Mark—surprisingly followed by Matthew[20]—toward the end of the Olivet discourse faithfully records

---

[20] The surprise factor is that Matthew, while absolutely true to the tradition regarding Jesus' full humanity, is also well known to have 'softened' moments in

the word of Jesus that 'about that day or hour no one knows, not even the angels in heaven, nor the Son' (Mark 13:32; Matt. 24:26). Even a brief glance through the Fathers makes it clear that this is the sentence that has tended to put the fox among the chickens.

But such a sentence is quite consistent with the overall picture presented by all three Synoptic evangelists. Jesus is portrayed not as acting out of a position of divine power, but as a truly human figure who is totally dependent on God his Father. He is thus seen as constantly engaged in prayer;[21] and at the end he even prays to be delivered from the very reality that he came early on to recognize as his own prophetic 'fate'—death at the hands of the political and religious authorities. Thus his well-known words: 'Abba, everything is possible for you. Take this cup from me. Yet not what I will, but what you will' (Mark 14:36). The faithfulness of the evangelists to this dimension of the tradition, when it is equally clear from other moments (birth narratives; Immanuel; the centurion's exclamation, etc.) that they know well who he really is, is a sure mark of their historical reliability.

But further word is needed about Luke's presentation, since his Gospel narrative is purposefully presented as part 1 of a two-part story. Despite his omission of the saying about 'not knowing the hour', his narrative is the most thoroughgoing in terms of portraying a 'kenotic' Jesus. For example, there is no question that part of the purpose of Luke's birth narrative is to make known Jesus' divine origins at the outset (virgin birth through the instrumentality of the Holy Spirit). Yet equally prominent in this narrative is the fact that his birth meant the coming of the awaited messianic deliverer (Luke 1:32–3, 49–55, 69–75; 2:28–35, 38). So important is this for Luke's narrative that it tends to supersede the divine dimension of Jesus' origins in every way; indeed, the birth narrative itself ends on this

---

Mark which might be understood as diminishing his deity; thus, e.g. all of Jesus' questions in Mark that might suggest he didn't know something are either eliminated or turned into indicatives (see 8:29–30//Mark 5:9; 9:21–2//Mark 5:30; 14:15–17// Mark 6:37–8; 17:14//Mark 9:16; 17:17–18//Mark 9:21; 18:1//Mark 9:33). Yet if you were to read Matthew on his own without access to Mark, you would hardly notice such things.

[21] This is especially true of Luke's Gospel, a feature that is in keeping with his emphasis that Jesus is totally dependent on the Spirit (see below). Thus Jesus is described as praying at every crucial turn in the narrative (3:21; 5:6; 6:12; 9:18, 29; 11:1; 22:41; 23:46).

note: 'Then he went down to Nazareth with [his parents] and was obedient to them.... And as Jesus grew up, he increased in wisdom and in favor with God and people' (2:51–2).

Thus everything about the presentation of Jesus to Israel is under the guidance and empowering of the Spirit: the Spirit who descends on him at his baptism (3:22) leads him into the desert for the testing (4:1) and back to Galilee to begin his ministry (4:14). In Luke's narrative art Jesus is then actually presented to Israel—in the programmatic Nazareth narrative (4:16–20)—as fulfilling Isaiah 61:1–2, with its special emphasis, 'the Spirit of the Lord is on me, because he has anointed me to proclaim good news to the poor' (4:18). That Luke intends us to read the rest of his Gospel narrative with 'by the Spirit' as the proper modifier of all Jesus' mighty words and deeds is made clear in part 2 (the Book of Acts). Not only does the prologue pick up this motif (Acts 1:2), but at the two crucial 'turning points' of the narrative (2:14–41, the presentation of the crucified and risen Jesus to the Jews; and 10:38, the presentation to the Gentiles), the Apostle Peter says explicitly that 'Jesus of Nazareth was a man accredited by God to you by miracles, wonders and signs, which God did among you through him' (2:22) and that 'God anointed Jesus of Nazareth with the Holy Spirit and power, and [that] he went around doing good and healing all who were under the power of the devil, because God was with him' (10:38). And this by the one who also narrates that Jesus' ultimate origins are divine (Luke 1:35) and that he has currently assumed his place of authority as the Lord, sitting at the right hand of the Father (Acts 2:33).

It is hard to imagine a more truly 'kenotic' presentation of the Incarnation than this, and it is precisely such a presentation which presents so much tension for ordinary readers when they move from Luke to John's Gospel, to which we now turn at the end.

5. HUMANITY AND DEITY IN THE GOSPEL OF JOHN

I think it is fair to the data to suggest that if the Fourth Gospel had been the only narrative of Jesus that had been preserved in the church, the Workshop that led to this book would very likely never have happened. That is, since in John the 'kenotic' dimension of Jesus' earthly life is generally missing—and this for a number of reasons—the 'tensions' that one feels between John and the Synoptics would simply not have emerged, and this discussion, therefore, would tend to be moot at the Scriptural level and carried on altogether at the theological and philosophical level.

But that having been said, one seriously misreads John's Gospel, as Ernst Käsemann in fact did,[22] who would imagine John to be uninterested in Jesus' being genuinely and fully human. Precisely the opposite. Granted that his narrative is expressly written from his post-Easter understanding of the pre-Easter Jesus. After all, it is 'after [Jesus] was raised from the dead, [that] his disciples recalled what he had said' (2:22; cf. 12:16; 13:7); and this is also where the coming of the Spirit is so important to John's narrative (14:26; 16:14). Nonetheless, John's concern is that it was the truly human Jesus, 'whose parents [people] knew' (6:42), who was at the same time the ultimate locus of God's self-disclosure on our planet.

Whatever else is true of John, he cares immensely about Jesus' real humanity: the eternal Word became *flesh* and tabernacled among us (1:14); during the regular course of his earthly life he grew tired and hungry as the result of travel by foot (4:6); he wept (for whatever reasons) at the graveside of a friend (11:35); his family origins were known (1:45–6; 6:41–2, etc.); and his death was that of a shepherd laying down his life, from whose pierced side came both blood and water.

So it is hardly true that John's presentation is of a 'naively docetic' Christ. Indeed, his concern lies on the other side of things, namely that it is precisely in *the One who became flesh* that people could now behold the glory of God (1:14).[23] To lose touch with his true humanity is to lose touch altogether with the locus of revelation.

---

[22] See *The Testament of Jesus: A Study of the Gospel of John in the Light of Chapter 17*, 2nd edn., trans. Gerhard Krodel (Philadelphia: Fortress Press, 1968). His well-known critique of the Gospel, that it is 'naively docetic', has been ably refuted by Marianne Meye Thompson, *The Humanity of Jesus in the Fourth Gospel* (Philadelphia: Fortress Press, 1988).

[23] This, of course, is the point where the Gospel and 1 John share a similar *Sitz im Leben*. The concern of the latter is with some false prophets who 'deny the Son' (2:18–23), which later is expressed in terms of denying that 'Jesus has come in the flesh'

At the same time, however, John is intensely concerned that the truly human One is indeed the One who had come from the Father and was going to return to Him. Hence, very much as in Hebrews, John's emphases lie on both sides simultaneously; but in contrast to Hebrews there is very little emphasis on the 'kenotic' nature of his human life. John's passion is that the human being known as 'Jesus, son of Joseph' is none other than the Jewish Messiah, the Son of God (20:31),[24] who very well knew his 'whence and whither' (13:3; 17:5, cf. 6:33, 38; 7:29; 8:23 et al.), and who 'manifested' the Father in all that he was and did (17:6).

And this double reality, that in Jesus' earthly life God's glory was being clearly manifested—which is now seen all the more clearly from the post-Easter, post-Pentecost side of things—accounts at the same time for John's frustration, if I may be allowed such a word. This is articulated first in his programmatic prologue and then found throughout the narrative: that 'the true light that gives light to everyone [came] into the world, and though the world itself was made through him, the world did not recognize him' (1:9), that 'he came to that which was his own, but his own did not receive him' (1:11). This is then picked up, *inter alios*, in 3:19: 'light has come into the world, but people loved darkness rather than light,' and finds final expression in the double summary at the end of the Book of Signs (12:37–50).

Thus, because John's emphasis is on revelation and redemption through Jesus, the Son of God, he intentionally highlights the reality of the divine in the earthly Jesus. The earthly was plainly there, and absolutely crucial to his telling of the story; so how could some have

(4:1–2). The essential difference between the two (besides the obvious difference in genre) is the clearly 'Jewish' dimension of the Gospel, where the purpose is expressly that 'you might believe that Jesus is the Messiah, the Son of God' and the narrative is framed altogether by the Jewish festival calendar (see 2:13; 5:1; 6:4; 7:2; 10:22; 11:55–12:1; 13:1).

[24] So rightly TNIV. This is one of John's more important 'double meaning' of words, so that the confession of Nathanael (1:49), by one who is designated by Jesus as a 'true Israelite', is the most explicitly Jewish in the Gospel, picking up the messianism of Psalm 2 as it does: 'the Son of God, the King of Israel'. Thus, throughout the 'Book of Signs' (2:12–12:50) Jesus is presented as the One who fulfils all the messianic expectations associated with the Jewish feasts; but at the same time the language of 'Son of God' takes on the added dimension of 'the Son of the Father', who is 'one with the Father', and thus becomes language pointing to his divinity.

missed it? But because Jesus' followers had come to believe that he was Son of God in both senses—the Jewish Messiah and the eternal Son of the Father—John's interest is ultimately, and especially, in the eternal Son as the one who revealed the Father most truly and perfectly.

This is the reason also why the element of self-limitation is so often missing from the picture. It is simply not relevant to John's concerns. Nonetheless, one dimension of it is forcefully expressed throughout the narrative, which is quite in keeping with his primary concern; namely, in the repeated emphasis that in his Incarnation Jesus the Son is totally dependent on the Father. This emphasis begins in the Sabbath controversy in chapter 5, the first open conflict with 'the Jews': as with the Father, Jesus 'is always at his work to this very day' (5:17); yet he 'can do nothing by himself; he can do only what he sees his Father doing' (v. 19), and this because 'by myself I can do nothing' (v. 30). Thus throughout the narrative Jesus functions not on his own authority (14:10). Rather he speaks only what he has heard from the Father (12:49; 14:24; 17:8) and 'can do only what he sees his Father doing' (5:19), because he came to do the Father's will (5:30; 6:38–40), thus obeying the Father's commands (10:18; 15:10) by doing the Father's works (10:32, 37–8; 14:10). So, divine Jesus is indeed, but in his Incarnation he is totally dependent on the Father.

The point to make is, that if John has thus become a primary, if not *the* primary, source for orthodox Christology, one should not make more of his tendency *not* to tell the story in 'kenotic' terms than is merited by the overall picture. Lack of concern in this direction may indeed be seen as Christological, but not in the sense that the later church has taken it. That is, he does not write to 'correct' or 'enhance' the Synoptic picture, but to make sure that his readers do not miss the essential matter about Jesus—that as redeemer of the world he is also the one who most fully and truly reveals the Father.

6. CONCLUSIONS

So where does this overview of the biblical data leave us? Let us return for a moment to the beginning of this chapter, where I suggested that many orthodox believers feel no tension at all in these data. They begin with the perspective of John's Gospel and simply and easily read that perspective into the Synoptic account, but often do so in such a way as to miss—or dismiss—the Synoptic picture altogether. That is, they find no conflict because they subsume the one set of data under the other, rather than let them sit side by side in happy tension.

This is a view of Scripture that I call 'progressive canonical', which turns out to be another form of having a 'canon within the canon', a view that was asserted unabashedly by E. J. Carnell in *The Case for Orthodox Theology*.[25] In a five-step programme of hermeneutics, he argued that the New Testament interprets the Old, that the Epistles interpret the Gospels, and that 'systematic passages interpret the incidental', which for him meant that the whole canon was finally interpreted on the basis of Romans and Galatians!

While it is true that for the Christian (as with Jesus and Paul) the New interprets the Old, I reject the rest of this view as unworthy of Carnell's own 'high view' of Scripture. Since the biblical texts themselves do not provide us with this key for reading, it means that the key has been brought to the texts from the outside and expresses a prior theological commitment before one reads the texts themselves. I urge that the canon itself be the deciding factor; and the canon embraces both Luke and John side by side. Equally inspired of the Holy Spirit, they must equally play their roles in our Christological theologizing. And in this case we get little help from the Epistles, which do not speak systematically to our Christological concerns.

All of this to say that an orthodox biblical Christology almost certainly must embrace some form of a 'kenotic' understanding of the Incarnation, that the One who was truly God, also in his Incarnation lived a truly human life, a life in which he *grew* both in stature and in wisdom and understanding (Luke 2:52), learned obedience through what he suffered (Heb. 5:8), and who as Son of the Father did not know the day or the hour (Mark 13:32).

Could such a one also have gone 'zap' and produced instant hamburger in his hand? That is, could he have turned stones into bread at his own behest, as Satan tested him to do? That remains in

---

[25] Philadelphia: Westminster Press, 1959. I am here contending with the content of chapter 4, 'Hermeneutics', 51–65.

the category of the unknown. But to believe that he *could* have done so would mean that his own powers during his humanity were limitless, as over against his being fully dependent on the Father through the power of the Spirit. The overall evidence of the Gospels seems to imply that he *could not*, since, in contrast to the apocryphal gospels, they offer us no evidence of an Incarnate God who used his powers for his own selfish ends. But at this point theology takes over, because the same evidence, I must allow, could also be understood in terms of *would not.*

3

The Odyssey of Christ: A Novel Context for Philippians 2:6–11

Bruce N. Fisk

The Hellenistic context of early Christianity is back. After several post-Holocaust waves of preoccupation with the Jewish roots of early Christianity, the current vogue among NT scholars is to attend to matters Hellenistic,[1] including Roman imperial politics, Graeco-Roman religion, sophistic rhetoric and, to lesser degrees, the social world of the early Greek novels.[2] Riding this wave with abandon, my

[1] The best scholarship, of course, refuses to choose between Jewish and Hellenistic contexts since 1st-century Judaism was so thoroughly Hellenized, as was early Jewish Christianity. See further A. F. Segal, *Paul the Convert: The Apostolate and Apostasy of Saul the Pharisee* (New Haven: Yale, 1990) 84; W. D. Davies, *Paul and Rabbinic Judaism* 4th edn. (Philadelphia: Fortress, 1980) 320; S. Neill and N. T. Wright, *The Interpretation of the New Testament: 1861–1986* 2nd edn. (New York: Oxford, 1988) 370, 375–6; and recently Troels Engberg-Pedersen, ed., *Paul Beyond the Judaism/Hellenism Divide* (Louisville, KY: Westminster/JKP, 2001). Contrast the forced dichotomy between 'Greek' and 'Jewish' in the portrait of Paul presented by C. J. den Heyer, *Paul: A Man of Two Worlds*, trans. J. Bowden (Philadelphia: Trinity Press International, 2000).

[2] As a barometer of interest among biblical scholars in the early Greek novels, see esp. the work of the SBL *Ancient Fiction and Early Christian and Jewish Narrative Group* (formally organized in 1992), and the selection of the Group's essays, edited by R. F. Hock, J. B. Chance, and J. Perkins, published in *Ancient Fiction and Early Christian Narrative* (Atlanta: Scholars, 1998). Also of note is the recently launched e-journal, *Ancient Narrative* [http://www.ancientnarrative.com/] which continues and expands the *Petronian Society Newsletter* [http://www.ancientnarrative.com/PSN/index.htm]. For a concise but trustworthy guide for biblical scholars to the world of the novels, see Ronald F. Hock, 'The Greek Novel' in David E. Aune, ed., *Greco-Roman Literature and the New Testament*, SBLSBS 21 (Atlanta: Scholars Press, 1988) 126–46.

contribution shall amount to an exercise in Hellenistic reader response. I pose the following question: how might the so-called *kenōsis*
narrative of Philippians 2:6–11 sound in the sort of world that
produced, and consumed, Graeco-Roman fiction? Where, in other
words, might we situate Paul's narrative about the self-emptying
and subsequent exaltation of Christ within the broader social context—the mythic landscape—of the early Greek romance novels? If
this reading strategy seems initially rather odd—rather like holding a
hymn book in one hand and a Harlequin romance in the other—the
hope is that it might nevertheless expose or at least highlight aspects
of the hymn that might otherwise go unnoticed.

To pursue these sorts of questions, we shall identify several central
features of the *Christ hymn*[3] and explore the extent to which these
elements find counterparts among the generic conventions of early
romance literature. This is not, *nota bene*, a search for literary
influences or echoes. Neither is it an exercise in intertextuality nor
a test case in *mimesis*.[4] Still less are we concerned with the prehistory
of the hymn, nor shall we evaluate proposals about a pre-Christian
Heavenly Redeemer myth.[5] We seek only to hear Paul's *hymn* in the
reading chamber of Graeco-Roman fiction, arguably an important

---

[3] Throughout this paper, I use the term *hymn* in an unguarded, non-technical
sense. Notwithstanding the popularity of the view that Phil. 2:6–11 is a pre-Pauline
hymnic fragment, I find the evidence less than persuasive. For judicious (and
similarly negative) assessments of the evidence, see esp. G. Fee, 'Philippians 2:5–11:
Hymn or Exalted Prose?' *BBR* 2 (1992) 29–46, and S. E. Fowl, 'The Story of Christ in
the Ethics of Paul', *JSNT* Sup. 36 (Sheffield, 1990) 31–45. Cf. M. Bockmuehl, ' "The
Form of God" (Phil. 2:6) Variations on a Theme of Jewish Mysticism' *JTS* 48 (1997)
2–4, 1–23. For the purposes of this paper, we might point out that the poetic,
rhythmical hymn-like quality of Phil. 2:6–11 finds a parallel in the early novels, in
Longus' ode to Eros (*Daphnis and Chloe* 2.7), on which see T. Hägg, *The Novel in
Antiquity* (Berkeley: UC Press, 1983) 37–8. Thanks to Ron Hock for drawing my
attention to this passage.

[4] Intertextuality differs from *mimesis* insofar as the latter refers (in its primary
sense) to the Hellenistic practice of 'training of students to write through the
imitation of recognized models' (Dennis R. MacDonald, ed., *Mimesis and Intertextuality in Antiquity and Christianity* (Harrisburg: Trinity Press Int., 2001) 1). Cf. idem,
The Homeric Epics and the Gospel of Mark (New Haven: Yale, 2000).

[5] For orientation to the (now largely passé) debate on this last question, see Peter
T. O'Brien, *The Epistle to the Philippians*, NIGTC (Grand Rapids: Eerdmans, 1991)
193–4, and R. P. Martin, *A Hymn of Christ: Philippians 2:5–11 in Recent Interpretation
& in the Setting of Early Christian Worship* (Downers Grove: Inter-Varsity, 1997 (1967,
1983)) 90–2.

yet long-neglected part of what has been called the 'imaginative economy' (Peter Brown) of Paul's world.

To represent the corpus of ancient Greek novels, we shall limit ourselves to some of the oldest exemplars, which is to say three works composed during the first and second centuries of our era.

1. Chariton's *Chaereas and Callirhoe*, dubbed by B. P. Reardon 'the first European novel', is a twisting saga of love lost and regained that likely emerged in mid-first century CE.[6]

2. *An Ephesian Tale* by Xenophon, similarly convoluted and melodramatic, probably dates from the second century, though we know little if anything about its author.[7]

3. Achilles Tatius' *Leucippe and Kleitophon*, apparently popular in its day, is an erotic, eclectic tale of eloping lovers from the third quarter of the second century CE.[8]

None of these works could have been known to the Philippian congregation, the first audience for Paul's Christ story.[9] But each of

[6] Bryan P. Reardon, ed. *Collected Ancient Greek Novels* (Berkeley: UC Press, 1989) 17. Reardon bases his dating on the admittedly unreliable criterion of style: since Chariton's Greek is non-Atticized, it would seem to reflect the period prior to the late first century CE. A. Heiserman, *The Novel Before the Novel* (Chicago: University of Chicago Press, 1977) 75, represents the consensus view when he dates the work around 50 CE. Cf. R. Hock, 'Greek Novel', 128. For the standard text and translation of Chariton, see G. P. Goold, ed. *Callirhoe*, LCL (Cambridge, MA: Harvard U.P., 1995). For an excellent, slightly older translation, see B. P. Reardon, *Ancient Greek Novels*, 17–124.

[7] The evidence for a second-century date is helpfully summarized in Gareth Schmeling, *Xenophon of Ephesus* (Boston: Twayne, 1980) 18–19. For the Greek text we follow Georges Dalmeyda, *Xénophon d'Éphèse, Les Éphésiaques (ou Le Roman d'Habrocomès et d'Anthia)* (Paris: Société d'Édition 'Les Belles Lettres', 1962). English translations generally follow Graham Anderson, in B. P. Reardon, *Ancient Greek Novels*, 125–69.

[8] We may infer the work's popularity from the survival in Egypt of seven papyri, ranging from the 2nd to the 4th centuries. See John J. Winkler, in B. P. Reardon, *Ancient Greek Novels*, 170–1. For Greek text, we follow S. Gaselee, *Achilles Tatius*, LCL (Cambridge, MA: Harvard U.P., 1947 (1917)). English citations generally follow J. J. Winkler's translation in Reardon, ibid., 170–284.

[9] Quite apart from uncertainties regarding the dates of these compositions, the challenges of identifying the audience and of assessing the popularity of these novels are formidable. Recent essays on this subject have tended to dispute the standard claim (represented by, e.g. Tomas Hägg and B. E. Perry) that these works aim at the young and the restless, the frivolous, the newly literate, the women, etc. According to Susan A. Stephens, 'Who Read Ancient Novels?', in James Tatum, ed., *The Search for*

them reflects, arguably, the moral and literary sensibilities of Paul's day. In them we encounter stock conventions of Graeco-Roman morality, standard notions of propriety, social constructions of class and gender, and expressions of religious piety. And they all share certain narrative expectations. Against this backdrop, five features of the Christ hymn stand out: its plot structure, narrative beginnings, the place of choice and freewill, the centrality of death, and the role of divine intervention. After examining each of these features, we shall consider the theological pay-off of reading Paul in this 'novel' context.

1. PLOT: THE STORY IS V-SHAPED—FROM HUMILIATION TO EXALTATION

Whatever else Paul is doing in Philippians 2:6–11, he is surely telling a story—one that begins and ends in splendour, and that in between traces a journey of abject humiliation followed by exaltation. This V-shape is clearly marked: verses 6–8 move progressively downward,[10] culminating in Christ's death by crucifixion; verses 9–11 announce a sudden but fitting reversal of fortunes, culminating in the universal recognition of Christ's lordship. Paul's account of Christ's exaltation is not narrated in progressive stages, yet the series of clauses in verses

---

the Ancient Novel (Baltimore: Johns Hopkins, 1994), 405–18, they could not have been widely read and would have circulated primarily among the upper classes. Similarly, Ewen Bowie, 'The Readership of Greek Novels in the Ancient World', ibid. 435–59. Cf. B. P. Reardon, *Ancient Greek Novels*, 10–11.

[10] Thus, my reading differs from Robert Gundry's proposal ('Style and Substance in "The Myth of God Incarnate" According to Philippians 2:6–11' in S. E. Porter, P. Joyce, and D. E. Orton, eds., *Crossing the Boundaries: Essays in Biblical Interpretation in Honour of Michael D. Goulder* (Leiden: Brill, 1994) 271–93) that Phil. 2:7a (*he emptied himself, taking the form of a slave*) refers not to Christ's Incarnation but to Christ's death on the cross. On Gundry's reading, verses 7a and 8 (*he humbled himself and became obedient to the point of death—even death on a cross*) are parallel descriptions of the same event: Christ's 'slave-like death' (p. 274). If Gundry is correct, the hymn becomes not a sequential narrative of descent and ascent, but rather a declaration of 'the contrast between the high of pre- and postexistent divine honor and the low of a shameful human death' (pp. 274–5).

9–11 do seem designed to provide a measure of balance to verses 6–8, as the following display (following the *NRSV*) might suggest:

6 Though he was in the form of God,
   he did not regard equality with God as something to be exploited,
7   but emptied himself,
           taking the form of a slave,
           being born in human likeness.
       And being found in human form,
8   he humbled himself
               and became obedient to the point of death—
                   even death on a cross.
9   Therefore God also highly exalted him
               and gave him the name that is above every name,
10   so that at the name of Jesus every knee should bend,
           in heaven and on earth and under the earth,
11   and every tongue should confess that Jesus Christ is Lord,
   to the glory of God the Father.

Signalling the sudden reversal is the strongly inferential *dio kai* ('there-fore ... also') introducing verse 9, as well as the abrupt change in subject from *Christ* to *God*. Since at least Ernst Lohmeyer (1928), therefore, it has been customary to think of verses 6–8 as Christ's *katabasis* and verses 9–11 as Christ's *anabasis*.[11]

All of this corresponds rather nicely, as it turns out, to the symbolic world of the ancient novels, where a descent–ascent sequence is not only foundational but also explicit, and routinely captured in concise narrative summaries of similar size and substance to the condensed account set forth in Philippians 2. The Greek romance followed a basic pattern, as B. P. Reardon explains: 'initial felicity rudely broken by journey and separation; danger to life, limb, and chastity; rescue by divine agency; and eventual reunion through similar

---

[11] Ernst Lohmeyer, *Kyrios Jesus: Eine Untersuchung zu Phil. 2,5–11* (Heidelberg: Winter, 1928, 1961). See further R. Martin, *A Hymn of Christ*, 25–30, 38–9. I am thus not persuaded by J. Jeremias, 'Zur Gedankenführung in den paulinischen Briefen' in J. N. Sevenster and W. C. van Unnik, eds., *Studia Paulina in Honoerem J. de Zwaan* (Haarlem: Bohn, 1953), 139–54, that the structure is tripartite (6–7a, 7b–8, 9–11).

means'.[12] Heiserman offers a similar summary of these ancient tales: the protagonists 'suffer the direst threats to their lives and values, ... but ... they survive all their perils to live happily ever after'.[13] Most helpful, for our purposes, is Hock's description of the novels' structure:

This structure entails *humiliation* of the novel's protagonists and then their *exaltation* at the end. A summary of the plot of these novels will point out this structure: hero and heroine come from aristocratic families but after they fall in love they *lose this status* and become *slaves*. In addition to the psychological *humiliation* of being treated as a slave they endure assorted physical hardships, usually as a result of their maintaining fidelity to their beloved. But in the end they are *raised up to their former status* by the aid of some gracious deity, after which they live happily ever after.[14]

These novels tell stories, in other words, of descent and ascent, of humiliation and exaltation, of tragic defeat followed by glorious victory. Of course, this V-shaped pattern is by no means unique to the early novels. Homer's *Odyssey,* inspiration to every aspiring Hellenic troubadour, tells how Odysseus endured countless trials and humiliations—shipwreck, Cyclops, adverse winds, cannibals, the enchanting Circe, descent into Hades, Poseidon's wrath, the Sirens' sound, the twin perils of Scylla and Charybdis—on his return to Ithaca, and even donned the garb of a beggar to suffer ridicule from Penelope's many suitors before gloriously reclaiming his rightful estate. A descent–ascent pattern was clearly established long before the early novelists emerged, and endured long after.[15]

---

[12] Reardon, *Ancient Greek Novels,* 125.

[13] Heiserman, *Novel Before the Novel,* 6.

[14] Hock, 'Greek Novel,' 134 (emphasis added). See also Dale Martin, *Slavery as Salvation: The Metaphor of Slavery in Pauline Christianity* (New Haven: Yale University Press, 1990) 35.

[15] Northop Frye, *The Great Code: The Bible and Literature* (San Diego: Harcourt Brace, 1983) 169, contends that 'the U-shaped pattern, approximate as it is, recurs in literature as the standard shape of comedy, where a series of misfortunes and misunderstandings brings the action to a threateningly low point, after which some fortunate twist in the plot sends the conclusion up to a happy ending.' For a seminal discussion of this pattern or 'monomyth', as it appears across ages and cultures, see Joseph Campbell, *The Hero with a Thousand Faces* (Princeton: Princeton U.P., 1972; orig. 1949). For an influential adaptation of Campbell with an eye toward popular culture, see Christopher Vogler, *The Writer's Journey: Mythic Structure for Storytellers & Screenwriters* (Studio City, CA: Michael Wiese Productions, 1992).

This is not to say that our ancient novels track a smooth, clean down–up storyline. On the contrary, they are notorious for their interminable sub-plots, multiple endings, and unwieldy plot structures. Yet readers cannot help but detect a basic pattern across this corpus and, as we shall see, we are justified in calling it V-shaped.

Chariton's tale of *Chaereas and Callirhoe* is largely the story of the couple's relentless descent from highest honour to unimaginable shame, a pattern Heiserman has called 'erotic suffering'.[16] Twice Callirhoe is falsely accused of infidelity. She is physically assaulted, mistakenly buried alive, captured and enslaved by brigands, almost thrown into the sea (1.12), and then sold into slavery. As the tyrant's ship carries her away, the irony of this stark reversal is not lost on Callirhoe: 'I must be a slave—I, who was born noble' (1.11). Indeed, Callirhoe seems almost eager to chronicle the stages of her descent:

Fortune, your curse is on me! You are pursuing me on land and sea. You have not had your fill of my misfortunes. First you made my lover my murderer ...; then you gave me [*me... paredōkas*] into the hands of tomb robbers and brought me out from the tomb onto the sea, and set over me the pirates, who were more frightening than the waves. My celebrated beauty I was given to this end, that the brigand Theron should get a high price for me. I have been sold in a deserted spot and not even taken to a city like any other bought slave [*hōs allē tis tōn argyrōnētōn*]—Fortune, you were afraid people might see me and think me nobly born! That is why I have been handed over like a mere chattel [*dia touto hōs skeuos paredothēn*] to I know not whom, Greeks or barbarians or brigands once more (1.14).[17]

To all of this she would soon have to add unwanted pregnancy. 'Fortune, you have added this as well to my misfortunes,' says Callirhoe, 'that I should become a mother too—mother of a slave!' (2.8). As she considers whether or not to take the life of her child, she takes comfort in a familiar narrative pattern: 'How many stories are there', she asks, 'of sons of gods and kings born in slavery [*theōn*

---

[16] A. Heiserman, *The Novel Before the Novel*, 75–116. The phrase 'erotic suffering' (*pathos erōtikon*) comes from Chariton, *Callirhoe* 1.1.

[17] Cf. Callirhoe's prayer of dedication to Aphrodite: 'I beg you, mistress, be at peace with me now; I have had enough misfortune! I have died and come to life again. I have been taken by pirates and made an exile; I have been sold and been a slave; and I reckon my second marriage a greater burden yet than all this' (3.8). Except where stated, English citations from the novels follow the translation and versification of B. P. Reardon, *Ancient Greek Novels*.

paidas kai basileōn en douleia gennēthentas], then coming into their rightful ancestral rank?' (2.9). Note the basic pattern: a son of god first becomes a slave and then acquires his rightful rank—lofty status, then descent and humiliation, and finally exaltation.[18]

Callirhoe's ascent out of slavery seems to be under way, at last, when she reluctantly agrees to marry Dionysius, a nobleman from Ionia. Chariton has a temple attendant highlight the irony for us: 'That woman was a *slave*', she says, 'and Aphrodite has made her *mistress of all of us*' (*Hautē doulē men ēn, hē de Aphroditē pantōn hēmōn kyrian pepoiēken autēn*; 3.6). With appropriate modifications this remark could slide neatly into several books of the New Testament.[19] Readers of Paul's Christ hymn may understandably experience déjà vu. Callirhoe's trials are not yet over, however, for the men in her life determine to defend their claim on her in a Persian court. News of this development prompts yet another bitter outburst from Callirhoe—an outburst that chronicles her now-familiar descent into slavery:

'Oh,' she cried, 'that was all I needed, in my misfortunes—to be taken to court! I have died and been buried; I have been stolen from my tomb; I have been sold into slavery—and now, Fortune, on top of that I find myself on trial! You were not satisfied with traducing me to Chaereas; you have led Dionysius to suspect me of adultery! The first time, your slander led me to the tomb; now it brings me to the royal court of justice!' (5.5)[20]

When Persian king Artaxerxes falls for beautiful Callirhoe—take a number—she refuses to flinch, preferring rather to rehearse, one more time, her many previous setbacks:

'It will not be my first experience of suffering,' she said. 'I am acquainted with misfortune. What disposition can the King make for me that would be worse than I have already suffered? I have been buried alive; the tomb is

---

[18] Even when Dionysius readily agrees to marry her, not as *slave* but as *nobility*, she hesitates, fearing some further humiliation must be in store: 'I trust you, Dionysius,' she said. 'It is my own fortune I do not trust. It has brought me low before now, from greater fortune; I am afraid it has not yet settled its quarrel with me' (3.2).

[19] Cf. Acts 2:22–36; Rom. 1:3–4; Heb. 2:9; Rev. 5:12.

[20] We encounter a parallel yet briefer account of her downward spiral in a bitter remark about the burden of beauty: 'How many times have you handed me over—to pirates, to the sea, to the tomb, slavery, judgment! But the heaviest burden I have had to bear is the King's love' (6.6).

narrower than any prison cell. I have been delivered into the hands of pirates. And now I am suffering the worst of my torments: Chaereas is near me and I cannot see him' (6.7).

Meanwhile the descent of her beloved Chaereas begins when he is captured by Persians, sold into slavery and forced to work the land in heavy chains (3.7). Adding injury to insult, he is wrongly sentenced to death, by crucifixion no less, for allegedly attempting to escape (4.2). Only the quick thinking of sidekick Polycharmus saves him from a grisly death (4.3). When he subsequently learns that his wife now belongs to someone else, despair descends:

I have been sold into slavery on account of you; I have dug the earth; I have carried my cross; I have been handed over to the executioner—and you were living in luxury, you were celebrating your marriage, while I was in chains! (4.3)[21]

We reach an even lower moment—the crook of the V—just before the trial, when Chaereas, assuming Callirhoe will reject him for Dionysius, attempts to end his own life (5.10). With the unexpected onset of war, however, Chaereas trades in his despair and passivity for courageous activism. Eager to lay down his life and to avenge his lost love, he sides with Egypt against Persia, setting the stage, finally, for his glorious vindication. Chariton, though himself showing signs of authorial fatigue, trumpets Chaereas' long-awaited ascent from exile and estrangement:

Aphrodite took pity on him; having harassed by land and sea the handsome couple she had originally brought together, she decided now to reunite them. And I think that this last chapter will prove very agreeable to its readers: it cleanses away the grim events of the earlier ones. There will be no more pirates or slavery or lawsuits or fighting or suicide or wars or conquests; now there will be lawful love and sanctioned marriage. So I shall tell

---

[21] Compare the summary of his fate in the letter he addresses to Callirhoe: 'I was sold, enslaved, put in chains. Do not harbor malice against me for kicking you, in my temper—in my turn I ascended the cross because of you and did not say a word against you' (4.4). Likewise he rehearses his downward trek to his friend Polycharmus who won't let him commit suicide: 'I should have been spared what followed—being sold, attacked by robbers, put in chains, crucified—and a king more cruel than the cross! How sweet death would have been after I heard that Callirhoe had married again!' (6.2; cf. 7.1).

you how the goddess brought the truth to light and revealed the unrecognized pair to each other. (8.1)

The return to Syracuse is without incident, and the couple's emotional reunion with family and friends is described in glowing detail. The crowds cannot withhold their praises (8.7) and all redounds to the greater glory of Aphrodite and the hosts of heaven (8.8). Once again we discern broad parallels to the narrative pattern of Paul's Christ hymn.

That Xenophon's *Ephesian Tale* conforms to this same V-shape is confirmed early and explicitly. The oracle of Apollo, sought by two anxious fathers regarding their lovesick children, offers a preview of coming attractions:[22]

But for them I see terrible sufferings and toils that are endless;
Both will flee over the sea pursued by madness;
They will suffer chains at the hands of men who mingle with the waters;
And a tomb shall be the burial chamber for both, and fire the destroyer;
The savior you will afterwards offer rich gifts;
But still after their sufferings a better fate is in store (1.6).

The narrative sequence is now familiar: suffering—death—divine deliverance—final bliss.[23] As with Chariton's tale (which this one is thought to emulate[24]), the downward journey of Habrocomes and Anthia is protracted and complex. Together they are captured and enslaved by Phoenician pirates (1.13) and threatened by jealous suitors (1.16). When falsely accused of attempted rape (2.5), Habrocomes is tortured and imprisoned (2.6–7). When he is released to embark on a quest to reclaim his bride (2.10), it leads only to slavery in Egypt (3.12), and then to crucifixion on false charges (4.2). After

---

[22] On the device of foreshadowing in Xenophon, see G. Schmeling, *Xenophon*, 89–90. Schmeling (ibid. 27) not only sees in this oracle an outline of the entire plot but also regards this structure as foundational to the genre: 'It seems certain from this that Xenophon had either some general scheme in mind from the beginning or that the architectonic unity of the novel form is so stereotyped that the same outline is appropriate to almost every novel. While there are surely many differences among the various Greek and Roman novels, a general outline, like the one found in Xenophon, would yield most plots.'

[23] For a more complex (though not incompatible) structural analysis, see Schmeling, *Xenophon*, 82–3.

[24] On the rather complex and unresolved relationship between these two works, see Thomas Hägg, *The Novel in Antiquity*, 18–26.

narrowly escaping death, he is recaptured and almost burned alive (4.2).

Meanwhile, Xenophon has Anthia carried off to Syria and delivered to a lowly goatherd (2.9). She narrowly escapes death as well but only to be sold as chattel to Cilician merchants (2.11), shipwrecked, captured by robbers (2.12), almost sacrificed to Ares (2.13), and almost forced to marry Perilaus, the irenarch of Cilicia (2.13–14). From this last predicament she seeks escape through suicide but the poison only makes her *appear* dead (3.5–6). She is buried—alive, as it turns out—then stolen by another band of pirates (3.8), sold again, and threatened by one master after another (3.11; 4.5; 5.4; 5.9). If this isn't enough, Anthia must also escape a trench full of wild dogs, and somehow avoid defilement when sold to a pimp (5.5).

Like Chariton, Xenophon depicts the upward journey—the couple's restoration to glory—with much greater economy. Habrocomes' quest ends abruptly when he arrives in Rhodes and meets up with Anthia, appropriately near the temple of Isis (5.13). The reunion delights the crowds who respond with praise to the goddess. The couple's reflex is likewise theocentric. 'To you, greatest goddess [*ō megistē thea*],' they cry to Isis, 'we owe thanks for our safety; it is you, the goddess we honor most of all [*ō pantōn hēmin timiōtatē*], who have restored us' (5.13). With their sufferings finally behind them, they return to Ephesus to enjoy city-wide acclaim and the 'better fate' promised in the oracle. Their very first act back home is to head for the temple where they pray and sacrifice to Artemis, while setting up an inscription in her honour (5.15).[25] Thus, the story concludes with universal honour for the couple, and increased glory to the gods.

The differences between Achilles Tatius' composition and the (evidently) earlier works of Chariton and Xenophon are substantial. Along with Longus and Heliodorus, Achilles Tatius writes in the shadow of the so-called Second Sophistic, the Greek cultural revival that flourished in the second century and that produced refined works of literature instead of pulp fiction.[26] The downward–upward

---

[25] The story thus comes full circle, concluding (5.15) as it began (1.2), with a festival to Artemis.

[26] See further Tomas Hägg, *The Novel in Antiquity*, 34–73.

trajectory of *Leucippe and Kleitophon* is, nevertheless, clear and similarly marked by periodic summary statements. A few representative excerpts should suffice.

In the wake of shipwreck (3.1–5) and imprisonment (3.9), Kleitophon finds himself in bitter turmoil:

O gods and spirits, if you do exist and hear our prayers, what great crime did we commit, to be overwhelmed by this avalanche of adversities? ... But I feel less sorrow for my own troubles—overwhelming though they be—than for yours, Leucippe.... What a resplendent wedding: your bedroom is a prisoner's cell; your mattress is the ground; your garlands and bracelets are hawsers and wrist ropes; the bride's escort is a brigand sleeping at the door! Instead of the wedding march we hear a funeral song (3.10).

And then, in a scathing aside:

We confessed our gratitude too soon, O sea. I reject your philanthropy: you were more humane to your dead victims than to us whom you saved only for a worse death. You spitefully decided that our death would be incomplete without bandits (3.10).

Some time later, when Leucippe succumbs to delirium, Kleitophon offers another backward glance at the stages of their descent:

Did Fortune rescue us from robbers for you to become dementia's pawn? Our good fortune in each case has proved bad luck: we have escaped domestic danger only to suffer shipwreck; we have survived the sea and eluded the outlaws, yes—because you were being groomed for delirium. And if you ever do recover your wits, my dearest, I can only fear that god must have some other calamity in store [*phoboumai palin ton daimona, mē ti soi kakon ergasētai*]. Who could be more disaster-prone than we, who are even frightened of good fortune? But if only you would return to sanity and self-possession, let Fortune begin a new round of her game [*paizetō palin hē Tychē*] (4.9).

After her recovery, Leucippe offers a similarly bitter rehearsal of her past, in a secret letter to Kleitophon:

You know well all that I have suffered for you, yet now I am obliged to refresh your memory. For your sake [*dia se*] I left my mother and undertook a life of wandering. For your sake [*dia se*] I went through shipwreck and captivity at the hands of pirates. For your sake I have been a sacrificial victim, an expiatory offering, and twice have died [*dia se hiereion gegona kai katharmos kai tethnēka ēdē deuteron*]. For your sake I have been sold and shackled in iron; I have wielded the hoe, scraped the earth, endured the lash—and was all this in order to become another man's wife, as you are now another woman's husband? (5.18)

Our couple's situation cannot remain desperate, of course, for in these tales ascent must follow descent. Thus, from apparent ritual slaughter Leucippe must return to life (3.17), and of charges of infidelity she must be acquitted (8.13–14). In the end, then, our two lovers are joyfully reunited to celebrate their marriage, at which point the novel abruptly ends.

This survey of three Greek novels warrants several generalizations:

a. *complexity:* one crisis or trial is never enough; there must be multiple episodes and stages, at least of descent, and multiple mini-rescues before the denouement.

b. *predictability:* these stories suffer from routine predictability (though with occasional incoherence) and exploit all the standard topoi (jealous suitor, pirate attack, shipwreck, enslaved nobility, falsely accused lover, etc.).

c. *extravagance:* various elements loom much larger than life: physical beauty, trials, dangers, popular reactions.

d. *injustice:* trials are inflicted, often disproportionately, on the undeserving.

e. *passion:* romance and sex figure prominently, as does the couples' zeal for fidelity.

f. *status and honour:* the institution of slavery appears regularly, as do instances of status reversal (from free to slave or vice versa) and the myth of temporarily hidden nobility.[27]

Only some of the structural parallels between our three exemplars can be explained in terms of literary influence (e.g. of Chariton on Xenophon). It seems more likely that these ancient storytellers felt constrained—or unleashed—by a shared set of narrative conventions. To the extent that Paul's readers enjoyed a measure of familiarity with the generic structures and constraints that generated the early novels, the broad outline of his Christ story—with its movement in stages from descent to ascent, and from dishonour to

---

[27] See R. Hock, 'Greek Novel', 143–4, and Dale Martin, *Slavery as Salvation*, 35–42.

honour—would seem not only *appropriate* but also *familiar.*
Whether our readers would detect, within this *familiar* story, certain
foreign or *inappropriate* elements remains to be seen.[28]

2. BEGINNINGS: THE HERO BELONGS, AND BEGINS, AT THE TOP

With this basic narrative shape before us, we turn to consider specific
elements within Paul's Christ story. The opening clause of verse 6
describes Christ existing *en morphē theou.* It lies beyond the scope of
this chapter to moderate the debate over this phrase. Did Paul and
the early Christians imagine a god with quasi-physical features?[29] Are
we to recall here the glory of Yahweh's appearances to Israel?[30] Should
we think of God's *form* much as Aristotle thought of a thing's
substance, so that Jesus is here said to share in the *essence* of
deity?[31] Might these words be intended to recall Adam, the first

---

[28] I suspect readers familiar with the V-shaped plot structure would intuitively
construe the hymn as a narrative of *sequential* stages rather than as an a-temporal
depiction of 'the character of Christ's whole life', as argued by J. D. G. Dunn,
Christology in the Making (Philadelphia: Westminster, 1981) 120. Likewise, the
nuances of Gundry's structural analysis ('Style and Substance,' above, n. 10) might
have been lost on such readers. Cf. L. Hurst, 'Re-enter the Pre-existent Christ in
Philippians 2:5–11?', *NTS* 32 (1986) 452–3 (449–557).

[29] The word *morphē* occurs only a handful of times in the Greek Old Testament,
almost always with reference to the visible appearance of something. See Judg. 8:18;
Job 4:16; Isa. 44:13; 52:14 (Aquila); Dan. 3:19; 4:33; 5:6, 9, 10; 7:28 (Theodotion);
Tobit 1:13; Wis.18:1; 4 Macc.15:4. For a defence of this position, see M. Bockmuehl,
'Form of God', 19, who concludes that 'Paul stands in a ... Jewish mystical tradition
in which it was possible to speak of the Lord's majesty and greatness by alluding to the
inconceivable size and beauty of his bodily appearance.'

[30] When God *appears*—on Mt. Sinai (Exod. 19:18–25; 24:15–18; 33:18–23), over
the Temple (2 Chr. 7:1–3), among God's people (Isa. 40:5)—God appears *in glory.*
Similarly, recall the various quasi-physical descriptions of God, e.g. in Isa. 6:1; Ezek.
1:26–8; Dan. 7:9. Thus John Calvin found the key to Phil. 2:6 in John 17:5. See also
Heb. 1:3. Paul himself uses *doxa* of God's visible splendour in Rom. 1:23; 1 Cor. 11:7;
2 Cor. 3:18; 4:6. On this view, see esp. O'Brien, *Philippians,* 208–11 and Martin,
Hymn, 104–5; S. Fowl, *Story of Christ,* 53–4.

[31] This view was popular among 19th-century British scholars, including J. B.
Lightfoot (*St. Paul's Epistle to the Philippians* (1868; 1913; repr., Zondervan, 1953)),
M. R. Vincent (*Epistles to the Philippians and Philemon,* ICC (Edinburgh: T. &

human, who was made according to God's *image* and *likeness* (Gen. 1:26–7)?[32] Does the hymn portray Jesus' repudiation of Adam's quest to be (even more) like God (Gen. 3:5, 22)?[33] Whatever the force of *en morphē theou*, it must surely be taken closely with the divine status

T. Clark, 1897)), and H. C. G. Moule (*Studies in Philippians* (Cambridge: CUP, 1899; repr. Kregel, 1977)). For Lightfoot (110), *morphē* implied 'not the external accidents but the essential attributes'. A more recent variation on this view comes from Gerald F. Hawthorne (*Philippians*, WBC 43 (Waco: Word, 1983) 84): 'This somewhat enigmatic expression, then, appears to be a cautious, hidden way for the author to say that Christ was God, possessed of the very nature of God ..., without employing these exact words.'

[32] This view is defended by R. Martin (1983, 1997) 119, 161–4, J. D. G. Dunn, *Christology* (1980, 1989) 114–21, N. T. Wright, *The Climax of the Covenant* (Minneapolis: Fortress, 1991) 57–62, and others including J. Hering (1936), O. Cullmann (1957), and C. K. Barrett (1962). Paul compares Jesus and Adam in Rom. 5:12–21 and 1 Cor. 15:20–2, 45–7, on which passages see again Wright, *Climax*, 26–40. For Christ as the *eikon* of God, see 2 Cor. 4:4 and Col. 1:15. For critique, see David Steenburg, 'The Case against the Synonymity of *morphe* and *eikon*,' *JSNT* 34 (1988) 77–86, and M. Bockmuehl, 'The Form of God', 8–11.

[33] Dunn argues that Adam Christology in Phil. 2 offers no support for a doctrine of pre-existence. For Dunn, the passage depicts Jesus facing 'the same archetypal choice that confronted Adam'. The difference is that Jesus 'chose not as Adam had chosen (to grasp equality with God). Instead he chose to empty himself of Adam's glory and to embrace Adam's lot, the fate which Adam had suffered by way of punishment' (*Christology*, 117). Thus, according to Phil. 2:6–11, Christ 'undid Adam's wrong'. He 'rejected Adam's sin, but nevertheless freely followed Adam's course as fallen man to the bitter end of death; wherefore God bestowed on him the status not simply that Adam lost, but the status which Adam was intended to come to, God's final prototype, the last Adam' (ibid. 119). The narrative Christology of J. W. McClendon, Jr. (*Systematic Theology: Doctrine* (Nashville: Abingdon, 1994) 267) arrives at much the same conclusion; 'the dominant feature of 2:5–11 has never been a heavenly–descent myth, for it is not a passage about the pre-incarnate acts of God, but one that juxtaposes Messiah Jesus' earthly vicissitudes with the vast claim of his Lordship.' McClendon understands *morphē theou* as 'Godlike image' (267), as his paraphrase of v. 6 indicates: 'who, mirroring God on earth, turned back the temptation to rival God' (268). For problems with a thoroughly 'anthropological' approach, esp. as articulated by Dunn, see O'Brien, *Philippians* (1991) 266–8; Wright, *Climax*, 90–7; Hurst, 'Re-enter the Pre-existent Christ', 449–557; and Fee, *Paul's Letter to the Philippians*, NICNT (Grand Rapids: Eerdmans, 1995) 203 n.41 & 209 n.73. To agree that Christ is something of an Adam-figure in this passage (reminiscent of Rom. 5:12–21 and 1 Cor. 15:20–8) is not necessarily to grant that the hymn chronicles *only* Christ's earthly descent (i.e. faithful obedience, righteous choices, voluntary submission to God's will). Adam–Christ parallelism may be real without being strict; typology may be illuminating without being determinative. Christ's life of righteous obedience need not be the only thing that distinguished him from Adam. If the hymn celebrates Christ-as-Adam, it also depicts someone greater-than-Adam. Adam Christology does not preclude pre-existence Christology.

language (*to einai isa theō*) in the next clause (2:6b), and defined over against *morphē doulou* in what follows (2:7). To be *en morphē theou*, then, apparently entails being *isa theō*, equal with God,[34] which status Christ enjoyed *before* donning 'a slave's form', that is, *before* taking on 'human likeness' (*en homoiōmati anthrōpon*).[35] Interpretive disputes notwithstanding, Paul's Jesus story clearly begins with glory and with Christ's exalted, (quasi-)divine status. For aficionados of the ancient novel, where heroes and heroines routinely loomed larger than life, all of this is precisely as it should be.

Chariton's Callirhoe, daughter of Hermocrates the heroic general, was the sweetheart of all Syracuse and, before long, happily wed to her heart's desire. Chariton never tires of recalling her noble rank (1.11, 14; 2.1, 3, 5, 9, etc.). Thus, during Callirhoe's funeral procession (premature, as it turns out), she lay on a golden bier, escorted by cavalry, infantry, and city officials en route to a magnificent seaside vault. Surpassing her family's wealth and social rank, however, was her beauty: 'more than human, it was divine (*ouk anthrōpinon alla theion*), and it was not the beauty of a Nereid or mountain nymph at that, but of the maiden Aphrodite herself' (1.1). When she first emerged as the bride of Chaereas, it was 'as when Artemis appears to hunters in lonely places' (1.1). Even when presumed dead, her body appeared 'bigger and lovelier than in life', making everyone note 'how like the sleeping Ariadne she looked' (1.6). And grave robbers with purely mercenary interests could see that her beauty was 'more valuable than anything else' (1.9) and that it wasn't human (*oude anthrōpinon to kallos*; 1.10).

Callirhoe's proper rank and status never fully disappear from view, for, throughout her descent into humiliation, her countenance continually betrays her: 'Shall we say she's a slave?' asked one of the pirates. 'Who's going to believe that once he sees her?' (1.10). Callirhoe even complains to Fortune, when sold privately outside the city: 'you were afraid people might see me and think me nobly born!' (1.14). Apparently one could tell slaves from nobles in a crowd, based

---

[34] So Fee, *Philippians*, 207: 'both [phrases] point to the same reality.' On the mutually illuminating relationship between these expressions, see Wright, *Climax*, 82–3, and Fowl, *Story of Christ*, 56.

[35] See Fee, *Philippians*, 204.

solely on their physical attributes.[36] Even fellow slaves are awestruck. 'Lady,' says one of the countrywomen, 'when you look at Aphrodite, you'll think you're looking at a picture of yourself.'[37] Most striking of all are the comments of nobleman Dionysius when first he laid eyes on Callirhoe by Aphrodite's temple:

'Aphrodite,' he cried, 'be gracious to me! May your appearance be propitious to me!' He was in the act of prostrating himself when Leonas caught him up and said: 'Sir, this is the woman I bought—don't be alarmed. Woman, come to your master!' ... Dionysius struck Leonas. 'Impious man!' he cried. 'Do you speak to gods as if they were humans [*hōs anthrōpois dialegē tois theois*]? Are you calling her a bought slave? No wonder you couldn't find the man who offered her for sale! Have you not heard what Homer tells us? "And the gods, taking the shape of strangers (*kai te theoi xeinoisin eoikotes*) from other lands, observe the insolence and the orderly behavior of mankind" ' (2.3).

Dionysius insists to Leonas that Callirhoe must be divine:

It is a nymph or Nereid who has come up from the sea. Even divine beings are at certain times caught in the grip of destiny and compelled to associate with human beings—poets and historians tell us that (2.4).

Central to this story, then, is the virtual divinity of Callirhoe. The crowds spontaneously direct their worship toward her (3.2, 3, 9; 4.1, 7; 5.2, 3, 9; 6.2, 3), and even her husband concludes, when her tomb is discovered empty, that Callirhoe must have been divine, borne away by some jealous god (3.3). Chaereas himself does not enjoy the same level of adulation, though he too has the world by the tail. The son of the politically powerful Ariston, of noble rank and similarly

---

[36] Even slaves held such assumptions about physical appearance, as when Leonas, slave of Dionysius of Ionia, says of Callirhoe: 'a look at her will tell me whether she is fit for my master to possess or just suitable for people like us' (1.12). Most explicit are the remarks of Dionysius: 'a person not freeborn cannot be beautiful. Don't you know that the poets say beautiful people are the children of gods? All the more reason for their human parents to be nobly born' (2.1). The correlation between physical form and intrinsic nature goes back at least to Plato and Aristotle, and dominated the popular imagination of our period. See esp. B. J. Malina and J. H. Neyrey, *Portraits of Paul: An Archaeology of Ancient Personality* (Louisville: Westminster John Knox, 1996) 100–52 (esp. 103–4).

[37] Likewise, they 'admired her face as divinely beautiful' though 'when they saw what her clothes uncovered, her face went quite out of their thoughts' (2.2). Reardon (*Ancient Greek Novels*, 39, n. 36) suspects textual corruption here, though the general sense is clear.

pleasant to behold, he was, we are told, 'surpassingly handsome, like
Achilles and Nireus and Hippolytus and Alcibiades as sculptors and
painters portray them' (1.1).

Xenophon is similarly eager to announce the elevated status of his
lead characters. Habrocomes' father Lycomedes is 'among the most
influential citizens of Ephesus' (1.1) and such enviable social standing is invariably accompanied by physical beauty and intelligence.
The appearance of Habrocomes himself was, we read, 'phenomenal'.
The boy excelled in hunting, riding, and fighting, and was generally
so impressive that the people treated him *hōs theō* (*like a god*); some
'prostrated themselves and prayed at the sight of him' (1.1) and
others described him as the 'incomparable image of a handsome
god' (*kai hoios oude heis kalou mimēma theou*; 1.1).[38] Likewise the
beauty of the young Anthia was 'an object of wonder', moving some
to 'worship her as Artemis' (*prosekunēsan hōs Artemin*), to identify
her outright as the goddess (*tēn theon einai*), or to declare her 'made
by the goddess in her own image' (*hypo tēs theou peripoiēmenēn*;
1.2).[39]

Although our third novel (Achilles Tatius) does *not* highlight the
wealth and nobility of its central characters, it does emphasize their
beauty. One glimpse of Leucippe is more than enough to intoxicate
Kleitophon for life (1.4, 7, 9; 2.6).[40] Even when Leucippe is reduced
to slavery in Ephesus, the noble Melite perceives her true status:
'Even in fallen circumstances', she says, 'your beauty proclaims you
a person of no mean birth' (5.17). Here again we encounter the
notion that certain physical attributes would cause freeborn citizens
to stand out in a crowd.

So two of our three exemplars amount to *celebrity* biographies—
lives of the rich and famous—insofar as they describe society's elite,
the bluebloods who have it all and therefore have much to lose. The
third is the woeful tale of a supermodel. Common to all three is the

---

[38] Literally, 'and a copy of the good god like no one [else]'. Habrocomes was so
self-important that he baldly refused to acknowledge Eros until overcome with
passion for Anthia.

[39] The Greek here should perhaps be translated 'but others [thought she was]
someone else [i.e. not actually a god], kept by the goddess for herself.' Dalmeyda,
Xénophon d'Éphèse, indicates the text has been altered here, though he translates it
much like Reardon: 'C'est l'image de la déesse façonnée par elle à sa ressemblance.'

[40] Cf. the reaction of the general in 4.3, 6–7.

regularity with which lead characters are compared to the gods, particularly in physical appearance. In this respect, Paul's story of a godlike hero would resonate with his readers, whether the hymn was understood to highlight Jesus' elevated status on earth, or was thought to assign him a place, from the outset, among the gods. Readers inhabiting the thought-world of the novels would, we imagine, read *en morphē theou* and *isa theō* metaphorically, as descriptions of Christ's stunning countenance and noble family of origin.

3. CHOICE: THE HERO DETERMINES TO EMBRACE HUMILIATION

A central element in the first half of the hymn is Christ's initiative in his descent. Two details are crucial. First, the semantic force of the participle *hyparchōn* (*being, existing*) in 6a is tricky to pin down. It has often been taken *concessively*: '*although* existing in the form of God', as in the *NRSV* above (cf. *RSV, NASV*). Since C. F. D. Moule, however, a number have opted for *causal* force: '*[precisely] because* he existed in the form of God'.[41] On this view, Christ's decision to give of himself and to embrace humiliation was precisely what we might expect from divine beings; acts of self-sacrifice are what most clearly reveal divine nature. Questioning this increasingly popular *causal* reading, however, is G. Fee who proposes instead the less loaded *circumstantial* sense: '*who, in the circumstance of being...*'.[42] Likewise, for R. Gundry, the logic of divine 'compensation' introduced by *dio* (*therefore*) in verse 9 fits better with the older concessive reading.[43] As we shall see, our imaginary audience of novel enthusiasts might be inclined to agree with Gundry.

Second is the thrust of verse 6b—a notorious crux that has single-handedly fuelled a cottage industry in New Testament studies. Christ, Paul contends, 'did not consider his equality with God to be *harpagmos*'.

---

[41] 'The Manhood of Jesus in the NT' in S. W. Sykes and J. P. Clayton, eds., *Christ, Faith, and History* (Cambridge: CUP, 1972) 95–110. Cf. N. T. Wright, '*Harpagmos* and the Meaning of Philippians 2:5–11' *JTS* 37 (1986) 345; G. Hawthorne, *Philippians*, 85.

[42] *Philippians*, 202, n. 40   [43] 'Style and Substance', 283.

What, precisely, does *harpagmos* mean? An *act of seizing*? *Stolen booty*? A *prize gained*? A *thing to take advantage of*?[44] I find myself drawn to the trajectory of interpretation charted by C. F. D. Moule, Roy W. Hoover and N. T. Wright, according to which Christ 'did not regard equality with God as *something to be exploited*'.[45] On this reading, the hymn portrays Christ refusing to take full advantage of his position. He refused to equate glory with self-promotion.[46] And rather than exploiting his lofty position, he humbled himself. The word order of verse 7 is emphatic: 'it was *he himself* that he emptied,' and the thrust of verse 8 is parallel: 'he humbled *himself*.' Whether or not the verb *humble* (*etapeinōsen*) borrows from Isaiah 53:8 (*en tē tapeinōsei*), the self-humbling of Christ would seem to be the distinctive contribution of Paul's hymn.[47]

So as not to miss the point, it may be worth considering how the story *might have* gone. Paul's logic (or the logic of an earlier composer) *could have* run as follows:

---

[44] Following the *NRSV*. *Harpagmos* occurs only here in the Greek Bible, and rarely in Hellenistic literature. The interpretive options in this passage are conveniently outlined in Lightfoot, *Philippians*, 133–7, Roy W. Hoover, 'The Harpagmos Enigma: A Philological Solution' *HTR* 64 (1971) 95–119; and N. T. Wright, '*Harpagmos*,' 321–52; idem, 'Jesus Christ is Lord: Philippians 2:5–11' in his *The Climax of the Covenant* (Minneapolis: Fortress, 1991) 56–98. Parallel though not identical expressions (employing cognates *harpagma* and *harpazein* and similar predicate accusative constructions) occur in Heliodorus (Aethiopica VII.11, 20; VIII.7), Plutarch (Timoleon 23; Philopoemon 15.2; Dion 26.1), Josephus (War 4.2.4); Eusebius (Comm. in Luc. 6; Eccl. VIII.12.2; Vita Constantini 31.2); and Cyril of Alexandria (De ador. I.25).

[45] For variations of this view, see C. F. D. Moule, 'Further Reflections on Philippians 2:5–11' in W. W. Gasque and R. P. Martin, eds., *Apostolic History and the Gospel* (Grand Rapids: Eerdmans, 1970) 264–76; Hoover, 'Harpagmos Enigma,' Wright, 'Harpagmos'; idem, 'Jesus Christ is Lord'; O'Brien, *Philippians*; and Fee, *Philippians*, 205–7.

[46] Cf. Rom. 15:3; 2 Cor. 8:9.

[47] On this point see further O'Brien, *Philippians*, 228, and Martin, *Hymn of Christ*, 212. Among those confident of an Isa. 53–Phil. 2 linkage we might mention R. Strimple, 'Philippians 2:5–11 in Recent Studies: Some Exegetical Conclusions' *WTJ* 41 (1978/79), 247–68; N. T. Wright, *Climax* (1991) 60–1, and R. H. Gundry 'Style and Substance,' 271–93. (Cf. H. W. Robinson (1926), J. Jeremias (1953, 1963), L. Cerfaux (1954).) The unpersuaded include M. Hooker, 'Philippians 2:6–11' in E. E. Ellis and E. Grässer, eds., *Jesus und Paulus* (Göttingen: Vandenhoek und Ruprecht, 1975) 151–64, and O'Brien, *Philippians*, 1991. Uncertain is R. Martin *Hymn of Christ* (1997 (1983)).

a. Christ enjoyed exalted status,
b. he willingly accepted his fate,[48]
c. he was humiliated and killed at the hand of his enemies, and
d. he was subsequently exalted by God.[49]

But this is *not* the story Paul tells. For Paul, it matters that Christ himself took the initiative and willingly stepped downward. At the centre of Paul's Jesus story we find *voluntary self*-abasement. Here, perhaps for the first time, Paul's story would bring our novel amateurs up short, for no hero in our secular corpus ever chooses to step down into humiliation. Setbacks and hardships in the novels are always imposed involuntarily, by some external force, be it Fortune or Eros or Envy, or some brazen suitor or lustful master who fails to grasp that No means No.

The opening scene of Xenophon's *Tale* depicts Habrocomes as the double victim of his own arrogance and a vengeful deity. Smitten by Eros he cries out: 'What catastrophe has befallen me, Habrocomes, till now a man, despising Eros and slandering the god? I have been captured and conquered and am forced to be the slave of a girl' (1.4). And when Habrocomes and Anthia embark on their ill-fated voyage, it is only to *accept*—surely not to *seek*—whatever disasters lie ahead (1.11). Likewise, Chariton portrays Callirhoe buried alive or captured by brigands or sold as a slave, but never of her own free will. Always she is ready to bemoan her fate (1.8, 14; 2.2) and we are not surprised when, finally agreeing to marry Dionysius, she uses the occasion to climb back up out of humiliation:

I have suffered misfortune, but I still have my pride.... So if Dionysius wants to have me as his concubine, ... I will hang myself rather than give my body up to outrage fit for a slave. But if he wants me as his legal wife,

---

[48] For accounts of Jesus' passion that highlight his willing (if perhaps reluctant) *acceptance*, but not *self*-humiliation see, e.g. Matt. 26:38–9, 42; Mark 14:36; Luke 22:42; John 18:1–11. Divine necessity in Christ's death is central in Matt. 16:21; Mark 14:49; Luke 24:7, 26, 44–6; Acts 3:18; 1 Pet. 1:11.

[49] The story of Isaac's 'humiliation' at the hands of his father (Gen. 22), especially as retold in post-biblical traditions, might have fuelled the imaginations of early shapers of the Christ story. On the state of Aqedah traditions in first-century Judaism and on the attention given to Isaac's active, willing participation, see my 'Offering Isaac Again and Again: Pseudo-Philo's Use of the Aqedah as Intertext' *CBQ* 62 (3, 2000) 481–507, and 'Do You Not Remember? Scripture, Story and Exegesis in the Rewritten Bible of Pseudo-Philo', *JSP* Sup. 37 (Sheffield, 2001) 249–63.

then I too want to be a mother so that Hermocrates' line will be continued (3.1).

So also the spiralling plight of Achilles Tatius' Leucippe is not of her own choosing: 'Have mercy on me,' she tells Milete, 'I am free by birth, though now a slave, as Fortune chooses' (5.17; cf. 3.5, 10–11). When someone *voluntarily* embraces a lowly position, it reflects either a passive resignation to Fortune or a final attempt to salvage personal dignity. Thus, shame drives Chaereas, when charged with killing his own wife, to call for his own humiliation:

Stone me to death in public; I have robbed our community of its crowning glory! ... try to find some unspeakable way to punish me. I have done something worse than any temple robber or parricide. Do not give me burial; do not pollute the earth—plunge my criminal body to the bottom of the sea! (1.5)[50]

And when Chaereas finally sets out in search of Callirhoe, he assures Poseidon that he would choose slavery with his wife over returning without her (3.5). Later, when sentenced to death allegedly for attempting to escape, Chaereas goes readily, 'glad to be leaving a life of misery and ill-starred love' (4.3). Then, when rescued from death on a cross, he pleads to be hoisted back up rather than to live on with the knowledge that his Callirhoe is the wife of another man (4.3). Less masochistic, but similarly self-deprecating, an enslaved Callirhoe resists the inclination of her fellow slaves to dote over her: 'Give me a slave's tunic; why, *you* are superior to me!' (2.1) And when Dionysius asks her to tell her story, she is initially reluctant to admit her noble birth: 'What happened before is a dream, a fable. Now I am what I have come to be—a slave, and a foreigner.'

Notwithstanding such self-abnegation in moments of shame or despair, our lead characters' first instinct is always to resist humiliation. No clear-thinking aristocrat would ever choose slavery.[51] The

---

[50] We witness a similar embrace of humiliation in Leucippe and Kleitophon when Menelaus, their Egyptian travelling companion, tells how he sought for himself the harshest punishment for having caused the death of his lover: 'I did not resist. I took the stand and made no defense. Rather I demanded the death penalty for myself' (2.34).

[51] This not to suggest that all forms of slavery were thought equally shameful, nor that emancipation inevitably improved one's social status. On the complexities and

contrast between Paul's story and the novels could hardly be more stark; to read Paul through the lens of the Greek novels is, it appears, to see in Christ's descent a shocking, counter-intuitive act by one whose lofty status would seem to rule out even the thought of downward mobility. 'Even though Christ had it all', they might hear Paul saying, 'he nevertheless did the unthinkable: he chose to subject himself to shameful humiliation and slavish death.'

4. DEATH: THE HERO'S HUMILIATION IS ABSOLUTE

The descent of Christ—from equality with God to the form of a slave, from human likeness to humble obedience—reaches rock bottom with his death, death by Roman crucifixion. The end of verse 8 hints, but just barely, that Christ's death was particularly humiliating. *Stauros*, the final word in the verse, belongs to a three-word appositional phrase supplied to emphasize the shameful manner of Jesus' death.[52] Death by crucifixion was the single most barbarous form of execution the ancients could dream up and everyone knew it.[53] But the hymn scarcely lingers here; there is no move to depict the cross as a dastardly deed perpetrated by malevolent cosmic forces. It is not portrayed as a great evil, nor as the ultimate violence, nor even as a lamentable tragedy. Nor does Paul show any inclination to finger the earthly villains responsible. We are simply told that Christ died, and that he died in willing obedience, presumably in obedience to the

---

ambiguities of slave status in the Roman empire, see Dale Martin, *Slavery as Salvation*, 1–49, and James S. Jeffers, *The Greco-Roman World of the New Testament Era* (Downers Grove, IL: IVP, 1999) 220–36. For rare examples of voluntary enslavement for socio-economic gain, see Martin, *Slavery as Salvation*, 41–2.

[52] Although some contend that these three words are a Pauline gloss on a pre-existing hymn, a plausible case can be made for including them in the original composition (whether Paul's or not). See O'Brien, *Philippians*, 230–1.

[53] For a valuable introduction to the subject, see Martin Hengel's *Crucifixion* (Philadelphia: Fortress, 1977) and Gerard S. Sloyan, *The Crucifixion of Jesus: History, Myth, Faith* (Minneapolis: Fortress, 1995) 9–23. Also useful is R. A. Horsley and N. A. Silberman, *The Message and the Kingdom* (Minneapolis: Fortress, 1997) 85–7, and several chapters in John T. Carroll and Joel B. Green, *The Death of Jesus in Early Christianity* (Peabody, MA: Hendrickson, 1995).

Father.[54] *Emptying* language, in other words, is the poet's lyrical way of declaring that Christ descended all the way to the cross—that Christ poured out his life in obedience to God.[55]

Death is highly prominent in the early novels. Major characters are routinely presumed dead and suffer one near-death experience after another. Chariton's Callirhoe barely survives the assault of her husband, almost dies in the dark of her tomb, and almost drowns at sea. But she does not remain in the grave. Indeed, she who had 'died' 'came back to life' (1.8). The one who was buried alive escaped her tomb.[56] Likewise, although Chaereas survives an attack at sea, both Callirhoe (3.7, 10) and Phocas (3.9) consider him dead, and Callirhoe even erects a tomb in his honour (4.1). Evidently Chariton felt his readers would enjoy the twist that allows Chaereas and Callirhoe to 'bury' each other: 'First you buried me, in Syracuse', we hear Callirhoe say, 'and now I am burying you in Miletus' (4.1). Meanwhile, Chaereas manages to get himself sentenced to death by crucifixion (4.2) only to find a last-minute reprieve (4.3) so that when he appears suddenly before the Persian king it is like one returned from the dead. In distress Dionysius cries out: 'What Protesilaus[57] is this who has come back to life to plague me? What god of hell have I offended that I should find a rival in a dead man—dead, and buried on my land?' (5.10)

We have already described how often Xenophon nudges both Habrocomes and Anthia to the brink of death, if not by crucifixion then by poison or pyre or ritual murder or burial or suicide. Similarly, Achilles Tatius' story includes no less than three episodes in which Leucippe, the heroine, dies (so to speak) and comes back to life. Book 3 finds Kleitophon, survivor of storm at sea and capture by bandits, watching from afar as his lover appears to be bound, disembowelled, and placed in a coffin. Only later does Kleitophon discover

[54] Students of Paul will recognize here the sort of Gospel shorthand found elsewhere in his correspondence (e.g. 1 Cor. 1:17–18; Gal. 5:11; 6:12). See further Sloyan, *Crucifixion of Jesus*, 46–7.

[55] See esp. Fee, *Philippians*, 210.

[56] Cf. Callirhoe's reminiscence at 5.5. Her unborn child barely escapes death as well (2.9).

[57] Protesilaus was an early, royal casualty of the Trojan War. As the story goes, his wife Laodamia was so distressed that the gods agreed to give them a brief reunion, after which she took her own life to join him in Hades.

that the ritual slaying was actually a ruse and that Leucippe was very much alive.[58] A tap on the coffin and she rises up from the grave into the arms of an astounded Kleitophon (3.17). In book 5, the hapless Leucippe is carried off by pirates who appear to behead her, as Kleitophon again looks on, and toss her torso into the sea (5.7). It wasn't her, of course, and she turns up six months later as an Ephesian slave girl. In disbelief, Kleitophon wonders whether his beloved might have 'come to life again' (*palin anebiō*, 5.19; cf. 5.11). In book 7, finally, the imprisoned Kleitophon is persuaded that jealous Milete had paid for Leucippe's murder. Not surprisingly, his friend calls the report into question: 'Who knows whether she is alive this time too?' he asks. 'Hasn't she died many times before? Hasn't she often been resurrected?' (7.5)

So common is the theme of death, or near-death, that it might be called a stock feature—a predictable *topos* in early romance literature. For those at home in this symbolic world, Paul's description of Christ as obedient *unto death*—even unto a grisly, humiliating death—would seem completely appropriate. The obvious difference, of course, is that Christ's was no near-death experience. It was not a close call. God did not intervene at the last moment to rescue the hero from the enemy. The early novelists, with an eye toward verisimilitude, could conjure only *apparent* death for their lead characters. With a similar concern for historical plausibility, Paul's story had to acknowledge Jesus' actual death by crucifixion.

5. DIVINE INTERVENTION: GOD RESPONDS TO RESTORE AND EXALT

We noted earlier that with verse 9 the grammatical subject of Paul's hymn abruptly shifts from Christ to God. God has been lurking in the background all along, but only after the death of the hero does

---

[58] Before explaining how his trick worked, Menelaus the Egyptian playfully announces to Kleitophon, 'Leucippe will now come to life again (*anabiōsetai*)' (3.17). This episode is followed by another rescue from the brink: Leucippe suffers a drug overdose—from an aphrodisiac administered by an inept lover—and lapses into madness, from which she is rescued by an elixir (4.15–17).

God step forward to play an active role: 'Therefore God also highly exalted him and granted to him the name that is above every name.' We should probably not think of this exaltation as a divine *reward* for heroic deeds but rather as a divine *response* to genuinely humble obedience. In a God-ordered world, this is how the story *should* go. Every knee *should* bow and every tongue *should* acknowledge that Jesus is Lord because this is the way God works.[59]

How would this satisfying, happy ending to the Christ story strike those who inhabited the moral universe of the early novels? Two observations. First, the hymn depicts Christ's exaltation as sudden and immediate. Unlike the account of Christ's descent, which proceeded in incremental stages (from equality with God, to self-emptying, human appearance, humiliation, obedience, and death), we find here no corresponding stages of ascent, no stories of victory over enemies, no allusion to the resurrection or the ascension. One moment Christ is dead, the next he is exalted above all. For those familiar with the early novels, this would occasion little surprise, for the ancient novelists were similarly prone to condense and accelerate their endings. Having given scrupulous attention to the hero's trials and humiliations, they devote surprisingly little space to the details of the end. Perhaps their creative energies were spent. Perhaps they dared not demand any more of their readers. For whatever reason, the details of the couples' restoration and safe return rarely take up more than a few pages.[60]

Secondly, the god of Paul's hymn arrives on the scene rather late, is unaccountably silent while the hero suffers humiliation, and intervenes only to bring vindication. This aspect of the story would stand out, I suspect, since the gods of the novels are not only present but extraordinarily active throughout the story. We know, of course, that Paul's god is actively involved at every stage of redemption, including the crucifixion (cf. Rom. 3:25; 5:8; 2 Cor. 5:18–21), but our privileged access to Paul's reflections elsewhere cannot gainsay the fact that

---

[59] The divine propensity to deliver the oppressed and to elevate the lowly is a common theme in the NT: Matt. 5:5; 16:25; 18:4; 20:16; 23:12 (cf. Luke 14:11; 18:14); Luke 1:52–3; Jas. 4:6 (cf. Ps. 138:6).

[60] See Schmeling, *Xenophon*, 84: 'Xenophon concentrates his inventiveness on the episodes; he stumbles into them... and gets out of them ..., as best he can.'

God, in the story told in verses 6–8, seems absent or at least passive. The contrast with the novels on this point is striking.

Chariton's gods are never far from the action. Eros arranges the very first 'chance' encounter between Chaereas and Callirhoe, and inspires the crowds to lobby for their wedding. Jealous suitors do not act alone but enlist Eros to help them break up the marriage (1.2). Likewise, when Leonas, slave in the household of Dionysius, hears Theron offer to sell Callirhoe, he exclaims: 'Some god has delivered you to me to be my benefactor' (1.12). And when he learns that Theron's boat is already moored on his master's land, he concludes: 'Fortune is already leading you to Dionysius' (1.13; cf. 2:2). Callirhoe's prayer to Aphrodite is refused since the goddess had additional plans for her (2.2). Eros fans the flame of love in the hearts of both Dionysius (2.4) and Artaxerxes, the Persian king (6.4, 7). And when Callirhoe resists Dionysius' every effort to woo her, Fortune intervenes (2.8). Before her wedding to Dionysius, Callirhoe beseeches Aphrodite to keep secret the paternity of her unborn child (3.2). Fortune is credited with the calamity that humbled the pirates (3.3), and we learn that some unnamed divinity discovers Theron's false testimony (3.4). It is in a temple—the temple of Aphrodite in Ionia—that Chaereas, after saying his prayers, discovers a golden image of Callirhoe and learns that she lives (3.6). In his darkest moment, Chaereas chalked up his woes to divine malice: 'In dream and in reality alike, the gods hate me!' (6.2) Likewise, King Artaxerxes declares himself a victim of 'a massive plot ... laid by a god, not by human beings' (6.3). The war between Babylon and Egypt is provoked by Fortune (6.8) and Fortune insists on delaying the inevitable reunion between Chaereas and his dear Callirhoe (7.6–8.1). Only when Aphrodite decides that enough is enough do the two lovers find each other (8.1).

The celestial powers are also busy in the tale of Achilles Tatius, though they move more often behind the scenes.[61] Looking back upon his life, Kleitophon bemoans 'all the indignities Love [Eros] has made me suffer' (1.2) and recounts how 'Fortune began her drama' by giving him a dream (1.3; cf. 4.1). Fortune is blamed for the tragic

---

[61] The less prominent role of the gods in this novel is likely due, in part, to the first person voice of the narrator who, as a character within the story, does not enjoy omniscience.

death of Charikles (1.14), and Eros and Dionysos are credited for fanning the flames of love between Leucippe and Kleitophon (2.3). Even unknown deities get into the act: thanks to 'some kind god' (*daimōn* ... *tis agathos*), a chest full of theatre props washes ashore just in time to help Kleitophon stage Leucippe's escape from certain death (3.20; cf. 3.22).

Especially in Chariton and Xenophon, but also in Achilles Tatius, divine intrusion into human affairs is frequent, complex, often inscrutable, and by no means limited to vindication. These gods intrude and react. They subvert and reward. One minute they are charged with injustice and impotence (Chariton 4.4), the next they are praised for aid and protection (Xenophon 5.15). By contrast, Paul's story portrays a god whose role is far more limited, positive, and consistent. This god does not punish and humiliate, it only exalts and bestows; it does not initiate and meddle, it responds and delivers. The difference between the coherent god of Paul's narrative and the arbitrary, duplicitous gods of the novels would scarcely be lost on Paul's readers. There is, however, one thing on which all parties agree: when the story comes to an end and the hero is exalted, the highest praise is carefully directed toward heaven.

6. NOVEL PERSPECTIVES

To read Paul's Christ hymn alongside the early Greek novels is, first of all, to enter the narrative world Paul shared with his contemporaries. The heroic tale Paul tells, with its lofty beginnings and triumphant ending, would have met (we imagine) with broad approval among those who knew how these sorts of stories were supposed to work. Divine-like beings are *supposed* to fall headlong from the heights. Heroes are *expected* to suffer hardship and humiliation. And the gods *must* respond with deliverance and vindication. Of course, Paul's brief account is nothing like the protracted, predictable, at times tedious novels we have considered, but the main contours of Paul's story fit neatly within the world that produced them.

But our exotic exercise in 'co-reading' has yielded more than a renewed appreciation for Paul's storied frame of reference. We have also witnessed ways in which Paul's narrative *doesn't* fit the paradigm. Two deviations stand out among the rest. First is the counter-intuitive role Christ plays in his own descent. Very little in the Hellenistic popular culture could have prepared Paul's readers for the self-humiliation of Christ depicted in Philippians 2:6–8. Too much value was attached to honour and status; too many Roman institutions shielded the elite from the masses; too many risks attended disruptions of the status quo, for Christ's voluntary descent into slavery and death to make sense. If the *cross itself* was 'foolishness' to Greeks (1 Cor. 1:18–25), Christ's *wilful embrace* of that cross would have been virtually incomprehensible.

A second deviation—a corollary of the first—concerns the equally distinctive role God plays in Paul's story. We observed above how routinely the novels appeal to divine causation and intervention. Whether the divine role is literal or metaphorical; whether the gods propel the action or interrupt it; whether they forewarn with dreams or respond with answered prayer; whether deities are malicious or propitious—the plot trajectory of the novels is punctuated with manifestations of the divine. This Graeco-Roman religious backdrop highlights the limited role of Paul's god who is active in Philippians 2:9–11 but essentially absent from 2:6–8. The god of Paul's hymn is neither frustrated nor duplicitous. Ironically, the whirling machinations and interventions of the Roman gods serve only to advertise their imperfections and moral weakness, while the more restrained response of Paul's god signals only moral perfection, unrestricted power, and universal sovereignty.[62]

[62] This chapter has emerged in stages. Preliminary musings on the narrative shape of Phil. 2 took the form of a plenary address delivered for *Kenosis: A Campus Reflects*, at Westmont College on 25 Sept. 2000. I'm grateful to Randy VanderMey and Telford Work for the kind invitation and thoughtful interaction on that occasion. Stage two was a paper presented at the *SBL Pacific Coast Region Annual Meeting* (St. Mary's College, Moraga, CA) on 25 Mar. 2002, entitled ' "After their sufferings a better fate is in store": Philippians 2:6–11 and the Conventions of Greek Romance'. For the lively exchange that followed, thanks to Ronald F. Hock and the members of the *New Testament Epistles and Apocalypse Section*. That paper evolved, finally, into this, my contribution to the *Kenotic Christology Workshop* sponsored by the *Calvin Center for Christian Scholarship*, and convened at Calvin College, 29 May to 1 June 2002. The wonderfully charitable sparring over those four spring days reminded me of all that is good in the academy. Thanks to Steve Evans for a place at the table.

4

Nineteenth-Century Kenotic Christology: The Waxing, Waning, and Weighing of a Quest for a Coherent Orthodoxy

Thomas R. Thompson

Every Christology of Incarnational tack celebrates a kenotic motif. Only the most docetic of Christological models depreciate the deigning grace of God the Son, who though rich became poor for our sakes. Such impugn the gospel witness: that the wisdom of God is uniquely cruciform, and therefore humble and meek—a refinement in the doctrine of God that many Greeks found unpalatably foolish. At the heart of its confession, the catholic church has long affirmed the humbling, self-accommodating, lisping humanity of God. In this broad thematic sense a 'kenotic Christology' is rather a tautology, much like a 'theology of hope'.

But if there has been an enduring consensus regarding this basic gospel motif, there arose in modern times an acute controversy over the exact nature of this kenosis in respect to the person of the Son. Kenotic Christology in the more proper, historiographical sense of the term belongs to a distinctive model of the Incarnation that flourished in the seven decades prior to the First World War— initially on the Continent, then in Britain. Its characteristic trademark was the attempt within the bounds of Chalcedonian orthodoxy to construe the incarnate person of Christ in a way that would account for his full humanity and complete unity of person—both of which kenoticists, among others, regarded as docetically impaired by the regnant version of a two-natures model—by means of toning down the more maximal features of his divinity. The kenosis of Philippians 2:7 and context (vv. 6–11) was therefore taken as a real self-relinquishing, limiting, or emptying of divine attributes, powers, prerogatives, and/or glory by the pre-existent Logos upon the event of Incarnation. And though this poetic text became, quite naturally, the *locus classicus* of the Christology to which it lent its name, kenoticists of all stripes were quick to assert that their doctrine contained nothing more or less than the Christological implications of that broader kenotic motif to which all of Scripture testified, and thus was a viable interpretation of the poetry of the Incarnation.[1]

This chapter will survey the waxing and waning of nineteenth-century kenoticism and then weigh this Christological project in the balance of current theological concern and debate. The first section will sketch out the kenotic venture from its rise and through its greater half-century reign of popularity by paying special attention to the statements of major kenoticists who represent important variations on its theme. The second section will identify the central reasons for kenoticism's fall in fashion, by way of both theological objection and theological trend. The concluding section will then evaluate this Christological project in view of our present theological

---

[1] The assertion by nineteenth-century kenoticists that the action of kenosis is performed by the *logos asarkos*—the pre-Incarnate Christ—constituted a different interpretation of the Philippians passage from that of the inherited exegetical tradition. Friedrich Loofs notes that though a figure like Hilary seems to broach such an interpretation, 'The truth is that no theologian of any standing in the early church ever adopted such a theory of the *kenosis* of the Logos as would involve an actual supersession of His divine form of existence by the human—a real "becoming-man", i.e. a transformation on the part of the Logos.' 'Kenosis', *Encyclopedia of Religion and Ethics*, 683. Though such an understanding was frequently entertained on a more popular level, the reigning theological and orthodox view was to interpret the kenosis as a *krypsis* or voluntary concealment of divine powers by the *logos ensarkos*—the historical Christ. Considerations of divine immutability, it is agreed, played no small part in such an interpretation. Concerning the independence of the kenotic project from the Philippians passage, H. R. Mackintosh states, representatively, that 'discussion has made it clear that Kenoticism, be it right or wrong, does not in the least depend for its cogency on two or three isolated passages in St. Paul.' In *The Doctrine of the Person of Jesus Christ*, 2nd edn. (Edinburgh: T & T Clark, 1913; repr. 1978), 469. Granting his point, this chapter will not engage in any discussion of the exegetical issues surrounding this complex pericope. The range of these issues and the variety of interpretations taken on Phil. 2:5–11 can be seen in Ralph P. Martin's *Carmen Christi: Philippians 2:5–11 in Recent Interpretation and in the Setting of Early Christian Worship* (Grand Rapids: Eerdmans, 1983).

climate and concerns. I will argue finally that, for those committed to an Incarnational approach with basic Chalcedonian convictions, the largely dismissed kenotic project not only deserves reconsideration, but that more recent theological developments provide even greater warrant for its viability. The most successful retrieval of the kenotic strategy, however, may have to take that tack harder and in a more rigorous direction than its typical nineteenth-century expression.

1. THE WAXING OF NINETEENTH-CENTURY KENOTICISM

Historians speak of a 'stampede' to kenotic models of the Incarnation in the nineteenth century, and that in two basic phases: first on the Continent,[2] and then later in Britain.[3] In the estimate of one observer, the kenotic endeavour was a movement of such mass and distinction as to constitute 'the fourth great attempt at theological explanation of the being of Christ'—after the biblical, conciliar, and scholastic endeavours.[4]

The distinctly modern provenance of kenotic Christology has not escaped notice—by critic or advocate. The nineteenth century was, of course, a time of great theological flurry and Christological reconstruction. Lingering Enlightenment scepticism towards conciliar pronouncement, followed by the heightening of historical consciousness and its attendant critical methodology, made history as never before a central category of theological thought and concern. Thoroughly scrutinized was Christianity's original Saint. For some, like David Friedrich Strauss, such an inquiry seriously impugned the Christ of history as a valid object of faith; but for others, the quest

---

[2] Claude Welch treats of this 'stampede' in the German context in his *Protestant Thought in the Nineteenth Century*, vol. 1 (New Haven: Yale University Press, 1972), 233–40. Major kenoticists on the Continent include Thomasius, Hofmann, Liebner, Frank, Ebrard, Martensen, and Gess.

[3] Arthur Michael Ramsey addresses this 'stampede' in Britain in his *From Gore to Temple: The Development of Anglican Theology between Lux Mundi and the Second World War, 1889–1939* (London: Longmans, 1960), 30–43. Major kenoticists in Britain include Gore, Fairbairn, Weston, Gifford, Forsyth, and Mackintosh.

[4] P. Henry, 'Kénose', *Dict. de la Bible, Supplément*, v. 156.

for the historical Jesus reaped delightful dividends: 'But we feel Him more in our theology because we know Him better in history. His historical reality and significance have broken upon us with something of the surprise of a discovery, and He has, as it were, become to us a new and more actual Being.'[5] It was this latter attitude to the historical Jesus that the kenoticists embraced, but they did not combine this textual rediscovery of the *humanum* of Christ in all its observed limitations and development with the growing anti-metaphysical sentiments or lingering creedal scepticism of the day. Rather, theirs was the attempt to mediate this new historical accent on Christ's humanity with the confessions of the past—hence the ambiguity of classifying kenotic Christology as a *mediating*[6] or *confessional*[7] theological endeavour.

It is this mixture of the modern, virtually apologetic attempt to construe the person of Christ in all his historical and unitive integrity (the new non-negotiable Christological axioms) with the classical doctrine of the Trinity and its corollary of the eternal, personal pre-existence of the Son, that distinguishes nineteenth-century kenotic Christology not only from all other neo-confessional and mediating efforts, but also from those more speculative attempts in the same century that are also fond of the kenotic motif. Pre-eminent among the latter is the Christology of Hegel, whose system it would be better to characterize as an all-inclusive kenotic *theology*, since he made the self-divesting of the unitarian God and the finitization of absolute Spirit central concepts in his philosophy.[8] But from Thomasius to Mackintosh, it is precisely a commitment to the pre-existence of the personal Logos, presupposing a Trinity distinguished *ad intra* from *ad extra*, that sets modern kenoticism apart from all other monist-tending speculations. For it is the goal of a kenotic Christology to make a little more understandable how it is that the pre-existent Son can enter into a fully human condition while retaining both his

[5] A. M. Fairbairn, *The Place of Christ in Modern Theology* (New York: Charles Scribner's Sons, 1916), 3.

[6] As does, for instance, Donald G. Dawe in *The Form of a Servant: A Historical Analysis of the Kenotic Motif* (Philadelphia: Westminster, 1963), 90–1.

[7] As does, for instance, Welch in *Protestant Thought*, 233.

[8] See Martin Breidert, *Die Kenotische Christologie des 19. Jahrhunderts* (Gütersloh: Gütersloher Verlagshaus Mohn, 1977), 291ff.

divinity and unity of person. And it attempts to explain this if not in terms of, then in a sensitive dialogue with, the church's traditional language of 'two natures'.[9] Thus nineteenth-century kenoticism must be distinguished both from that of the traditional interpretation of kenosis as *krypsis* and from more modern kenotically motived *theo*logies.

To get a good flavour of this nineteenth-century project, it will be helpful to look at some of its important statements: primarily that of Thomasius at the beginning of this Christological wave as its first articulate systematic statement, and Mackintosh at the end who retrospectively offers a more modest British statement; but also briefly at a few major kenoticists in the middle. These will afford a good lay of the land of nineteenth-century kenoticism—its characteristic concerns and variations on a theme.

A. Gottfried Thomasius (1802–75)

Even before Gottfried Thomasius' first Christological statement appeared in 1845 as *Beiträge zur kirchlichen Christologie*, there had already been some kenotic stirrings in the century by Sartorius, Gaupp, and König.[10] But the laurels go to Thomasius for first articulating this distinctly new approach in Christology in any significant systematic fashion. Thomasius' definitive kenoticism, however, is found in his *Christi Person und Werk*, which constitutes his 'Dogmatics from the Midpoint of Christology'.[11] It is his statement

---

[9] Kenoticists, whether expressly or tacitly, employ a distinction between 'two-natures' *doctrine* and 'two-natures' *model*. Whereas kenoticism considers itself an alternative to the model, it regards itself as an interpretation of the doctrine—that is, in the spirit of the non-negotiables of Chalcedonian orthodoxy.

[10] And a century earlier by Zinzendorf, who may well have been the first modern kenoticist, unsystematically so. See Breidert, *Kenotische Christologie*, 30–51.

[11] As reads the subtitle in part. This work was both an expansion and revision of Thomasius' earlier *Beiträge* and appeared in three editions over the years 1858–88. The most salient texts of Thomasius' kenoticism from the second of the three sections of this work, entitled 'The Person of the Mediator', have been translated and edited by Claude Welch in his *God and Incarnation in Mid-Nineteenth Century German Theology* (New York: Oxford University Press, 1965) and will be the basis of the following discussion of Thomasius' Christology. References to Thomasius' *Christi Person und Werk* are cited in this section intratextually from Welch's translation by page number only.

here of the person of Christ that has been heralded as 'the classic form of the Kenotic theory'.[12]

Thomasius is careful in this work initially to lay out his confessional presuppositions. Chief among these for a kenotic Christology is his advocacy of a strong enough trinity doctrine so as to affirm the personal pre-existence of the Son. For Thomasius this requires that the trinitarian relations be conceived of not as 'rigid, immovable forms of existence but as living, personal positions' (81). His endorsement of the immanent/economic distinction means that God is 'as such complete in himself, and humanity is his creature and as such is no element of the concept of God' (32). Here he consciously distances his position from those Hegelian, speculative Christologies of Strauss and Baur. For Thomasius the Incarnation is no absolute necessity of the historical process, but a gracious response by God to remedy a world torn by sin.

Given these larger confessional claims, Thomasius then lays out his basic Christological axioms concerning the person of Christ: 'Accordingly, for the treatment of Christology, we can set down the canon that every conception of the person of the mediator that endangers either the reality of his deity, or the truth of his humanity, or the unity of his person, is an erroneous one' (37). True deity, true humanity, and the real unity of Christ's person are for Thomasius 'the basic pillars of Christology' (59). To hold all three of these together in the most coherent possible way requires in his opinion a kenotic construal: 'Always, apart from the presupposition of some kind of self-limitation of the divine, one or the other of the canons set down above is violated' (55).

Thomasius has tersely circumscribed his project. His primary motivation is to give greater play to both the humanity of the *logos ensarkos* and his unitary ego, which two elements he thinks have heretofore not been satisfactorily integrated by any Christological tradition. The former has been a strong emphasis of the Reformed tradition, but when combined with a maximal understanding of the Logos's divinity has compromised the *una persona* (via the so-called 'extra Calvinisticum'[13]). But the Lutheran tradition,

---

[12] Mackintosh, *Doctrine of Christ*, 267.

[13] David Willis has shown that this pejorative term could rightly be supplanted by a better one, something along the lines of 'extra Catholicum', since the Reformed

asserts Thomasius, errs precisely in the opposite way: strongly emphasizing the unity of Christ's person, a maximal view of his deity 'divinizes' and thus obliterates the *vere homo*. Given the more favourable climate for church union in Germany between Lutheran and Reformed, which prompted much of this Christological dialogue, Thomasius interacts with these two traditions and posits that a more coherent and mediating position between them lies in a real kenosis of the *logos asarkos*. Being a representative of the Erlangen School, however, Thomasius consciously works within a neo-confessional Lutheranism and views his efforts as a continuation of its doctrinal tendency, especially as a constructive furthering of the sixteenth-century kenotic debate between Giessen and Tübingen.[14]

So it is no surprise when Thomasius begins his actual construal of the Incarnation with a very traditional formulation: the second member of the Trinity, the divine Logos, *assumed* a human nature. Thomasius here affirms that the Logos, the Son of God, is the person-forming principle or ego of the divine-human person in the Incarnation. Therefore the human nature he assumed is *anhypostatic*. The Logos appropriated a generic human nature fraught with all the weaknesses of the flesh so as to be fully homogeneous with our own existence as conditioned by sin, but not volitionally determined by it. So far, so traditional.

But, he immediately adds, the language and conceptuality of *assumption* does not go far enough to secure the historical person of the Logos. An actual kenosis is also necessary: 'We shall have to say that *assumtio* of human essence does not by itself completely express the concept of Incarnation, but that the latter must be conceived at

---

assertion that prompted the Lutheran objection was really that of a standard teaching of the Christian tradition going all the way back at least to Athanasius—namely, that in the incarnate state the eternal Son of God, though united to his humanity, was not completely circumscribed by it. In *Calvin's Catholic Christology: The Function of the So-called Extra Calvinisticum in Calvin's Theology* (Leiden: E. J. Brill, 1966), esp. 60.

[14] The kenosis debate in the 1620s between Giessen and Tübingen, which schools lined up behind the Christological emphases of Chemnitz and Brenz respectively, concerned whether in the state of humiliation the Incarnate Christ's ubiquitous humanity was merely concealed (*krypsis*—Tübingen) or actually relinquished of use (*kenosis*—Giessen), in order to address a peculiarly Lutheran problem. Note, however, the big difference with Thomasius in that he is advocating a self-limitation of the *logos asarkos*.

the same time as divesting of the divine' (56). To posit no real sense of kenosis as an act of the *logos asarkos* concomitant with the assumption of human nature is to be led, asserts Thomasius, into the heretofore-regnant Christological conundrums. For, on the one hand, if the Son of God retains his maximal mode of divine being in the state of humiliation (the 'extra Catholicum'), the humanity of Christ is threatened by a docetic depreciation, and his—by all gospel appearances—unitive consciousness is endangered by a certain duplicity of person where the divine always 'surpasses', 'hovers above', or 'lies beyond or behind' the humanity producing a 'twofold mode of being, a double life, a doubled consciousness' (46–7). Such a position, he asserts, 'threatens to annul even the truth of the Incarnation' (54). But on the other hand, any Lutheran dickering with the *communicatio idomatum* of the *genus majestaticum* will not do either. Though perhaps retaining the unity of the person (which Thomasius considers the genius of Lutheran Christology), there is such a docetic *appreciation* of Christ's humanity that it can no longer in any real sense of the word be appreciated as such. Any supposition of the full actuality of divine attributes makes a chimera of the human experience and development of the historic Jesus.

The only resolution to this impasse, asserts Thomasius, is a construal of the *assumtio humani* by the divine Logos of kenotic proportions:

And thus we shall have to posit the Incarnation itself precisely in the fact that he, the eternal Son of God, the second person of the deity, gave himself over into the form of human limitation, and thereby to the limits of a spatiotemporal existence, under the conditions of a human development, in the bounds of an historical concrete being, in order to live in and through our nature the life of our race in the fullest sense of the word, without on that account ceasing to be God. Only so does there occur an actual entrance into humanity, an actual becoming-one with it, a becoming-man of God; and only so does there result that historical person of the mediator which we know to be the God-man (48).

For Thomasius, the kenosis of the divine Logos consists precisely in this: 'a divesting of the divine mode of being in favor of the humanly creaturely form of existence, and *eo ipso* a renunciation of the divine glory which he had from the beginning with the Father' (48). In other words, the Logos is reduced to the rank and measure of a human person; his divine Ego is now 'humanly determinate in its consciousness and life' (57); the Son *became* flesh, and therefore 'like us in the fullest, most literal sense of the word' (51).

A theological principle that this translation from the divine to the human requires, and which becomes as essential to a kenotic model as that of the twofold states of Christ, is the assumption of a kinship or susceptibility between divine and human persons. Thomasius strongly asserts that *natura humana capax divinae.* Such a capacity, he insists, was established in creation, since humanity was fashioned in the divine image—and more precisely, in the image of the Logos. Consequently, 'when the Son enters into humanity he does not betake himself into a sphere inadequate for him but transposes himself into (or appropriates to himself) a nature which he created in his image for the purpose of his self-revelation' (40). This kinship between God and humanity not only makes a kenotic Christology possible, Thomasius maintains, but it is on this supposition alone that any meaningful sense of the Incarnation becomes possible. For if God and humanity are so qualitatively different, then the Incarnation must of necessity take on a docetic cast.

Throughout his proposal Thomasius is almost obnoxious in his insistence that the Incarnate Logos is in no way diminished in his being truly divine. While in the Incarnation the Son divests himself of the divine mode of being, this is by no means a divesting of what is *essential* to divinity; though the Son assumes a human nature, which is at the same time a kenosis of the divine nature, Thomasius reassures us, 'Nothing is lacking to him which is essential for God to be God' (56).

Thomasius actually ventures three different strategies of how to maintain the essential divinity of the Incarnate One who has divested himself of the divine mode of being. The first consists quite simply of a distinction between essence and attribute. That is, Thomasius so characterizes the divine essence by one absolute quality that it relativizes, and thus makes more accidental, those other qualities that are generally taken to be essential to deity. This supreme quality he posits, along with the Nominalist tradition, in God's will or self-determination: 'in God being and will are not different' (81). Therefore, since the Son's kenosis is based on the act of free self-limitation, an expression of the will, Thomasius reasons that such a kenosis is 'not a denial but rather a manifestation of the [divine] essence' (59). Rather than a contradiction of divinity, the Son's self-determined divesting of attributes typical to the divine mode of being is supremely commensurate with the divine essence; for, even 'in the deepest self-abandonment the subject thereof nevertheless remains integrally itself' (74).

A second, but brief, way Thomasius attempts to differentiate essential divinity in the kenotically Incarnate Son from that which he divests himself of is by way of the distinction between 'potence' (*Potenz*) and 'actuosity' (*Aktuosität*). In the Incarnation, he maintains, the Logos relinquished the possession of the divine glory *actually* and now only possesses it *potentially*. The Incarnation is thus described as a 'withdrawal to potence'. Note in the following quotation how this distinction dovetails with the preceding strategy:

A withdrawal of the Logos to potence thus means nothing else than this, that he, the Logos, withdrew by virtue of an act of self-limitation (= self-determination) from the periphery of self-revelation and actuosity to his innermost center, humanly speaking to the root of his concrete being, which is essential absolute will ... but in terms of my concept the eternal being is so little annulled by the withdrawal to potence, which is an act of will (= essence), that it rather conserves and maintains itself in the act (96–7).

It is Thomasius' third strategy, however, that has been taken to be his classic answer how the kenotically Incarnate Son maintains his essential divinity. This involves a distinction in the attributes themselves—namely, between those that are 'immanent' and those that are 'relative'. Attributes that pertain to the former, such as absolute power (of self-determination), truth, holiness, and love are essential to deity and thus retained by the Son in his incarnate state; those that pertain to the latter, such as omnipotence, omniscience, and omnipresence are deemed not essential to deity by Thomasius and can thus be relinquished by the Incarnate Son without any loss of divinity.[15] He reasons that since in God there are personal and trinitarian distinctions, certain attributes that manifest these relations are immanent, essential, or metaphysical to God—apart from the created

---

[15] Thomasius' division in the divine attributes here is dependent on his definition of an attribute as an aspect of a being's expression which arises only in distinguishable relationship with another being. For this see Welch's helpful discussion, *God and Incarnation*, 67–9, n. 10.

world. But with creation there arise other attributes that are expressive of God's relationship uniquely to it and which are thus nonessential to God *qua* God. It is this panoply of relative attributes that the Son divested upon Incarnation, but which in no way diminishes his essential divinity:

> Omnipotence is no 'more' of the absolute power, omniscience is no addition to the immanent divine knowledge, omnipresence is no enhancement of the divine life. Thus if the Son as man has given up these attributes, he lacks nothing which is essential for God to be God. And he has given them up by virtue of free self-determination; thus among us he was not omnipotent, not omnipresent, not omniscient—because he willed not to be (73).

Note here again the confluence with Thomasius' first distinction: the divine essence as self-determining will plays a leading role in his kenoticism.

Besides a radical paring down of essential attributes, Thomasius' construct also takes to task the traditional understanding of divine immutability. There is no question that from Patristic and Chalcedonian times the insistence upon the strict ontological unchangeableness of the divine nature played a very important role in positing and maintaining the full actuality of divine attributes in the Incarnate Christ. To this tradition Thomasius rejoins that any strict view of divine immutability can actually constitute a 'divine imperfection', since it would severely restrict God in determining what God wills; moreover this axiom, if logically pushed, would even preclude the sheer possibility of Incarnation, since 'such a God will certainly also be incapable of becoming man' (100).

Of course Thomasius never asserted that the Son would remain indefinitely denuded of his world-relative attributes. Rather, once his salvific task is accomplished, what was divested is regained: 'The transition into this state, the act of exaltation, occurs by an operation of the Father on the humiliated one. As reward for the demonstrated obedience, God gives him the glory of which he divested himself' (78). The Son receives back his omni-attributes, but possesses them now as the God-man. Here it is evident that a kenotic Christology lives or dies by the distinction of a twofold state of Christ's mediation, as it attempts to view in greater historical relief the more statically construed two-natures doctrine.

We close this brief exposition of Thomasius' kenoticism by looking at some of its implications for the doctrine of the Trinity. The first
thing we notice with Thomasius' model in respect to the Trinity is
that it demands a greater cooperative effort of all divine members
than a more 'substantialist' view of Christ allows. That is, since the
Son is restricted in power to the dimensions of the human condition,
his dependence upon the Father through the Spirit becomes more
explicit. This also highlights the necessary obedience of the Son and
his human struggle to overcome sin and temptation. Consequently, a
greater role is accorded the Spirit in the development, ministry, and
suffering obedience of the Son (cf. 65–7).

Throughout the kenosis of the Son, however, the immanent Trinity suffered no interruption, asserts Thomasius, since in the Incarnation the Son remained one with the will of the Father, and thus one
with the essence of God (81–2). Nevertheless, the Trinity did undergo
a modification; but for us this is a reorientation of the most won-
drous sort: humanity, it seems, now has a permanent place in the
inner life of the Trinity by virtue of the God-man (83).

Thomasius also maintains that since the inner-trinitarian relations
suffered no vacancy during the Son's kenosis, neither did the maintenance and rule of the world. Though it may appear that the Son's lack of
omni-attributes in the state of humiliation would entail that the main-
tenance and rule of the cosmos could not occur temporarily through
him, the fact is, Thomasius asserts in a questionable tour de force,
Christ was more than ever at the centre of these world-ruling functions.
For it is in his world-redeeming activity that the true rule and susten-
ance of the cosmos is accomplished since redemption sets creation
aright. Besides, the true rule of God is that over and within the pious
heart; and this Christ was making possible in and through his kenosis
(85–7). On this more tranquil, though perhaps question-begging,
note, we conclude our basic exposition of Thomasius' kenoticism.

B. Other Continental Kenoticists: Ebrard, Martensen, Gess

Thomasius' proposal was soon joined by a flurry of statements on the
Continent in the effort to shore up the kenotic model in respect to
Christ's deity, humanity, or unity of person—each a perceived area of

vulnerability in Thomasius by one critic or another. While this proliferation of statements eludes easy categorization, given the range of Christological issues and theological variables involved, A. B. Bruce, an early kenotic watcher, identified three other major types of the kenotic model in addition to the 'Thomasian'. These have as their major representatives Ebrard, Martensen, and Gess. A glance at their basic proposals will illustrate the various speculative strategies employed by the Continental kenoticists.[16]

J. H. August Ebrard (1818–88), a Reformed theologian, interpreted Christ's kenosis as an exchange of his pre-existent eternal form or mode of being (*Ewigkeitsform*) for a temporal one (*Zeitlichkeitsform*). Rather than relinquishing certain divine attributes *à la* Thomasius, the Incarnate Logos retains all his attributes but possesses them only in proportion to a human mode of existence. The omni-attributes were therefore available to Jesus but only in an applied, space-time form: omnipotence, for example, becoming his ability to work miracles at will within his own limited sphere of influence; omniscience, his ability to see through objects and persons; omnipresence, his ability to go wherever, over land or sea. The evident weakness of Ebrard's model is the *vere homo*.[17]

Bishop H. Martensen of Denmark (1808–84), out of primary concern for Christ's mediatorial function in creation, worked with a distinction between the 'Logos revelation' and the 'Christ revelation'. As the essential world-Logos, the Son's revelation is generally and everywhere present. In the Incarnation, however, the eternal Logos supplements that revelation in a special and personal way by

---

[16] A. B. Bruce, *The Humiliation of Christ*, 5th edn. (Edinburgh: T & T Clark, 1900), 138–63. First delivered as the Cunningham Lectures in 1876, in it Bruce calls the Thomasian model the *absolute dualistic type* and reckons among its advocates König, Delitzsch, and Kahnis, 386–94. Since Thomasius understood the kenosis as a relinquishing of some divine attributes but not others, he was criticized by certain kenoticists for denuding Christ's deity and by others for not securing his full humanity. Thomasius was also criticized for not insuring the unity of Christ's person since he worked with both a kenotic and assumption model in which the depotentiated Logos assumed both a human nature *and soul*, repudiating therefore a metamorphosis of the Logos into a human soul, leaving in question the relationship between the divine and human personhood in Christ. On the latter see Bruce, 141–2.

[17] Ibid. 152–9. Bruce calls Ebrard's model the *absolute semi-metamorphic type*. He cites no other advocates of this model.

becoming human. The kenosis consists in the self-limitation or concentration of the Logos in the man Jesus as the Christ revelation—the
revelation of the Logos in limited human form and weakness. But
while the Logos in the Christ revelation is encompassed within the
concrete bounds of a human life, his revelation in nature is not
diminished. The Logos therefore lives a double life in certain conscious
ways, which identifies the Achilles' heel of Martensen's model: the
una persona.[18]

Wolfgang Friedrich Gess (1819–91), a German Lutheran theologian, runs the kenosis all the way empty: in order to effect the
Incarnation the Logos relinquishes all divine attributes, powers, prerogatives, and glory. The pre-existent Word *becomes* flesh, literally.
Having been transformed into a human soul, the Son gains consciousness of his divine identity and mission only in the gradual course of
human development, a life of faith lived in complete dependence on
God the Father in the power and energies of the Spirit, a life which also
included the possibility of a fall into sin. Gess is recognized as the most
consistent of the nineteenth-century kenoticists. He is also routinely
cited for his vulnerability in securing the *vere Deus*.[19]

C. Hugh Ross Mackintosh (1870–1936)

H. R. Mackintosh offers a version of kenotic Christology that stands
at the end of the greater half-century of this theory's popularity, his
Doctrine of the Person of Jesus Christ first appearing in 1912.[20] Being

---

[18] Ibid. 159–63. Bruce calls Martensen's model the *real* but *relative* type and
reckons as other advocates Schoberlein and Hutton, 415–21.

[19] Ibid. 144–52. Bruce calls Gess's model the *absolute metamorphic* type and
reckons as other advocates Gaupp, Hahn, Schmieder, Reuss, and Godet, 394–400.
Another kenotic watcher, Oscar Bensow, divides the Continental kenoticists into
three chief parties: those that view the kenosis as (1) the relinquishing of certain
divine attributes, of which Thomasius is the chief representative; (2) the relinquishing of all divine attributes, of which Gess is the chief representative; and (3) the
exchange of the divine mode of existence, all attributes intact, for a human mode of
existence, under which he classifies both Ebrard and Martensen. Oscar Bensow, *Die
Lehre von der Kenose* (Leipzig: A. Deichert Verlagsbuchhandlung, 1903), 123ff.

[20] As the basis for the following discussion of Mackintosh's Christology, *The
Doctrine of the Person of Jesus Christ*, 2nd edn. (Edinburgh: T & T Clark, 1913; repr.
1978) is cited intratextually by page number only.

one of the last modern kenoticists, Mackintosh helpfully serves as a filter that highlights for us the major concerns and features of this discernible movement, since he both gives this venture a discerning historical read, as well as offers his own carefully constructed statement of it.

Mackintosh is cognizant that the kenotic discussion in the English context is a sort of second wave to that of its course on the Continent, since he mentions a 're-opening' of the kenotic debate by a number of English theologians, most notably P. T. Forsyth. Mackintosh is not convinced that the criticisms levelled against that initial wave are decisive, and especially censures such critics for not distinguishing between the kenotic 'principle' and its various 'forms' of articulation (463–5). Whereas Mackintosh passionately holds to the former, to which he will give his own formal voice and expression, he feels no responsibility to defend the latter—namely, all the specific proposals put forth by previous, mostly Continental theologians. He is especially sympathetic to Thomasius, however, since his Christological form represents the first significant articulation of the principle, in addition to proposing a more conservative version of kenotic Christology than many of his more speculative counterparts (266–9).

Much has been made of the non-speculative character of English kenotic Christology, that compared with the rigour of Continental thought, the Isles offer a thinner theological gruel. Mackintosh himself notes this shift in tenor: 'There are obvious differences between the older Kenotic theories and the new. For the Christian thinker of today is more reserved and proportionally less vulnerable on points of speculation' (468). In this vein, Mackintosh appears especially enamoured of the tenor of Forsyth's kenoticism, which it seems has been duly tamed by 'the moralizing of dogma'.[21] Thus moral and personalistic categories of thought will edge out philosophic and ontological ones in Mackintosh's model, whose treatment everywhere betrays a careful tentativeness. A theological reasoning that is more a posteriori, viewing kenosis as a necessary interpretive

---

[21] Forsyth's programmatic call for reformulating Christian doctrine in more personalistic and ethical categories. See his *The Person and Place of Jesus Christ, The Congregational Union Lecture for 1909* (Philadelphia: The Westminster Press, 1910), especially Lecture 8, 'The Moralising of Dogma'. The anti-speculative spirit of Ritschlianism is certainly here in the air.

key to the historical fact of the Incarnation, will take precedence over any speculation a priori; for, insists Mackintosh, it is simply not 'given to man to watch God as He becomes incarnate' (470). Mackintosh will make more modest claims than Thomasius and his Continental colleagues.[22]

Nevertheless, though Ritschl's influence be rife and Forsyth's on the rise, there is still a necessity, asserts Mackintosh, to engage a theoretical, indeed metaphysical, interpretation of the person of Christ; for one cannot for ethical concerns alone beg the question of the real: 'a metaphysic of the conscience is none the less metaphysical.... Between the ethical and the metaphysical view of Christ, then, there is no final antagonism' (303–4).[23]

In his historical survey of Christological development, Mackintosh gives the following summary description of the kenoticism that has gone before him:

The Kenotic theologians, one and all, proceed upon orthodox assumptions as to the Trinity and the two natures present in the one person of our Lord. Their object is to show how the Second Person of the Trinity could so enter into human life as that there resulted the genuinely human experience that is described by the evangelists. To this problem they are unanimous in replying—of course with individual variations—that the eternal Logos by a wonderful suspension or restriction of His Divine activities reduced Himself

---

[22] Mackintosh appears driven to Christological reconstruction more out of the need to account adequately for the biblical portrait of an integrally human Jesus than any other philosophical considerations—a rationale that generally characterized the biblically and empirically inclined English from their more speculative counterparts across the Channel.

[23] Of Ritschl's influence on the then current state of Christological debate, Mackintosh says: 'Many writers on doctrine at the present moment are either dubious as to the value of systematic thought or afraid of their own minds; Ritschlianism, with all its service to faith, has a little disparaged the use of reason in theology; and of nothing are we more in need than of a wise and instructed courage' (301). It should go without noting that both Mackintosh and Thomasius, as all the other kenoticists, argue for an intimate unity between Christ's person and work, yet warrant a distinctive ontological treatment of the former as the necessary presupposition and illumination of the latter. As Mackintosh puts it, 'If ... the work is the *ratio cognoscendi* of the nature, not less true is it that the nature is the *ratio essendi* of the work' (342). Although the kenotic model of Incarnation centres discussion principally on the person of the Mediator, its assertion of self-divestment has obvious implications for the work of the Mediator, and vice versa.

within the limits and conditions of manhood. Somehow He laid aside His Divine mode of existence in order to become man (266).

Mackintosh would accept such a description, along with its attending assumptions, as characterizing his own kenoticism. What is only implied in this description of the kenotic task, however (by the word 'wonderful'), and which really attracts and impels Mackintosh to embrace its principle, is the way kenosis accentuates the lengths to which divine love suffered for human salvation: 'This I believe to be the profoundest motive operating in the Kenotic theories—this sense of sacrifice on the part of a pre-existent One' (265).[24] It is not that divine love cannot be manifested apart from the Incarnation, he asserts, 'It is rather that, apart from Incarnation His love is not exhibited so amazingly.'[25] This display of love in and through identification with the human condition, he contends, can only be truly appreciated by a kenotic model of Christ's person.

Thus Mackintosh sets about formulating his own reconstructive statement. Like Thomasius before him, he is dissatisfied with the practical legacy of Chalcedon. Although committed to Chalcedon's intentions—axioms he will enumerate—Mackintosh is not convinced that its particular 'theoretically-tending' form has best served the church. What he has in view here is the doctrine of the two natures. While Mackintosh does not object to the concept of natures per se, he insists that their particular construal in the Chalcedonian formulation and subsequent interpretation has resulted in two undesirable effects. In the first place, this formulation 'imports into the life of Christ an incredible and thoroughgoing dualism' (294). For if the divine nature is fully actualized concurrently with that of the human nature—and doctrines such as the immutability and impassibility of the Godhead make it necessarily so—this inevitably results in a duplicity of Jesus' person (294–5). In the second place, such an abstract delineation of natures, coupled with the assertion that the

---

[24] In an address delivered the year before, in 1911, Mackintosh virtually offers this 'motive' as the only satisfying answer to the problem of evil: 'How shall we assure men in their agony that God veritably is love? For my part, I find the one completely satisfying solution in the certainty that Christ, the Son of God, has indeed suffered in our behalf.' *The Person of Jesus Christ* (London: Student Christian Movement, 1912; repr. 1925), 90–1.

[25] Ibid. 102.

Logos is the person-forming principle of the man Jesus, whose human nature is thus anhypostatic, has resulted in a depreciation of his humanity (295–6). Given the terms of Chalcedon, insists Mackintosh, we are faced with a veritable dilemma whose two horns are sharp indeed:

This dilemma, then—the Scylla of a duplex personality and the Charybdis of an impersonal manhood—has invariably proved fatal to the doctrine of two natures. If it takes Jesus' manhood seriously, as the New Testament of course does by instinct, it makes shipwreck on the notion of a double Self. If, on the other hand, it insists on the unity of the person, the unavoidable result is to abridge the integrity of the manhood and present a Figure whom it is difficult to identify with the Jesus of the Synoptic Gospels (296–7).

Here, as with all kenoticists, the Achilles' heels of both Alexandria and Antioch—docetism and duplicity—become the inherited obstacles to be overcome.

So with the conviction that the traditional articulation of the two-natures doctrine 'is detachable from the believing estimate of our Lord' (299), and in no way constituting a renunciation of its intention, Mackintosh sets out to 'stamp the mintage freshly'. Though rejecting the ancient form of Christological currency, he contends that the substance of his proposal 'has the same meaning as of yore' (305). That substance Mackintosh distils into the following four axioms, which parallel Thomasius' 'pillars of Christology': (1) the deity of Christ; (2) his personal pre-existence; (3) his true humanity; and (4) the unity of his person (469–70). And with Thomasius, Mackintosh holds that these Christological non-negotiables cannot be held together in any true coherent fashion on any other assumption than a real divine kenosis:

Now it is impossible to think these four positions together save as we proceed to infer that a real surrender of the glory and prerogatives of deity, 'a moral act in the heavenly sphere', must have preceded the advent of God in Christ. We are faced by a Divine self-reduction which entailed obedience, temptation, and death. So that religion has a vast stake in the kenosis as a fact, whatever the difficulties as to its method may be. No human life of God is possible without a prior self-adjustment of deity (470).

It is clear from this quotation that Mackintosh does not consider the kenotic theory to be trouble-free. In fact, at one point he even states:

'The difficulties of a Kenotic view are no doubt extremely grave' (466). Nevertheless, Mackintosh contends that this Christological version alone best accounts for Christian belief about Christ and best satisfies the religious heart. The alternatives to it are few, and untenable: either some form of adoptionism, 'which is pagan'; or an unmodified divinity of the Logos, who then is prone to being a docetic, unhistoric Christ. Though we may not be able to specify his person in any precise manner, only a kenotic Christ, asserts Mackintosh, satisfies the historical facts before us (470–1).

So how does Mackintosh envision this kenosis? For one thing, he does not think that Thomasius' distinction between immanent and relative divine attributes can be maintained. For once the world is in place, 'the Divine relations of omnipotence, omniscience, and the like are as really essential as righteousness or grace' (476). Such attributes *ad extra* become necessary determinations of the Godhead and cannot be easily thought away without also dispensing of the very God–world relation itself. Thus Mackintosh considers the omni-attributes as essential to divinity. Yet Mackintosh also clearly says that there is no evidence from the Gospels that Jesus possessed such maximal attributes (e.g. 270). So how does he resolve such an apparent conflict? By positing a transposition of divine attributes from a state of actuality to that of potency:

Still, though not parted with, attributes may be transposed. They may come to function in new ways, to assume new forms of activity, readjusted to the new condition of the Subject. It is possible to conceive the Son, who has entered at love's behest on the region of growth and progress, as now possessing all the qualities of Godhead in the form of concentrated potency rather than of full actuality, *dunamei* rather than *energeia* (477).

Since it is not immediately evident what Mackintosh means by a transposition from actuality to potency, he attempts to illustrate what this might entail in respect to each of the omni-attributes. For example, in respect to omniscience, Mackintosh says,

in its eternal form the absolute intelligence of God acts as an intuitive and synchronous knowledge of all things; when the Eternal passes into time, however, knowledge for Him must take on a discursive and progressive character.... So Christ, who in virtue of His relation to the Father had Divine knowledge within reach, took only what was essential to His vocation. Though on many subjects He shared the ignorance as well as the knowledge of His contemporaries, yet He had at command all higher truth which can be assimilated by perfect human faculty (477).

But even with this clarification it is not easy to see how the kenotic Christ still possessed omniscience essentially, but only in potency and not in actuality. And Mackintosh is forced to engage in some rather strained redefinition of these attributes in the attempt to make this understandable (477–9). Although this manoeuvre never really becomes clear, what Mackintosh finally seems to be saying is that since the life of the person of the kenotic Christ was and still somehow is continuous with that of the life of God, whatever properties he willed to become latent in his kenotic state are quite readily and naturally available to him upon exaltation (cf. 479). Though Mackintosh does not want to denude the *logos ensarkos* of any essential divine attributes, which he accuses Thomasius of doing, neither does he want to say that the kenotic Christ merely refrained from their possible maximal use—for this 'would lead back to the old untenable conception of a krypsis' (482). For Mackintosh, the kenosis must be the supra-temporal act of the *logos asarkos*. But whether his transposition theory can have it both ways appears questionable.

In any event, Mackintosh's proposal implies, just as Thomasius' did, a redefinition of divine immutability. And much in the style of Thomasius, Mackintosh handles this by elevating one attribute of God to be supreme, an attribute which then alone defines God's unchangeableness, an attribute which also happens to be highly compatible with his kenotic programme—namely, love: 'What is immutable in God is the holy love which makes His essence' (473). Whereas for Thomasius divine love was the motive for the Incarnation and God's will or self-determination the immutable essence that allowed for such a self-limitation, for Mackintosh love is both the motive and the unchangeable divine essence that makes kenosis possible. Since the kenosis is an expression—better, the supreme expression—of divine love, it is wholly consistent with who God is and therefore no violation of divine immutability (472–3).

Mackintosh also follows Thomasius in assuming, as must all kenoticists, the personal commensurability between the divine and the human. For him, the Incarnation 'implies not the contrast, but the mutual affinity, of the human and the Divine. It implies that God is deeply kin to man who is made in his image, which man in turn is susceptible of God. To assume an ultimate dualism in this sphere is to condemn the Christologian to failure from the start' (439). Mackintosh sees no evidence in Scripture to contradict this view.

Does this mean that the Calvinist-tutored Mackintosh rejects the so-called extra Calvinisticum? Just what capacity does Jesus' humanity have for his divinity—a full one? Here Mackintosh shows his reserve, for it is an area he would prefer to 'pass over in silence'. He does, however, offer two comments. First, he doesn't think Scripture affords any concrete evidence to suppose that the life of the *logos ensarkos* also consciously transcended the bounds of his human condition—all passages so adduced having reference either to the historic or exalted Christ, not the *logos asarkos*. Secondly, he thinks that the doctrine of the Logos's existence *etiam extra carnem* in the state of humiliation has tendencies towards a certain 'ditheism' or 'tritheism'. What Mackintosh means by this is that to aver that the cosmos would fall into chaos if not for the universal activities of the Son even during his humiliation is to posit a crude understanding of a division of labour within the Trinity. 'After all,' he states, 'it is a fundamental truth that the world is upheld by God, not by a constituent or part of God' (485). This comprises Mackintosh's 'silent' answer to the question of Christ's cosmic functions during his kenosis; he contends that the kenoticist is not obligated to speculate on the *logos asarkos* or to give an answer to such 'remoter questions' (271; cf. also 270–1; 483–5).

But Mackintosh's own kenotic proposal raises some questions for the doctrine of the Trinity. For example, does not the strong notion of person presupposed by either a pre-existent Son or a kenotically Incarnate Christ suggest a sort of ditheism or tritheism itself? To deal with such issues Mackintosh turns in his last chapter to the implications of a kenotic model for the doctrine of the Trinity. And here he delicately attempts to steer a middle course between a more traditional western trinitarianism and a stronger social version of the Trinity. On the one hand, he considers the Augustinian psychological analogy of a single human self-consciousness inadequate to account for the historic Christ; on the other hand, he thinks that a fully social account involving multiple centres of divine consciousness compromises the monotheistic claim. Mackintosh opts for a weaker social version in the attempt to preclude the tritheist charge (523–6). Without our engaging its details, Mackintosh's discussion makes clear once more the intimate and reciprocal connection between Trinity and Christology.

2. THE WANING OF MODERN KENOTICISM

Mackintosh's attempt to sustain a kenotic model of the Incarnation was not greeted with the necessary enthusiasm, and shortly thereafter modern kenoticism experienced a discernible demise. This theological attempt to mediate an integrally human Jesus of more modern awareness and sensitivity with the Christ of confessions past was deemed unsuccessful, if history be the judge. While the reasons for this fall from fashion are many and varied, if we take the kenotic venture as a mediating theology (*Vermittlungstheologie*), we can more easily map out two basic angles of critique: objections from the confessional right that cite it for various violations of orthodoxy; and objections from the progressive left that censure it for not being modern or historical enough. The former proceed mostly by way of internal criticism of the kenotic project; the latter largely leave kenoticism behind in the wake of theological trend. We begin with the conservative reaction.

A. Objections from the Right

The criticisms of kenotic Christology from the orthodox right were as prompt and forthcoming as this movement's effusion of forms; they were also as multiple and nuanced as the broad range of theological aspects involved. Since the kenotic model was no monolith of form, but admitted of variations on its principal theme, the so-called orthodox opponents of kenoticism can also be found within the ranks of the kenoticists themselves—one kenoticist regarding another's statement deficient on deity, humanity, or unipersonhood, and so on, which accounts for the variety of models and types we have briefly documented. But when the dust had finally settled on the project as a whole, these are the major criticisms as to why kenoticism was ruled out of bounds by the more confessionally oriented.

The major doctrinal complaint, with little surprise, was that the kenotic model did not sufficiently account for the deity of the Incarnate Christ. Francis J. Hall, an ardent opponent of kenoticism, put it quite typically this way: 'Was He God or not? If he possessed the fulness of the Godhead—i.e., all Divine attributes—He was God. But, if He was lacking in any of these attributes, He certainly was not God. It is possible to fail in perceiving the fact, but the logic of kenoticism is utterly inconsistent with a real acceptance of the Christian dogma that Jesus Christ was very God.'[26] The various attempts to formulate the deity of the kenotically Incarnate Son did not satisfy the orthodox majority that God was essentially still or sufficiently in Christ reconciling the world. It is this perceived mitigation of the event of salvation—that is, the dubious implications of the kenotically weakened Son for his redemptive work—that caused the gravest of concerns. The words of Karl Barth, another opponent of kenoticism, best sum up this important consideration: 'God is always God even in His humiliation. The divine being does not suffer any change, any diminution, any transformation into something else, any admixture with something else, let alone any cessation. The deity of Christ is the one unaltered because unalterable deity of God. Any subtraction or weakening of it would at once throw doubt upon the atonement made in Him.'[27] For, 'If in Christ—even in the humiliated Christ born in a manger at Bethlehem and crucified on the cross of Golgotha—God is not unchanged and wholly God, then everything that we may say about the reconciliation of the world made by God in this humiliated One is left hanging in the air.'[28] Although Barth credits the venture with good and noble intentions, he articulates the more orthodox consensus that with a kenotic construct it is not so evident that it is truly God who greets us in Christ. And such a fear

[26] Francis J. Hall, *The Kenotic Theory* (New York: Longmans, Green and Co., 1898), 221-2.

[27] Karl Barth, *Church Dogmatics*, vol. IV/1: The Doctrine of Reconciliation, eds. G. W. Bromiley and T. F. Torrance, trans. G. W. Bromiley (Edinburgh: T & T Clark, 1956), 179–80.

[28] Ibid. 183.

was augmented when it was suspected that the consistent and logical conclusion of kenoticism was found in the position espoused by Gess who was considered to have stripped the incarnate of all divinity whatsoever.

Closely related to the deity issue, and again with little surprise, kenotic Christology was cited for violating the doctrine of divine immutability. Eugene Fairweather sums up this objection when, after relating the goals of the kenoticists, he states:

> We must ask, however, whether any ultimately defensible doctrine of the Incarnation could conceivably meet these Kenotic requirements. Certainly the traditional Christology declines to try to meet them, on the ground of the principle of divine immutability, and as long as that principle stands there can be no place for a Kenotic doctrine in Christian thought ... [since] ascriptions of mutation and composition to God run counter to the eternal changelessness and the perfect simplicity of infinite and transcendent Spirit, in which Christian theology has commonly found the very meaning of deity.[29]

Thomasius took this as Dorner's chief objection to his kenoticism, to which Thomasius replied that divine immutability, strictly defined, relegates the very notion of Incarnation to a rather dubious status.

Friedrich Loofs associates kenoticism's impugning of divine immutability with its denial of the so-called extra Calvinisticum. This is another oft-repeated criticism, given famous voice by William Temple:

> What was happening to the rest of the universe during the period of our Lord's earthly life? To say that the Infant Jesus was from His cradle exercising providential care over it all is certainly monstrous; but to deny this, and yet say the Creative Word was so self-emptied as to have no being except in the Infant Jesus, is to assert that for a certain period of history the world was let loose from the control of the Creative Word, and 'apart from Him' very nearly everything happened that happened at all during the thirty-odd years, both on this planet and throughout the immensities of space.[30]

Loofs observes that kenosis theory is consistent only if it 'surrenders everything in the nature of an "Extra Calvinisticum" '—an additional

---

[29] Note in this quotation as well the objection from divine simplicity. Eugene R. Fairweather, 'The "Kenotic" Christology', Appended Note in F. W. Beare, *A Commentary on the Epistle to the Philippians* (New York: Harper & Row, 1959), 170–2.

[30] From his *Christus Veritas*, 1924. Quoted by Dawe, *Form of a Servant*, 142.

price it must pay for its denial of immutability.[31] The adjustments offered by kenoticists for this doctrinal contingency were generally not found to be adequate.

If kenotic Christology does not adequately account for the deity of the incarnate, earthly Christ, then this constitutes, quite obviously, a violation of the doctrine of the Trinity. Hall lays out this simple arithmetic for us quite bluntly: 'Moreover, the doctrine of the Trinity is violated by Kenoticism. Whatever the Trinity is It is eternally. The three Persons are co-eternal and co-equal. But if the Son of God was at any time lacking in Divine attributes He was not then coequal with the Father and the Holy Spirit.'[32] And such trinitarian criticisms of kenosis doctrine came in a variety of forms—from the accusation that it left the Trinity temporarily binitarian, as suggested above, to the objection that it implies an unacceptable tritheism, since it posits such a false and crude separation between divine persons.[33] Again, the objections here are as varied as the objectors' views of the Trinity and how exactly it is that kenosis violates the divine essence, attributes, or functions of the triune God.

Many other concerns were also voiced. Regarding the other pole of Christ's ontology—his humanity—came objections of the sort that kenotic theory was unable to affirm the abiding humanity of the ascended Christ.[34] Some also chided the kenotic effort for being too rationalistic, for overreaching its speculative bounds.[35] Others, conversely, mocked it for being a complete kenosis of reason.[36] So, from

---

[31] Loofs, 'Kenosis', 687.   [32] Hall, *The Kenotic Theory*, 234–5.

[33] As seen already in Mackintosh's treatment, and as implied by Donald Baillie's first objection to kenoticism in his widely read and cited *God Was In Christ: An Essay on Incarnation and Atonement* (New York: Charles Scribner's Sons, 1955), 96.

[34] Cf. for example, Baillie, who presents this as his third and final objection to kenosis. Ibid. 97.

[35] Loofs, for example: 'Moreover, the modern theory of the Kenosis, in all its forms, still carries an air of presumption, inasmuch as it ventures upon constructions which would have a meaning only if God's relation to the world, or, let us say, the relation of the Logos to God, and His divine and divine-human self-consciousness, could be grasped—and analyzed—by the finite mind of man.' 'Kenosis', 687.

[36] A. E. Biedermann's quip concerning Gess's model: 'With this version of the kenosis doctrine, of the logically complete sharpening of the church's doctrine, there is also completed the kenosis of the reason, its divesting in the service of dogma to the point of absolute absurdity. Gess's Logos, which divests itself to the point of being a human soul, is the perfect contradiction in terms. Reason finds itself translated into the land of absolute fairy tale.' In Welch, *God and Incarnation*, 306.

pious concern for mystery to intellectual scorn for casuistry, the kenotic model was routinely criticized and generally dismissed as an untenable orthodox project.

B. Objections from the Left

Critics on the left, it should first be noted, tend to echo with approval those criticisms from the right—most generally, that the kenotic project is untenable based on orthodox suppositions, as this grants further warrant for dispensing with the latter. Donald Dawe, for instance, who has written one of the significant surveys of kenotic Christology, offers this assessment: 'Throughout the nineteenth century many of the mediating theologians in Germany and the English-speaking world had tried to preserve some form of the orthodox doctrine of Christ in the modern world by use of the kenotic motif. But the outcome was always the same. While they used kenosis to save part of the house of orthodoxy, another part always seemed to be undermined.'[37] While Dawe agrees with the range of conservative criticisms that stymied the pre-World War I endeavour, such agreement is a bit duplicitous since he himself advocates a more Arian interpretation of the kenosis hymn and strongly objects to the viability of a kenotic construal within the framework of traditional trinitarian theology. Dawe proposes instead a rehabilitation of the kenosis *motif* for what it teaches a posteriori about the redemptive love of God—much along the lines of Barth. I say 'a bit duplicitous' because while he feels free to use the kenosis motif in a considerably modified doctrine of God and Christ, he does not afford the modern kenoticists any degree of the same latitude, but holds them to historic orthodox standards strictly conceived, features of which the kenoticists themselves attempted to reinterpret, albeit with greater sensitivity to confessional matters. Similar to Dawe on this score is Martin Breidert who has written another important survey of kenoticism, though limited to the more German, Continental scene. He rejects the idea of any possible reconstruction of modern kenoticism since he finds any 'Christology of identity' problematic. Instead he opts for

---

[37] Dawe, *Form of a Servant*, 141.

a 'Christology of relation': Jesus is not God, but God is in some sense in Jesus. Such a perspective, he contends, circumvents the unsolvable problems that arise with a kenotic model.[38]

From a historical point of view, the most significant trend from the 'mediating left' that helped dampen the flames of kenoticism, primarily on the Continent, was the rise of Ritschlianism, with its ties in Schleiermacher's theology and full flowering in so-called classical liberalism.[39] This modern theological strain rendered moot the problems that the kenotic model attempted to resolve, since it no longer shared the same set of confessional presuppositions. Ritschl and his school resisted speculative inquiries, confining their reflections to the practical aspects of God's activities toward us (value judgements) and declaring out of epistemological bounds the divine essence *in se*. They had little concern therefore with issues such as Christ's dual nature. As the last great Ritschlian, Harnack, put it, such dogmatic formulations were the weedy intrusion of Greek philosophy on the pure soil of the Gospel. Moreover, the classical liberals had no real kenotic problem because they had no real pre-existent Christ who came down to earth. For Ritschl, Christ 'pre-existed' only in the sense of an eternal idea or intention in God's mind; he was not prior to his humanity a subsistent personal entity. Which is also to say that the classical liberals had no traditional doctrine of the Trinity. Rather, they conceived of God as the one, eminent personality, a personalist unitarianism that served to replace any metaphysical notion of God as supreme being or substance. In light of this set of commitments, the traditional notion of the Incarnation appeared mythological—a myth that at best could be husked for a kernel of religious or moral truth.

There is one other aspect of the 'mediating left', implicit in the above, that needs highlighting, since it has served as a lingering bias against the kenotic project. With the modern turn to anthropology, subjectivity, and history came a shift in Christological method from 'above' to 'below', from an Incarnational approach to an emphasis

---

[38] Breidert, *Die Kenotische Christologie*, 308ff.

[39] I speak here of Liberal Protestantism as a 'mediating theology' in a broad and extreme sense, since it was largely an attempt to accommodate Christian belief to the presuppositions of the modern world, primarily in conformity to a rationality based on restrictive scientific and historical models.

on Jesuology that begins its reflections with Jesus of Nazareth and only allows the question of his divinity (as distinguished from deity) to emerge at inquiry's end. Inaugurated by Schleiermacher, and carried on by Ritschl, this 'Christology from below' was reinvigorated in more recent times by Pannenberg. His assessment of the kenotic project rings true for all those who sound the death knell of an Incarnational approach:

Even the kenotic Christology of the nineteenth century was thus unable to overcome the fundamental difficulty of an Incarnational Christology. It, too, could only conceive the humanity of Jesus, bound to a limited space, limited in power and knowledge, to the degree it ignored his divinity.... The impasse reached by every attempt to construct Christology by beginning with the Incarnational concept demonstrates that all such attempts are doomed to failure.[40]

This Christological method has continued to hold sway in much of modern theology and biblical scholarship especially given the Baillie battle cry that 'docetism is dead'. In modernist theological circles the humanity of Christ (supposing his unity of person) has become the non-negotiable Christological axiom with which the deity claim must contend.

In western theology the mediating baton was handed to neo-orthodoxy once classical liberalism had largely run its course. But even for those neo-orthodox who were Incarnationally minded, such as Barth, modern kenoticism was considered to be a misplaced project—witness Barth's polemic against it. By and large, neo-orthodox theologians continued the embargo of classic metaphysical

---

[40] Wolfhart Pannenberg, *Jesus—God and Man*, 2nd. edn., trans. Lewis L. Wilkins and Duane A. Priebe (Philadelphia: The Westminster Press, 1977), 312, 322 resp. Of course a 'Christology from below', now considered by many an infelicitous phrase, can be pursued as a historical method that need not conflict with a high Christology, since there is indisputably in the biblical record an ascending (adoptionistic) Christological strain. The early church certainly followed this *ordo cognoscendi* of Christ's personal identity before clarifying his pre-existence in the *ordo essendi*. Most ascending (from below) Christologies, however, never reach such a height but remain adoptionistic in presupposition, positing only a degree of 'divinity' in Jesus the adopted Son of God. The early Pannenberg claimed to have overcome such adoptionism by virtue of a 'retroactive ontology'—a mysterious conception indeed. The later Pannenberg, however, seems to afford greater play for an Incarnational approach. See his *Systematic Theology*, vol. 2, trans. Geoffrey W. Bromiley (Grand Rapids: Eerdmans, 1991), 363ff.

constructions and paid little attention to the doctrine of the Trinity. Barth, of course, is the exception to the latter, but his particular trinitarianism does not seem to require a kenosis of a second person of the Trinity.

3. WEIGHING CLASSIC KENOTICISM

Certainly the kenotic motif did not suffer the eclipse that formal kenoticism did, as this theme, we observed, is in some form or fashion as constant as Christology itself. And so kenosis continued to be a very salient feature in the explication of the gospel. Witness Barth, Bonhoeffer, and a host of others, who make much of the kenotic themes of divine love, sacrifice, and humility, which together attest to 'the humanity of God'. But all resisted the label of 'kenotic Christology' given its association with the distinctive nineteenth-century approach and its specific set of questions.

So it is not surprising that a considerable amount of time elapses before one again hears talk expressly of 'kenoticism' or 'kenotic Christology'. But now, with the greater historical distance from its modern—one can now say 'classic'—expression, the term is able to bear a notable revision in meaning. Kenoticism is now applied to various Christological projects that differ significantly from the intent and strictures of its nineteenth-century advocates. For example, John Macquarrie,[41] Graham James,[42] and Lucien Richard[43] all advocate kenotic Christologies that are united in their methodological approach from below, constituting a 'reformed kenoticism ... [that] disposes of the old stumbling block of pre-existence'.[44] As a conse-

[41] John Macquarrie, 'Kenoticism Reconsidered', *Theology*, 77 (1974), 115–24. To be read in conjunction with his 'The Pre-existence of Jesus Christ', *Expository Times*, 77 (1966), 199–202.

[42] Graham James, 'The Enduring Appeal of a Kenotic Christology', *Theology*, 86 (1983), 7–14.

[43] Lucien J. Richard, *A Kenotic Christology: In the Humanity of Jesus the Christ, the Compassion of Our God* (Washington, DC: University Press of America, 1982). This book is expanded and revised (though not changed in Christological basics) in *Christ: The Self-Emptying of God* (Mahwah, NJ: Paulist Press, 1997).

[44] In the apt words of James, 'Enduring Appeal', 13.

quent, but also parallel development, the kenotic has taken on broader theological connotations and applications that shade in meaning into any divine or human moment of love, humility, self-giving, letting-be, enabling-to-be, and the like, in reference to the inner-trinitarian life, creation and providence, God's revelation or grace-laden initiatives, the Christic pattern of life, basic human freedom or relations, and such. Kenosis has now become a highly fruitful but diffuse motif of manifold application. Such a prolific promiscuity of the kenotic can be seen in the recently published *The Work of Love: Creation as Kenosis*,[45] whose kenotic focus runneth over into all areas in, around, and under Creator and creature, with a modicum of attention to, but no sustained sympathy for, the nineteenth-century project.

So does this indicate that the theological consensus which first tolled the death knell of modern-now-classic kenoticism continues in unshaken unison today?—that the best we can do is to exploit the motif apart from any tougher ontological questions that inevitably arise from a faithful dialogue with the creedal Christological tradition? Not quite. Amid a tacit consensus, there does seem to be a minority report gaining some hearing. Stephen Davis,[46] Ronald Feenstra,[47] David Brown,[48] and Stephen Evans,[49] among others, have argued for a reconsideration of the classic kenotic project. Feenstra, for example, in analysing the major issues involved in the debate, contends that credible responses can be offered to the major arguments against kenosis, whose doctrinal untenability he thinks has mostly been asserted rather than demonstrated.[50] David Brown,

[45] Edited by John Polkinghorne (Grand Rapids & Cambridge, UK: Eerdmans & SPCK, 2001).

[46] Stephen T. Davis, *Logic and the Nature of God* (Grand Rapids: Eerdmans, 1983), 118–31.

[47] Ronald J. Feenstra, 'Pre-existence, Kenosis, and the Incarnation of Jesus Christ', Ph.D. thesis (Yale University, 1984) and 'Reconsidering Kenotic Christology', in Ronald J. Feenstra and Cornelius Plantinga, Jr., eds., *Trinity, Incarnation, and Atonement* (Notre Dame, IN: University of Notre Dame Press, 1989), 128–52.

[48] David Brown, *The Divine Trinity* (London: Gerald Duckworth & Co. Ltd., 1985), 220ff.

[49] C. Stephen Evans, *The Historical Christ and The Jesus of Faith* (Oxford: Clarendon Press, 1996), 132–6.

[50] In his dissertation, Feenstra specifically looks at four major areas of contention and argues (1) that kenosis doctrine does not necessarily imply a denial of the

for another example, defends the 'kenotic model' in addition to a classical two-natures approach with this rationale: 'first, the model is like TNC [two-natures Christology] at least in this respect, that it instantiates what is incontestably an Incarnational identity claim, that the human Jesus was the same person as the divine Christ or Word; secondly, the model is not obviously incoherent; finally, it is a plausible interpretation of the historical evidence.'[51] Though it is an alternative to two-natures Christology, Brown does not defend kenoticism as a rival. He contends that no definitive choice can be made between the two as to which is more correct, though one must of necessity be.[52] Similarly Thomas Morris, who has articulated a strong philosophical defence of a classical two-natures model in his 'two-minds' Christology.[53] Though he generally finds a kenotic model wanting in view of his own preferred Christological portrait, he concludes a related article by saying,

Something like one or the other of these pictures of the Incarnation is necessary, I think, if we are to make full sense of the manifest earthly career of Jesus from the perspective of a high Christology; or, to put it the other way around, if we are to make full sense of a high Christology from the perspective of the manifest, earthly career of Jesus. From either point of view, we need some such account of the metaphysics of God Incarnate.[54]

I agree. Given the confessional non-negotiables—say, Thomasius' pillars or, better, Mackintosh's axioms that make pre-existence explicit—these appear to me the only two Incarnational games in town. And for those who find Morris's 'two-minds' construct less than satisfying in a Nestorian sort of way, the kenotic approach is still an attractive alternative. I concur therefore with those who wish to reconsider nineteenth-century kenoticism, and in this final section

divinity of the Incarnate Son; (2) nor does it imply a denial of Christ's true humanity in either the state of humiliation or exaltation; (3) that pre-existence in general is a coherent notion and does not create insurmountable problems for affirming Jesus' full humanity; and (4) that a social analogy of the Trinity resolves many a trinitarian problem otherwise considered to be entailed by a kenotic doctrine.

[51] Brown, *The Divine Trinity*, 231.   [52] Ibid. 271.

[53] Thomas V. Morris, *The Logic of God Incarnate* (Ithaca, NY: Cornell University Press, 1986).

[54] Idem, 'The Metaphysics of God Incarnate', in Feenstra and Plantinga, *Trinity, Incarnation and Atonement*, 127.

I want to highlight some theological developments and considerations, mostly with a view to the confessional right, that especially warrant its revaluation. I will then conclude with some observations concerning what we may learn from that project in particular.

With the modern heightening of historical consciousness, there was a significant rethinking in the twentieth century of the God–world relation in more historical and dynamic terms. Whereas the old axiom of divine immutability weighed heavily against the kenotic project, this is not the case today. The virtually new axiom of divine passion—that God indeed suffers, not out of deficiency of being but connaturally out of love—both exhibits and parallels the reassessment of immutability, cut as they are from the same metaphysical cloth: God can and indeed does change in significant respects, but never in contradiction to God's character, understood along the lines of God's faithfulness to the good, the true, and the beautiful that God essentially is. The linchpin of a fixed and plenary set of essential divine attributes therefore has been loosened, particularly when thinking about the Incarnate Son. Hence the warranted discussion of *true* deity (or even *sufficient* deity) as opposed to *full* deity, and of what attributes are essential to deity, which are compatible with humanity, and which incompatible that would necessitate relinquishing in order to affirm the true humanity of a kenotically Incarnate Son. The classic kenotic question remains: To what extent could God change without becoming untrue to God's essential self? Put trinitarianly, could a divine person become truly human without becoming inauthentically divine? Put biblically, could one say of Jesus of Nazareth *tout court* that one essentially has seen God the Father?

The trinitarian renaissance of the last three decades—roughly, since Karl Rahner's thankfully heeded lament that Christians were for all practical purposes 'mere monotheists'—has also brought new perspectives and possibilities to the kenotic question. In general, this resurgence has boasted more differentiated doctrines of the Trinity that challenge the regnant psychological analogy in the western trinitarian tradition. The most differentiated of these proposals sail under the flag of social models of the Trinity, on which there have boarded a broad range of advocates. The greater play accorded in such models to the divine persons in contrast to the Trinity of supreme substance (confessional right) or absolute subject (progressive

left)—both of which finally favour a singularity of divine personhood—bolsters the classic kenotic project. Indeed, it is hard to conceive
that project consistently or coherently without some sort of social
trinitarianism, since a robust kenosis of a unitarian God would leave
in question who's minding the celestial store (the death of God atheo-
logians, who were also fond of the kenotic motif, were happy to
proclaim it was vacant).

Granting its defensibility from the tritheist charge (which would
recount another strike against classic kenoticism), a more differentiated
or social doctrine of the Trinity would better facilitate the truth of a
Spirit-Christology. I have reference here to a Spirit-Christology compatible with a classical Incarnational claim, not a Spirit-Christology of
adoptionistic proportions (the more typical association), though the
truth they both incarnate is the same: by title, Jesus the Christ, Jesus the
Messiah, the Anointed One was a man specially endowed with God's
Spirit, who by all gospel appearances lived dependently upon his Father
and amazingly among his neighbours in pneumatic power and energies.
This rather basic biblical theme, neglected by the confessional right,
obviously warrants greater space for Christ's true, full, even radical
humanity as offered by a kenotic construal.

A well-differentiated trinitarianism also affords other possibilities
for thinking about Christ's role as mediator of creation, even if or
when kenotically incarnate. Though it is a complex issue that I can
merely broach here, one need not think of Christ's mediation of
creation in largely Stoic terms as that of a Logos-substance inherently
shouldering a material creation, without which Atlas—if kenotically
incarnate—the world would fall into chaos. Though surely I carica-
ture, certain objections to kenoticism on this score virtually assume
such a crude structural immanentism. Recall William Temple's famous objection. While there are a variety of avenues available in
addressing this 'doctrinal contingency', an especially fruitful one
centres on the role of the—again neglected—Spirit, who as the
Creator-Spirit is also identified as the sustaining Wisdom immanent
in creation, as for instance Moltmann develops in his Christology.[55]

[55] See, for example, Jürgen Moltmann, *The Way of Jesus Christ: Christology in
Messianic Dimensions*, trans. Margaret Kohl (New York: HarperCollins, 1990), esp.
287–90.

These more dynamic and relational developments in the Christian doctrine of God point towards new possibilities in ontology (read also metaphysics), speculation on which has been considered a liability of a kenotic Christology by the mediating left, a prejudice that continues to be reinforced by 'Christologies from below' as well as by postmodernist strains of thought. Many simply regard it passé to employ in a more straightforward fashion the essentialistic language and conceptuality of the trinitarian and Christological heritage. But the ontological issues involved here are unavoidable. The embargo on metaphysical questions in much modern theology, though touted since Kant as an epistemic humility (itself a default metaphysics of subjectivity), is largely a reaction against a certain sort of metaphysics: the classical Greek variety. But this is to confuse form for content. Christopher Stead, who has done considerable study on the classical notion of divine substance, assures us that ancient talk about substance in general and the divine *ousia* in particular was anything but hard and fixed, but admitted a range of meanings not necessarily tied to a Platonic or Aristotelian metaphysic.[56] He informs us that the association of substance with a 'static ontology' that views God as strictly immutable, impassible, apathetic, timeless, and the like, is just that: a product of association; that in regard to the issue of God and change, for instance, it is not the description of deity in terms of substance that precludes a dynamic divinity, it is the doctrine (i.e. supposition) of divine immutability.[57] Stead himself, who as an admirer of Wittgenstein cannot be accused of linguistic naiveté, recommends the continued *regulative value* of essentialistic discourse: if we ascribe attributes to God, then God is properly described in entitative terms as a substance, which reminds us as well that deity is an abiding reality not proscribed by human experience.

While I applaud the modern ascendancy of a personalist metaphysics vis-à-vis a substance metaphysics, the former does not cancel

---

[56] Concerning the notion of divine *ousia*, Stead states: 'It is used ... to express the fact of God's existence ... to pose or answer extremely general questions about God's nature ... to place him in the category of substance ... to suggest that he has something comparable to a constituent material ... or to pose a verbal definition.' 'The Concept of Divine Substance', in *Substance and Illusion in the Christian Fathers* (London: Variorum Reprints, 1985), 13; see esp. 11ff.

[57] Idem, *Divine Substance* (Oxford: Oxford University Press, 1977), 274–5.

out the latter, but serves its qualification. Such a personalism, however, must be rigorously trinitarian—grounded in and exemplified by
the triune God (classical liberal personalism was too individualistic
and not dialogical enough, grounded as it was in a unitarian conception of God). Here I agree with theologians like John Zizioulas
that *Being* ought ultimately to be conceived along the lines of
Communion—prioritizing persons-in-relations and therefore the dynamic of community.[58] And even if Zizioulas is not quite right that
the Cappadocians actually effected this revolution in ontology on the
basis of the Trinity, this is a revolution called for by trinitarian
theology and justly fought for in the recent renaissance. What this
means for Christology and a kenotic Christology in particular is this:
from a confessional point of view one cannot avoid ontological
issues; one cannot beg the question of Christ's personal ontology. If
Jesus of Nazareth is identical in person with the eternally existent Son
of God, one hypostasis of three in the Christian conception of God,
that is, if God's presence in Christ is a 'substantial presence' of the
Logos, then there must be *some* description of his transition in status
from an exclusively divine mode of being to a human mode of being.
This is to say, the basic ontological intent of the Chalcedonian
description in all its essentialistic discourse cannot be disregarded.
The recent gains in a trinitarian ontology warrant such a question
and such a conceptuality, or conceptual tools, albeit in a modified—
more dynamic and relational—doctrine of God.

This begging of the ontological question of the Incarnation can be
seen, for instance, in Barth's Christology. While Barth loudly asserts
against kenoticism that 'God is always God even in His humiliation',
he tends to avoid the question how this is thinkable in the one person
of Jesus Christ.[59] Given his revelational model of the Trinity, which

---

[58] John Zizioulas, *Being As Communion: Studies in Personhood and the Church*
(Crestwood, NY: St. Vladimir's Seminary Press, 1985).

[59] It is interesting to note, however, that Barth's affirmation of the Incarnation—
e.g. 'He appropriates unto himself the being of man in contradiction to himself, but
he does not share that contradiction' (*Church Dogmatics* IV/1, 202)—is largely
justified by his understanding of God's essential being as 'the One who loves in
freedom', which bears a remarkable similarity to what Thomasius (freedom) and
Mackintosh (love), taken together, considered as essential deity. For Barth's avoidance of the harder ontological issues of the Incarnation, see also Pannenberg, *Jesus—
God and Man*, 312–15.

prefers to view Christ as a 'mode of being' (*Seinsweise*) of the event of God's singular subjective revelation, Barth's Christology, as Pannenberg puts it, 'knows of no temporal succession of the two "states" of humiliation and exaltation'.[60] Hence, the issue of the kenosis of the second Person does not arise.

Moltmann provides a more striking example of this avoidance, since he clearly advocates an eternal Trinity of three distinct, discrete persons (post *The Crucified God*) and does not in any way want to dissolve Christology into anthropology by way of an adoptionistic Jesuology. Though he proposes a Spirit-Christology as a via media between descending (above) and ascending (below) Christologies, he affirms, for all I can see, the basic 'axioms' or 'pillars' of an Incarnational approach. But Moltmann is reluctant to use the language of 'pre-existence' (though the notion is clearly implied) or to talk about any initial act of kenosis by the Incarnate Son. Perhaps this is tact given the Christological tack he wants to elaborate—the neglected messianic and therefore pneumatic dimensions of Christ's life and ministry. But it does seem peculiar to me that whereas he talks freely about the general divine kenosis in the creation of the world as a self-limitation of omni-attributes,[61] and even more particularly about the kenosis of the Spirit,[62] he does not expressly entertain this same fruitful move in the Incarnation of the Son. My point here is this: the classic kenotic approach in principle seems to me not only eminently compatible with Moltmann's Christology, but his Christology actually appears to presuppose it. If Jesus Christ is the eternal Son of God who as the Messiah lives a fully integrated and docetically unimpaired human life in dependence upon the Father in the power and energies of the Spirit, this seems to require a kenosis of ontological dimensions. Why shy away from the issue?

Nineteenth-century kenoticism was a quest for a coherent Christological orthodoxy. After an account of its flourishing, I outlined the main reasons for its decline, and in this last section have sketched some theological developments and concerns that warrant a serious reconsideration of this basic project. What we therefore learn most

---

[60] Ibid. 313, n. 86.
[61] 'God's Kenosis in the Creation and Consummation of the World', in Polkinghorne, ed., *The Work of Love*, 137–51, esp. 147–8.
[62] Moltmann, *The Way of Jesus Christ*, 91–4.

generally from this Christological venture is that it cannot be quickly dismissed; the fundamental issues it addresses persist and are implicit in any construal of the Incarnation. A kenotic model of the Incarnation may yet be the best of all possible Christological worlds, of articulating more coherently the truth of the church's confession of the person of Christ, which is at the same time the truth of both a descending and ascending Christology, the truth of both the Incarnational and adoptionistic strains of Scripture. Moreover, while I applaud the application of the kenotic motif in its current theological breadth, a revisitation of its original Incarnational context and event might disclose the integrating and intensive source of its redolence. If the Son of God for the sake of an other really crossed the great metaphysical divide between God and humanity, this provides a powerful propaedeutic for all those other affirmations of kenosis. The kenotic posture of Christ upon his Incarnation would then provide the keynote for his earthly ministry, which then becomes 'keynotic' for understanding the inner-trinitarian life of love, humility, self-deference, enabling-to-be, and such, that divine life vis-à-vis creation, the Christic pattern for human relationships, and so on. To neglect or dismiss this possibility may be to risk a depreciation of the gospel—the lengths to which God in Christ reached out to empower an impoverished humanity en route to glorifying all of creation.

Finally, what might we learn from nineteenth-century kenoticism in particular? If this project was a quest for a coherent orthodoxy, it was an attempt to eliminate what were considered the debilitating paradoxes of the two-natures model. Those who esteem paradox per se, usually on the basis of principle (e.g. *finitum non capax infiniti*), will continue to have little sympathy for the kenotic approach, perhaps even declaring it *ab initio* an illegitimate theological endeavour. But while the *acceptance of* paradox may be a virtue, because inevitable, there is a legitimate discussion as to what constitutes a paradox—by definition no clear and distinct idea, but admitting a range of connotations from appearance to essence—and where exactly this applies in theology. The kenoticist is typically not fond of paradox *qua* contradiction (essential paradox). *Credo quia absurdum est* is surely the death of theology as a 'logy'—as a science employing all the logical tools of analysis. *Credo ut intelligam*, however, is a warrant for pushing beyond contradiction, if possible.

The nineteenth-century kenotic venture was largely judged to run aground on its own quest, making wreck on the paradoxes it set out to eliminate—one model not accounting for Christ's true humanity, another his unity of person, and so forth. Even Mackintosh at the retrospective end was resigned to certain tensions and inconsistencies within his own account. So perhaps the particular lesson we learn from this endeavour is that we finally must live with Christological paradox even if we want to assert a real kenosis of the Incarnate Son, *à la* the British kenoticists. But if there is still an opening for a more coherent kenotic read of the Incarnation—and this might constitute the 'parabolic surprise' of this chapter—it would lie in the approach of ... Gess? Wolfgang Friedrich, that is, whose model took the kenotic tack harder and in a more rigorous direction than its other nineteenth-century expressions since it posited a strict identity (*una persona*) between the Logos and human rational soul of Jesus of Nazareth, of the Word who *became* flesh, of the pre-existent one who *was made* like his brothers in every way. For this Gess is universally acclaimed as the most consistent and coherent of the kenoticists, but who was dismissed for not securing the necessary deity claim. I think that claim can be secured on the Gessian model. But that is the argument of another work.

5

Is Kenosis Orthodox?

Stephen T. Davis

1

This chapter addresses the question whether kenotic Christological theories are orthodox[1]. Naturally, this will require discussion of what makes a Christological theory count as kenotic. It will also require discussion of what makes a Christological theory orthodox as opposed to, say, unorthodox or even heretical. Roughly, I will use the word *orthodox* in such as way as to imply that 't is orthodox' (where 't' is some theological theory or claim) means roughly 't is acceptable for belief by the people of God.' It does not mean 't is *required* for belief by the people of God.'

It should be noted that in the present chapter, I am presupposing the truth of a 'high' Christology, that is, one that is consistent with the decrees of Nicaea I and Chalcedon. I do not argue for such a Christology here (as I have done elsewhere[1A]). This is because my intended audience primarily consists of those who also hold to a high Christology, but are suspicious of kenosis. I make this point because many biblical and theological scholars today reject the 'truly human and truly divine in one person' formula, argue instead for a minimal Christology, and would doubtless reject the kenotic theory as *too* orthodox.

---

[1]   The argument of this essay is largely similar to Chapter 10 of Stephen T. Davis, *Christian Philosophical Theology* (Oxford: Oxford University Press, 2006).

[1A]   For example, in my contributions to Stephen T. Davis (ed.), *Encountering Jesus: A Debate on Christology* (Atlanta: John Knox Press, 1988).

What then is a *kenotic* Christological theory? Roughly, let us say that such a theory is one that explains the Incarnation in terms of the Logos 'giving up' or 'laying aside' or 'divesting itself of' or 'emptying itself of' certain properties that normally belong to divinity. Some kenotic theorists take this divestment to be temporal and temporary, with the period of divestment corresponding to the time-span of the earthly life of Jesus. After Jesus' earthly life, that is, in the exaltation, the Logos resumes possession of all divine properties. What is always emphasized, however, is the voluntary and redemptive aspect of kenosis: it was out of love for us and for the sake of our redemption that the Logos 'emptied himself'.

It should go without saying that kenotic theories have no necessary connection whatsoever with (1) denying that Jesus really performed the miracles attributed to him in the gospels or attempting to explain them rationalistically; (2) arguing that Jesus Christ was a mere man, not really and essentially God;[2] (3) making Jesus Christ a sort of demigod by enlarging his humanity with a few divine properties;[3] (4) implying that the Logos, shorn of many of its divine attributes in the Incarnation, is temporarily excluded from the Trinity;[4] (5) affirming pantheistically that God and human beings are different forms of the same thing or are at least not very different; (6) claiming that we too, like Jesus, can be Incarnations of God; or (7) insisting that women should be subordinate to men.[5] I can confidently state that no contributor to the present volume holds, asserts, or argues for any of these items.

A kenotic theory of the Incarnation should be understood as contrasting with what I will call a *classical* theory of the Incarnation, which makes no reference to the Logos giving up any properties.

---

[2] Donald Baillie describes the kenotic theory as follows: 'He who formerly was God changed Himself temporarily into man, or exchanged his divinity for humanity.' See his *God Was in Christ: An Essay on Incarnation and Atonement* (New York: Scribner's, 1948), 96.

[3] As is charged by Dietrich Bonhoeffer in *Christ the Center*, trans. John Bowden (New York: Harper & Row, 1966), 97.

[4] As is charged by Wolfhart Pannenberg in his *Jesus—God and Man*, 2nd edn., trans. Lewis L. Wilkins and Duane A. Priebe (Philadelphia: Westminster Press, 1977), 311.

[5] See the critique of kenosis in Daphne Hampson, 'On Autonomy and Heteronomy' in Daphne Hampson (ed.), *Swallowing a Fishbone? Feminist Theologians Debate Christianity* (London: SPCK, 1996), 1–17.

Classicists argue that, in the Incarnation, the Logos simply took on a new, that is, human, condition. Some classical theorists add that the human nature was amplified or enhanced in order to make it fit for unity with the divine nature.

Kenotic theories of the Incarnation differ on whether the Incarnation of the Logos is to be distinguished from the kenosis, and on (so to speak) how long each lasts. The view that I am defending is that the kenosis is indeed distinct from the Incarnation, with the kenosis lasting only for the some thirty years of Jesus' lifetime, and the Incarnation lasting from the moment of Jesus' conception to eternity. That is, the statement, 'The second person of the Trinity is God Incarnate' is after (say) 4 BC always true, while the statement, 'The second person of the Trinity is kenotically incarnate' was only true from about 4 BC until about AD 29, and indeed is now (i.e. as I write this sentence in the twenty-first century) no longer true. The Incarnation accordingly begins in time and, unlike the kenosis, does not ever cease.[6]

Kenotic Christological theories were first proposed in the early nineteenth century, although 'kenotic' notions can be found much earlier in Christian tradition, and of course in scripture itself, as kenoticists always insist. The first explicit kenotic theologians were the Germans, Gottfried Thomasius (1802–75) and W. F. Gess (1819–91).[7] Then the theory was defended by a series of able British theologians, including P. T. Forsyth (1848–1921), Charles Gore (1853–1932), H. R. MacKintosh (1870–1936), and Frank Weston (1871–1924).[8] Interestingly, one of the themes emphasized by the early kenoticists, namely, that Jesus' temptations and sufferings were real, is now considered commonplace. Within the last thirty years, kenosis has enjoyed a renaissance among a small group of theologians

[6] See C. Stephen Evans, 'The Self-Emptying of Love: Some Thoughts on Kenotic Christology', in Stephen T. Davis, Daniel Kendall, S.J., and Gerald O'Collins, S.J. (eds.), *The Incarnation: An Interdisciplinary Symposium on the Incarnation of the Son of God* (Oxford: Oxford University Press, 2002), 246–72.

[7] See Ch. 4 by Thomas R. Thompson, 'Nineteenth-Century Kenotic Christology', for a fuller account. For a book-length treatment, see Claude Welsh (ed. and trans.), *God and Incarnation in Mid-nineteenth Century German Theology* (New York: Oxford University Press, 1965).

[8] See, for example, Frank Weston, *The One Christ: An Enquiry into the Manner of the Incarnation* (London: Longmans Green, 1907).

and philosophers of religion, including Hans Urs von Balthasar,[9] Brian Hebblethwaite,[10] as well as several of the contributors to the present volume. Some kenotic theories were doubtless intended by their authors as substitutes for, rather than interpretations of, Chalcedon. But as noted, the version that I am defending presupposes the full humanity and divinity of the one person of Christ. Accordingly, I am suggesting a kenotic theory as a way of interpreting Chalcedon.

The name and essence of the theory derive from the great Christological hymn of Philippians 2:6–11, where Paul says of Christ (in the NRSV): 'who, though he was in the form of God, did not count equality with God a thing to be grasped, but emptied himself [the Greek term Paul uses here, *ekenosin*, is a derivative of the word *kenosis*], taking the form of a servant, being born in the likeness of men'.

2

Let me now sketch out a possible kenotic theory of the Incarnation.[11] The basic idea is that Christ was indeed simultaneously truly divine and truly human, possessing as he did all properties that are essential to divinity and humanity, and that this was made possible by the Logos emptying itself, during the period of Jesus' earthly life, of those properties that normally characterize divinity but are inconsistent with humanity.

Now all things or substances have properties. Some properties are essential to them and some are accidental to them. An *essential property* of x is an attribute that x has and cannot lose without ceasing

---

[9] In such works as *Mysterium Paschale: The Mystery of Easter*, trans. Aidan Nichols, O.P. (Edinburgh: T. & T. Clark, 1990), *Theo-Drama III: The Dramatis Personae: The Person in Christ*, trans. Graham Harrison (San Francisco: San Francisco Press, 1992), and *Theo-Drama IV: The Action*, trans. Graham Harrison (San Francisco: Ignatius Press, 1994).

[10] See Brian Hebblethwaite, *The Incarnation: Collected Essays in Christology* (Cambridge: Cambridge University Press, 1987), esp. 27–44.

[11] It is explained in more detail in my *Encountering Jesus* and in Chapter 8 of my *Logic and the Nature of God* (Grand Rapids: Eerdmans, 1983).

to exist or to be x. Three-sidedness is an essential property of any triangle; if a given triangle were to lose its three-sidedness, it would no longer be a triangle. An *accidental property* of x is an attribute that x has but can fail to have and still be x. Being a philosophy professor is presumably an accidental property of mine; it seems that I could both exist and still be the very thing or person that I am if I stopped being a philosophy professor. A *common property of a kind k* is an attribute that all members of k have (e.g. for the natural kind 'human being', *having been born on earth* is a common property).

Let us list some properties of God and human beings:

God	*Human beings*
1 Being necessary.	1' Being contingent.
2 Living for ever.	2' Living only for a finite time.
3 Being omnipotent.	3' Being non-omnipotent.
4 Being omniscient.	4' Being non-omniscient.
5 Being incorporeal.	5' Being corporeal.

Now here is a problem for all orthodox views of the Incarnation: if properties 1–5 are essential to God; and if properties 1'–5' are essential to all human beings; and if the orthodox doctrine of the Incarnation (which includes the 'truly human and truly divine' clause) affirms that Jesus Christ must simultaneously possess all the members of both sets of properties; and if (as it surely seems) it is logically impossible for any being simultaneously to have all the members of both sets of properties; then the orthodox doctrine of the Incarnation spelled out at Nicaea and Chalcedon is incoherent.

But how do we go about deciding which properties of human beings are essential to them? And how do we go about deciding which divine properties are essential to God? 1'–5' certainly seem to be properties of human beings (although 2' can be debated); and 1–5 certainly seem to be properties of God, at least as Christians conceive of God. But must we affirm that 1'–5' are *essential* properties of human beings? And must we affirm that 1–5 are *essential* properties of God?

Again, how do we know which of a being's properties are essential to it and which are accidental to it? With abstract or mathematical objects (e.g. circles, sets, etc.) the decision is sometimes fairly easy. For concrete things such as human beings, it is rarely easy. Now

Christians accept the orthodox doctrine of the Incarnation; they hold that Jesus Christ is 'truly human and truly divine'. Accordingly, Christians will be much inclined to *deny* that the properties listed in the chart above are essential properties of God and human beings, respectively. Indeed, Christian theology has always insisted that Jesus Christ is both the pre-eminent revealer of God and the model human being. Looking at the Incarnation of Christ, then, is one fruitful way (maybe the best way) of finding out about divinity and humanity, of discovering which properties of God and human beings are essential and which are accidental. If Jesus Christ is 'truly human and truly divine', then perhaps the properties listed above are either not essential properties or else are consistent with all the others.

Thomas Morris, who is not a defender of kenosis, has nevertheless made a helpful suggestion that kenoticists can use: perhaps the 1'–5' properties are essential properties not of *being human* but of *being merely human*.[12] And of course orthodox Christians do not want to affirm that Jesus Christ was 'merely human'. Perhaps then the 1–5 properties are essential properties not of *being divine* but of *being divine simpliciter* (i.e. being divine without also being human). And of course orthodox Christians do not want to affirm that God is 'God simpliciter'. Indeed, Christians hold that there never has existed any 'God simpliciter'; the one and only God who exists is a God who becomes incarnate in a human being. Accordingly, what Christians want to say about Jesus Christ is that he was *truly human* but not *merely human, truly divine* but not *divine simpliciter*.

Here is where kenosis comes in. The core idea is that Jesus Christ was 'in the form of God' as the Logos, or the Second Person of the Trinity, and that at a certain point in human history he voluntarily and obediently 'emptied himself' both of the divine glory and of certain other divine properties; he then took on 'human form', that is, became a human being. That is, in the Incarnation, Jesus Christ 'emptied himself' by temporarily giving up those divine properties that are inconsistent with being truly human while retaining sufficient divine properties to remain truly divine; and he did not assume those common human properties that are inconsistent with

---

[12] See Thomas V. Morris, 'Divinity, Humanity, and Death', *Religious Studies*, 19 (1983), 457.

being truly divine but assumed sufficient human properties to be truly human. In the Incarnation, then, Jesus Christ was not *a mere human* but truly human; he was not God *simpliciter* but rather truly divine. Perhaps one cannot simultaneously be a mere human and truly divine; and perhaps one cannot simultaneously be God *simpliciter* and truly human. But Christians hold that it is possible to be 'truly divine and truly human'.

The whole kenotic scheme depends on there not being any essential divine properties that no human being can have and on there not being any essential human properties that no divine being can have. And following another acute suggestion from Morris,[13] a coherent kenotic theory will accordingly hold that what is essential to God is not, for example, omniscience, but rather the more complex property of being omniscient-unless-freely-and-temporarily-choosing-to-be-otherwise. The same point will then be made with other divine properties such as omnipotence, omnipresence, and so on.

What does it mean for God to 'give up' a property? Well, as long as the property in question is accidental, there is no big problem. We certainly give up properties constantly, for example, the property of having long hair whenever we cut it short, or the property of being seated whenever we stand. 'God gives up property p' would roughly mean, then, that at a given point God has property p but at a later point, of God's own free choice, God does not have property p. Suppose, for example, that God is in fact omniscient but that God could still exist and still be divine if God were slightly less than omniscient (if there were, say, some few things that God does not know). That is, suppose that omniscience is a property of God, but an accidental one. Then 'God gives up the property of omniscience' means that at one point God is omniscient and that a later point God voluntarily becomes non-omniscient, while still existing and remaining God.

But there is a problem here. While some properties can surely be given up (e.g. having long hair, being seated), others, whether essential or accidental, seem to be (so to speak) 'ungiveupable'. These are time-indexed properties or properties one has because of events that

---

[13] See Thomas V. Morris, *The Logic of God Incarnate* (Ithaca: Cornell University Press, 1986), 75.

occurred in the past, for example, properties such as *not having been created, having existed in the sixteenth century,* and *being the creator of the heavens and the earth.* Without arguing that these properties are essential to any being who has them (they may or may not be essential properties), the point is that they cannot be given up. Any being who has them at one temporal point has them at all temporal points. Thus kenosis is in trouble, because it makes no sense to say, for example, that the Logos gave up the property of *not having been created* in order to be truly human or that Jesus Christ gave up the property of *having been created* in order to be truly divine.

In response to this problem, defenders of kenosis can refer to a traditional way of making Christological affirmations, namely, that Jesus Christ has some properties *as* God and some *as* a human being. The Chalcedonic Definition itself seems to imply something of the sort: 'of one substance with the Father *as regards his Godhead,* and at the same time of one substance with us *as regards his manhood*' (italics added). This way of making Christological affirmations has been explored in a preliminary way by P. T. Geach,[14] who calls them reduplicative propositions. He distinguishes what we ought to say that God *as God* can do from what we can say that God *as a human being* can do. In sentences such as 'A as P is Q,' Geach says, we are not to think of Q as a predicate attached to the complex subject 'A as P'— rather, we ought to read the sentence as 'A is, as P, Q.' Thus we can sensibly say such things as 'Jesus Christ is, as God, unable to die' and 'Jesus Christ is, as a human being, able to die' without nonsense.

There are dangers here: if the notion is pushed too far, Christ might seem divided into two persons, one of which was and the other of which was not able to die. To divide Christ like that would be to fall dangerously close to the Nestorian heresy, condemned at the Synod of Ephesus in AD 431. And if the unity of Christ's person is emphasized, the following objection might arise: 'Well then, is the one person Jesus Christ able to die or not? Surely it must be one or the other: which is it? If he is able to die, he is not divine; if he is not able to die, he is not human.'

---

[14] P. T. Geach, *Providence and Evil* (Cambridge: Cambridge University Press, 1977), 25–8.

Suppose a certain person named Malan is both mayor of the town and director of athletics at the local college. (Similar to an example given by Geach, this one describes an actual person whom I know.) Malan has certain rights and responsibilities as mayor (e.g. signing into law resolutions passed by the city council) and certain rights and responsibilities as director of athletics (e.g. approving expenses covered by the athletics department budget). Someone might then ask: 'Well then, is this one person Malan able to sign resolutions into law or not?' In one sense, the answer is yes—the one person Malan does have that ability. But in another sense, the question is ill-formed. It ought to ask: 'Does Malan, as mayor, have that ability?' Then of course the answer is yes (just as the answer to 'Does Malan, as athletics director, have that ability?' is no). Similarly, the objection raised at the end of the previous paragraph is ill-formed. In one sense (a sense that will lead to paradox), the one person Jesus Christ both was and was not able to die. Better, however, to say: he was, as human, able to die; he was not, as divine, able to die. Jesus Christ does not possess those inconsistent properties in the same way.

The analogy between Malan and the Incarnation is not exact. The main difference is this: there is no great logical or metaphysical difficulty in an athletics director also serving as mayor; but there is a logical or metaphysical difficulty in God's becoming a human being. Thus, sentences such as, 'The athletics director of the college signs resolutions into law in this town' seem, though puzzling, logically possible. But sentences such as, 'The Second Person of the Trinity is able to die' seem both puzzling and logically impossible. Nevertheless, I will stand by the claim that when the sentence is well-formed ('The Second Person of the Trinity is, as a man, able to die, and is not, as God, able to die'), it is true.

There is no escaping the fact that there is paradox involved in the notion of Incarnation. We will not be able to use kenosis, or any other theory, to remove all mystery from the doctrine. But kenosis does help us toward a coherent way of understanding Incarnation. It helps provide a sense in which we can legitimately (although admittedly somewhat paradoxically) say: 'Jesus Christ is truly divine.' It helps provide a sense in which we can legitimately (although admittedly somewhat paradoxically) say: 'Jesus Christ is truly human.'

It is important to note that the kenotic theory defended here has nothing whatever to do with a human being becoming or turning into God in the sense that he formerly was human but then relinquished humanness to achieve divinity (or relinquished divinity to become human) or with human properties changing into divine ones (or the reverse). Nor does it end up with the kenotically incarnate Logos as a lessened or reduced God. If the theory could be shown to deny the *homoousious* principle of Chalcedon, it would not be worth defending. But it does not do so. The kenotically incarnate Logos is indeed 'of one substance with the Father' because the Father's nature or substance just is the set of his essential properties, which the theory insists Christ had. And since we do not accordingly have a minimized deity who dies on the cross, there are no untoward salvific implications in the theory either.

Let me make three last points before concluding my explanation of the kenotic theory that I am defending. First, kenosis is based on the idea that the human essence or nature has a natural receptivity to the divine nature. In this way, it is quite unlike a coyote nature or an amoeba nature. It is possible for a human nature and a divine nature to be united in one person because human beings, unlike coyotes and amoebas, were created 'in the image of God' (Gen. 1:27).

Secondly, many kenotic theorists (call them 'irenic kenoticists') are disinclined to claim that Incarnation can *only* be explained via kenosis. Accordingly, they are not to be seen as enemies of classical theories of the Incarnation. Those kenoticists must be irenic who agree that (1) the Incarnation of the Logos is everlasting after Jesus' conception (i.e. it is still—in the twenty-first century—true that 'The Logos is God Incarnate'); and (2) the kenosis lasted only for the period of Jesus' earthly life. Thus such kenoticists face the question how Incarnation without kenosis is possible. Accordingly, they will have to appeal to non-kenotic theories to understand how it is true in the twenty-first century that 'The Logos is God Incarnate.'

Thirdly, every orthodox Christologist is a kenoticist in some sense. Even those who criticize and reject kenosis either explicitly or implicitly allow that in the Incarnation the Logos divested itself of at least *some* divine properties. Almost everybody admits that, in the Incarnation, the Logos gave up certain divine prerogatives like the divine glory (this point seems a clear implication of the kenosis hymn).

And even determined rejecters of kenosis seem, on close analysis, to be implying (whether openly or not) that the Logos gave up certain other divine properties. Even Tom Morris, defender of his own decidedly non-kenotic 'two-minds' theory, seems to me to be an unwitting kenoticist. What the 'two-minds' theory entails that the Logos 'gave up' or 'emptied itself of' in the Incarnation was invulnerability to human pains and sufferings.[15]

3

How do we go about discovering whether kenosis—or any theological theory—is orthodox? On this question, Catholics and Protestants differ, and it will be important to consider both viewpoints. Protestants classically recognize but one source of theological authority, namely, scripture. Accordingly, a Protestant will typically try to show that a given theological theory or claim is orthodox by showing that it is scriptural. That is, the theory or claim is either explicitly taught or else is entailed by one or more properly interpreted texts of scripture. Catholics classically recognize two sources of theological authority, namely, scripture and tradition. Accordingly, a Catholic will typically try to show that a given theological theory or claim is orthodox by showing that it is to be found in, or agrees with, or is entailed by what is found in either scripture or tradition or both.

Let us first consider the Roman Catholic notion of theological authority. A preliminary point is that the term 'tradition', even in its theological uses, can mean different things. In the present context, it refers either to unwritten teachings of Jesus that were said to have been passed down by word of mouth in the church, or to the entire Roman Catholic theological and ecclesiastical system and history ('the Catholic tradition'). For Catholics, this second usage refers pre-eminently to decisions of church councils and *ex cathedra* pronouncements of popes, with emphasis placed on the Holy Spirit's

---

[15] This seems a clear implication of the argument of pp. 88–107 of Morris, *The Logic of God Incarnate.*

gracious guidance of the church throughout history. Catholics also typically distinguish between *traditio passiva*, which is the changeless deposit of faith that is passed on from generation to generation, and *traditio activa*, which is the constantly changing beliefs and practices of the church.

But how are scripture and tradition related? There are two Catholic theories, what I will call the older theory and the revisionist theory. The older theory derives from the Council of Trent (1545–63). Although Catholics interpret Trent differently, the Council's basic claims are that scripture and tradition are two functionally equal sources of religious truth, and that theological theories or claims can be justified by appeal to either source. That is, divine revelation is materially divided—some of it is found in scripture and some in unwritten tradition. And scripture is inferior to the church, both because the canonization of scripture was an act of the church and because scripture by itself is functionally insufficient for salvation, since it needs to be authoritatively interpreted by the church.[16]

After Vatican II, the revisionist theory (of people like Joseph Geiselmann, George Tavard, and Karl Rahner[17]) has replaced the older theory among most Catholics (except very conservative ones). Revisionists still hold (1) that scripture and tradition constitute two sources of religious truth; (2) that scripture is the creation of the church (in the sense that it was the church that canonized the texts that Christians call 'the Bible'); and (3) that scripture needs authoritative interpretation by the church. But revisionists do not subordinate scripture to tradition, and the material insufficiency of scripture is no longer affirmed. What is instead insisted on is the unity of scripture and tradition. Both flow from the same source

[16] Thus Catholics have occasionally appealed to tradition as the authoritative source of dogmas not found in scripture. For example, in the promulgation of the dogma of the assumption of the Blessed Virgin Mary in 1950, no scriptural support for the dogma was cited (although such support was claimed); what was instead appealed to was the consensus of the church.

[17] See, for example, George R. Geiselmann, 'Scripture, Tradition, and the Church: An Ecumenical Problem', in D. Callahan, H. Oberman, and D. O'Hanlon, S.J. (eds.), *Christianity Divided* (New York: Sheed and Ward, 1961); George H. Tavard, *Holy Writ or Holy Church* (New York: Harper & Brothers, 1959); for an excellent summary of his views, see Rahner's own article on 'Scripture and Tradition', in his (ed.) *Encyclopedia of Theology: The Concise Sacramentum Mundi* (New York: The Seabury Press, 1975).

(God) and move toward the same goal. Materially, it is now held that scripture witnesses to all revealed truth. Catholic doctrine is now said to develop under the guidance of the Holy Spirit, as the church works to unfold the implications of scripture and tradition. It is the function of the magisterium, or church teaching office, authoritatively to interpret scripture and tradition, and decide what Catholic teaching is, that is, to explain, apply, and sometimes revise Catholic teaching.

Let us turn to the Protestant approach. For Protestants, 'Scripture alone' was a motto of the Reformation. It appears to connote a whole constellation of related claims: (1) There is no source of religious truth that rivals scripture in its authority, accuracy, and power to convince; tradition is only a secondary authority, and is a norm only to the degree that it agrees with scripture.[18] (2) Scripture is the final criterion of all religious claims; scripture does not receive its authority from the church but rather from God, its author or inspirer; accordingly, every theological, moral, or liturgical development in the church is to be tested by scripture. (3) Scripture is intrinsically clear and needs no infallible church or tradition to interpret it; individual believers are capable of reading and understanding it; and scripture is the judge of tradition and sometimes stands over against tradition as a critique of beliefs and practices in the church. (4) Nothing can be added to scripture; the Bible tells us all that is necessary for our salvation.

As a Protestant myself, I tend toward accepting at least some version of 'Scripture alone'. But I also want to retain an important place for tradition in determining which theological theories or claims are orthodox. Let us see what can be said along those lines.

As noted, there are various things that 'Scripture alone' might be said to mean. Sometimes it is said to mean that *Scripture is our only source of religious truth.*[19] But that claim cannot be true. The Protestant Reformers themselves insisted that some knowledge of God

---

[18] As Luther argued in his disputation with John Eck in 1519, popes and councils can and do err, so they cannot constitute the highest authority for theology.

[19] Something very similar to this seems suggested in the Second Helvetic Confession (1566): 'And in this Holy Scripture, the universal church of Christ has the most complete exposition of all that pertains to a saving faith, and also to the framing of a life acceptable to God; and in this respect it is expressly commanded by God that nothing be either added to or taken from the same.'

can be gained by contemplating the creation. Moreover, many people come to believe certain truths about God without ever having read the Bible, or indeed without ever having heard of it. But then perhaps 'Scripture alone' should be said to mean that *Scripture is our only salvifically sufficient source of religious truth.* Now, few Christians want to deny that scripture is *the* source of saving religious truth, or the source of religious truth *par excellence.* But the difficulty here is that many people have apparently been saved in Christian terms, that is, have been converted and baptized, quite apart from any exposure to the Bible. Note the case of the good thief on the cross (who was apparently converted but surely not baptized) (Luke 23:43) and the Philippian jailer (Acts 16:25–34). They had no exposure to scripture because, obviously, the book that Christians call the Bible did not then exist.

Switching from the notion of scripture as a source to scripture as a norm, perhaps 'Scripture alone' means something like: *Scripture is our only sure norm or guide to truth in matters of religion.* In other words, truth in the area of religion might come from the Bible or from elsewhere, but only the Bible is a sure test for approval or rejection of religious claims.[20] This formulation seems almost, but not quite, right. I surely want to affirm that scripture, properly interpreted, is our primary criterion or test for truth in matters of religion. But it cannot be our *only* criterion. Why not? Because scripture does not tell us what scripture is: Catholics are right that the canon of scripture was established by the church. Also, scripture does not clear up corruptions that have appeared in the text of scripture; it is the scholarly community that does that. Finally, scripture does not decide whose interpretation of scripture is to count as correct and authoritative. That (as I will argue below) is an act of the entire Christian community, past and present. The scriptures are the book of the church, and hence find their proper place to be lived, interpreted, prayed over, and obeyed within the church.

---

[20] Thus the Geneva Confession (1536) says: 'We affirm that we desire to follow scripture alone as a rule of faith and religion, without mixing it with any other things which might be devised by the opinion of men apart from the word of God.'

Then perhaps we ought to say that 'Scripture alone' means: *Once scripture is canonically and textually established and correctly interpreted, scripture is our only sure norm or guide to truth in matters of religion.* I do not wish to argue against this interpretation of 'Scripture alone'; indeed, I think the statement is true. But since in the case of many texts there is room for doubt whether we have arrived at their correct interpretation, I would prefer to interpret 'Scripture alone' in some such way as this: *Scripture is our source of religious truth above all other sources, our norm or guide to religious truth above all other norms or guides.* In other words, all other sources of theological truth are subordinate to scripture and are to be tested by scripture. Scripture has the last word, the final say. There may be other criteria of religious truth—for example, tradition, reason, experience—but scripture is the final test, the sure norm, the infallible rule of what we are to believe. When it is correctly interpreted, whatever scripture says, goes.[21] Perhaps the phrase *prima scriptura* would be a better way of making this point than the traditional *sola scriptura.*

There are, of course, various degrees of 'being scriptural' or 'agreeing with scripture'. Some theological claims will have the status of being *required* by scripture, some *allowed* by scripture, some *forbidden* by scripture. A certain degree of flexibility in applying the 'Scripture alone' formula is surely required. Take some theological claim, statement, or theory p. It seems that there are five large categories into which scriptural approval of p might fit:

1. p is a consensus of the teachings of the whole of scripture, that is, p is either taught or presupposed everywhere in scripture (or in every text that is relevant to the truth or falsity of p).

2. p is either taught or presupposed in places in scripture (though perhaps not everywhere or in every relevant text), and is inconsistent with nothing that is either taught or presupposed elsewhere in scripture.

---

[21] Thus the Westminster Confession of Faith (1646) says: 'The Supreme Judge, by whom all controversies of religion are to be determined, and all decrees of councils, opinions of ancient writers, doctrines of men, and private spirits, are to be examined, and in whose sentence we are to rest, can be no other but the Holy Spirit speaking in the Scriptures.'

3. p is nowhere either explicitly taught or presupposed in scripture, but can be considered the best interpretation of the witness of the whole of scripture or of various scriptural texts taken as a whole.

4. p is consistent with what is either taught or presupposed in scripture, that is, nothing in scripture contradicts p.

5. Some scriptural texts can be interpreted as supporting p, although other texts can also be interpreted as rejecting p.

What sort of or degree of 'scripturalness' is required or desired in the case of various theological claims will vary greatly. It will depend on factors like: which theological topic is being considered; how important it is; who is the intended audience of the theological statement in question; and whether the statement is being recommended as merely theologically acceptable or as theological mandatory for the Christian community.

Despite the flexibility that I have argued for in interpreting and applying the 'Scripture alone' formula, I reject the idea (as do most Catholics today) that tradition alone can justify a theological claim, that scripture is materially insufficient. There are no revealed truths that are found in tradition but not in scripture. Still, I want to argue for an important place in theology for tradition. This is because there has been an alarming de-emphasis on tradition in recent years at both ends of the Protestant theological spectrum. Some on the right wing pay insufficient attention to the great creeds and thinkers of the past because they believe the Bible is all that we need. The idea seems to be that Christians today should just read their Bibles, believe what it teaches, and they will end up believing correctly. To pay much attention to Athanasius or Aquinas or Luther is deemed unnecessary. Some on the left wing pay little attention to the great creeds and thinkers of the past because they find them outmoded and irrelevant to a new age. We need a new paradigm for Christian theology, they say, freed from pre-scientific theories or patriarchal attitudes or western imperialism. To pay much attention to Augustine or Calvin or Schleiermacher is not deemed particularly interesting.[22]

---

[22] The essential problem for such folk, in my view, is how to remain cognitively Christian. If both the Bible and tradition are taken to be, at best, only tenuous norms, we are left with a Christian faith in which virtually 'anything goes'.

In my view, tradition remains indispensable in interpreting scripture. I believe that all who do serious exegesis or theology must be knowledgeable about the history of Christian thought and practice. This creates a barrier against private or eccentric interpretations of scripture. The church must have criteria for rejecting off-beat interpretations. Tradition is the church's best protection against the misuse of the Bible always found in heresies and cults. Indeed, the use of tradition in this way is (so I would argue) something nearly everybody engages in. Even the staunchest defenders of 'Scripture alone' tend to interpret the Bible through the lens of certain doctrines, creeds, or biblical texts that are considered hermeneutically foundational.[23]

Indeed, some sort of strategy like this is unavoidable. Tradition shows us that certain texts of scripture take hermeneutical priority over others, and shows us how to interpret them. Tradition also helps us grasp—as we see pre-eminently in the doctrine of the Trinity— that a doctrine can be deemed normative for Christians despite the absence of any clear proof texts specifically teaching it. We see it also (for Catholics, the Orthodox, and certain Protestants) in infant baptism.

It is frequently said that differences between Catholics and Protestants on the issue of theological authority have narrowed considerably in recent years. Indeed, Karl Rahner said: 'The "Scripture alone" of the Reformation is no longer a doctrine which distinguishes and separates the churches.'[24] This statement is almost true, in my opinion, but not quite. Fortunately, many of the differences between Catholics and Protestants have indeed narrowed, on this and other issues. Most Christians rejoice in that fact. What remains is not whether scripture needs to be interpreted. All can agree that it does. But Catholics and Protestants give different answers to the question whether scripture must be *authoritatively* interpreted. Prot-

[23] This point is argued further in my 'Tradition, Scripture, and Theological Authority', in Stephen T. Davis (ed.), *Philosophy and Theological Discourse* (London: Macmillan, 1997). See also C. Stephen Evans, 'Tradition, Biblical Interpretation, and Historical Truth', in Craig Bartholomew, C. Stephen Evans, Mary Healy, and Murray Rae (eds.), *'Behind' the Text: History and Biblical Interpretation* (Grand Rapids: Zondervan, 2003; UK: Paternoster, 2004).

[24] Karl Rahner, *Foundations of Christian Faith* (New York: Crossroads Publishing Co., 1984), 378.

estants hold, contrary to Catholics, that scripture needs no binding interpreter rather than the Holy Spirit. All who interpret scripture, including those in church teaching offices, stand under scripture.

My own view, then, is both that tradition is necessary for interpreting scripture and that scripture takes priority over tradition, because it is our highest source and norm of religious truth. Christians believe that ideally (i.e. except in those cases where the church has erred) scripture and tradition agree. But in fact, the two probably never completely coincide, and that is why scripture's role, whenever necessary, is to correct tradition. Tradition guides the interpretation of scripture, but never controls it. Protestants can affirm the Roman Catholic notion of the Holy Spirit's gracious guidance of the church in doctrinal matters. But the reality of human depravity, as well as a glance at the history of doctrine, convinces most Protestants that no human institution has been kept free from error. So all institutions, including the church, must stand under the collective authority of scripture.[25]

4

Our central concern in this chapter is whether kenotic Christological theories are orthodox. It now seems that in order to answer that question we must ask three other questions: (1) Is kenosis as a Christological theory scriptural? (2) Does kenosis agree with the Christological tradition? And (3) can defenders of kenosis successfully reply to criticisms of the doctrine, especially those criticisms that explicitly or in effect impugn its orthodoxy? These are the questions that will be taken up in this and the following two sections of the chapter.

So far as question (1) is concerned, I will not say much. Other contributors to this book are professional scripture scholars (as I am not) and will address this question. Let me begin my discussion of this point with an autobiographical note. As a teenage convert to

---

[25] These views are developed further in 'Tradition, Scripture, and Theological Authority', 47–68.

Christianity, I believe it was several years before I learned that the doctrine of the Incarnation meant that Jesus was 'truly God and truly human'. But I had read the gospels by then, and as a child had of course heard many of the stories about Jesus. I found myself naturally thinking of the Incarnation along (what I later found were called) kenotic lines. Indeed, to this day the fit of kenosis with the New Testament picture of Jesus is its greatest attraction for me. I have in mind points like the fact that Christ grew in wisdom (Luke 2:52), did not know who had touched his cloak (Mark 5:29–31), and did not know the date of the Parousia (Mark 13:32).

Nevertheless, so far as a Christological theory is concerned, we would not expect to find it explicitly taught in scripture. Whether in the Incarnation the Logos emptied himself of certain properties normally characteristic of divinity or else simply added a new human nature (perhaps an enhanced human nature) to his already existing divine nature is not a question that concerned the biblical writers. What we would be looking for, then, would be (so to speak) scriptural *permission* for the theory. And that is precisely what defenders of kenosis claim that we do have, both in Philippians 2 and elsewhere.

Despite disagreement on each point, there is, I believe, some degree of consensus among Pauline scholars that Philippians 2:6–11: (1) is a unified text, and (2) contains a 'high' Christology. And although not much rides on these next points for present purposes, there is also significant opinion that this text (3) is in the form of a hymn;[26] and (4) with the possible exception of a few words (e.g. 'death on a cross'), is from a pre-Pauline Christian source. That is, Paul is citing words that he did not compose; accordingly, the hymn reflects beliefs of the very young church. So the text has the authority of both Paul and the pre-Pauline community. But unfortunately the text is also an exegetical and especially lexical minefield, and there has been controversy about it from the early church until today.[27]

---

[26] Some would dispute this point. For assessments of the evidence, see Stephen E. Fowl, 'What Is A Hymn?', *Journal for the Study of the New Testament*, Supp. 36 (Sheffield, 1990) and Marcus Bockmuehl, ' "The Form of God" (Phil. 2:6): Variations on a Theme of Jewish Mysticism,' *Journal of Theological Studies*, 48/1 (1997), 1–23.

[27] See the essays in Ralph P. Martin and Brian Dodd (eds.), *Where Christology Began: Essays on Philippians 2* (Louisville: Westminster John Knox Press, 1998), especially the essays by Larry J. Kreitzer and Richard Bauckham.

Here would be my own rough summary of the text. It is important to note that Paul starts off with the intention of expressing an ethical imperative: (1) that the Philippians should behave in the same sort of self-giving and even self-sacrificial way that Christ Jesus did, in his Incarnation. (2) Exploring that last point further through the use of the pre-Pauline hymn, Paul says that Christ Jesus was at one time, that is, before his appearance in the form of a servant, in the form of God (*en morphe theou*). (3) But he did not count the status of equality with God (*to einai isa theo*) something to be grasped or held on to or exploited (*harpagmos*—a 'thing to be seized'). (4) Rather, he obediently emptied himself (*heauton ekenosen*), taking the form of a servant, being born in human likeness, and being obedient to God even to the point of death by crucifixion. (5) Accordingly, God has highly exalted him (*auton huperuphosen*) and has given him the name that is above every name (*to onoma to huper pan onoma*); that at the name of Jesus every knee should bow and every tongue should confess that Jesus Christ is Lord (*kurios Iesous Chistos*) to the Glory of God the father. That is to say, within the context of Jewish monotheism, Jesus Christ is made God's equal as worthy of praise and worship. Language that the Old Testament would apply only to God is here applied to Jesus.

So far as our purposes in the present essay are concerned, we can rejoice along with all who affirm the full divinity of Christ, whether their Christology is classical or kenotic, in the high Christology of the kenosis hymn. A plausible exegetical case can be made here that part of what Christ Jesus emptied himself of in the Incarnation was the divine glory and majesty. This was at least part of what was involved in taking on human likeness. But the specific issue we are interested in—whether in the Incarnation the Logos 'emptied' himself of some of the properties God normally has—does not appear to be answered by exegetical considerations alone.

He 'emptied himself, taking on the form of a servant', the text says. Some who oppose the kenotic interpretation insist that since the text does not precisely say what Christ Jesus emptied himself of (which is true), it follows that he did not empty himself *of* anything, and thus certainly not of any divine attributes. But that is not a very impressive argument. Both in English and in Greek, some verbs, when used, immediately cry out for a direct or indirect object. If I say, 'I repeat', you can sensibly wonder what I am about to repeat. If I say, 'I listen', you can sensibly wonder what I am listening to. (This is not true of all verbs, of course, e.g. 'I stand.') Now any vessel that is 'emptied', whether that vessel be a bottle, a room, a human life, or even a divine life, must be emptied 'of' something. So what the hymn implies or presupposes that Christ Jesus 'emptied himself' of is still an open question.

Some who resist kenotic theories of the Incarnation insist that what Christ Jesus emptied himself of was not any of the divine *attributes* but rather certain divine *prerogatives*, like the divine glory. And that solution can work, that is, this may be a possible reading of the text, but only if one can formulate a coherent distinction between the divine attributes and the divine prerogatives. (It will seem to some that 'having the divine glory' is just as much an attribute or property as 'being omnipotent' or 'being omniscient'.) And if that distinction cannot be coherently formulated, and if the text implies that he at least emptied himself of the divine glory, we are already halfway there to a kenotic interpretation of the Incarnation.

Others who resist kenoticism argue that the 'emptying' spoken of in Philippians had nothing to do with the Incarnate Logos temporarily *no longer possessing* certain attributes (like, say, omnipotence or omniscience). It had to do instead with the Incarnate Logos *voluntarily not exercising* those attributes for the duration of Jesus' earthly life. Again: maybe so. Here the crucial issue is not exegetical but philosophical: is a person who at any time has the ability to be omnipotent but voluntarily and temporarily decides not to call on that ability 'truly human' (as the creed insists)?

But it would be a mistake to believe that the only biblical basis for the kenotic theory is Philippians 2. Note also John 17:4–5, where Jesus prays, 'I glorified you on earth by finishing the work that you gave me to do. So now, Father, glorify me in your own presence with the glory that I had in your presence before the world existed.' What exactly is being said here? Possibly several things: first, that Jesus Christ once had divine glory and complete oneness with the Father (cf. John 17:11, 20–6); secondly, that at the time of his prayer (i.e. during his earthly ministry) he did not possess the fullness of divine glory; and thirdly, he looked forward to regaining it. (See also 2 Cor. 8:9; 12:9; Heb. 2:9, 17.)

I conclude that exegetical considerations do not explicitly confirm the kenotic theory. But neither do they rule out the idea that the Logos temporarily gave up certain properties that God normally possesses. The theory seems to be allowed by scripture.

5

Let us then turn to our second question: Are kenotic interpretations of the Incarnation consistent with church tradition? In this case, the texts we must look to, by almost universal consent, are the Creeds of Nicaea I (AD 325) and Chalcedon (AD 451). These are the creeds that the church has always taken as spelling out the limits of orthodoxy in Christology. The relevant part of the Nicene Creed reads:

And in one Lord Jesus Christ, the only-begotten Son of God, begotten of the Father before all worlds, God of God, Light of Light, Very God of Very God, begotten, not made, being of one substance with the Father by whom all things were made.[28]

And the relevant part of the Creed of Chalcedon declares that Jesus Christ is

At once complete in Godhead and complete in manhood, truly God and truly man, consisting of a reasonable soul and body; of one substance with the Father as regards his Godhead, and at the same time of one substance with us as regards his manhood; like us in all respects, apart from sin; one and the same Christ, Son, Lord, Only-begotten, recognized in two natures, without confusion, without change, without division, without separation; the distinction of the two natures being in no way annulled by the union, but rather characteristics of each nature being preserved and coming together to form one person and subsistence.[29]

The core ideas here appear to be that (1) Jesus Christ is one unified person (2) in whom two natures coexist, a divine nature and a human nature; (3) these natures are neither confused with each

---

[28] *The Book of Confessions* (New York: Office of the General Assembly of the Presbyterian Church (USA), 1983), 1.1–3.

[29] Henry Bettenson (ed.), *Documents of the Christian Church* (New York: Oxford University Press, 1960), 72–3.

other nor separated from each other in him; and (4) he is accordingly at once truly divine and truly human. What the church fathers produced, in my opinion, is not an explanation of the Incarnation (that was wisely left for individual theologians), but rather a guideline or boundary. It was a way of letting the church know what is acceptable and what is not acceptable in Christology. At heart, it says: any Christology is acceptable that affirms the divinity, the humanity, and the unity of the person of Christ.

Sarah Coakley points out that some of the crucial terms in the Chalcedonian definition (terms like *physis* ('nature') and *hypostasis* ('person')) are left undefined, which leaves the statement somewhat open-ended. No attempt is made to explain precisely how two natures can cohere in one person, let alone a divine nature and a human nature. She argues that Chalcedon should be viewed as a theologically regulatory and binding text, as a grid through which reflections on Christology must pass. The statement, she says, intends to rule out aberrant Christologies (e.g. Apollinarianism (in which the two natures are mixed because the human nature is 'taken up' into the divine nature), Eutychianism (in which after the union there is but one nature, the divine nature), and extreme Nestorianism (in which there are two different persons in Christ, two separate subjects, linked only by a union of love)); it does not 'intend to provide a full systematic account of Christology, and even less a complete and precise metaphysics of Christ's make-up. Rather, it sets a "boundary" on what can, and cannot be said.'[30]

There are, then, many important Christological issues that Chalcedon cannot solve. As Coakley says, Chalcedon does not tell us in what the divine and human 'natures' consist, what *hypostasis* and *physis* mean and how the two are related to each other in Christ, how many wills Christ has, whether the *hypostasis* is identical to the pre-existent Logos, or what happens to the human *physis* at Christ's death and in his resurrection.[31] I would only add that since kenotic theories of the Incarnation have nothing whatever to do with Apollinarianism, Eutychianism, or extreme Nestorianism, and affirm the two

---

[30] Sarah Coakley, 'What Does Chalcedon Solve and What Does it Not? Some Reflections on the Status and Meaning of the Chalcedonic "Definition" ', in *The Incarnation: An Interdisciplinary Symposium on the Incarnation of the Son of God*, 161.
[31] Coakley, 162–3.

unmixed natures and the one person, the Chalcedonic definition does not rule out kenosis. Kenosis may be mistaken as a Christological theory; maybe there are better Christological theories in the neighbourhood; but kenosis is orthodox.

6

But perhaps kenosis is unorthodox at some deeper level. The best way to test for that possibility is to consider those criticisms of the theory that intentionally or in effect impugn its orthodoxy. Let me now turn to that task. I will discuss three such criticisms.

1. *In the kenotic theory, the earthly Jesus is not really divine.* This is a standard criticism of kenosis, and impugns the orthodoxy of the theory because orthodoxy requires that the earthly Jesus Christ is indeed 'truly divine'. The objection revolves around an insistence on the part of the critic that such divine properties as omnipotence and omniscience are essential properties of God. Since on kenosis the kenotically incarnate Logos 'emptied himself' of such properties, it follows that Jesus Christ was not, as orthodoxy insists, 'truly divine'.

But this is surely too quick. It is true that the one and only God is omnipotent and omniscient. The statement, 'All Gods in existence are omnipotent and omniscient' is true. But it does not follow that these are essential properties, that is, that a being who was nearly but not quite, say, omnipotent cannot go on existing or cannot be God. Returning to a point made earlier, perhaps these are *common* divine properties but not *essential* divine properties. (Similarly, the property of *having been born on earth* is a common human property but not an essential human property.) Again, perhaps what is essential to God is having the property of being omnipotent-unless-freely-and-temporarily-choosing-to-be-otherwise. If this property is essential to God, kenosis remains untouched by the present criticism.

And to repeat a point made earlier, Christians believe that Jesus was 'truly divine and truly human'. So if the claim that omnipotence *simpliciter* is an essential property of God is inconsistent with Jesus Christ being 'truly divine and truly human', Christians will be inclined to say: 'So much the worse for the doctrine that omnipotence *simpliciter* is an essential property of God.'

2. *In the kenotic theory, the glorified Logos is not truly human.* This criticism too impugns the orthodoxy of kenosis for those who accept the permanent embodiment and humanity of the Logos. There is (so it is said) a kind of necessary reverse 'emptying' in kenosis, where the glorified Logos, on returning to heaven, emptied itself of humanity.

There are two ways in which kenoticists can answer this objection.[32] The first, which has been defended by Evans as possibly true, claims that the kenosis of Christ continues in his glorification; Christ receives some of his former properties in his glorified state, not because this is metaphysically necessary, but because it is fitting that he be rewarded in this way for his obedience. Thus the glorified Christ may be omniscient and no longer ignorant of any truths, but enough human properties (such as the possession of a body) are retained to remain fully human. So there are kenotic theories that fully accept the idea of everlasting kenosis; they are accordingly not vulnerable to the present criticism.

The second, which has been defended by Feenstra,[33] claims that kenosis is not necessary to *being incarnate*, although it might be necessary to *becoming incarnate*, or at least to becoming incarnate for the purposes of redemption. So it is at least possible that the kenosis cease while the Incarnation continues. Christ remains fully human but the kenosis ends. The Incarnation and the kenosis are conceptually distinct. The Incarnation is the Second Person of the Trinity everlastingly becoming human at the point of his human birth; and the kenosis is that same Person temporarily sharing our lot. And since I stated earlier my own view that the Incarnation is distinct from the kenosis, I find this second reply to the criticism attractive. It should be noted that adopting this reply requires defenders of kenosis to accept the idea that Incarnation apart from kenosis (or after least *after* kenosis) is possible—indeed, actual. As also noted earlier, I fully accept that implication; accordingly,

---

[32] They are skilfully explored by Evans. See 'The Self-Emptying of Love,' pp. 263–7. Note that Evans also endorses as a possibility the Feenstra strategy discussed below. See Ch. 8, 'Kenotic Christology and the Nature of God', pp. 200–2.

[33] See Feenstra 'Reconsidering Kenotic Christology', pp. 148–9.

I have never seen myself as an enemy of non-kenotic theories of the Incarnation.

3. *In the kenotic theory, divine immutability must be given up.* This criticism is raised by John Hick, who earlier in his career had argued that all orthodox Christologies are logically incoherent.[34] His point now is that the kenotic theory 'clashes with any traditionally orthodox understanding of God' by requiring rejection of divine immutability.[35] It is odd that Hick of all people raises this criticism, because throughout his career he has rejected traditional Christian doctrines right and left. Still, perhaps his point is that kenoticists want to be orthodox, but cannot be, since their own doctrine requires them to jettison divine immutability, which they themselves take to be orthodox.

It is true that in the tradition we can find notions of divine immutability that seem inconsistent with kenosis. Suppose we say that 'strong immutability' is the notion that no statement about God's possessing a certain property can have different truth values at different times. It certainly seems true that anybody who holds *that* doctrine will be singularly unattracted to the kenotic theory of the Incarnation (in which the statement, 'The Logos is kenotically incarnate in a man,' was once true but is now false). But what if we accept 'soft immutability', that is, the doctrine that God is not fickle, capricious, mercurial, or moody; God's holy and benevolent nature remains ever and eternally the same; God is faithful in keeping God's promises; God's aims and intentions for human beings do not change? Now I have no idea whether Hick would find soft immutability attractive, but I do. And it is perfectly consistent with kenosis.

It seems, then, that all three objections can be answered. Accordingly, we are within our rights in concluding that the kenotic theory of the Incarnation is orthodox.

---

[34] John Hick (ed.), *The Myth of God Incarnate* (Philadelphia: The Westminster Press, 1977), 178.

[35] John Hick, *The Metaphor of God Incarnate: Christology in a Pluralistic Age* (Louisville: Westminster John Knox Press, 1993), 75. Hick also mentions divine aseity, which for lack of space I will not discuss.

7

In this chapter I have presented a version of the kenotic theory of the Incarnation. I have argued that it is within the bounds of Christian orthodoxy. My argument for that point has consisted of three parts: (1) kenosis is allowed by scripture; (2) kenosis is consistent with the great Christological creeds; and (3) kenosis can be defended against three criticisms that charge it with being non-orthodox.

Despite being a Protestant, I believe, as Catholics do, that there exists, and must exist, a magisterium. This is an authoritative church teaching office, an office that normatively decides which teachings are orthodox and which are not. But I do not believe that the magisterium is anything remotely like a committee that holds meetings in a room somewhere. Indeed, I believe the real Christian magisterium consists of the voice of the entirety of the people of God, past, present, and future. They together constitute the authoritative interpreters of the Christian tradition.

Of course the church can err. It has doubtless done so at many times in the past. But so far as those Christian traditions that earnestly desire to be faithful to the apostolic traditions and ecumenical creeds are concerned, I believe God will preserve them at crucial points from dangerous theological error. So in the final analysis, whether the kenotic theory is orthodox depends on whether the people of God accept it as orthodox.[36]

[36] I would like to thank Sarah Coakley, Stephen Evans, Gordon Fee, Bruce Fisk, Ron Feenstra, Edward Oakes, S.J., Gerald O'Collins, S.J., and Susan Peppers-Bates for their helpful comments on earlier drafts of the present essay.

6

A Kenotic Christological Method for Understanding the Divine Attributes

Ronald J. Feenstra

Although kenotic Christology comes in many forms, the versions that seem most promising attempt to articulate an orthodox (Chalcedonian) view of Jesus Christ: that he is one person, truly divine and truly human. This chapter will outline elements of orthodox Christology and then develop a version of kenotic Christology that attempts to adhere to Christological orthodoxy, arguing that such a kenotic Christology can account for perplexing biblical claims such as that the Word humbled himself or emptied himself in the Incarnation (Phil. 2:7), that he grew in wisdom (Luke 2:52), and that the Incarnate Son did not know the time of the end of the world (Mark 13:32). Against this background, the chapter will take note of some recent criticisms of kenotic approaches to Christology and consider the important methodological point these criticisms raise about how our understanding of the divine attributes should be formed. The chapter will conclude with observations about how the method employed by kenotic Christology can help to correct or supplement our view of the attributes of God. In sum, this chapter argues that an orthodox kenotic Christology not only can account for some perplexing biblical claims about Jesus Christ but also offers a fruitful method for deepening our understanding of the divine attributes.

THE CHALCEDONIAN DEFINITION

The touchstone for Christological orthodoxy is the Chalcedonian definition of faith, promulgated by the Council of Chalcedon on 25 October 451. Building on conciliar decisions at Nicaea in 325 and Constantinople in 381 as well as on the Formula of Reunion between Cyril, bishop of Alexandria, and John, bishop of Antioch, the assembly at Chalcedon made this affirmation:

Following, therefore, the holy fathers, we confess one and the same Son, who is our Lord Jesus Christ, and we all agree in teaching that this very same Son is complete in his deity and complete—the very same—in his humanity, truly God and truly a human being, this very same one being composed of a rational soul and a body, coessential with the Father as to his deity and coessential with us—the very same one—as to his humanity, being like us in every respect apart from sin.[1]

Expanding on the Formula of Reunion's statement that in Jesus Christ two natures had been united in an 'unconfused union',[2] the Chalcedonian definition speaks of him as

Christ, Son, Lord, Only Begotten, acknowledged to be unconfusedly, unalterably, undividedly, inseparably in two natures, since the difference of the natures is not destroyed because of the union, but on the contrary, the character of each nature is preserved and comes together in one person and one hypostasis, not divided or torn into two persons but one and the same Son and only-begotten God, Logos, Lord Jesus Christ.[3]

According to this pivotal statement of Christological orthodoxy, not only is Jesus Christ truly divine and truly human, but also the character of each nature (divine and human) 'is preserved and comes together in one person and one hypostasis'. But how do these natures come together in one person?

---

[1] 'The Council of Chalcedon's "Definition of the Faith"', in *The Christological Controversy*, trans. and ed. Richard A. Norris, Jr. (Philadelphia: Fortress, 1980), 159.
[2] Cyril of Alexandria, 'Cyril's Letter to John of Antioch', in *The Christological Controversy*, 142.
[3] 'The Council of Chalcedon's "Definition of the Faith"', in *The Christological Controversy*, 159.

THE COMMUNICATION OF ATTRIBUTES

The standard view of orthodox Christianity is that the attributes of both the divine nature and the human nature are 'communicated to' or predicated of the one person, Jesus Christ. The concept of the 'communication of attributes' (or *communicatio idiomatum*) appears as early as the thought of Tertullian (*c.*160–*c.*225).[4] As Aloys Grillmeier points out, the concept of the communication of attributes was an important feature of fifth-century Christological debates.[5] In the period leading up to Chalcedon, it was affirmed by such figures as Athanasius of Alexandria, Cyril of Alexandria, and Pope Leo I.

When he predicates both human and divine properties or attributes of Jesus Christ, Athanasius of Alexandria (*c.*296–373) assumes and affirms the concept of the communication of attributes. Along with affirming that Jesus Christ has divine attributes because of his divine nature, Athanasius says that Jesus Christ has certain properties because of his human nature: the Logos is said to hunger, thirst, suffer, and be weary on account of the flesh he had taken on, although these are not 'the works proper to the Word Himself'.[6] He adds that, in taking on human flesh, the Lord 'put it on whole with the affections proper to it; that, as we say that the body was His own, so also we may say that the affections of the body were proper to Him alone, though they did not touch Him according to His Godhead'.[7] Recognizing that people might be scandalized by the divine Word's possession of human characteristics, Athanasius says that Christ suffered 'not in His Godhead, but "for us in the flesh"' so that the passions might be seen to be proper not to the Word, but to the flesh. Thus the Logos remains impassible, 'yet because of that flesh which He put on, these things are ascribed to Him, since they are proper to

---

[4] Aloys Grillmeier, *Christ in Christian Tradition, 1: From the Apostolic Age to Chalcedon (451)*, 2nd edn., trans. John Bowden (Atlanta: John Knox, 1975), 122.

[5] Grillmeier, *Christ in Christian Tradition*, 1:436.

[6] Athanasius of Alexandria, 'Four Discourses against the Arians', in *A Select Library of Nicene and Post-Nicene Fathers of the Christian Church*, 2nd series, eds. Philip Schaff and Henry Wace, vol. 4 (Edinburgh: T. & T. Clark and Grand Rapids: Eerdmans, n.d.), III.31.

[7] Athanasius, 'Four Discourses against the Arians', III.32.

the flesh, and the body itself is proper to the Saviour.'[8] Here is the heart of the doctrine of the communication of attributes: the Incarnate Son of God has the divine attributes essentially and from all eternity and has the essential human attributes (which do not include being sinful) because he took on human nature in the Incarnation. In Athanasius's employment of the doctrine of the communication of attributes an important issue also arises: how can Christ be both impassible and have passions predicated of him? Is he both impassible and passible? As will be seen below, concern over apparent incompatibilities such as this are a motivating factor for kenotic Christology.

Two central figures in the Christological controversy of the fifth century were Cyril (d. 444), bishop of Alexandria, and Nestorius (d. c.451), bishop of Constantinople. In a letter to Cyril, Nestorius says that, although the body is the 'temple of the Son's deity' and is conjoined to his deity, we must not 'attribute to him, in the name of this association, the characteristics of the flesh that has been conjoined with him—I mean birth and suffering and death'.[9] It is an 'insane heresy', says Nestorius, 'to make the divine Logos have a part in being fed with milk and participate to some degree in growth and stand in need of angelic assistance because of his fearfulness at the time of the passion. I say nothing about circumcision and sacrifice and tears and hunger, which, being joined with him, belong properly to the flesh as things which happened for our sake. These things are taken falsely when they are put off on the deity.'[10] We cannot, he says, attribute birth, circumcision, tears, hunger, suffering, and death to the divine Logos or Son of God. Nestorius's comments are somewhat puzzling, since he seems to be under the mistaken impression that the communication of attributes involves attributing to the divine nature (not simply to the person of the Son) properties Christ had by virtue of having become human.[11] Nevertheless, Nestorius quite

---

[8] Athanasius, 'Four Discourses against the Arians', III.34.

[9] Nestorius, 'Nestorius's Second Letter to Cyril', in *The Christological Controversy*, 139.

[10] Nestorius, 'Nestorius's Second Letter to Cyril', in *The Christological Controversy*, 139.

[11] Grillmeier concludes that Nestorius misunderstood the teaching about the communication of attributes (*Christ in Christian Tradition*, 1:504).

clearly denies that properties or characteristics of the flesh the Son of God has conjoined to himself—properties such as birth, suffering, and death—can be attributed to the impassible divine Son of God.

In his response, Cyril of Alexandria affirmed the communication of attributes. He says that, since the body the Logos took on suffered, the Logos is 'said to have suffered these things for our sakes, for the impassible One was within the suffering body'.[12] In a letter describing the terms of agreement (known as the 'Formula of Reunion' of AD 433) between Cyril and John, bishop of Antioch, Cyril says that the divine Logos is impassible, although as the agent of salvation he 'is seen to attribute to himself the passions that occur in his own flesh'. Cyril repeats the point as follows: 'Christ refers the passions of his own flesh ... to himself by means of an appropriation which occurs for the sake of our salvation.'[13] As with Athanasius, Cyril affirms that the Incarnate Son of God has the properties of both the divine nature he had from eternity and the human nature he took on. Like Athanasius, Cyril also does not clarify how the one person or Son of God can be said both to be impassible and to suffer the passions of his flesh.

Following a fifteen-year lull in the Christological controversy that ensued upon the Formula of Reunion, the debate raged once again. In response, Leo I (d. 461), bishop of Rome, entered the debate with a document that eventually contributed to the settlement of the debate at Chalcedon. In a statement that is echoed in the Definition of Chalcedon, Leo offers a straightforward description of the 'communication' of properties from the natures to the person of the Son:

Because of this unity of person, which must be understood to subsist in a twofold nature, we read that the Son of man came down from heaven (since the Son of God took on flesh from the Virgin of whom he was born), and conversely we say that the Son of God was crucified and buried (even though he endured these things not in that divine nature in virtue of which, as Only Begotten, he is coeternal and consubstantial with the Father, but in the weakness of his human nature). Consequently we all also confess in the

---

[12] Cyril of Alexandria, 'Cyril of Alexandria's Second Letter to Nestorius', in *The Christological Controversy*, 133.
[13] Cyril of Alexandria, 'Cyril's Letter to John of Antioch', in *The Christological Controversy*, 144.

creed that the only-begotten Son was crucified and buried, in accordance with the words of the apostle: 'For if they had known, they would never have crucified the Lord of glory' [1 Cor. 2:8].[14]

So the unity of two natures in one person implies that whatever properties comprise the two natures of Christ are predicable of Christ himself. But given the disparity of the natures, the communication of properties results in the union of disparate properties in the one person of Christ: 'Since, therefore, the characteristic properties of both natures and substances are kept intact and come together in one person, lowliness is taken on by majesty, weakness by power, mortality by eternity, and the nature which cannot be harmed is united to the nature which suffers.'[15] But how should we understand the coming together in one person of these apparently incompatible properties?

Leo I seems to offer at least two distinct suggestions. First, he suggests that incompatible properties of both dying and being incapable of death are predicated of the one person. Thus he says that the 'mediator between God and human beings, the human being who is Jesus Christ, can at one and the same time die in virtue of the one nature and, in virtue of the other, be incapable of death'.[16] In contrast with this suggestion that Christ simply possesses incompatible properties, Leo I offers a second suggestion:

What he did was to enhance humanity not diminish deity. That self-emptying of his, by which the invisible revealed himself visible and the Creator and Lord of all things elected to be reckoned among mortals, was a drawing-near in mercy not a failure in power.... Each nature retained its characteristics without defect, and just as the 'form of God' does not remove the 'form of a slave', so the 'form of a slave' does not diminish the 'form of God'.[17]

Here, along with the insistence that each nature remained intact as it was united in the person of the Incarnate Son, Leo I (reflecting views

[14] Leo I, 'Pope Leo I's Letter to Flavian of Constantinople', in *The Christological Controversy*, 151.

[15] Leo I, 'Pope Leo I's Letter to Flavian of Constantinople', in *The Christological Controversy*, 148.

[16] Leo I, 'Pope Leo I's Letter to Flavian of Constantinople', in *The Christological Controversy*, 148.

[17] Leo I, 'Pope Leo I's Letter to Flavian of Constantinople', in *The Christological Controversy*, 148–9.

held by Athanasius and others) adds the proposal that the self-emptying of the Son in the Incarnation involved an elevation of humanity, not a diminishment of his deity.

Thomas Aquinas reflects and clarifies the orthodox consensus on the communication of attributes. In reply to the question whether it is true that 'God is man', Aquinas says, 'since the Person of the Son of God for Whom this word *God* stands, is a suppositum of human nature, this word *man* may be truly and properly predicated of this word *God*, as it stands for the Person of the Son of God'.[18] Conversely, one may also say 'Man is God', according to Aquinas, since 'this word *man* may stand for any hypostasis of human nature; and thus it may stand for the Person of the Son of God, Whom we say is a hypostasis of human nature', and the person of the Son of God is properly called God.[19] So the Son of God may properly be called human and he may properly be called divine. The properties that comprise each of those natures may also be predicated of the person of the Son of God, since there is one hypostasis of both natures. But Aquinas notes that we can distinguish the *reason* that various properties are predicated of Christ, 'since those things that belong to the Divine Nature are predicated of Christ in His Divine Nature, and those that belong to the human nature are predicated of Christ in his human nature'.[20] Nevertheless, Aquinas insists that 'the union of the human nature with the Divine was effected in the Person, in the hypostasis, in the suppositum, yet observing the distinction of natures; so that it is the same Person and hypostasis of the Divine and human natures, while each nature retains that which is proper to it.'[21] Hence Christ's suffering or 'Passion belongs to the *suppositum* of the Divine Nature by reason of the passible nature assumed, but not on account of the impassible Divine Nature.'[22] So Aquinas holds that both human and divine properties are predicated of the Son of God, since he has both human and divine natures. As a result of taking on human nature

---

[18] Thomas Aquinas, *Summa Theologica*, rev. edn., trans. Fathers of the English Dominican Province (New York: Benziger, 1948; rpt. Westminster, MD: Christian Classics, 1981), IIIa.16.1.

[19] Aquinas, *Summa Theologica*, IIIa.16.2.

[20] Aquinas, *Summa Theologica*, IIIa.16.4.

[21] Aquinas, *Summa Theologica*, IIIa.46.12.

[22] Aquinas, *Summa Theologica*, IIIa.46.12.

then, Christ, the divine Son of God, suffers. This is one of the significant consequences of the orthodox Christian view of the communication of attributes.

INCOMPATIBLE ATTRIBUTES?

As was noted in the previous section, predicating properties of both divine and human natures to one person raises some perplexing questions. For example, how can the Incarnate Son be both 'impassible by nature', as Athanasius says, and yet have passions such as suffering predicated of him? How can he both have divine omniscience and yet be able to say, when speaking about the end times, 'But about that day or hour no one knows, not even the angels in heaven, nor the Son, but only the Father' (Mark 13:32, TNIV)? Given the importance of the latter question to kenotic Christology, this section will note briefly several types of responses to this question.

First, some theologians resolve the apparent conflict between the Son of God's omniscience and Scripture's report that he claimed not to know something, by reinterpreting what Scripture says. Thus Athanasius argues, since Jesus in Mark 13 describes circumstances that will precede the events of the return of the Son of Man, he in fact 'knows exactly, nor is ignorant, when the hour and the day are at hand'.[23] And Aquinas holds that Christ is said not to know the day and hour of the final judgement because he was unwilling to reveal it, although in fact this is something 'the Son knows, not merely in the Divine Nature, but also in the human'.[24] Quoting Origen, Aquinas says that even when Christ asked questions, he did so 'not in order to learn anything, but in order to teach by questioning'.[25] On this view, would it follow that Jesus never needed to ask questions as his father 'taught' him carpentry, since he knew the answers already? Would he, already at six months of age, have known about subatomic particles? In the end, this response seems less than adequate, given its willingness

---

[23] Athanasius, 'Four Discourses against the Arians', III.42.
[24] Aquinas, *Summa Theologica*, IIIa.10.2, ad 1.
[25] Aquinas, *Summa Theologica*, IIIa.12.3, ad 1.

to hold a view of Jesus' knowledge that stands in significant tension with what the New Testament says about him.

A second response to the apparent conflict between the omniscience and non-omniscience of the Son is simply to accept it. Louis Berkhof, for example, describes the properties of the person of Christ as follows: 'The person can be said to be almighty, omniscient, omnipresent, and so on, but can also be called a man of sorrows, of limited knowledge and power, and subject to human want and miseries.'[26] In addition, Berkhof denies that any of the properties of one nature are communicated to the other nature. Thus, he says, 'The deity cannot share in human weaknesses; neither can man participate in any of the essential perfections of the Godhead.'[27] Here he seems to treat a nature not as a set of properties (how can a set of properties share in human weakness?) but as something more like a reality (an Aristotelian 'primary substance' rather than a 'secondary substance'). Berkhof does not seem troubled by, or try to resolve, the question of how contradictory properties such as being omniscient and being limited in knowledge may be predicated of the person of the Son.

A third—or perhaps it is a variant of the second—response to the problem of apparently conflicting properties in the Incarnate Son of God appeals to the logic of reduplication. Drawing from Aristotle and Aquinas, Peter Geach proposes that we 'distinguish between what God can do *simpliciter*, and what we say God *as God* can do, using the reduplicative form of proposition'.[28] On this view, one might say that the Son as God is omniscient, but the Son as human does not know the day or the hour of the end of the world. But this position seems puzzling or problematic. If, on the one hand, the ultimate referent or 'primary substance' being referred to here is the one person, the Son of God, then it seems to follow that this person is both omniscient and unaware of the time of the end of the world. This position would then be a more sophisticated version of the second response, since in both cases contradictory properties apply

[26] Louis Berkhof, *Systematic Theology*, 4th edn. (Grand Rapids: Eerdmans, 1939), 324.

[27] Berkhof, *Systematic Theology*, 324.

[28] Peter Geach, *Providence and Evil*, The Stanton Lectures, 1971–72 (Cambridge: Cambridge University Press, 1977), 27.

to the Logos or Son of God. If, on the other hand, 'Son as God' and 'Son as human' are two distinct referents or primary substances, then no contradictory properties apply to either referent. But another problem does arise. Who is the agent of salvation? The 'Son as God' would lack human nature and thus would not be able to be our substitute. And the 'Son as human' would lack divine nature and thus would be unable to bring about reconciliation. So, initially at least, it appears that the third response is either a sophisticated version of the second response or unacceptable theologically. Although it may be possible to revise the reduplicative strategy in order to account for these problems, doing so lies outside the purposes of this chapter.

Still a fourth response to the apparent incompatibility of properties of the Incarnate Son is to reject or reinterpret the Chalcedonian claims that lead to such an outcome. Thus, in a volume that provoked considerable controversy in 1977, John Hick says that orthodoxy has not been able to give any content or meaning to the idea of two natures, human and divine, co-inhering in the one historical Jesus Christ:

For to say, without explanation, that the historical Jesus of Nazareth was also God is as devoid of meaning as to say that this circle drawn with a pencil on paper is also a square. Such a locution has to be given semantic content: and in the case of the language of Incarnation every content thus far suggested has had to be repudiated. The Chalcedonian formula, in which the attempt rested, merely reiterated that Jesus was both God and man, but made no attempt to interpret the formula.[29]

More recently, Hick has clarified his point here. Rather than asserting that 'the idea of a God-man is a self-contradiction', Hick's point is that, if it is to be believable, the doctrine of the Incarnation must be intelligibly explained, and no explanation has yet succeeded.[30] In his 1977 article, Hick suggests that the purpose of Incarnational doctrine is 'not to assert a metaphysical fact but to express a valuation and

[29] John Hick, 'Jesus and the World Religions', in *The Myth of God Incarnate*, ed. John Hick (Philadelphia: Westminster, 1977), 178.
[30] John Hick, *The Metaphor of God Incarnate: Christology in a Pluralistic Age* (Louisville: Westminster John Knox, 1993), 3.

evoke an attitude'.[31] He also claims that it is not literally true to say that Jesus was the Son of God Incarnate; this is a *myth*. The real significance of Jesus, according to Hick, is that in following Jesus 'we have found ourselves in God's presence and have found God's meaning for our lives. He is our sufficient *model* of true humanity in a perfect relationship to God.'[32] By 1993, Hick prefers to speak of the Incarnation as a metaphor rather than a myth. According to him, although Jesus saw himself as an eschatological prophet, he was transformed by Christian thought into 'God the Son come down from heaven to live a human life and save us by his atoning death'.[33] As Hick describes things, 'A good metaphor—Jesus as a "son of God", one in whom the divine Spirit was powerfully present and whose life has revealed to others the reality and love and claim of God—was turned into the metaphysical theory that Jesus had two natures, one human and the other divine'.[34] In short, confronted with the apparent contradiction of properties in the Incarnate Son of God, Hick rejects the Chalcedonian understanding of the Incarnation and proposes another view of what the Incarnation is. For those who believe Chalcedonian Christology to be faithful to Scripture, Hick's response is not acceptable.

Although each of the above responses to the Son's possessing apparently incompatible properties raises fascinating and important issues, exploring those issues goes beyond the scope of this chapter. Given the constraints of space and time, this chapter will focus on kenotic Christology as yet another way to try to resolve the apparent incompatibility of the Incarnate Son's properties.

[31] Hick, 'Jesus and the World Religions', 178.

[32] Hick, 'Jesus and the World Religions', 178–9 (emphasis added). In a response that was first published in 1977, immediately after *The Myth of God Incarnate* was published, Herbert McCabe responds to Hick. McCabe, who is a Dominican priest, responds as follows: 'It is part of the *meaning* of a circle that it is not a square or any other shape; so saying something is both a circle and a square is to say it both is and is not a circle which says nothing at all.' But 'it cannot be part of the *meaning* of man that he is not God' ('The Myth of God Incarnate', in *God Matters* (London: Chapman, 1987), 57–8). So, as McCabe argues, there is not the same contradiction in saying that Jesus is both human and divine as there would be in saying that a square is a circle.

[33] Hick, *The Metaphor of God Incarnate*, 5.

[34] Hick, *The Metaphor of God Incarnate*, 79.

KENOTIC CHRISTOLOGY[35]

Although kenotic Christology, which flourished in German and British theology during the half century prior to the First World War, comes in a variety of forms, this chapter articulates a version of kenotic Christology that attempts to be faithful both to Scripture and to Chalcedonian orthodoxy. After the statement of a Chalcedonian kenotic Christology in this section, the next two sections will examine some recent criticisms of kenotic Christology and will respond to those criticisms by defending the method of discerning the divine attributes that one finds in kenotic Christology.

Kenotic Christology draws from a number of biblical passages. The term 'kenosis' comes from Philippians 2:7, which appears in a hymn that says that Christ Jesus did not consider equality with God something to be 'used to his own advantage' (TNIV), but 'made himself nothing' (*ekenosen*) by taking the nature of a servant, being made in human likeness, and also by humbling himself by becoming obedient to a humiliating death on a cross. A similar idea appears in 2 Corinthians 8:9, which says that Jesus Christ, though rich, became poor so that his people might become rich through his poverty. But what does it mean that he humbled himself, or emptied himself, or made himself nothing? What was the effect of that self-emptying or self-abasement? One part of the answer to such questions seems to appear in Mark 13, where Jesus, after predicting the destruction of the Temple, responds to a question about when the end times will occur. In his response he describes several signs of the end times and then adds a puzzling comment: 'But about that hour no one knows, not even the angels in heaven nor the Son, but only the Father' (Mark 13:32, TNIV). In the light of this statement that the Son (at least during his incarnate life on earth) does not know something, Luke's comment that, as Jesus grew, 'he increased in wisdom' (Luke 2:52) seems to take on added significance. And the assurance in Hebrews

---

[35] Parts of this section borrow from Ronald J. Feenstra, 'Reconsidering Kenotic Christology', in *Trinity, Incarnation, and Atonement: Philosophical and Theological Essays*, eds. Ronald J. Feenstra and Cornelius Plantinga, Jr., Library of Religious Philosophy, vol. 1 (Notre Dame: University of Notre Dame Press, 1989), 128–52.

that Jesus was tempted suggests another aspect of his self-emptying: 'For we do not have a high priest who is unable to empathize with our weaknesses, but we have one who has been tempted in every way, just as we are—yet he did not sin' (Heb. 4:15). Even Jesus' prayer to the Father that he be glorified with the glory he had in the presence of the Father before the world existed (John 17:5) suggests that the Incarnation involved a giving up of some aspect of divine glory. Given passages such as these, exploring the self-emptying or self-humiliation of the Son of God in becoming human seems likely to yield some insights into Christ's divine and human natures, and especially into his possession of apparently incompatible properties, such as being omniscient and being unaware of the time of the end of the age.

In confronting the question of whether Christ possesses incompatible properties, kenotic Christology acknowledges the limitations in Christ's knowledge and resists attributing incompatible properties to him. But if the Incarnate Son of God is not omniscient during his life on earth, how can he be fully divine? The kenotic answer is that if the Son of God, during his life on earth, was not omniscient and yet fully divine, then the concept of God must be understood to include an attribute other than simple omniscience. Recognizing that God has a high degree of knowledge—even omniscience, in some sense— kenotic Christology attempts to develop a concept of God that allows predicating both the divine knowledge attribute and non-omniscience to Jesus Christ during his earthly life. But what sort of knowledge attribute could be essential to the divine nature and yet possessed by a person who lacks at least one item of knowledge for at least part of his existence?

In a ground-breaking treatment of this question, Stephen T. Davis says that his belief 'both that Jesus Christ was God and that Jesus Christ was non-omniscient leads me to deny that omniscience is essential to God'.[36] While denying that 'omniscience *simpliciter*' is an essential divine attribute, Davis suggests that 'omniscience *in some sense*' is an essential divine attribute.[37] Thus the Son of God could

[36] Stephen T. Davis, *Logic and the Nature of God* (London: Macmillan and Grand Rapids: Eerdmans, 1983), 124.

[37] Davis, *Logic and the Nature of God*, 125–6.

possess the divine knowledge attribute of 'omniscience *in some sense*' even when temporarily becoming non-omniscient during his life on earth.[38] In this work, Davis follows the kenotic Christological method of reconceiving the divine attributes in the light of the Incarnation.

Thomas V. Morris, although preferring another Christological approach over kenotic Christology, has helped to articulate a kenotic understanding of divine attributes such as omniscience. In working out a kenotic Christology, he proposes the following analysis of the essential divine attributes: 'What would be claimed . . . is that it is not precisely *omniscience* which is a requisite of deity. It is rather a distinct property, the property of being omniscient-unless-freely-and-temporarily-choosing-to-be-otherwise, which is a logically necessary condition of deity. . . . It will be this compound property rather than omniscience *simpliciter* which will be said to be an essential property of any individual who is God.'[39] On this view, the kenotically Incarnate Christ is omniscient *in some sense* because even during his earthly life he has the property of being omniscient-unless-freely-and-temporarily-choosing-to-be-otherwise. And Christ can be essentially omniscient in this sense even though he is also temporarily non-omniscient.

Despite having developed an important restatement of kenotic Christology, Morris offers several criticisms of the view. I will focus on one criticism in this section of the chapter and another in the next section. On the version of kenotic Christology that he has developed, says Morris, it 'fails to be true that any divine person is logically or metaphysically immune to states of extensive ignorance concerning important truths about the world'.[40] On this analysis, God could have the essential divine knowledge attribute and also freely choose to be non-omniscient for an extensive period. His proposal also seems to leave open the possibility that all three divine persons could simultaneously be freely and temporarily non-omniscient. In short, this statement of the essential divine attribute of omniscience is too

[38] Davis, *Logic and the Nature of God*, 126.

[39] Thomas V. Morris, *The Logic of God Incarnate* (Ithaca and London: Cornell University Press, 1986), 99–100.

[40] Morris, *The Logic of God Incarnate*, 100–1.

permissive because it does not adequately specify the occasions on which a divine person might be temporarily non-omniscient.

An advocate of kenotic Christology could therefore revise the concept of the essential divine attribute in question by proposing that the attribute of omniscience-unless-kenotically-incarnate (where a kenotic Incarnation is understood as freely chosen and temporary), not the attribute of omniscience *simpliciter*, is essential to deity. On this analysis, the kenotically Incarnate Jesus Christ, although temporarily non-omniscient, would still be able to possess the attribute of omniscience-unless-kenotically-incarnate. In order to address the further concern that perhaps all three divine persons could simultaneously be kenotically incarnate, the kenotic position could specify that, since the Incarnation of the Son was for the purpose of atonement or reconciliation between God and fallen creatures, a divine person can become kenotically incarnate only for the purpose of reconciliation.[41] Since the reconciliation of fallen creatures has been accomplished through the life, death, and resurrection of Jesus Christ, there is neither a need nor a possibility of another divine kenotic Incarnation. On this view, once the Son of God has become kenotically incarnate and brought about reconciliation, no member of the Trinity can become similarly incarnate. As a result, since the Son is no longer *kenotically* incarnate (that is, self-humbled as he was during his life on earth) all three divine persons are now unalterably omniscient.

In sum, on the revised kenotic proposal, the property of being omniscient-unless-kenotically-incarnate (where a kenotic Incarnation is understood as freely chosen, temporary, and for the purpose of reconciliation) is an essential property of each divine person. So when the Son freely, temporarily, and for the purpose of reconciliation becomes kenotically incarnate, it is no longer a live option for either the Father or the Holy Spirit to become incarnate in this way. And once the Son has accomplished the work of reconciliation, then

---

[41] This statement should not be taken as rejecting the view that there could have been a divine Incarnation even if no fall had occurred. The point here is that, since the Incarnation described in Scripture was for the purpose of reconciling God and fallen creatures (a reconciliation that it brought about), there could have been no more than one such Incarnation.

Father, Son, and Holy Spirit can be said to be unchangeably and unalterably omniscient.

This section has argued, focusing on the divine knowledge attribute, that by rethinking our concept of the divine attributes it is possible to affirm that Jesus Christ during his life on earth was both truly divine and, during his freely chosen, temporary, redemptive self-humiliation, not omniscient. In contrast to those who hold that Jesus really was omniscient during his earthly life but pretended not to be, or that he possessed conflicting properties, kenotic Christology works from what God has revealed through and about the Incarnate Christ to revise the concept of God accordingly.

RECENT CRITICISMS OF KENOTIC CHRISTOLOGY

Revising the concept of God is a serious matter, and some recent criticisms of kenotic Christology have focused on this issue. These criticisms help to raise an important methodological point about how our understanding of God's attributes should be formed. Following this section's analysis of several criticisms of kenotic Christology along these lines, the next section will defend the method kenotic Christology uses for understanding the divine attributes.

In spite of his sympathies for kenotic Christology, Morris eventually decides against it. In addition to the concern (noted above) that kenotic Christology allows for extensive ignorance on the part of a divine person, he also criticizes kenotic Christology for conflicting with 'Anselmian intuitions' about the nature of God as a greatest possible being. Anselmian intuitions, says Morris, might hold that 'it is better to be absolutely immune to states of avoidable ignorance than to be capable of such states, and thus that it is omniscience *simpliciter* which is a requisite of deity, as well as a property any particular divine being must have essentially, and hence immutably.'[42] Although Morris recognizes that intuitions, including Anselmian ones, are defeasible, nevertheless intuitions do count for something.[43] In sum, since kenotic Christology 'requires significantly

---

[42] Morris, *The Logic of God Incarnate*, 101.
[43] Morris, *The Logic of God Incarnate*, 133–4.

altering the traditional conception of deity', and in particular since it seems to conflict with Anselmian views of God, Morris is reluctant to accept it.[44] Morris's objection is similar to the first of three concerns stated by Richard Swinburne.

Swinburne objects to kenotic Christology because it is incompatible with (some forms of) natural theology, it departs from Chalcedon, and it is overly complex. All three of these objections point to the need to consider whether kenotic Christology follows an appropriate method in discerning what the divine attributes are.

After considering the kenotic Christology of the nineteenth-century theologian Gottfried Thomasius, Swinburne points out the incompatibility between the kenotically Incarnate God and the God of natural theology:

> The difficulty with such a [kenotic] theory is that all the arguments to the existence of God are arguments to a simple source of all ... to whom omnipotence and omniscience belong essentially; and any being who was divine would have to have the same essential properties as such a creator—otherwise he would be less than the creator source of all, and there would be no Incarnation of God.[45]

In short, since kenotic Christology posits a God who does not have omniscience essentially, its 'God' is less metaphysically exalted than the essentially omniscient God posited by the arguments of natural theology. But if the being who was incarnated is metaphysically less exalted than the essentially omniscient (and omnipotent, and so on) creator of the world, then the Incarnation is not an Incarnation of God.[46] This criticism raises the question whether natural theology provides the best means for determining what the essential divine attributes are.

By interpreting kenotic Christology as in some way undermining or diminishing the full divinity of the Incarnate Christ, Swinburne arrives at a second criticism: kenotic Christology departs from the

---

[44] Morris, *The Logic of God Incarnate*, 149.

[45] Richard Swinburne, *The Christian God* (Oxford: Clarendon Press, 1994), 232.

[46] As Stephen T. Davis pointed out at the Kenotic Workshop, Swinburne's criticism shows that a conflict of intuitions underlies his disagreement with kenotic Christology. Some would say that a God who can undergo the limitation described by kenotic Christology is more exalted than a God who cannot undergo such limitation.

Chalcedonian Definition. As he sees it, kenotic Christology supposes that God could humble himself and live 'a human life' only by 'God the Son ceasing in some way to have the divine properties; the humility involved a giving up. Chalcedon, by contrast, affirms that the humility involves a taking on. The king humbles himself by becoming a servant as well as being a king.'[47] Of course, this criticism depends on the premiss that, according to kenotic Christology, the Incarnation involved the Son's giving up or ceasing to have divine properties. But kenotic theologians who adhere to Chalcedon hold that the Incarnation shows that the essential divine attributes must be rethought, not that the Son gave up divine attributes in the Incarnation.

Swinburne's third criticism is that kenotic Christology is overly complex. Suppose, he says, that in order to be divine, a person must have such traditional divine properties as being the creator and sustainer, being omnipresent, omnipotent, omniscient, perfectly good, a source of moral obligation, eternal, and necessary 'unless he chooses to abandon them for a prearranged interval'.[48] But then Swinburne wonders whether in such a case God the Father could 'temporarily abandon the traditional properties at the same time as God the Son and God the Spirit'.[49] His response to this suggestion leads to the criticism that kenotic Christology involves an excessively complex hypothesis:

If so, then there can (metaphysically) be a universe without there being a God in control at that time. If that be admitted, what argument could there be from the universe for supposing that there is a God since his control would not be needed to explain its existence, and what reason would there be for believing that God would ever be in control again? And if we suppose that there is some mechanism to ensure that one divine being is always in control, our hypothesis is beginning to become very complicated and for that reason less likely to be true. The hypothesis of the existence of a being who has the divine properties essentially (and of any other such being whose existence is entailed thereby) is much simpler than the hypothesis of the existence of a kenotic God.[50]

---

[47] Swinburne, *The Christian God*, 233.
[48] Swinburne, *The Christian God*, 232.
[49] Swinburne, *The Christian God*, 232.
[50] Swinburne, *The Christian God*, 232–3.

On the principle that a simple hypothesis is more likely to be true than a complex one, Swinburne doubts the validity of kenotic Christology. Of course, simplicity alone cannot decide the matter. Given the depth of mystery surrounding God and our inability to comprehend God fully, one might expect some subtlety and complexity in our understanding of the divine attributes.

John Hick sets his criticisms of the effects of kenotic Christology on the concept of God within the context of a concern for what is essential for genuine religion. 'In adjusting the concept of God to make divine Incarnation possible', he says, 'one may jettison aspects of the concept that are religiously essential.'[51] Thus the evidence that leads to denials of Jesus' omnipotence, omniscience, and incorporeality also leads to denials of his omnipresence, uncreatedness, being the creator, and aseity.[52] Hick criticizes Davis for rejecting 'much of the traditional Christian understanding of God' in order to make 'conceptual space for divine Incarnation', and argues that Morris's kenotic theory shows that one problem (Incarnation) can be solved only by creating 'a new and equally formidable problem elsewhere' (that is, in the doctrine of God).[53] Of course, in advocating a metaphorical (not metaphysical) conception of the Incarnation whereby Jesus, like others who respond to God's loving presence, 'Incarnated' divine love to an eminent degree, Hick has decisively departed from the traditional Christian understanding of the Incarnation. For Hick, then, retaining a concept of God that he regards as 'religiously essential' is more important than adhering to Chalcedonian orthodoxy. But must we choose between these? Or is it possible to formulate a concept of God such that both divine and human properties can be predicated of Jesus Christ during his earthly life?

In sum, all three of Swinburne's objections, like the concern expressed by Morris, indicate the need to examine the validity of kenotic Christology's method for understanding the divine attributes. And Hick's concern that kenotic Christology's adjustments in the concept of God will lead to rejecting 'religiously essential' aspects of the concept of God also points to the importance of

---

[51] Hick, *The Metaphor of God Incarnate*, 73.
[52] Hick, *The Metaphor of God Incarnate*, 73.
[53] Hick, *The Metaphor of God Incarnate*, 73, 75.

examining the basis for a proper Christian understanding of God. This will be the project of the next section.

A METHOD FOR UNDERSTANDING THE DIVINE ATTRIBUTES

How should Christian theologians formulate their concept of God? What status should be accorded to Anselmian views of God, or concepts of God rooted more broadly in natural theology? If one uses Christian belief in the Incarnation as a control for one's concept of God, does that imply that the divine attributes are formulated on an ad hoc basis? This section will argue that it is right and proper for Christian theologians to use Christian beliefs that Jesus Christ was truly divine and truly human and biblical statements about his knowledge as controls in formulating their understanding of God.

In an important piece of advice to Christian philosophers, Alvin Plantinga offers a key methodological insight. Christian philosophers, he argues, need not engage only in an effort to determine whether belief in God is probable or plausible, but may start from the existence of God in doing philosophical work.[54] His point is that Christian philosophers may—and even should—start from what they know as Christians. Their views about human freedom, for example, should be informed by their views of God's action and God's holding people accountable for their actions.[55] Morris makes a similar point regarding the Incarnation:

If we develop our philosophical anthropology and our doctrine of God in isolation from each other and from the central tenets of Christian faith, it is no surprise that conflicts may arise, that 'impossibilities' be generated. But it is a perfectly proper procedure (some would even say—rightly, I think—mandatory) for the Christian philosopher or theologian to develop his idea of human nature, his conception of what the essential human properties are,

[54] Alvin Plantinga, 'Advice to Christian Philosophers', *Faith and Philosophy*, 1 (1984): 260–1.

[55] Plantinga, 'Advice to Christian Philosophers', 264–7.

with certain presuppositions or controls derived from his doctrine of God and his belief in the reality of the Incarnation.[56]

Although in this passage Morris only points out that the Incarnation can affect our view of *human* nature, elsewhere he also says that Christian belief in the Incarnation properly acts as 'a control over the precise specification of what God is like'.[57] Christian theologians who follow Plantinga's advice, then, should not first devise concepts of God and of human nature and then try to determine whether, given these concepts, a divine person can become incarnate. Rather, they should start with what they know, namely, that the divine Son of God has become incarnate as described in the New Testament, and then work to what they do not know as clearly, namely, the best way to state the divine and human attributes.

This important point of theological method has been noted by such figures as Tertullian, Karl Barth, and N. T. Wright. In opposition to Marcion, who said it was impossible or unsuitable for God to be born, enfleshed, and suffer, Tertullian responds: 'With God, however, nothing is impossible but what he does not will.'[58] Strictly speaking, Tertullian engages in overstatement, since some things that God does not will are possible for him, but his central contention is correct: if God wills to do something, then doing that is possible for God. Putting the point the other way, Christians must not follow Marcion in deciding in advance, based on a concept of God, what God can and cannot do. Tertullian even goes so far as to say that if God had chosen to be born of a mere animal, it would be foolish 'if we are to judge God by our own conceptions'.[59] It is also 'foolish' to believe 'in a God that has been born, and that of a virgin, and of a fleshly nature too, who wallowed in all the before-mentioned humiliations of nature'.[60] But, quoting Paul, Tertullian says that 'God chose the foolish things of the world to shame the wise; God chose the weak things of the world to shame the strong' (1 Cor. 1:27, TNIV). Although the

---

[56] Morris, *The Logic of God Incarnate*, 64.

[57] Morris, *The Logic of God Incarnate*, 88.

[58] Tertullian, 'On the Flesh of Christ', in *The Ante-Nicene Fathers*, eds. Alexander Roberts and James Donaldson, vol. 3 (Edinburgh: T. & T. Clark; Grand Rapids: Eerdmans, n.d.), ch. 3.

[59] Tertullian, 'On the Flesh of Christ', ch. 4.

[60] Tertullian, 'On the Flesh of Christ', ch. 4.

Incarnation is unworthy of God, says Tertullian, it is of benefit to me.[61] Tertullian is not intimidated by Marcion and others who find Christian claims about the birth, suffering, and death of God the Son to be shameful and impossible. We should not decide in advance what God can or cannot do, he says, but should look at what God has done. Then, in the light of what God has done, we know that even *this* is possible for God, although it may seem impossible to us.

Similarly, Karl Barth says that we should not decide what God is like independently of the revelation of God in Jesus Christ. He criticizes Protestant orthodoxy for constructing a doctrine of God apart from God's revelation in Jesus Christ.[62] We should rather, says Barth, form our understanding of God in the light of the Incarnation. In a passage that is key to understanding Barth's view of the divinity of Christ, he says, 'The meaning of His [Christ's] deity—the only true deity in the New Testament sense—cannot be gathered from any notion of supreme, absolute, non-worldly being. It can be learned only from what took place in Christ', where we see that 'God as God is able and willing and ready to condescend, to humble Himself in this way.'[63] Again, 'Who God is and what it is to be divine is something we must learn where God has revealed Himself and His nature, the essence of the divine.'[64] God humbles himself 'without being in contradiction to his divine nature', but 'in contradiction to all human ideas about the divine nature'.[65] We must therefore 'learn to correct our notions of the being of God', including any thoughts that God can only be the 'Wholly Other', in the light of the Incarnation.[66] The key to the concept of the 'divine nature', says Barth, lies in the fact that 'Jesus Christ was obedient unto death, even the death of the cross.'[67] We should not decide apart from Jesus Christ what God is like, says Barth, but should correct our understanding of God in the light of the reality of Jesus Christ's taking our nature

[61] Tertullian, 'On the Flesh of Christ', ch. 5.

[62] Karl Barth, *Church Dogmatics*, 4 vols., eds. G. W. Bromiley and T. F. Torrance (Edinburgh: T. & T. Clark, 1956–75), II/1, 242.

[63] Barth, *Church Dogmatics*, IV/1, 177. It is worth noting that Barth himself was quite critical of kenotic Christology.

[64] Barth, *Church Dogmatics*, IV/1, 186.

[65] Barth, *Church Dogmatics*, IV/1, 199.

[66] Barth, *Church Dogmatics*, IV/1, 186.

[67] Barth, *Church Dogmatics*, IV/1, 199.

and his obedient suffering even to death on the cross. If Jesus Christ is God's decisive and clearest revelation to humanity, then our understanding of God will need to be shaped by what is revealed through and by him.

Like Tertullian and Barth, N. T. Wright notes that since God's 'self-revelation has taken place supremely in Jesus, the crucified and risen messiah of Israel', God is known in Jesus, 'the human being who lived, worked, and died in first-century Palestine'.[68] Given this reality, Wright makes what he calls a 'shocking claim': 'not that we know what the word *God* means and can discover the extent to which this "God" was present in, or revealed through, Jesus; rather that, by close attention to Jesus himself, we are invited to discover, perhaps for the first time, just who the creator and covenant God was and is all along'.[69] Taking seriously the Christian claim that Jesus was the Incarnate Son of God should move us to a new and deeper understanding of who God is. Thus, in the context of discussing Philippians 2:5–11, Wright notes the insight Christ's humiliation gives into the nature of God:

The real humiliation of the Incarnation and the cross is that one who was himself God, and who never during the whole process stopped being God, could embrace such a vocation. The real theological emphasis of the hymn, therefore, is not simply a new view of Jesus. It is a new understanding of God. Against the age-old attempts of human beings to make God in their own (arrogant, self-glorifying) image, Calvary reveals the truth about what it meant to be God. Underneath this is the conclusion, all-important in present Christological debate: Incarnation and even crucifixion are to be seen as *appropriate* vehicles for the dynamic self-revelation of God.[70]

If the incarnate and humiliated Christ is a revelation of God, then even in his humiliated condition something of God's nature is revealed. At the very least, we learn that a divine person, the Son of God, can take on this humiliated condition, including even suffering,

[68] N. T. Wright, 'The Truth of the Gospel and Christian Living', in *The Meaning of Jesus: Two Visions*, Marcus Borg and N. T. Wright (San Francisco: HarperCollins, 1999), 214.

[69] Wright, 'The Truth of the Gospel and Christian Living', 214–15.

[70] N. T. Wright, *The Climax of the Covenant: Christ and the Law in Pauline Theology* (Edinburgh: T. & T. Clark, 1991; Minneapolis: Fortress Press, 1992), 84.

death, and—the point that has been the focus of this chapter—a lack of omniscience.

Wright also notes that the apostle Paul's understanding of monotheism was redefined by the appearance of Christ. Thus after affirming that there is but one God (1 Cor. 8:4, echoing the *Shema* in Deut. 6:4) and observing that there are many so-called gods, Paul says, 'yet for us there is but one God, the Father, from whom all things came and for whom we live; and there is but one Lord, Jesus Christ, through whom all things came and through whom we live' (1 Cor. 8:6, TNIV). As Wright observes, Paul here redefines monotheism Christologically, placing Jesus within a text that affirms that 'Israel's God is the one and only God, the creator of the world.'[71] For the apostle Paul, then, what monotheism is must be redefined in the light of the appearance of Jesus Christ, the Lord. In Christian theology, this redefinition of monotheism eventually led to the view that God is triune—one God in three persons.

Just as the Christian understanding of the number of persons in God is rooted not simply in what can be known about God by natural revelation and through the work of natural theology, but is based on God's special revelation, especially in the belief that God was incarnate in Jesus Christ, so too our view of the attributes of God needs to be open to input from the nature of God as it was revealed in Jesus Christ. If Christians use Anselmian methods to articulate their concept of God, they must use these methods only insofar as they reflect what Scripture says about God. And if there is any conflict between the deliverances of Scripture and the deliverances of the Anselmian method, Christian theologians should favour what Scripture says. In fact, it would be odd if the Incarnation of God contributed to our knowledge that God is triune, but contributed nothing to our understanding of the divine attributes. If Jesus Christ is the most direct revelation of God, as Christians believe he is, then surely our understanding of what God is like seems likely to need revision in the light of what is revealed through his presence and teaching. So we need to be willing to revise our concept of God in the light of the Incarnation.

---

[71] N. T. Wright, *The Climax of the Covenant*, 129. I am grateful to Bruce Fisk for having pointed out Wright's comments on this point.

By what method, then, should Christian theologians develop their understanding of God's attributes? The place to start, of course, is Scripture, which describes God as unsurpassably great, powerful, all-knowing, sovereign over all creation (that is, not confined to certain localities), without beginning of days or end of life, dependent for existence on no one outside God, creator of every non-divine being, perfectly good, supremely just, and more loving than the most gracious father or mother. Anselm offers a helpful principle by which to express such attributes: God is that than which nothing greater can be thought.[72] The Anselmian method, then, is to attribute to God great-making properties, that is, properties that it is better to have than to lack, and then to say that God has these properties to a superlative degree. So in an attempt to develop and summarize the biblical depiction of God, Anselmian theology describes God as the greatest possible being who possesses great-making properties such as maximal power (omnipotence), knowledge of every truth (omniscience), and perfect goodness. But Anselm's method can only be a guide, not the final word on the divine attributes.

Given what Scripture says about Jesus' growing in wisdom and about the Son's lack of knowledge (during the time of his self-emptying on this earth) of the time of the end of the age, and given the teaching of Scripture and the creeds that Jesus Christ is fully divine, the divine knowledge attribute must be understood in such a way that the Son can be divine and non-omniscient during the time he was humiliated for the purpose of bringing about reconciliation. The term 'omniscient-unless-kenotically-incarnate' (where a kenotic Incarnation is understood as freely chosen, temporary, and for the purpose of reconciliation) is a way of expressing the divine knowledge attribute in order to account for what has been revealed by and through the Incarnate Christ. If God's knowledge is supremely exalted and perfect, yet the divine Son can, without giving up his divinity, be less than omniscient for a time during his life on earth, then our understanding of the essential divine knowledge attribute needs to be modified accordingly.

[72] Anselm of Canterbury, 'Proslogion', in *The Major Works*, eds. Brian Davies and G. R. Evans (Oxford: Oxford University Press, 1998), ch. 2.

Of course, given our inability to comprehend God fully, we can assume that a statement of the divine attributes that has been modified in the light of the Incarnation is still inadequate. Surely the reality of God's nature is beyond our ability to grasp fully. Yet we must do our best to describe God's attributes on the basis of God's revelation to us. The claim that the essential divine knowledge attribute is that God is omniscient-unless-kenotically-incarnate is an attempt to do just that.

CONCLUSION

This chapter has argued, in the light of the Chalcedonian Definition and standard Christian claims about the communication of attributes, that kenotic Christology offers a way of understanding the divine attributes that remains faithful to both Chalcedonian orthodoxy and biblical claims about Jesus Christ. In response to recent criticisms, the chapter argues that kenotic Christology follows a proper method for understanding the divine attributes. Just as God's revelation in the Incarnation has led Christians to the belief that God is triune, so too the revelation of God in the Incarnation, as attested by Scripture, leads to the belief that God has unsurpassable knowledge that can, during the Son's humiliation for the purpose of redemption, take a form that involves non-omniscience. Following the method for understanding the divine attributes used by kenotic Christology offers a fruitful method for deepening our understanding of the divine nature.[73]

[73] I am indebted to the members of the Kenotic Workshop for many valuable comments and suggestions offered during discussion of an earlier draft of this essay. Richard Muller and David Rylaarsdam offered helpful advice on historical matters. I am especially grateful to C. Stephen Evans for having organized the workshop.

7

Trinity and Kenosis

Thomas R. Thompson and Cornelius Plantinga, Jr.

More obvious even than love and marriage, or horse and carriage, do the doctrines of Trinity and Incarnation 'go together', as it was the event of the Incarnation that first gave rise to the distinctive Christian conception of God-as-Trinity, its transcendental ground. The revelation of Jesus Christ, the eternally begotten, but now enfleshed Son of the Father, compelled the Christian confession of a personal plurality within the one, true God.

Given their vital union, a weakening of one of these confessional fundaments will result in the attenuation of the other. A modalistic construal of the Trinity, for example, typically results in a docetic impairment of the Incarnation; adoptionistic Christologies, conversely, are almost invariably accompanied by a unitarian conception of God.

But even within confessional parameters one finds variations on these doctrinal themes, as this volume illustrates in respect to the Incarnation, exploring the viability of both a two-natures and kenotic model. This is also true of the Trinity, as the discussion ranges within creedal space today over a number of debatable models. As with all the loci in general, to tweak one of these doctrines in a particular way will suggest modifications in the other. The basic question we pursue in this chapter is: What particular shape does trinity doctrine take with a kenotic model of the Incarnation?

Our query is all the more serious since one of the recurrent criticisms of kenoticism is that it violates the very doctrine of the

Trinity. Such criticism is complex, ranging from the more general, virtually analytic judgement that a kenotically weakened Son no longer qualifies as a divine denizen:

It means a virtual destruction of the Trinity, and therefore takes away our very God. The humanized Son, self-emptied of His divine attributes, could no longer be a divine subsistence in the trinitarian life.[1]

to the objection that it sunders the *indivisa* of trinitarian operations:

The doctrine of the Trinity is violated by denying the uninterrupted Divine fulness of the Son, and by neglecting the truth of Divine coinherence and the indivisibility of the Eternal, Three in their operations.[2]

to the most serious charge that kenotic theories entail a tritheism:

They avowedly operate by the actual withdrawal of the Son, either in respect of His physical, or of all His attributes, or in respect of a field of His consciousness, from the Trinitarian fellowship. If one of the Persons of the Blessed Trinity can be temporarily withdrawn from the intercommunion of the Deity either in respect of the whole or of any portion of His being, Monotheism can scarcely be preserved. The distinction between the Persons of the Godhead becomes at least as sharply individualistic as that between finite personalities. Thus we have no longer one God but three Gods.[3]

This is not to say that confessional trinitarians one and all do not embrace, even relish, a kenotic motif in their theology. But the kenotic model is another thing.

This chapter will contend for an obvious connection, a marriage which critics of the kenotic model, as witnessed above, have been quick to denounce: that the most consistent kenoticism requires a well differentiated doctrine of the trinitarian persons, one too differentiated for critics. Put more simply and provocatively, we will argue that the viability of the kenotic model is dependent on a social understanding of the Trinity—that the success of the former requires

---

[1] Louis Berkhof, *Systematic Theology,* 4th edn. (Grand Rapids: Eerdmans, 1939), 329.

[2] Francis J. Hall, *The Kenotic Theory* (New York: Longmans, Green and Co., 1898), xviii.

[3] E. Digges La Touche, *The Person of Christ in Modern Thought,* Donnellan Lectures 1911–12 (London: James Clarke & Co., 1912), 363.

the success of the latter.[4] After tracing out this evident conceptual connection between a kenotically Incarnate Son (Section 1) and social trinitarian form (2), we will flesh out a trinitarian concept of personhood that is compatible with the Incarnation, especially a kenotic one (3), and conclude by offering a brief defence of the resulting social conception of the Trinity against its most serious charge—that it entails an unacceptable tritheism (4). At last call, those inclined to the tandem kenotic Incarnation–social Trinity might argue that this particular union only accentuates the original genius of these doctrines: that God stoops low for our salvation and by so doing is revealed to be no undifferentiated and therefore indifferent monad, but an open, outstretched community of Love. And one might further argue that such ground needs to be reclaimed in the Christian tradition against theological pressures that docetically depreciate the Incarnation and defeat the trinitarian distinctions.

1. THE INCARNATE PERSON OF CHRIST

The claim to theological fame of the kenotic model is that it secures the Chalcedonian non-negotiables regarding the person of Christ— think of Thomasius' pillars or Mackintosh's axioms[5]—in a historic- ally unprecedented way, especially preserving Christ's humanity and

---

[4] But not necessarily vice versa. Richard Swinburne, for example, defends a social analogy of the Trinity while rejecting kenoticism on the grounds that divine attributes such as omnipotence and immutability are non-negotiably essential to divinity. See his *The Christian God* (Oxford: Clarendon Press, 1994), 170–91; 230–3. Stephen Davis, on the other hand, advocated early on a kenotic model of the Incarnation, while rejecting a social doctrine of the Trinity. See his *Logic and the Nature of God* (Grand Rapids: Eerdmans, 1983). Recently, however, Davis has in conversation re-evaluated his position on a social trinitarianism, and his modification of views can also be seen in a not-yet published critique of Brian Leftow's 'Anti Social Trinitar- ianism', in Stephen T. Davis, Daniel Kendall, and Gerald O'Collins (eds.), *The Trinity: An Interdisciplinary Symposium on the Trinity* (Oxford: Oxford University Press, 1999), 203–50.

[5] From Thompson's essay, pp. 79 & 91. Mackintosh distilled the non-negotiable substance of Chalcedon into the following four axioms: (1) the deity of Christ; (2) his personal pre-existence; (3) his true humanity; and (4) the unity of his person.

unity of person, by means of reconceiving his deity (which critics
rather claim it fudges). Some review of the Chalcedonian formulation is therefore necessary.[6]

It is interesting to note historically that the official trinitarian
terminology was clarified prior to the Christological. The so-called
Cappadocian settlement of the Trinity (c. Constantinople 381) preceded Chalcedon (451)—the conciliar high water mark of patristic
Christology and esteemed benchmark concerning the person of
Christ. The artful inversion of their respective definitions has often
been noted: whereas the trinitarian formula prescribes a plurality of
persons in a unity of nature, the Christological formula prescribes a
unity of person in a plurality of natures. What concerns us most
particularly is the notion of person, which formally ought to be
univocal between Trinity and Incarnation, since it is identical in
respect to one person of the Trinity, the Incarnate One.[7]

To simplify a long and complicated doctrinal story, the real trick in
attempting to negotiate the Chalcedonian definition[8] in some coherent

---

[6] For reference, we quote the text in full here:

Following therefore the holy Fathers, we unanimously teach to confess one and the
same Son, our Lord Jesus Christ, the same perfect in divinity and perfect in humanity,
the same truly God and truly man composed of rational soul and body, the same one
in being (*homoousios*) with the Father as to the divinity and one in being (*homoousios*) with us as to the humanity, like unto us in all things but sin (cf. Heb 4:5). The
same was begotten from the Father before the ages as to the divinity and in the latter
days for us and our salvation was born as to his humanity from Mary the Virgin
Mother of God (*theotokos*).

We confess that one and the same Lord Jesus Christ, the only begotten Son, must
be acknowledged in two natures (*physis*), without confusion or change, without
division or separation. The distinction between the natures was never abolished by
their union but rather the character proper to each of the two natures was preserved
as they came together in one person (*prosopon*) and one hypostasis. He is not split or
divided into two persons, but he is one and the same only-begotten, God the Word,
the Lord Jesus Christ, as formerly the prophets and later Jesus Christ himself have
taught us about him and as has been handed down to us by the Symbol of the Fathers.

J. Neuner and J. Dupuis (eds.), *The Christian Faith in the Doctrinal
Documents of the Catholic Church* (Dublin: Mercier Press, 1973), 614–15.

[7] This is assuming that the Incarnation is a true revelation of the *person* of the Son,
which we assume, and which also seems to be assumed by Chalcedon in employing
the Cappadocian language for trinitarian personhood for 'one and the same Lord
Jesus Christ'—namely, one *prosopon* and one *hypostasis*.

[8] We take the Chalcedonian 'definition' in the original, etymological sense of *de-
finire*—that of setting bounds or limitations on what can be said—which translated

way is to maintain the unity of Christ's person, the integration point of both his divinity and humanity. In the Chalcedonian formula Christ's singular 'person' has two principal foci, though the first is more principal than the second: from the side of his true deity, Christ, in being *homoousios* with God the Father, is the eternally begotten and (pre-) existing Son, most commonly and technically designated in Christological discussion as the *Logos*; from the side of his true humanity, Christ, in being *homoousios* with us, is begotten of the Virgin, and designated a *rational soul*, meaning a human rational soul or human person (not just body) in pointed exclusion of Apollinarianism. These two—the divine Logos and the human rational soul—are held to be the identical person in Christ, 'one and the same', as Chalcedon puts its, one ontological subject. At the same time, the person-forming principle in the very human Jesus of Nazareth *is* the eternally (pre-)existent Logos. In the later clarifying words of tradition, the human nature of Christ is *anhypostatic* (without its independent personal existence) but is *enhypostatic* (personalized/animated) in the Logos. The human soul of Jesus of Nazareth is not independent from, but one and the same with, the eternal Logos. But how can this be?

Advocates of a two-natures *model* can only declare ineffable the union of the Logos and the rational soul, invoking the theologoumenon of the 'communication of the attributes' (*communicatio idiomatum*) which merely predicates both divine and human attributes of one ontological subject of the Son ('merely predicates'—that is, doesn't offer an explanatory model). In such discussions, the 'entity' of the rational soul appears to be animated when-or-as activated by the human nature, whereas the Logos animates (or is animated by?) the divine nature. (Which is prioritized: person or nature? Sometimes it is hard to tell.) But the Logos and the rational soul are nonetheless declared one and the same, a union chalked up to the mystery of the Incarnation. The general tendency in this two-natures construct that kenoticists find objectionable is its vulnerability to docetism, and therefore personal duplicity. If the Logos remains in undiminished realms and dimensions of deity, the divine personhood of Christ

---

to Christology means ruling out of bounds specific Christological proposals, principally the Arian, Apollinarian, Nestorian, and Eutychian.

tends to overwhelm his humanity qua human person; similarly, when Christ's human attributes are in view, such accounting for his human soul appears in duplicitous tension with his undiminished deity and divine personhood.

The *basic* kenotic strategy is for the Logos to limit his divine powers, prerogatives, attributes, and/or glory so as to be compatible with a humanity as animated by a human rational soul—that is, to be and live as a human person. But even here the kenoticists were not consistent. Recall for a moment A. B. Bruce's early typology of kenotic proposals that categorized the models into four types, based on major representatives Thomasius, Ebrard, Martensen, and Gess.[9] Within this tactical variety, it is quite clear that Martensen's model falters on the *una persona*, as does Ebrard's, since the latter's inability to secure the true humanity also implies a disunity between the Logos and a human rational soul. But even Thomasius blinked on this issue. As Thompson noted, since Thomasius worked with both a kenotic and assumption model, he posited that the Logos assumed both a human nature *and soul*, which put in real question the unity or singularity of Christ's personhood.[10] Given Bruce's typology, it is really only the Gessian model that consistently posits the strict identity between the Logos and Christ's human rational soul and attempts to ensure the integrity of the latter by positing a proportional limitation of the former. It is the basic strategy of this model with its strict personal identity that seems to be assumed by the majority of those who advocate a kenotic model in this volume.

If we take this particular kenotic tack consistently, while assuming a univocal notion of personhood formally between Incarnation and Trinity, it becomes clear why this requires a more social doctrine of the Trinity—or conversely, why critics think it violates the doctrine of the Trinity in the direction of tritheism—since it accentuates in bold the distinction of trinitarian persons. The Logos *qua human person* is delineated an ontologically discrete person from God the Father. If

---

[9] Bruce called the Thomasian model the *absolute dualistic* type, the Ebrardian the *absolute semi-metamorphic* type, that of Martensen's the *real* but *relative* type, and the Gessian the *absolute metamorphic* type. A. B. Bruce, *The Humiliation of Christ*, 5th edn. (Edinburgh: T & T Clark, 1900), 138–63. For a brief summary of these specific tacks, see Thompson's Ch. 4, pp. 86–7 above.

[10] Ibid. p. 86, n. 16.

the eternal Son really becomes human, a human soul by self-limitation, one unitive consciousness within the bounds of a human body and experience without docetic excess, as kenoticists believe jibes with the biblical record, then his is a sentient life lived vis-à-vis the Father in the power and energies of the Spirit (as the Messiah). In this fashion the kenotic model would actually secure the same distinction of persons that is posited by adoptionistic and Spirit-Christologies—in which kenoticism recognizes valid moments—without the reductionistic price of a sheer adoptionism. At the same time, we note parenthetically, one could argue that this distinction among trinitarian persons is already implied in the revelation of the trinitarian name of Father, Son, and (less evidently) Spirit, reminding us again that a well-differentiated doctrine of the Trinity is not dependent per se on a kenotic model of the Incarnation. But a kenotic model certainly accentuates these distinctions and is clearly dependent on them.

Thomasius, for example, saw early on the 'kenotic need' for a greater dynamic within the Trinity in which 'the trinitarian relations are not to be thought of as rigid, immovable forms of existence but as living, personal positions' that even imply a 'threefold form of consciousness';[11] and Mackintosh at the end of the nineteenth-century kenotic wave struggles for a trinitarian mean between an Augustinian psychological model of a single self-consciousness, which he finds out of sorts with the biblical Christ, and a 'social' doctrine of discrete persons, which he assumes is polytheistic or tritheistic. His own proposal falls to the paradoxical, in which Father, Son, and Spirit are viewed as 'members or manifestations of a single Divine life beyond the limits of time, forming together the supreme instance of individuality'.[12] This chapter argues essentially that Mackintosh qua kenoticist need not be so paradoxical in his approach to the Trinity, that a consistent kenoticism fits well with a social doctrine of the Trinity, and that a responsible defence of the latter against the tritheist charge is possible.

---

[11] Gottfried Thomasius, 'The Person of the Mediator', in Claude Welch (ed. and trans.), *God and Incarnation in Mid-Nineteenth Century German Theology* (New York: Oxford University Press, 1965), 81–2.

[12] H. R. Mackintosh, *The Doctrine of the Person of Jesus Christ*, 2nd edn. (Edinburgh: T & T Clark, 1913; repr. 1978), 525.

2. THE SOCIAL MODEL OF THE TRINITY

Social models of the Trinity have become increasing popular within the recent renewal of trinitarian thought. This trinitarian renaissance of the last three decades found its rallying cry in Karl Rahner's lament of the late sixties that the Trinity had little play in the vast majority of Christian thought or spirituality—that, indeed, despite their orthodox confession of the Trinity, Christians were for all practical purposes 'mere monotheists'. A subsequent groundswell of trinitarian thought has answered Rahner's jeremiad with the growing conviction that the Trinity is an eminently practical doctrine with crucial implications for both church and society.

A leading motif, if not primary motive, in this western resurgence of trinitarian thought has been a more differentiated understanding of the divine persons, a tendency that shows a greater affinity with the eastern trinitarian tradition. By taking more seriously the narrative history of Father, Son, and Spirit as the primary point of departure for the Christian doctrine of God, in contrast to any supervening notion of divine unity or oneness that would impair their distinctions, trinity doctrine has been freed from its subordination to a more philosophical theism (think of the tradition since Thomas of treating first the doctrine of the One God, and divine attributes that pertain thereto, before that of the Triune God). That is the gist of Rahner's famous axiom: 'The economic Trinity is the immanent Trinity and vice versa', which Rahner offered as a methodological corrective to bring into greater congruity our understanding of the historical actions of God with the being of God. Of course, Karl Barth had initiated this move earlier in the century by treating the Trinity as prolegomena in his *Church Dogmatics*, thereby elevating this largely languished doctrine as both the framework and touchstone of his entire theology.

Such a theological tack has sponsored a more dynamic or historically tempered doctrine of God. A trinitarian theism, let us call it, has led the way in rethinking certain classical divine attributes, particularly those derived *via negativa*—indivisibility, immutability, impassibility, apathy, eternality. Construed within a traditional

(Greek) metaphysical framework, such attributions conspired to paint a more static image of God as remote, distant, and impervious to a world of suffering and absurdity, a theistic portrait that excited much of modern atheism, especially of the protest variety. By contrast, trinitarians propose a more dynamic picture of the God–world relationship, one in which divine persons deeply participate in history's ebb and flow in sympathetic affirmation of creation. In this way the Trinity has assumed an important apologetic role in the Christian dialogue with modernity.

The trinitarian renaissance has also championed more relational accents in theology. Pre-eminent among these has been the forging of a more social view of the human person. Given the intrinsic connection between theology and anthropology, that doctrines of God reinforce certain perceptions and patterns of human personhood, a more trinitarian theism that intonates the communion and fellowship (perichoresis) of the divine persons has been rallied to accentuate an interpersonal view of humanity created in the divine image (as 'male and female'). Many welcome this development as a healthy corrective to the 'autonomous individual' of modernity. This more relational anthropology has resulted in the waning popularity of Augustine's long-standing psychological analogy for the Trinity in favour of Richard of St. Victor's full-orbed love analogy, as 'Love' has become the preferred language for the 'divine essence' among trinitarians today. Few are the major statements on the Trinity today that do not find in 'God is Love' (1 John 4:8) a most compelling description of and entrance into God's trinitarian being and action in history.

With such developments, it is not surprising that more social doctrines of the Trinity have gained a considerable hearing. Recalling the Cappadocian Fathers who employed social analogies,[13] social trinitarians have emerged from a broad range of theological traditions in the belief that the Trinity is best likened to a family, community, or society of persons. Though hardly immune to controversy or debate, the social analogy promises many advantages over

---

[13] The Cappadocian penchant for social models is both striking and suggestive— be it Gregory of Nyssa's 'three man analogy' of Peter, James, and John (*Tres Dei*), Gregory of Nazianzus' 'family analogy' of Adam, Eve, and Seth (*Fifth Theological Oration*), or Basil of Caesarea's contention that God is like a continuous and indissoluble community (*Epistle 38*).

other trinitarian constructs. For one, it claims to be the most consistent outcome of those more recent—dynamic and relational—gains in the doctrine of God in revision of more Greek-influenced categories. For another, it offers a more coherent account of the Trinity's threeness–oneness relation than the western tradition has bequeathed us, one which by the standards of the Athanasian Creed (verse 4) falls in the fair territory of 'neither blending the persons' (*à la* Modalism), 'nor dividing the essence' (*à la* Arianism). As a more accessible understanding of the Trinity, the way becomes clearer to see how the Trinity can function as an exemplary model for both the church and society at large, underscoring the relational nature (being) and benevolent task (act) of human personhood created in the divine image (cf. Gen. 1:26–8) and recreated in Christ (cf. John 17:20–3). The social conception of the Trinity offers a fundamental vision of God as a giving and open community of divine persons, one that invites us through Christ's sonship into its loving embrace as our true home. So conceived, the Trinity grounds a personalist metaphysics of communion and love that appeals to the deepest longing of the human heart—the desire to love and be loved.

In current trinitarian debate, the social analogy has two principal foils. These are best discussed by employing a typology of trinitarian models centred on the issue of personhood—the most difficult of trinitarian issues, but the one which goes to the heart of the intersection of Incarnation and Trinity and the models distinguished in this chapter. Our typology works with a very low-level *description* of personhood, however, one on which most could agree applies to both God and humanity. If we suppose that a person, divine or human, constitutes a centre of thought, will, act, love, and consciousness—that a person is essentially a sentient subject of thought and action—then we can map out three basic positions in debate today as to how such personhood applies to God trinitarianly. These would posit, differently, that God as Trinity is:

1. One Person existent (or manifest) as Father, Son, and Spirit
2. Three Persons—Father, Son, and Spirit—who are also One (Person?)
3. Three Persons—Father, Son, and Spirit—who together comprise the One True God

The first position takes such personhood singularly: in this sense of person, God is supremely one of these. What then of Father, Son, and Spirit? If they are considered *manifestations* of God-the-One-Person (the bracketed sense), then we are talking classic modalism in the fashion of Sabellius. But we have principally in mind here Barth's and Rahner's more sophisticated trinitarianisms in which Father, Son, and Spirit are all concurrently existent (purportedly, in some sense of 'eternal') as 'modes of being' (Barth) or 'manners of subsisting' (Rahner), designations they believe capture more accurately the trinitarian sense of personhood of the early church, since they are not convinced that it employed its personal language in our 'common sense' description here. Barth's and Rahner's similar trinitarianisms have been routinely criticized for their 'modalistic' tendency, as critics have found the terms 'modes' or 'manners' deficient in their ability personally to dignify Father, Son, and Spirit as objects of worship. The social trinitarian would concur. Given the Athanasian foul lines, this construct tends to 'blend the persons'.

The second type represents the traditional western 'paradoxical' position, which tends to answer the personhood question on both sides of the threeness–oneness ledger. While affirming with the conciliar tradition that the trinitarian members are 'persons'—for lack of a better term—any strong or distinguishable sense of the notion is ultimately overshadowed by an even greater unity claim. In this traditional model, strongly influenced by Augustine, the doctrine of God's indivisibility has tended to collapse any distinctions among divine persons into the simple, single, ineffable thing that God finally is. Although the 'persons' are ontologically distinguished within deity, they finally amount to little more than notional 'relations of opposition', since each 'person' is also strictly identical with the numerically one divine substance. The subtle theologizing involved in this long-considered 'orthodox' statement of the Trinity originated the still popular impression that the three persons of the Trinity also cash out into one (person), that three equals one by some supramundane arithmetic, a point at which the mystery and ineffability of the Trinity is typically invoked. The principal liability of this model is that it is very difficult to grasp since it appears to embrace a contradiction. Given its strong unity claim which reduces the trinitarian persons to sheer relations (something of which we have no experience), it also tends, by Athanasian standards, to 'blend the persons'.

The third option is also happy to ascribe personhood to the trinitarian members severally, but does this in its strongest, most eminent and unimpaired sense. It is this option that constitutes a social understanding of the Trinity, since the only appropriate analogies to convey it are those that are personally pluralist. God here is conceived of most fundamentally neither as one person *à la* (1), nor as three persons in some weak, highly equivocal sense, whose individuation is finally dubious *à la* (2); rather, God is conceived of quite unequivocally as three divine persons who co-exist as one God in a unity sublimely unique, but best likened to that of a family, or a community, or a society—for example, the church.[14] The basic problem this option sets up for itself methodologically is in securing the unity claim. By Athanasian standards the question is: Does it 'divide the essence'? Whether this can be resolved in a way that satisfies the conditions of monotheism suggests this model's principal liability: many consider it tritheist, or more tolerantly, tritheist-tending.

We will offer a defence against this charge in the final section. What needs further clarification is the concept of person appropriate to the trinitarian members, one which befits a social model of the Trinity as required by a kenotic model of the Incarnation. Given the univocal conception of person between Incarnation and Trinity, moreover, the kenotic strategy supposed here in which the Logos becomes a human rational soul offers express warrant for applying the 'trinitarian concept of person' to humanity—a parallel long suspected to be validated by the Incarnation and to have precedence in creation on account of humanity being fashioned *imago Dei*. That human persons bear a striking formal resemblance to trinitarian

---

[14] 'Best likened to' given our formal typology, not precisely like, since the sublime communion of divine persons cannot be fully mirrored in any human community. Among social analogies, the community of the church appears especially warranted given the paralleling unities Christ cites in his high priestly prayer between his oneness with the Father and the oneness among those who believe in him (John 17:20ff.) Indeed, here it is divine unity among divine persons that is offered as a model for ecclesial unity among human persons, since the church as the renewed image of God is increasingly to reflect trinitarian fellowship as an efficacious mark of its mission.

persons not only guarantees the relative success of the theological enterprise—given its necessary condition that we can only speak or think about God in any positive fashion (cataphatically) by way of analogy with our own experience—but it also bolsters the conviction that the basic western notion of the person as one clothed in uniqueness, rights, and dignity is in no small measure a Christian contribution, arising principally out of the early Christological and trinitarian debates.[15] Our 'trinitarian concept of person', therefore, applies to both divine persons and human persons, since it is only in the light of the former that the latter can truly 'know thyself'.

3. THE TRINITARIAN CONCEPT OF PERSON

Our working assumption is that in calling the trinitarian members 'persons' (*prosopoi, personae*), the early church chose the most appropriate *denotation* available, since one cannot pay Father, Son, and Spirit any higher distinguishing compliment. With no apologies for its personalist language therefore, it is the task of Christian theology to discern the appropriate *connotation* of divine personhood, in the same way that it does with all divine attributes and characteristics. In 'fleshing out' this 'trinitarian concept of person', we can identify three necessary dimensions: the ontological, the subjective-psychological, and the relational.

The ontological dimension possesses a certain logical priority in the concept of personhood and takes us back to the principal premodern conception of the trinitarian persons. Even if *prosopon* or *persona* derive etymologically from the theatre mask (cf. *dramatis personae*), a provenance that has, unfortunately, occasioned much doubt as to their propriety in trinitarian description, the equivalent term *hypostasis* guarantees their ontological depth, since the latter was originally distinguished from *ousia* by the Cappadocians to indicate a particular instance (or substance) of a general, common,

---

15 Thomas F. Torrance, for example, asserts: 'It cannot be stressed enough that it was this Trinitarian doctrine of God that actually gave rise to the concept of person, which was quite unknown in the world before.' 'The Goodness and Dignity of Man in the Christian Tradition', *Modern Theology*, 4/4 (July 1988), 320.

or universal nature.[16] In this vein, Boethius' definition of person became standard for scholastic treatments of the Trinity: *persona est rationalis naturae individua substantia*, which appears to be the equivalent of 'rational soul'.[17] The social trinitarian has no qualms in taking the Boethian definition rather straightforwardly as a needed constituent in the description of trinitarian personhood, as long as the rational soul or mind is understood synecdochically as a sort of *summa pars pro toto* of personhood (that is, a supreme part which would admit of other important constituents), and, more importantly, as long as the discrete, untransferable, substantial individuality of each divine member is maintained. This tended not to be the case in the scholastic trinitarian tradition since the *ousia* of God was taken to be the primary substance which admitted of no substantial distinctions whatsoever on account of the assumption of divine simplicity. When the persons (hypostases) are confessionally juxtaposed to the one indivisible divine nature, they lose their substantial personhood, they reduce to sheer relations (of opposition)—just as they do in Boethius, for example. Such is the bewildering legacy of trinitarian type (2).

With the rise of the modern world came a heightened importance of the individual and an increased awareness of the self, and thus the subjective or psychological dimension of personhood came to the fore. We cannot define a human person today without some reference to self-consciousness. But how the category of 'consciousness' is to be applied to the Trinity remains in sharp debate; in fact, it is the chief bugaboo of trinitarian personhood. Both of the first two models in our typology opt for a singular self-consciousness in God, contending that three of these would constitute tritheism: if personhood entails consciousness—as in our typological description—then God is supremely one subjectivity, state Barth and Rahner. So also the

[16] As is seen quite evidently in Basil's *Epistle 38* (now attributed to Gregory of Nyssa) among other letters.

[17] It is interesting to note that Boethius himself does not employ his 'standard definition' in reference to the Trinity (it does not occur in any of the trinitarian tractates), but only in reference to the person of Christ in 'A Treatise Against Eutyches and Nestorius'. While not much can necessarily be made of this, it does perhaps underscore in doctrinal development the univocal understanding of personhood across Trinity and Incarnation. We owe the textual observation to former Calvin and Calvin Seminary student, Matthew Lundberg.

western scholastic tradition, which, while admitting on the one hand that Father, Son, and Spirit are 'persons' in some ontological or Boethian sense, nonetheless places the divine consciousness in the singular nature or unity of God, an equivocation on personhood that fosters its paradoxical cast. The social trinitarian, however, predicates consciousness of each trinitarian person as a necessary constituent. If Father, Son, and Spirit are each response-able centres or subjects of thought and action, as appears the case from the biblical record, then this requires psychological equipage, such as will, understanding, and consciousness. Moreover, this seems to be implied by the Boethian definition of person, which itself harkens back to an eminent Greek anthropological tradition. The point of the rational soul, as opposed to an irrational one, is that it empowers a degree of self-transcendence over the ebb and flow of nature or chaos of the passions whereby one can self-consciously deliberate one's actions in pursuit of the good. Hence the Delphic credo, 'Know Thyself.' Moreover, it is hard to make one's way through Augustine's *De Trinitate* and not become lost in the self-conscious reflections of his rational soul in pursuit of trinitarian vestiges. While social trinitarians find Augustine's dominant psychological analogy for the Trinity wanting—because it is a single-person analogy—they are happy to concur that consciousness is an essential constituent of personhood, divine or human. But this need not be taken as a subjectivity in the fashion of the Idealistic tradition, which maintains that personal identity *is constituted* by self-consciousness, secured in a reflexive intra-subjectivity by bracketing all others out, a modern anthropology prone to a possessive individualism and culture of narcissism. Rather, it is a self-consciousness dependent upon *inter*-subjectivity, which anticipates our third dimension, the relational.[18]

---

[18] It is interesting to note that Barth's and Rahner's trinitarian formulations are significantly indebted to the Idealistic tradition of subjectivity. For a good discussion on how various degrees of consciousness and self-consciousness may appropriately apply to the trinitarian persons, see David Brown's essay, 'Trinitarian Personhood and Individuality' in Ronald J. Feenstra and Cornelius Plantinga, Jr. (eds.), *Trinity, Incarnation, and Atonement: Philosophical and Theological Essays* (Notre Dame, IN: University of Notre Dame Press, 1989), 48–78. Indeed, Brown's analysis of the issue suggests that there is an important sense in which Father, Son, and Spirit, while never ceasing to be distinct sentient beings, nevertheless share a unity of consciousness that qualifies and

We already noted that within the recent resurgence of trinitarian thought the doctrine of God has taken on more 'relational' hues. This includes the forging of a more relational definition of the person in application to the Trinity. Touted as a postmodern development, the conception of personhood as *interpersonal* or *social*, that a person is always a person-in-relation, is being proposed to counter the modern 'autonomous individual' and its considered deleterious social effects. Anticipated by Hegel, the idea that concrete personal existence is relationally mediated has been made much of in the twentieth century by 'personalists' such as Buber, Ebner, Macmurray, and others who emphasize that the 'I' arises only in responsible encounter with the 'Thou'. Applied trinitarianly, just as Adam is not Adam—humanity—without Eve (and Seth for that matter), so also the Father is not the Father—God—without the Son (and the Spirit for that matter). A humanity of social proportions reflects a divinity of social proportions who fashioned the former in sacramental relief 'in our image and likeness'. That 'person'—a qualitative concept as opposed to 'individual', a quantitative notion—entails by definition a 'person-in-right-relationship-to-others' recollects Richard of St. Victor's definition of the trinitarian person as 'an incommunicable existence (*eksistentia*—"a standing out") of the divine nature'—not to mention his intuition that 'God is Love' requires an immanent personal plurality within deity. Otherwise, we may add, creation and its history become necessary to God's essential Being as Love. The relational dimension appears to be a necessary constituent for both God and humanity, and precludes applying any inappropriate or crass anthropocentric connotation of personhood to the Trinity. And while trinitarians of all three types have largely embraced this relational emphasis on personhood in some form or fashion, social trinitarians have done so most consistently or coherently.[19]

modifies the nature of their own individuality in the direction of a corporate person (ality). This would be the one sense from a social trinitarian perspective that the Trinity could be thought of as one person—one corporate person(ality).

[19] Barth, for example, from the point of view of divine threeness plays up the relationality of Father, Son, and Spirit (just as he does *imago Dei* relationality which reflects trinitarian relationality); but from the point of view of their oneness, as 'modes' Father, Son, and Spirit lack ontological and psychological depth severally. Similarly many modern theologians who still work primarily with the traditional

Formally, all three of these dimensions are needed for an adequate concept of the trinitarian person. Some ontological description is necessary to substantiate and individuate Father, Son, and Spirit in their divine mode of being—as discrete *divine persons* (similarly human persons in a human mode of being). Their subjective differences are required by their narratological differentiation: in the scriptures they are revealed as cooperating but distinguishable actors, knowers, willers, lovers, and therefore sentient beings, which is to say conscious beings. And the relational dimension, which now appears quite axiomatic, provides the dialogical check to any excessive individuation of Father, Son, and Spirit. We might therefore summarize our 'trinitarian concept of person' by saying that a person—whether divine or human—is an ontologically discrete, responsible subject of thought, act, and relationship, endowed with understanding and will, and therefore consciousness. Such is our heuristic of trinitarian personhood.[20]

4. THE TRITHEIST CHARGE

Given this strong notion of the trinitarian person supposed by a social analogy and as required by a consistent kenotic model of the Incarnation, how does such a discrete individuation of the trinitarian persons not constitute tritheism? Can the social analogy satisfy the unity claim that there is, essentially, one true God? How does a social trinity not, by Athanasian standards, 'divide the essence'?

Cornelius Plantinga has offered the best defence against this charge by noting that the position ruled out of bounds by this Athanasian prohibition is Arianism.[21] Arianism 'divides the divine essence' *by*

---

scholastic construct, such as Walter Kasper, will highlight the relational dimension relative to the trinitarian persons, but are unable to carry this consistently over in their construal of divine unity. See, for example, Walter Kasper, *The God of Jesus Christ*, trans. Matthew J. O'Connell (New York: Crossroad, 1991).

[20] The term *heuristic* underscores that this is not an attempt at a definitive definition of personhood—divine or human—but a working definition or, better, working description that is open to expansion or revision.

[21] Cornelius Plantinga, Jr., 'Social Trinity and Tritheism', in Feenstra and Plantinga (eds.), *Trinity, Incarnation, and Atonement*, 21–47.

grading the divinity of the trinitarian members. Arius reasoned that the Father alone is Grade A divinity (because the divine essence is single, simple, and therefore incommunicable). The Son and Spirit therefore were accorded a lesser grade of divinity—a created degree of divinity. That there was a time when the Son 'was not' meant that he was a *creature*, but who nevertheless was *worshipped together* with the Father. Arianism therefore is tri- or poly-theistic because it *divided* its worship between Creator and creature.

The social trinity proposes no such thing; it does not grade the divine essence. Though discrete, distinguishable persons in the sense outlined above, Father, Son, and Spirit are all co-equal in deity and therefore co-essential (*homoousios*) with one another. This does entail, of course, taking the divine essence (substance or nature) in a secondary sense, to employ Aristotle's helpful distinction: Father, Son, and Spirit are each a primary substance (as in the Boethian definition: an individual substance of a rational [divine] nature), but who possess the same divine essence generically or secondarily conceived. They are the same sort of thing by nature—a *divine* person— in addition to being the same sort of thing hypostatically—a divine *person*. Thus is satisfied the classic definition of the Trinity: three persons in one essence. Here the social trinity neither blends the persons *à la* Modalism, nor divides the essence *à la* Arianism. It appears therefore a fair hit within the foul lines of confessional trinitarianism.

This generic construal of the divine essence, however, strikes many as an insufficient bond of divine unity (oneness). And perhaps it is. But the social trinitarian can offer other forms of divine unity beyond the essentialistic. One of these forms takes its hint from the trinitarian names in their processive relationships. Father and Son especially connote a relationship beyond the merely sortal, beyond the 'essential fact' that they are of the same divine class of person. Plantinga has termed this form of unity a 'quasi-genetic' unity referring to the relationships of derivation that unite Father, Son, and Spirit in a genetic sort of way—in human experience most akin to a family or blood tie.[22] The Son is not just a divine person like the Father but is

---

[22] Cornelius Plantinga, Jr., 'Social Trinity and Tritheism', in Feenstra and Plantinga (eds.), *Trinity, Incarnation, and Atonement*, 28–9.

eternally generated or begotten by the Father—hence his 'spit and image'. Likewise, though perhaps less evident by name, the Spirit is spirated or breathed from the Father (and/or through the Son, depending upon a western or eastern orientation). Father, Son, and Spirit are therefore bound together by something like the same spiritual blood.

These two senses of divine unity take us back to the paradigm case of the trinitarian determination of the divine *ousia*—the Nicene *homoousios*. In his important studies of this key creedal term, Christopher Stead notes that, while eluding simple definition, *homoousios* certainly does not reduce to what many have taken to be its 'orthodox' sense—namely, that it connotes that Father and Son are the same primary *ousia* or individual thing.[23] Rather, what was intended by the Nicene theologians was at least generic likeness, but most likely something even stronger—that connoting a relationship of derivation, such as a stream to its fountain source: 'To call a son homoousios with his father implies more than merely their common membership of the human race ... the term can evoke their whole biological and social relationship.'[24]

Apropos of the social relationship, it actually constitutes a distinct, third form of unity social trinitarians propose to shore up the oneness claim. The *perichoresis* or perichoretic unity of the trinitarian persons has become quite a fashionable way of articulating the divine unity when the distinction of persons is in view. But this is a venerable theological term that originally achieved wide trinitarian application through John of Damascus's *De fide orthodoxa* (8th century) to convey the 'mutual indwelling' (*circuminsessio*) or 'interpenetration' (*circumincessio*) of the divine persons on the basis of the 'in-ness' passages regarding Father and Son in John's gospel (e.g. 10:30). Though largely construed historically in ontological terms quite parallel to that of the divine *ousia* (if Prestige be right), perichoresis is now taken in a broadly voluntarist direction to connote the volitional, relational ties of life and love shared by Father, Son, and Spirit. In present trinitarian discourse, perichoresis highlights the unity of purpose, fellowship, communion,

---

[23] Stead has Prestige primarily in mind here, 'The Significance of the Homoousios' in *Substance and Illusion in the Christian Fathers* (London: Variorum Reprints, 1985), 399.
[24] *Divine Substance* (Oxford: Oxford University Press, 1977), 248; see esp. 245–50.

hospitality, transparency, self-deference, or just simply the love among Father, Son, and Spirit.

Thus our three essential dimensions of trinitarian personhood each have their complementary forms of unity that preserve the distinction of persons. To the ontological dimension correlates the essential divine unity, generically conceived (three hypostases of one divine *ousia*); the relational dimension corresponds principally (but not exclusively) to the quasi-genetic form of unity; and the subjective-psychological dimension jibes especially with the perichoretic unity of will, purpose, action, and love. While the various dimensions of personhood underscore the *distinction* and *discreteness* of Father, Son, and Spirit, the corresponding (and 'interpenetrating') forms of unity guarantee their distinction while securing against their *division* and *separateness*. Thus is honoured the wisdom of Tertullian's adage that the trinitarian persons are *distincti, non divisi; discreti, non separati* (*Adversus Praxean*).

Still, this trio of forms does not satisfy some that a sufficient account of divine unity has been given on a social model to preclude the tritheist charge. For those inclined to the first trinitarian type, as in Barth's trinitarianism, any triplicating of person in our heuristic sense above constitutes tritheism, since for Barth the primary locus of divine unity is in the singular subjectivity of God (de facto grounded in the 'Father'—the primary locus of personhood—and modally mediated by the 'Son' and 'Spirit'). With the Barthian we simply have a theological impasse on the description of person appropriate to the trinitarian members. But two things should be kept in mind here: one, it need be remembered that the Athanasian benchmark prohibits us to 'blend the persons,' since the failure of classic modalism was that it admitted only one person in God, the liability of the Barthian type; and two, the other Athanasian prohibition is not to 'divide the essence'—note well *essence*, not *persons*, since it is the latter that constitutes a popular conception of the tritheist error. Some simply think that to have more than one person in God is polytheistic. Formally, by trinitarian definition, it is not; it is the material determination of a divine person that is decisive. And while we have offered a meagre description of the trinitarian person that we deem requisite and appropriate, we realize that with some theological temperaments we are simply at an impasse.

A more established objection to the social model comes from trinitarian type (2), the traditional western scholastic model. In this construct 'dividing the divine essence' does not refer simply to the grading of the deity among the divine persons in the fashion of Arianism; it refers also (if not primarily or even exclusively) to any 'dividing the divine indivisibility'. If one reviews the list of post-Patristic tritheists—particularly John Philoponus, Roscelin of Compiègne, and Joachim of Fiore—it becomes clear that they have one theological peccadillo in common: their trinitarian constructs challenged a strict reading of the doctrine of divine simplicity. Philoponus and Joachim were especially concerned to overcome the 'quaternity problem' that dogged trinity doctrine: if Father, Son, and Spirit are concrete hypostases, they constitute three primary substances (and if they are not this, emphasized Roscelin, they are not distinct or discrete persons); but if the common divine nature is also construed as a primary essence—the single thing that God is— this adds up to four primary substances in God. Both Philoponus and Joachim therefore took the divine essence in a more generic sense. *Damnamus* was Lateran IV's response (1215) to Joachim's position, which then proposed to overcome the quaternity glitch by shoring up the divine unity in the strongest possible way—by insisting on the doctrine of divine simplicity, which makes each of the divine persons identical with the one simple primary divine essence.

From this traditional vantage point, whatever is considered proper to the one divine nature—itself the primary substance, the thing that God is—cannot be triplicated. This actually amounts to everything[25] *except* that novel hybrid category between substance and accident: the subsistent relation, identifiable only by virtue of the *relations of opposition* among the divine persons—namely, *paternitas, filatio, spiratio.* By definition, therefore, in type (2) trinitarianism, tritheism involves the triplicating of any general personal characteristic—such as 'mind', 'will', or 'consciousness'—or summary term—such as 'self', 'subject', 'centre of act', 'personality', or just simply 'person' in any commonsense, low-level description, since this would involve a

---

[25] Because, as Thomas would affirm, everything predicated of God is identical with the single undifferentiated substance which God is, since whatever is not the divine nature is a creature. *Summa Theologica* I, q.28a.2.

multiplying of the one divine essence. Here there is simply no allowance for three minds or wills or consciousnesses in God—though it needs to be noted that theologians of this persuasion will talk about such features in the plural, but only *relative* to the divine persons, not to the divine essence which has the final unitive say. Hence the logic of relative identity: in God-the-Trinity there are three consciousnesses (relative to the trinitarian persons), but only one consciousness (relative to the divine nature); hence the popular confusion over the Trinity that it is a mysterious, if not contradictory, doctrine.

While the doctrine of divine simplicity may have appeared axiomatic to theologians of the past, its truth is not so self-evident today. God's simplicity or indivisibility, a *via negativa* attribute, makes sense if God is principally conceived of as One supreme substance (or being) in contrast to the transient, decaying world of the Many. Unlike the ostensible world of the Many, whose parts break down, deteriorate, decay, and disappear into oblivion, Supreme Being must be immune to the physics of plurality-ergo-decay—that is, without parts, therefore one simple, single thing (from this also logically follows strict immutability, impassibility, apathy, as well as eternality construed as timelessness). While there are other reasons theologians have mustered for God's simplicity, which we wish not to oversimplify, the Greek metaphysics of the One and the Many remain, as far as we can sound, the deep grammar of indivisibility. And if this is so, there are a couple of assumptions implicit in this framework that can be questioned. First, should the category of substance, and here the divine nature construed as a primary essence, be prioritized over the category of personhood? Or should we be open to rethinking what a substance is in light of our understanding of persons as the primary examples of substances? If the former is the case, there is really no substantial room, as both Sabellius and Arius realized, for a plurality of persons of full divine status. And, in point of fact, we have cited the traditional western model for reducing the trinitarian persons to mere 'relations', dissolved as they substantially are into the one simple primary substance that God essentially is. The social trinitarian, without in the least eschewing the category of substance, would want to prioritize persons as primary substances as befits the biblical narrative in which God-the-Trinity is revealed in the personal.

Secondly, the assumption that God's nature as One must be con-
trasted with the world as Many appears nothing short of a gnostic
assumption that the material individuation in the world (matter as
the principle of individuation) is intrinsically defective. And here one
need only recall the first chapter of Genesis to refute such a supposition. If manyness, diversity, and otherness are, as a whole in creation,
'very good', then why not also essentially for God?

The notion of God's metaphysical indivisibility (simplicity) is, at
best, a datum of natural theology. We know of no biblical theologian
today—Old Testament or New—who would venture to read (exegete) this out of any biblical text. In point of fact, the Bible as a whole
says really little about the oneness of God, and when it does, its
metaphysical claim for such oneness is more basic. Take the famed
Shema (Deut. 6:4), for instance, the basic monotheistic creed. In its
original setting, it is surely a henotheistic injunction to monolatry,
and best translated along the lines of, 'Hear O Israel, Yahweh is our
God, Yahweh alone.'[26] To be sure, in the course of redemptive history
the Shema gets a fuller monotheistic connotation, as seen especially
in second Isaiah or Jeremiah. But what is that expanding connotation? Does it have reference to the inner constitution of God, as in an
ontological indivisibility? We think not; rather, the clear monotheistic development has everything to do with the Creator–creature
distinction: Yahweh it turns out is more than just Israel's national
god, Yahweh is actually the one true God because Yahweh is the
Creator of heaven and earth; every other claim to deity is a pompous
predication by a creature or a misplaced praise by a worshipper.[27]
Though we cannot elaborate this issue fully here, as far as we can see,
the biblical definition of monotheism has everything to do with the
Creator–creature divide. That is its basic metaphysical claim. If

[26] The variant reading, 'Hear O Israel, Yahweh is our God, Yahweh is one' is
grammatically acceptable, and even theologically acceptable *if* such oneness is understood to serve the unification of the manifestations of Yahweh from multiple pro-
vincialization—e.g. 'Yahweh of Samaria', 'Yahweh of Teman', etc. The latter could
easily lead to a division in the divine character and purpose. But even on this reading,
divine oneness has to do with *character and purpose*, not a quantity of divine persons
or ontological constituency. See, for example, Patrick D. Miller, *Deuteronomy*, Interpretation Series (Louisville: John Knox, 1990), 97–104.

[27] See, for instance, Jeremiah 10:1–16 for the basic aspects of this metaphysical
claim of Old Testament monotheism.

Yahweh alone is Creator, then Yahweh alone is the Sovereign Lord. The pretence of all other gods is the vacuous hubris of creatures.

If this is the basic sense of biblical monotheism, and if the basic Christian confession is that in the New Testament the God of Israel is revealed as Father, Son, and Spirit who are all on the side of the Creator, then the violation of the monotheistic confession would not have to do with the number of concrete divine persons revealed as the Creator God (creation being in Christian confession a trinitarian act of Father, Son, and Spirit) but rather with the transgression of the Creator–creature distinction. And if so, that would take us back to Arianism as the prime exemplar of 'dividing the essence', since it polytheistically violates the monotheistic confession by also *divinizing the creature* in its assessment of, and worship of, Christ, and, fightingly later, the Spirit.

So we are left with this basic theological question: What is the sufficient condition of tritheism as the violation of monotheism? If the sufficient condition of monotheism is the observation of the Creator–creature distinction, as we believe the Scriptures portray, then something akin to Arianism is the sufficient condition of tritheism. And in this case, the social trinity would not be tritheistic. But if another sufficient condition of tritheism is the abrogation of divine simplicity in the fashion of the post-Patristic tritheists condemned by Lateran IV, then the social analogy would have to be judged tritheistic. The social trinitarian thinks there are good reasons for challenging the axiom of simplicity, which, in truth, no longer appears axiomatic to most. Here is a long-sponsored datum of natural theology that can be trumped by Scripture.

A consistent kenotic model of the Incarnation posits a strict personal identity between the eternal Son of God and Jesus of Nazareth, of the Logos who became flesh in a human rational soul. Such a model quite obviously highlights the ontological discreteness of the trinitarian persons and has raised the objection that kenoticism violates the doctrine of the Trinity, a criticism that takes a variety of forms. While the debate will continue on just how a kenotically weakened Son continues to qualify as a divine denizen, this chapter has focused on the particular trinitarian form required by a consistent kenoticism. That form is some sort of social analogy of the Trinity that sponsors a strong notion of the trinitarian person, a heuristic of personhood we attempted to 'flesh out'. To the objection that this sunders the *indivisa* of trinitarian persons and their operations, we confess the transgression, if their indivisibility is understood in a strict ontological way that diminishes the substantial distinction of persons. Indivisibility, however, can be understood perichoretically, in the sense that the divine persons are volitionally undivided in purpose, life, and love. To the most serious charge that this entails a tritheism, we have offered a defence that we deem sufficiently biblical. We believe that the nexus kenotic Incarnation–social Trinity is not only a wedding of doctrines that cohere with and complement one another, but it may also be a union that brings out the very best in each other. Here is a doctrinal marriage that holds much promise in explicating, with all due appreciation, the God who is consummate Love and who has stooped low for our salvation.

8

Kenotic Christology and the Nature of God

C. Stephen Evans

Christians have traditionally believed that God is most fully revealed in the life, death, and resurrection of Jesus of Nazareth, understood as both fully human and divine. Because Jesus is fully human, we can attain some understanding of his life; because he is fully divine, this understanding gives us insight into the heart of God. If this line of thought is sound, it follows that our understanding of God's nature must be closely related to our Christology.

It is not surprising, then, that kenotic Christology, the account of the Incarnation that emphasizes the loving 'self-emptying' of God in Christ, first developed in the nineteenth century by such German theologians as Thomasius, with later elaborations by such British thinkers as Charles Gore and Frank Weston, should have inspired a 'kenotic theism' which sees the activity of 'self-emptying' to be a key to understanding the divine nature. In a recent volume edited by John Polkinghorne, *The Work of Love: Creation as Kenosis*, a diverse group of authors attempts to understand God's activity in creating and ordering the world in terms of the notion of a love that involves a costly giving on God's part.[1] What is surprising in that volume, however, is how little attention the authors actually pay to a kenotic understanding of Christ. In a helpful critical review article that concludes the book, Sarah Coakley distinguishes three types of meanings of kenosis: the term can be primarily Christological, primarily Trinitarian, or it can primarily refer to God's relation to

---

[1] *The Work of Love: Creation as Kenosis* (Grand Rapids, MI: Wm. B. Eerdmans, 2001).

creation. Coakley finds it to be a striking feature of *The Work of Love* 'that most of its contributors construe the significance of kenosis in this third, generalized sense—addressing God's relation to the world—and tend to turn to christological or trinitarian meanings only as a subsequent—paradigmatic or illustrative—move'.[2]

Most of the essays in that volume could be taken as illustrating Coakley's point. Ian Barbour, for example, writes about 'God's Power: A Process View' and attempts therein to show the ways in which process theism is congruent with themes in kenotic theism. Process theology 'offers a path between omnipotence and impotence by reconceptualizing divine power as empowerment rather than overpowering control'.[3] However, the life and death of Jesus do not, in Barbour's essay, play a prominent role, but seem rather to be something like a supremely important example: '[I]n the Incarnation and in Christ's death God participated in human suffering and showed the power of redeeming love.'[4] However, there is a gap even between the story of Jesus and the theological truths the story represents, since the voluntariness that is so crucial to Jesus' sacrificial life is not really present in the life of God. The limitations on God's power are metaphysical necessities for Barbour, not the result of an act of self-limitation on God's part.[5]

Arthur Peacocke and Holmes Rolston continue this trend of bringing in the Incarnation as a kind of illustrative paradigm by discussing kenosis primarily with reference to a scientific understanding of the natural world. Peacocke looks at the evolutionary processes as revelatory of God: 'The processes themselves, as unveiled by the biological sciences, *are* God-acting-as-Creator, God *qua* Creator'.[6] We come to understand God as participating in the suffering of the natural world by seeing the nature of the processes that go on in that world. The story of Jesus is seen by Peacocke as providing a 'warrant' for the beliefs about God's nature that the scientific story provides; without faith in Christ the account of God's nature rooted in science would be no more than a 'reasonable conjecture'. But this

---

[2] 'Kenosis: Theological Meanings and Gender Connotations', in Polkinghorne, *The Work of Love*, 193.

[3] Polkinghorne, *The Work of Love*, 20.   [4] Ibid. 8.

[5] Ibid. 12–13.

[6] 'The Cost of New Life', in Polkinghorne, *The Work of Love*, 23.

'conjecture' is 'reinforced, indeed overtly revealed—that is, communicated by God—if God is truly self-expressed in Jesus the Christ'.[7] A
similar tale is told by Holmes Rolston, who emphasizes that the
biological picture is not merely one of the 'selfish gene', but a story
that involves cooperation and even sacrifice, a story that gives us an
image of 'cruciform nature'.[8] (Though Rolston is careful to say that
the only true kenosis in the natural order is found in human moral
activity; there is no true kenosis in nature because there is nothing
voluntary there.)

   In this essay I wish, like the authors of *The Work of Love*, to look at
the links between kenotic Christology and kenotic theism. However,
taking Coakley's hint, I want to give greater attention than did those
authors to kenotic Christology. Rather than beginning with science,
as Peacocke and Rolston do, or metaphysical speculation about the
nature of God, and then turning to the Incarnation to illustrate or
vindicate the views proffered, I want to ask what it might mean for
our understanding of God's nature if Christ's Incarnation involves
kenosis and we truly believe that the Incarnation is the best means we
have for gaining insight into God's nature.

THE GOD OF THE PHILOSOPHERS AND THE BIBLICAL GOD

One way of looking at the issues that I shall address is in terms of the
often-discussed tension between the 'God of the philosophers' and
the 'God of Abraham, Isaac, and Jacob', to use Pascal's famous
terminology. The tension here has been crisply characterized by
William Alston as 'between God as "wholly other" and God as a
partner in interpersonal relationships, between God as the absolute,
ultimate source of all being and God as the dominant actor on the
stage of history'.[9] To what degree should a Christian understanding of

---

   [7] 'The Cost of New Life', in Polkinghorne, *The Work of Love*, 41.

   [8] 'Kenosis and Nature', in Polkinghorne, *The Work of Love*, 58.

   [9] 'Divine–Human Dialogue and the Nature of God', in *Divine Nature and Human Language: Essays in Philosophical Theology* (Ithaca, New York: Cornell University Press, 1989), 147.

God be shaped by considerations drawn from philosophical theology and to what degree from considerations drawn from Biblical theology?[10] I do not mean to suggest that these two kinds of considerations can be completely isolated from each other. We cannot read the Biblical revelation without bringing to it some philosophical assumptions. No serious Christian theologian, for example, infers from Exodus 33:18–23, in which God is said to allow Moses to see his back but covers Moses' eyes so Moses cannot see God's face, that God has a body. Nor is our philosophical speculation innocent and 'presuppositionless'. Those of us who are the product of many centuries of Christian culture can hardly pretend that our philosophical thinking is not shaped, at least unconsciously, by the Biblical narrative.

Neither do I mean to imply that the God of the philosophers is necessarily incompatible with the God of the Biblical revelation. The task of the systematic theologian is in part the task of producing an account of God that does justice to both sources of insight, and I certainly do not wish to suggest that this task is an impossible one. It is, however, a task that at times involves tension, since philosophical reflection and Biblical narrative do not always pull us in the same direction. The Old Testament is full of passages that speak of God 'repenting' and changing his mind, such as Genesis 6:7, where God says he is 'grieved' over his action in creating humans.[11] Such passages naturally suggest a God who has a successive mental life and is capable of changing his mind. Most Christian theologians have, however, under the influence of a conception of perfection heavily influenced by Greek philosophy, seen God as atemporally eternal and completely immutable. Therefore, while most Christian theologians may agree that both philosophical and Biblical considerations have force in developing an adequate view of God, there are lots of disagreements over the relative weighting of these kinds of considerations.

---

[10] This issue is a central theme in Ronald Feenstra's essay in this volume, 'A Kenotic Christological Method for Understanding the Divine Attributes'. As will become evident, I try in this essay to follow Feenstra's suggestion that Biblical considerations be given primary consideration in thinking about God's nature.

[11] For a good overview of these passages and some of the scholarly commentary on them, see John Sanders, *The God Who Risks: A Theology of Providence* (Downers Grove, Illinois: Inter-Varsity Press, 1998), ch. 3.

What I propose to do in this essay is to explore the consequences of allowing the Biblical story of Jesus as God Incarnate, interpreted kenotically, to have significant weight in determining how we conceive the nature of God. Rather than developing an account of the Incarnation that presupposes we have a fixed account of what it is to be God and which then tries to make sense of the possibility that God conceived in this way has become human, I want to see how a particular account of the Incarnation might require us to revise our understanding of the nature of God.

Someone might object to this procedure on the grounds that a kenotic interpretation of the Incarnation is hardly the only possible one, and that such an interpretation already presupposes certain philosophical views. I cheerfully concede both these points. Any particular Christological theory will always be just that: a particular theory to which there are alternatives. And no theory of the Incarnation, nor any reading of the Bible, can pretend to be philosophically innocent. However, for those who see kenotic Christology as plausible and worthwhile, it seems equally worthwhile to think about how taking seriously such a view of the Incarnation might push us towards a revised understanding of God. I do not, of course, want to claim that one could develop an account of the nature of God entirely by beginning with the Incarnational narrative, however interpreted; if we did not have some prior understanding of what the term 'God' means we could attach no meaning to the claim that Jesus was God. The fact that we must have such a prior understanding of God to formulate an account of the Incarnation does not, however, mean that our concept of God cannot be significantly reshaped in the light of that doctrine.

A SKETCH OF A KENOTIC CHRISTOLOGY

I do not intend in this chapter to give an extended argument for the plausibility or even the coherence of a kenotic account of Christ's Incarnation, though I have done so in a previous essay.[12] Rather, my

[12] 'The Self-Emptying of Love: Some Thoughts on Kenotic Christology', in Stephen Davis, Daniel Kendall, S.J., and Gerald O'Collins, S.J. (eds.), *The Incarnation*

essay has two main aims, and will therefore have two main parts. First, I will try to develop in this section and the next a version of kenotic Christology that will be ample enough to allow us to think about its implications. Having briefly developed a version of kenotic Christology, in the latter sections of the chapter I will try to explore what such a Christology might mean for our understanding of the nature of God. I want then to approach the question of what a kenotic theism might mean in light of kenotic Christology.

Let me say at the outset that I do not conceive of kenotic Christology as an alternative to Chalcedonian orthodoxy, but rather as one particular way of trying to make sense of the Incarnation and remain within the boundaries of orthodox Christian belief.[13] Kenotic Christology is inspired by Philippians 2:6–11, which speaks of Christ as one who 'being in very nature God' still 'emptied himself' or 'made himself nothing' (NIV).[14] The Greek verb for 'empty' (*kenoo*) is of course the source of the English noun 'kenosis' and its adjective form

(Oxford: Oxford University Press, 2002). For defences of kenotic Christology, also see R. J. Feenstra, 'Reconsidering Kenotic Christology', in R. J. Feenstra and C. Plantinga, Jr. (eds.), *Trinity, Incarnation, and Atonement* (Notre Dame, IN: University of Notre Dame Press, 1989), 128–53, and Stephen Davis, *Logic and the Nature of God* (Grand Rapids, Michigan: Wm. B. Eerdmans, 1983). Also see Davis's own contributions to *Encountering Jesus: A Debate on Christology* (Atlanta: John Knox Press, 1988).

[13] I am therefore fully supportive of Stephen Davis's argument in his essay in this volume that kenotic Christology is orthodox. I here follow Sarah Coakley's point that Chalcedon does not itself provide us with a particular theory of how Christ can be God Incarnate while being fully human, but rather establishes boundaries or parameters for views to be orthodox. In claiming my view is consistent with Chalcedon, I do not therefore mean to imply that it would have been acceptable to the authors of Chalcedon. I believe that there are probably numerous accounts of the Incarnation consistent with the Chalcedonian boundaries that the authors of Chalcedon would have rejected had they been presented with them.

[14] I am well aware that J. D. G. Dunn has given an influential interpretation of this passage in Philippians that eliminates the idea that the self-emptying of Christ involved a giving up of divine prerogatives by a pre-existent Son of God to become human in favour of the claim that the 'self-emptying' spoken of is entirely a matter of the voluntary acceptance by Jesus of servanthood and crucifixion with all that they involve. Dunn's interpretation seems unconvincing to me, because it does not cohere well with the apparent meaning of the clause that Christ 'was in very nature God' (NIV), and it loses some of the parallelism implicit in the 'descent and ascent' structure of the passage, which certainly concludes with a glorification that gives Christ divine or nearly divine status. It seems to me that Dunn's reading has obvious appeal to those who are convinced a priori that Paul (or whoever was the author of

'kenotic'. This self-emptying does not stop with Christ's becoming human but goes to the extreme of 'taking the very nature of a servant' and becoming 'obedient to death, even death on a cross'. As a consequence of this willingness to empty himself, God has rewarded Christ by giving him 'a name that is above every name'. Other New Testament passages that seem to support the idea that Christ's Incarnation involves a kenosis include 2 Corinthians 8:9, Acts 10:38, Luke 2:52, and Hebrews 5:7–9. In the final analysis, however, the idea of Christ's Incarnation as kenotic in character is supported not merely by individual passages of Scripture, but by the character of Jesus' life and death as a whole. The particular passages highlight a characteristic that is pervasively present in the entire narrative of Jesus' life and death.

Once Jesus is incarnate as a human person, the character of this self-emptying is readily apparent. The New Testament portrait of Jesus tells a story of a person who takes no thought for the ordinary personal interests that dominate most human lives. He has no wife or home, no career or interest in the accumulation of possessions. Instead he gives himself wholly to the proclamation of the kingdom of God and the nurture of his followers. He finally gives his very life as 'a ransom for many', not shirking a painful and shameful death for the sake of the redemption of human beings.[15]

Kenotic Christology affirms that the first and in some ways most decisive phase of this self-emptying process is seen in the second person of the Trinity's becoming a human being. In this act, God the Son chose to 'empty himself' of some of his divine prerogatives and fully enter into the life of a human being. When incarnated, God himself experiences the life of a finite, bodily being and all the limitations of such a life.

Philippians) could not have had a high concept of the Incarnation involving pre-existence at such an early date. However, to those who (like myself) think that the meaning of Scripture should be controlled by 'the rule of faith', and who believe that a passage should thus be construed in light of the overall Biblical message as this has been understood by the Church, there is no convincing reason to take Dunn's view of the passage. See J. D. G. Dunn, *Christology in the Making* (London: S.C.M. Press, 1980), ch. 4.

[15] Clearly, the narrative as I recount it here is heavily theologically coloured, but it should be recalled that kenotic Christology as I understand it is an attempt to understand the person of Jesus within the bounds of Chalcedonian orthodoxy.

Traditional understandings of the Incarnation have focused on God's becoming human as a process of addition. On such a view God adds to his divine nature a human nature, including a human soul and a human body, and through that human nature experiences the limitations of the common human life. From the point of view of orthodoxy, this perspective must be basically sound. The pre-existent Son of God already has a divine nature, and acquires a human nature in the Incarnation without ceasing to be divine. However, this does not mean that the Incarnation involves no substantive changes to the divine nature. We must ask the question what it means for the divine nature to become incarnate, to become enfleshed and live a bodily life. Certainly the Incarnation involves an addition to God, but we must ask whether the event is merely additive in nature or whether it also involves some kind of transformation of God the Son.

If one begins with the classical conception of God as timeless and absolutely immutable, the answer must be that the Incarnation involves no change at all in the divine nature. Christ's Incarnation is merely the temporal effect of a timeless divine intention. However, in this essay I want to see what kind of conception of God most naturally follows if we make the Incarnation itself the starting point for our thinking about God's nature. It seems safe to say that a conception of God as timeless and immutable would not be the most natural view of God if one took seriously the idea that the Incarnation itself is our primary window into God's being. For the Incarnation seems to shout to us that God is intimately involved in the temporal world and capable of change that is radical and even shocking in character. What is missing, in my view, if we think of the Incarnation merely as the temporal outcome of a timeless divine intention, is any sense that God himself *enters* the human condition, takes on human flesh, and experiences reality as a human does. If there is no change in God, what could it mean to say that God himself *takes on* human nature? A real Incarnation must not be merely an addition to God; it must make some difference to God and in God.

Once we are open to the possibility of change in God, then the further question arises what kind of change might be involved in God's becoming incarnate? The suggestion of the kenotic Christologist is that, in becoming human, God decided to divest himself at least temporarily of some of the divine properties, such as omnipotence, omniscience, and omnipresence. A decision to become a human being is, for example, a decision to be located in a particular place and this seems incompatible with omnipresence. Naturally, this view implies that such properties as omnipotence, omniscience, and omnipresence are not essential to be divine, since on an orthodox view Christ retains his divinity and thus divine nature during his earthly career. Contrary to what we might otherwise have thought, the kenoticist says that this provides us with good reason to think that what is essential to being divine is not the possession of such properties as omnipotence and omniscience, but rather such properties as 'being-omnipotent-unless-freely-choosing-to-limit-one's-power'.[16]

Some have objected that a being with such properties as 'being-omnipotent-unless-freely-choosing-to-limit-one's-power' would not be as 'perfect' as a being possessing properties such as omnipotence *simpliciter*, and God must be assumed to be 'a being than which none greater can be conceived', to use Anselm's memorable words.[17] However, it is by no means obvious that a being that is unable to restrict itself or limit itself in any way is more perfect than one that has such powers. I will later argue that a God not capable of self-limitation is in fact less perfect than a God who can limit himself. However, whatever our intuitions about divine perfections may be, one can question how reliable those intuitions are, especially intuitions about the three persons of a Trinitarian God. Suppose it is true that our a priori intuitions support the claim that a God with omnipotence would be more perfect than one with the corresponding kenotically qualified property (being-omnipotent-unless-freely-willing-to-limit-one's-power). (Though this is not the case for my own intuitions.) Also suppose, as I would, that God is the greatest possible being. If we believe the Incarnation is a reality and that it involved God's divesting himself of omnipotence, this might provide us with a

---

[16] This line of thought was suggested by Thomas Morris in *The Logic of God Incarnate* (Ithaca, New York: Cornell University Press, 1986), 75. It has also been taken by Ronald Feenstra and Stephen Davis in the works cited above.

[17] It is for this reason that Thomas Morris ultimately rejects a kenotic theory of the Incarnation in favour of a 'two-minds' theory.

reason to question our intuitions about perfection. In that case we would have a clear illustration of the ways in which faithfulness to the Biblical story might induce us to rethink our philosophically influenced conception of God.[18]

Kenotic accounts of the Incarnation have several strengths, I believe. One is that the religious power and meaning of the Incarnation are heightened. God's decision to become human is a costly decision to share fully in the human condition. Christ does not retain omnipotence and omniscience in reserve, so to speak, to be pulled out of the hip pocket in case of emergency.

A second strength is that a kenotic theory most naturally gives us a portrait of a unified Christ, certainly having two natures but constituting a single person with a single mind and body. Most rivals to a kenotic theory have postulated that Christ possessed 'two minds' or 'two systems of consciousness'.[19] With respect to his human mind Jesus is finite in knowledge and capable of ignorance and perhaps error, but with respect to his divine mind he is omniscient. But what does it mean to conceive of a single person with two minds? In what way is this person a unified single person?

Yet a third strength of the kenotic account is that it coheres well with the very human portrait of Jesus that we see in the gospels. An honest reading of the New Testament reveals a Jesus who seems to share the normal limitations all humans experience. Jesus is pictured as ignorant at times (Mark 13:31ff.). He is said to progress in his wisdom and knowledge in the way that all children do (Luke 2:52). Jesus is seen as a person who experiences hunger, feels weariness, and even expresses deep frustration (the latter in John 11:33). The writer of Hebrews says that Jesus was tempted in the same ways as other humans are, which seems to imply the possibility of moral failure (Hebrews 4:15). This sketch of the very human qualities of Jesus in the New Testament could easily be expanded of course.

---

[18] See Ronald Feenstra's chapter in this volume, 'A Kenotic Christological Method for Understanding the Divine Attributes', for a developed version of this methodological point.

[19] See, for example, Thomas Morris, *The Logic of God Incarnate*, and Richard Swinburne, *The Christian God* (Oxford: Clarendon Press, 1994), ch. 9.

KENOSIS AND GLORIFICATION: MUST KENOSIS BE
TEMPORARY?

Most kenotic theorists have conceived of the divestiture of such properties as omnipotence as temporary, and have thought that the glorified Christ has regained full omnipotence, omniscience, omnipresence, and other such properties. It is tempting to think of this temporary divestiture as a voluntary decision by God the Son not to exercise these properties during his earthly career, and this may indeed be one way of conceiving of the matter. However, I believe that for real kenosis the decision must not be thought of as a continuous decision to restrict the employment of these properties, a decision that can be revoked at any time. Such a continuous decision that can be revoked at any time does not look like a case of 'emptying' but rather simply a case of not using a power that one continues to have. I shall assume that a decision by God the Son to restrict the use of such properties must be in some way binding on himself.

One may ask whether and how Christ can reacquire such properties in his glorified state if they have really been given up. Critics have argued that if the glorified Christ retains his humanity and yet possesses the traditional divine properties, this shows that Incarnation does not require kenosis. Here there are several options for the kenoticist. One is to question whether the glorified Christ, assuming that he continues to be fully human, necessarily must possess all of the traditional divine properties. A second option is to agree that kenosis is not necessary for Incarnation; it is simply the particular way God chose to become incarnate. God's Incarnation can then continue even though the kenosis does not. The resumption of the traditional divine properties can be understood as accomplished by the power of the Father and the Spirit, who bestow glorification on the Son, who merits it by virtue of his sacrificial life and death, as Philippians 2:9 suggests.

This second option can be strengthened if we hold, as Ronald Feenstra has suggested, that kenosis might not be necessary for *being* incarnate, even though it might be necessary for *becoming* incarnate.[20] I think this idea is plausible, particularly if we understand the Son's decision to divest himself of some of the divine properties as equivalent to a decision to become incarnate in the kind of physical bodies humans currently have. Every account of the Incarnation must give prominence to the fact that God has assumed a bodily life; that is what Incarnation means. Athanasius, for example, in his classical work *On the Incarnation*, affirms over and over again that in Christ the divine Word 'took to himself a body, a human body even as our own'.[21] This human body is not a mere receptacle for Athanasius, but the 'instrument' that God chose to live through.[22] I do not of course mean to imply that Athanasius was an advocate of kenotic Christology, but merely want to emphasize how central the idea of 'taking a body' is to all accounts of the Incarnation.

The kenotic theorist wishes to ask what this decision on God's part to assume a bodily form of existence really entails, what it means to live through a body. It seems plausible that if the Son decided to live as a bodily human being, living his mental life as other humans do through the physical processes that occur in the brain and central nervous system, then he would be deciding to accept certain limitations. It seems likely that a being whose mental life depends on a finite physical brain could not be omniscient, and that such a being would have to be finite in physical power and limited in time and space. A decision to become incarnate in that kind of body may then require a kenosis, and I suggest that we understand Feenstra's suggestion to be the claim that becoming incarnate in an *ordinary* human body requires a kenosis.

However, the New Testament picture of Christ's glorified resurrection body, though sketchy to a high degree, includes the claim that this resurrected body is a 'spiritual body' that differs dramatically from our ordinary human bodies. It has, for example, the power to pass through a solid physical wall. Perhaps a continued Incarnation in such a glorified body would be compatible with reacquiring and possessing the traditional divine attributes. On this view Christ's Incarnation in an ordinary human body may have required a kenosis,

[20] R. J. Feenstra, 'Reconsidering Kenotic Christology'.
[21] St. Athanasius, *On the Incarnation*, trans. and ed. by a religious of C.S.M.V. (Crestwood, New York: St. Vladimir's Seminary Press), 34.
[22] Ibid.

but the kind of body he possesses in his glorified state may be compatible with the reassumption of all the traditional theistic properties.

KENOSIS AND DIVINE SELF-LIMITATION

If we take a kenotic account of the Incarnation to be at least roughly true, and if we assume that Christ's Incarnation should play a decisive role in shaping our understanding of God, what does this imply? I am going to focus on just one part of the answer to this question, by examining the idea that God's self-emptying in Christ tells us something fundamental about God's own capacity to limit himself. However, before this discussion, I want to note in passing how many avenues could be explored in looking at the meaning of a kenotic Incarnation for understanding God's nature. The implications of kenotic Christology for kenotic theism are broad and profound. I could focus, for example, on the meaning of the central Christian affirmation that 'God is love.' The nature of that love is most clearly shown in the selflessness shown by the Son of God both in his earthly life and death and in his willingness to give up the security of his heavenly mode of being to become incarnate as a human being.[23]

Another avenue that I would have liked to explore in this connection, but will only have space to mention, concerns the powerful relevance of thinking of God kenotically to the problem of evil, a theme that is well-addressed in *The Work of Love*. In responding to this problem many Christian thinkers today make a distinction between a theodicy and a defence. A theodicy would be an explanation of why God allows bad things to occur, a 'justification of the ways of God to humans'. A defence, however, has a more modest goal, arguing that it is reasonable to believe that God has a good reason for permitting evil even if we do not know what that reason is. Since God surpasses humans in power and knowledge even more than an adult

---

[23] See, for example, the essay by George Ellis, 'Kenosis as a Unifying Theme for Life and Cosmology', in *The Work of Love*. Also see the essay by Ruth Groenhout in this volume for a rebuttal to the feminist charge that selfless love is an ideal that is destructive for women.

human surpasses a human infant, it is reasonable to believe that humans may have no more ability to understand God's ways than a small child can understand all that adults do.[24]

It has long been recognized that God's Incarnation in Christ provides powerful backing to such a defence. For it is clear that for a defence to be successful, we need more than the bare possibility that God has good reasons for permitting evil. We need some reason to believe that God is good that justifies faith that he has such reasons even when we do not know what they are. An Incarnation that includes suffering to the point of painful death is powerful testimony to the goodness of God. If we believe God's character is revealed in Christ, we have reason to believe in God's love and goodness even if we do not understand all of God's actions. I believe that a kenotic understanding of the Incarnation significantly deepens the ground of this faith, for on the kenotic view God has in Christ completely identified with the human condition. He has made himself vulnerable to all the common ills of humanity, and has no hidden divine powers to be called forth in a pinch. In facing the frustrations and even terrors of human existence, Christ must depend entirely on the Father and the comfort of the Spirit. An assurance of love towards us as sufferers is far more powerful if it comes from one who has shown a willingness to share fully in our sufferings.

However, let me turn from these issues to the implication of kenotic Christology I do wish to explore: the way in which God's action in Christ powerfully demonstrates God's capacity and desire to limit himself out of love. This theme is addressed by the authors of *The Work of Love*, but these authors look primarily at God's activity in creation, highlighting the way in which God 'steps back' from the creation and respects its integrity, allows it to 'do its thing', so to speak. This 'stepping back' can also be powerfully seen in the human freedom that is a divine gift. God seems to go to great lengths not to override the human power to choose, tolerating horrendous evils and refusing to 'overawe' humans by a too-obvious manifestation of his glory that might induce a response to his will based on naked fear.

---

[24] See Stephen Wykstra, 'Rowe's Noseeum Argument from Evil', in Daniel Howard-Snyder (ed.), *The Evidential Problem of Evil* (Bloomington, IN: Indiana University Press, 1996) for a clear example of this line of argument.

I believe this characteristic divine activity of self-limitation comes into clearest resolution when we focus on God's Incarnation. God comes to humans in the form of a lowly servant. His outward appearance is not necessarily such as to command immediate respect. He performs mighty works as signs, but those signs are obviously ones that do not compel assent, since Jesus himself laments the fact that many who lived in the cities that have witnessed his greatest miracles have not responded with faith and repentance.[25] Even when God reveals himself in Christ, he does so in a way that allows those who do not wish to believe 'room' to reject him. Perhaps it is only in this way that we can see the love of God most clearly exhibited. We would doubtless respond to a God who dazzled us with glory or frightened us with his might, but would we really be responding to God's inmost nature if these scenarios were realized?

This self-limitation so clearly seen in the incarnate Christ undergirds almost all of the themes explored by the 'kenotic theists' in *The Work of Love*. If the notion of God 'stepping back' from creation or human choice is to be more than a metaphor, then we must be able to make sense of the idea that God is capable of limiting himself in some way. However, it has often been claimed that divine omnipotence cannot limit itself. For example, many of the resolutions favoured by philosophers for the 'paradox of the stone', the paradox posed by the question whether God could create a stone that he could not himself move, depend on the supposition that the possibility of such a stone is incoherent. God cannot create such a stone, because not even omnipotence can do what is logically incoherent, and the possibility of a self-imposed limitation on the part of God is indeed incoherent.

I do not wish to discuss the paradox of the stone itself at great length, because the problem posed in this form may seem to be trivial. However, the issue posed by the paradox is not trivial at all; it lies at the heart of our conception of God. It is at least not self-evident or obvious that an inability to limit oneself is a perfection. Kierkegaard, for one, doubts that this is so, and affirms that God's omnipotence affords him *greater* possibilities for self-limitation than lesser beings. In comparing God's Incarnation to Socrates' pose of ignorance and the king in the fairy tale who woos a peasant maiden

[25] See Matthew 11:20–4.

in disguise, Kierkegaard affirms that God can enter more deeply into the limited world of the one he wishes to have a relationship with, because God has what we might call a superior ability to limit himself: 'For this is the boundlessness of love, that in earnestness and truth and not in jest it wills to be the equal of the beloved, and it is the omnipotence of resolving love to be capable of that which neither the king nor Socrates was capable, which is why their assumed characters were still a kind of deceit.'[26]

If God the Son has in his Incarnation divested himself of such properties as omnipotence and omniscience, then self-limitation is not merely a possibility for God but an actuality. If God's Incarnation as Jesus of Nazareth is the primary window we have into the nature of God, then we would expect self-limitation not merely to be within the range of God's possibilities, but to be characteristic of God's actions, especially insofar as such self-limitation is an expression of love for what is genuinely other. All of the dimensions of God's kenotic activity discussed in *The Work of Love* depend on this possibility, and much else besides, for it is at least arguable that God cannot make promises and enter into covenantal relations if he cannot bind himself. If self-limitation lies at the heart of the Incarnation, then the Incarnation will be more than merely an illustration or paradigm of God's relations to the created world. It will be the revelatory event that gives us a picture of God's nature that illumines a central characteristic of those relations. The possibility of divine self-limitation is then a crucial issue not merely for kenotic Christology, but theology in general.

IS DIVINE SELF-LIMITATION POSSIBLE?

Many critics of belief in God have found the whole idea of an omnipotent God who allows any independence to his creation or

---

[26] Søren Kierkegaard, *Philosophical Fragments* (Princeton: Princeton University Press, 1985), 32. Strictly speaking, the voice here is not that of Kierkegaard's, but of his pseudonymous creation Johannes Climacus. For more on the relation between Climacus and Kierkegaard see my *Kierkegaard's Fragments and Postscript: The Religious Philosophy of Johannes Climacus* (Atlantic Highlands, NJ: Humanities Press, 1983), chs. 1–3, and *Passionate Reason: Making Sense of Kierkegaard's Philosophical Fragments* (Bloomington, IN: Indiana University Press, 1992), ch. 1.

freedom to his human creatures to be dubious or downright incoherent. A prominent example can be found in J. L. Mackie's much-discussed article 'Evil and Omnipotence'.[27] In the course of developing an attack on the popular 'free will solution' to the problem of evil, Mackie suggests that the idea that an omnipotent God can create free creatures leads to the 'paradox of omnipotence', which is essentially the question whether an omnipotent being can 'make things which he cannot subsequently control'.[28] Mackie says that an alternative and equivalent formulation of the paradox can be stated in terms of divinely made rules: 'can an omnipotent being make rules which then bind himself?'[29]

Mackie argues that this paradox is a genuine one, because we cannot answer the questions satisfactorily either positively or negatively: 'If we answer "Yes", it follows that if God actually makes things which he cannot control, or makes rules which bind himself, he is not omnipotent once he has made them: there are *then* things which he cannot do. But if we answer "No", we are immediately asserting that there are things which he cannot do, that is to say that he is already not omnipotent.'[30] Mackie's formulation of the problem is not entirely felicitous. For God to create free creatures, or to create a natural world that has its own independence and integrity, it does not seem necessary to affirm that God has lost the ability to intervene and directly control his creations. If this were so the voluntary character of kenosis that is expressed in self-limitation would only be present in the initial divine decision, though it is worth noting that the character would still be present. As Mackie has formulated the problem, subsequent to creating free creatures God would have no ability to take away the freedom he has granted. However, there appears to be no difficulty in saying that God might create free creatures, or a nature with its own 'integrity', and retain the power to take back that freedom or independence. What is not possible is for God to create free creatures and simultaneously completely determine their

---

[27] Originally published in *Mind*, vol. LXIV, no. 254 (1955). This article is frequently reprinted and the pagination used here is taken from William L. Rowe and William J. Wainwright (eds.), *Philosophy of Religion: Selected Readings*, 2nd edn. (New York: Harcourt Brace Jovanovich, 1989).
[28] Mackie, 'Evil and Omnipotence', 231.   [29] Ibid.
[30] Ibid.

behaviour, assuming that some incompatibilist account of freedom is true. However, it seems quite possible that God could create such creatures and retain the power to take away their freedom. The freedom would be real enough so long as God does not exercise this power.

However, though Mackie's formulation is not sound, I believe that the problem he is trying to articulate is still genuine. The heart of the issue lies here: Can God be the creator of things that have some real independence from himself? After all, on the theistic picture of things, human persons and the rest of the created order exist only because of God's creative will. Can any of the actions of humans (or the characteristics of nature) be truly *theirs* if this is the case? The classical picture of God as omni-determining every event in creation really rests on the intuition that the answer to this question is no. Though the classical picture tries to rescue freedom for humans and some independence for nature through the distinction between primary and secondary causality, it is hard to see how this distinction can overcome the implications of the classical understanding of divine providence as one eternal action in which God timelessly wills all temporal events to occur exactly as they do occur.

It is precisely at this point, I think, that philosophical intuitions must be subjected to critical evaluation by the revelation of God given in Christ's Incarnation. Kierkegaard makes the point in a typically memorable way: 'That God could create beings free over against himself is the cross which philosophy could not bear but upon which it has remained hanging.'[31] Theologians often give lip service to divine transcendence, and our human inability to understand God completely. Despite this, however, I believe that philosophical intuitions about such properties as omnipotence have powerfully shaped most theologies. We think we can grasp the notion of an all-powerful being by analogy with the powers we see exhibited in created objects. If I (or more plausibly, a scientist at MIT) created a robot, the powers and actions of that robot would be completely determined by the qualities given the robot by its human creator. Of course, if I am the creator, given my epistemological finitude, the

---

[31] *Kierkegaard's Journals and Papers*, vol. II, ed. and trans. by Howard V. Hong and Edna H. Hong (Bloomington, IN: Indiana University Press, 1970), 58 (entry no. 1237).

robot may well surprise me, and even become an 'out-of-control' monster, as in many science-fiction fantasies. God, however, being omniscient as well as omnipotent, would completely determine the powers and actions of his creations, and no surprises would seem to be possible for him. Relying on the analogy, we are driven to conclude that no part of God's creation can be truly independent of him.

Suppose, however, that it is precisely in this respect that God's power exceeds human power. God, and God alone, has the power to create things that have some real independence of himself. If this is the case, then philosophical intuitions that rely explicitly or implicitly on such analogies as the one sketched above will lead us astray, and we should be open to the possibility that our philosophical intuitions about divine power must be corrected. Once more, this is how Kierkegaard sees things:

> The greatest good, after all, which can be done for a being, greater than anything else that one can do for it, is to make it free. In order to do just that, omnipotence is required. This seems strange, since it is precisely omnipotence that supposedly would make [a being] dependent. But if one will reflect on omnipotence, he will see that it also must contain the unique qualification of being able to withdraw itself again in a manifestation of omnipotence in such a way that precisely for this reason that which has been originated through omnipotence can be independent. This is why one human being cannot make another person wholly free.... Only omnipotence can withdraw itself at the same time it gives itself away.[32]

Kierkegaard is in effect resolving Mackie's alleged paradox of omnipotence by rethinking the character of omnipotence. If God limits himself, this is not a loss of omnipotence, but an exercise of it. 'If in creating man God himself lost a little of his power, then precisely what he could not do would be to make man independent.'[33]

Mackie himself makes a promising distinction to help resolve his own paradox. He notes that the paradox of omnipotence has a parallel in what he calls the 'paradox of sovereignty', which arises over the question whether a legal sovereign, such as the Australian Parliament, can pass a law that restricts its own future power, for example, by passing a law that makes some other body sovereign.[34]

---

[32] *Kierkegaard's Journals and Papers*, vol. II, 62–3 (entry no. 1251).   [33] Ibid. 63.
[34] Mackie, 'Evil and Omnipotence', 231–2.

If we distinguish between first-order laws, or what we might call ordinary laws, and second-order laws, which are laws about laws, then Mackie says we can distinguish two kinds of sovereignty. Sovereignty (1) is authority to make first-order laws, and sovereignty (2) is the authority to make second-order laws. With this distinction in mind Mackie affirms that

[i]f we say that parliament is sovereign we might mean that any parliament at any time has sovereignty (1), or we might mean that parliament has both sovereignty (1) and sovereignty (2) at present, but we cannot without contradiction mean both that the present parliament has sovereignty (2) and that every parliament at every time has sovereignty (1), for if the present parliament has sovereignty (2) it may use it to take away the sovereignty (1) of later parliaments.[35]

After making a parallel distinction between omnipotence (1) (first-order power to perform any act) and omnipotence (2) (the power to restrict first-order powers), Mackie makes a similar conclusion about God:

Then we could consistently say that God all the time has omnipotence (1), but if so no beings at any time have powers to act independently of God. Or we could say that God at one time had omnipotence (2), and used it to assign independent powers to act to certain things, so that God thereafter did not have omnipotence (1). But what the paradox shows is that we cannot consistently ascribe to any continuing being omnipotence in an inclusive sense.[36]

Mackie's reasoning here closely parallels the resolution of the paradox of the stone developed by Richard Swinburne.[37] Swinburne argues that God indeed has the power to create a stone that he could not cause to move, but that if he did so, he would no longer be omnipotent. (Though Swinburne also claims that God would never in fact give up omnipotence.)

I wish to argue, however, that Mackie and Swinburne are wrong to think that if God limited himself in some way this would necessarily be a relinquishing of omnipotence. Rather, we should think of at least

---

[35] Ibid. 232.   [36] Ibid. 232.
[37] See Richard Swinburne, *The Coherence of Theism* (Oxford: Oxford University Press, 1977), 157–8.

some kinds of self-limitation on God's part as possibilities that are necessarily included in divine omnipotence. To see this we can start by noting the difference between the case of divine omnipotence and the case of political sovereignty. We speak of parliaments as if they were continuing institutions, but in one sense this is clearly untrue. The British Parliament in 2006 is quite a different body from the British Parliament in 1906, and it is different from the British Parliament that will exist in 2106, should this political institution continue to exist. A law passed in 2006 that would limit the powers of the Parliament in 2106 would clearly be experienced as a limitation on that later body, since that later Parliament would be composed of different legislators. Even the Parliament of 2008 would be significantly different, not merely because some members may have changed, but also because human beings are changeable creatures and quite capable of altering their views. Hence the will of the Parliament of 2006 may feel like and actually will constitute a restriction on a later Parliament.

The case of God is different, however. Not only does God continue to exist from one time to the next; he is also 'the same, yesterday, today, and forever'. I do not think this changelessness must be understood as absolute immutability, for even those who believe that God can respond differently to different circumstances can hold that these responses are governed by commitments that are fixed. God's basic character and purposes do not change. We may therefore in the case of God believe that if God wills to follow a certain policy, including a policy of 'stepping back' and allowing other beings some freedom of action, he is fully capable of consistently holding to that policy. In such a case, God's self-limitation would not be a sign of loss of divine power, but an expression of God's lack of fickleness, an embodiment of his covenantal faithfulness (*chesed*).

Can God bind himself? Can he, for example, make promises? As Mackie points out, one form a divine self-limitation could take would be for God to issue principles that are in some way binding on himself. If we think of a promise as an obligation generated by a principle external to God, then it seems problematic to say that God can make promises. This is especially true if we affirm, as I do, that moral obligations are themselves generated by divine commands.[38] God cannot have moral duties that hold independently of his will if we say that moral duties are generated by his will.

I therefore agree with William Alston that God cannot literally be bound by promises or incur 'obligations' in the way that humans do, because our obligations are grounded in something external to ourselves according to the moral theory I accept, and God cannot be bound by anything outside himself. Alston recognizes that this means 'if God has no obligations, it is not strictly true that He makes promises or covenants'.[39] When the Bible represents God as making promises or covenants, it is speaking analogically 'in so describing the transactions'.[40]

I concur with these sentiments. However, we must go on to ask (as Alston himself does) what is being expressed in this analogical way, and I think that the analogy turns out to be quite strong. Alston's answer is that a more strictly accurate expression of God's action would be that in making a promise to Abraham 'God *expressed the intention* to make Abraham's descendants as numerous as the dust of the earth'.[41] Merely expressing an intention is not the same as making a promise, though in this case 'we can count on an expression of intention from God as we can count on a promise from a human being; indeed can count on it much more, because of the utter dependability of God's character and purposes'.[42]

However, if God's will has this faithful character, then must we not think that God in having and expressing this intention is thereby limiting himself? God is in this case bound in the same way that a human being who makes a promise is bound, though God is not bound by anything outside himself. God is not bound by some moral duty that is external to his will; it is precisely his own will that binds him. God's intention in relation to Abraham can be said to limit God's freedom of action; there is a clear analogy to the binding effect a human person would create by making a promise, and thus the application of such human terms as 'promise' and 'covenantal

---

[38] For a defensible version of a divine command theory of moral obligation see Robert Adams, *Finite and Infinite Goods* (New York: Oxford University Press, 1999), chs. 10–11.

[39] William Alston, 'Some Suggestions for Divine Command Theorists', in *Divine Nature and Human Language* (Ithaca, NY: Cornell University Press, 1989), 265.

[40] Ibid.   [41] Ibid.   [42] Ibid.

obligation' to God is justified. Given God's 'promise' to Abraham, God is no longer free to disregard Abraham's descendants. He is limited, and the limits are no less real for being self-generated. In fact, we can say that the limits are powerful, precisely because the one who is limiting himself is all-powerful and completely faithful. No other limits could be effective than those generated by omnipotence itself.

The conclusion I wish to draw is that the 'paradox of omnipotence' that Mackie alleges to hold is best resolved by recognizing that true omnipotence is what Mackie calls omnipotence (2). A truly omnipotent being must have the power to limit himself. However, to think of this power of self-limitation as a loss of omnipotence is mistaken. If God chooses to limit himself and thereby is unable to perform certain acts, he has not necessarily lost any power at all. It is not like a case of a later parliament whose power has been limited by an earlier parliament. In this case God's power is limited by God's own *continuing* will to condescend to his creatures and relate to them in particular ways. A God who lacked the power to do this would be less powerful than one who has the power; there would be fewer courses of action open to a God who could not effectively will a course of action over time. A God who could not form intentions and act on them with consistency over time would be a God who is incapable of seeking long-term projects or having long-term goals.

SELF-LIMITATION AND THE INCARNATION

A critic might agree that a God who continuously wills to limit himself is conceivable, and that such a self-limitation is not an abrogation of omnipotence. However, one might object that this is not what is required by a kenotic theory of the Incarnation. If God the Son divests himself of such powers as omnipotence and omniscience to become human, this self-limitation is not merely a continuous will not to exercise those properties. For it is arguable that if Christ in his earthly career had the ability to exercise these properties, he must still have possessed them and had not really 'emptied himself'.

I agree that the self-limitation that is part of a kenotic Incarnation is different from the self-limitation involved in divine creational and covenantal relationships. A decision on the part of the Son of God to become a human person by assuming human nature and living in a bodily form would be a decision at a particular time with consequences that could not later be undone by the Son acting alone, once he has accepted the limitations involved in being an embodied, fully human entity. If he has given up omnipotence, he cannot use omnipotence to get it back. That is why the glorification of the Son is described by Scripture as accomplished by the power of the Father. The self-limitation in this case is more radical; the consequences are not grounded merely in the Son's own continuing will, but in the hard reality of the situation he has willed to create, once that situation is in place.

Nevertheless, there is a strong analogy between this act and the general capacity for God to limit himself. God the Son can foresee the limitations he will be accepting in becoming human and will to accept them. One might say that he knows the following hypothetical to be true: 'If during my human career I still possessed omnipotence, I would continually will not to exercise this power but to divest myself of it.' The antecedent may be contrary to fact, but the truth of the conditional ensures that the limits accepted by the Incarnate Christ have been freely accepted. He too is bound by his own will, only in this case his omnipotence (and other properties) have been actually given up; the self-limitation is of a more radical kind.

This is a significant difference, and it means that, in the case of the Incarnation, God the Son, at least temporarily, does not possess omnipotence (2) in Mackie's sense. In the case of the Incarnation, Swinburne's resolution of the paradox of the stone seems right. An omnipotent divine person would have the power to give up omnipotence, thus leading to the kenotic understanding of the proper divine property as 'being-omniscient-unless-freely-choosing-to-limit-himself'. Swinburne's mistake is to claim that a divine being could not possibly limit himself, for if he did, he would be giving up control of the universe. Perhaps this would be true of the Godhead, the divine Trinity understood as a unity; God as a whole would not and perhaps could not give up his divine power and leave the universe without a sustainer and providential orderer. However, that does not mean that *one* of the persons of the Trinity could not freely empty himself of such properties, secure in the knowledge that the Father and Spirit will continue providentially to guide creation, and perhaps even secure in the knowledge that he will someday be rewarded by them with the restoration of all the divine prerogatives.

If we learn from God's Incarnation that God is capable of this kind of radical self-limitation, we will have no difficulty accepting the idea that God is capable of self-limitation in the way required for him to bind himself by creating objects with some real independence and through making what we humanly term promises and covenants. The Incarnation truly does give us a window into God's powers that transforms our understanding of what God is capable of doing. If God the Son can, out of love, will to enter fully into the human condition, we should have no trouble understanding how the Godhead is capable of consistently willing the creation to 'do its thing' and exhibit a consistent character that is its own, and of consistently willing that humans have the freedom to perform actions that will truly be their own.

How does God perform such actions as giving humans freedom? I do not know. Perhaps to understand such power I would have to be God. All I can say is what I can say of any action X that God performs omnipotently: God wills X to occur, and by virtue of his power, X occurs. Normally, we understand the powers of a being by understanding the mechanisms whereby that being exercises those powers. However, even for finite beings, I believe there are basic powers substances possess that probably are not capable of explanation in this way. In any case I suspect that God's powers, at least his basic powers, are not mediated by mechanisms in this way, and thus our desire to understand will necessarily be frustrated. Part of the mystery of omnipotence is its power to 'withdraw itself' even as it 'gives itself'. However, this does not seem any more mysterious than the power to create a universe out of nothing.

IS INDEPENDENCE FROM GOD A CHARACTERISTICALLY MALE CONCERN?

Sarah Coakley, in the conclusion of her essay in *The Work of Love*, raises a provocative question. Coakley notes that the other writers in that volume all seem to assume a libertarian, incompatibilist conception of human freedom, and all seem anxious to ensure that God does not 'overpower' the creation. Her worry is that this anxiety might reflect a 'gendered' picture of the situation:

> But why and how is this picture of freedom 'gendered'? The answer lies in the significance granted, in this particular 'picturing' of freedom, to an act of total independence from restriction, conditioning, or the admission of dependence, and this is a vision deeply reminiscent, to those schooled in psychoanalytic theory, of the male child's repudiation of the power of the mother.[43]

Surely the same question can be asked about the picture of the divine nature that I have argued is inherent in kenotic Christology. For such a picture seems tremendously concerned with safeguarding the independence and freedom of the world and its human creatures, and thus emphasizes God's power to limit himself, seen most clearly in that radical act of self-emptying that begins with the Incarnation and culminates with death on the cross.

I am grateful to Coakley for posing this question, for it allows me to clarify both the kind of freedom and independence I have in view as well as the nature of God's self-limitation. Let me say first that no creature can be completely independent of its creator, and human freedom in relation to God cannot be absolute. We are finite, historically situated beings, and our freedom is similarly concrete and historical in character. As Kierkegaard repeatedly affirms, we have no *liberum arbitrium*: 'That a bare and naked *liberum arbitrium* is a chimera is best seen by the difficulty, the long, long continuous effort, which is necessary merely to get rid of a habit, even if one ever so earnestly has made a resolution.'[44] When human beings face choices, we always come to those choices with what we might call weighted interests. Our past choices, emotions, desires, and goals shape the reflection that typically precedes a choice and heavily push us in particular directions. Choices are made by actual human beings, not abstract 'powers of will'. And those actual human beings develop in and through relations with other persons; their identities are

---

[43] Coakley, *The Work of Love*, 205.
[44] Kierkegaard, *Kierkegaard's Journals and Papers*, vol. II, p. 67 (entry no. 1260).

thoroughly tied up with their relations to parents, their friends, their countrymen, and their relations with God.

Once we recognize that our choices have this character, and that freedom is situated and relational, why hold out for incompatibilism? What is the value of libertarian freedom if that freedom is enmeshed in this way? The affirmation of libertarian freedom, as I understand it, is not a claim that humans are or should be disconnected from others or their environment, social and natural. It is rather the claim that humans are not *purely* products of their environments and their own pasts. The deterministic alternative to libertarianism is one that implies that ultimately humans are simply a place through which causal lines flow; human choices are simply an inevitable sum of the causal vectors that feed into them. Libertarianism affirms that humans, though shaped by their pasts, are not the helpless victims of their pasts. It affirms that humans, though embedded in relations with others, are not simply products of those relations, but responsible, active participants in those relations.

A God who values freedom and independence is not necessarily a standoffish God, a God who is deistically unrelated to his creation. In fact, God's activity in limiting himself in relation to his creation, as I conceive it, is completely motivated by a desire for genuine relations with that creation. In an essay on the implications of prayer, William Alston rejects the thesis of what he calls divine 'omnidetermination' precisely because it undermines the possibility of genuine relations between God and his creatures: '[I]t [omnidetermination] seems to me plainly incompatible with genuine divine–human dialogue and much else in the Christian life as well.'[45] I believe that God limits himself, not to free humans from a relation, but to make them capable of having genuine relations with himself and others. The power on God's part to do this does not mean that he is weak; it is the kind of self-limitation only one who is absolutely strong and confident of that strength could undertake. The power of self-limitation seen in the Incarnation of love is one to which we have only dim human analogies, but one suggested by W. H. Vanstone is appealing:

---

[45] 'Divine–Human Dialogue and the Nature of God', in *Divine Nature and Human Language*, 148.

Trinitarian theology asserts that God's love for his creation is not the love that is born of 'emptiness'. . . . It is the love which overflows from fullness. Its analogue is the love of a family who, united in mutual love, take an orphan into the home. They do so not out of need but in the pure spontaneity of their own triumphant love. Nevertheless, in the weeks that follow, the family, once complete in itself, comes to need the newcomer. Without him the circle is now incomplete: his absence now causes anxiety: his waywardness brings concern: his goodness and happiness are necessary to those who have come to love him; upon his response depends the triumph or the tragedy of the family's love. . . . Love has surrendered its triumphant self-sufficiency and created its own need. This is the supreme illustration of love's self-giving or self-emptying—that it should surrender its fullness and create in itself the emptiness of need. Of such a nature is the Kenosis of God—the self-emptying of Him Who is already in every way fulfilled.[46]

To that I would add only that this kenosis of God occurs most decisively in the kenosis of Christ.

---

[46] W. H. Vanstone, *Love's Endeavour Love's Expense: The Response of Being to the Love of God* (London: Darton, Longman, and Todd, 1977), 69.

9

'He descended into hell': The Depths of God's Self-Emptying Love on Holy Saturday in the Thought of Hans Urs von Balthasar

Edward T. Oakes, S.J.

1

Any version of the Incarnation—the doctrine that somehow or another (meaning, however conceived) the infinite God *became* (meaning, *was transformed into*) a finite human being—requires by definition a correlative doctrine of kenosis (self-emptying) in order to be coherent. For that is what such a doctrine of infinite-becoming-finite entails in its very assertion. After all, the infinite can only become finite by emptying itself of its infinity, otherwise it will not have become, *been turned into*, the finite. In other words, without some notion along the lines of kenosis we are left with sheer paradox.

Not that Christian theology can ever dispense with paradox entirely, for everything about the Christian proclamation involves paradox in one form or another. Indeed, because of its doctrine of Incarnation, Christianity might be said to be *the* quintessentially paradoxical religion. For that reason, the subsidiary doctrine of kenosis cannot be said (at least in its usual guises) to attempt to *abolish* the paradoxes of Christian doctrine, only to leave them seeming less flagrantly self-contradictory. For example, to say 'the infinite has become the finite' is a paradox. To explain that paradox by saying 'the infinite has emptied itself to become finite' certainly resolves the paradox. But if one interprets self-emptying too univocally or too radically, the paradox is not just resolved but abolished. Thus, Christianity must continue to maintain that the infinite *remains* infinite while becoming (being turned into) something finite.

To alter Paul Ricoeur's famous line, who famously said 'the symbol gives rise to thought,' we may say of the relation of the Christian proclamation to later reflection, 'the paradox gives rise to theology.' But theology no more means to abolish paradox than thought intends to abolish symbol.[1] As an anonymous poem from the fifteenth century puts it, Christianity will always remain, as the title of the poem puts it, 'The Divine Paradox':

> A God and yet a man?
> A maid and yet a mother?
> Wit wonders that wit can
> Conceive this or the other.
> A God, and can he die?
> A dead man, can he live?
> What wit can well reply?
> What reason reason give?
> God, truth itself, does teach it;
> Man's wit sinks too far under
> By reason's power to reach it.
> Believe and leave to wonder.[2]

But wonder has proved in the long run to be an insufficient response to paradox, for Christians have also heard another version to the final line of that poem: 'Believe and leave to *theologize*.' Paradox gives rise to theology: and in such paradox-generated theology the concept of kenosis has proved time and again to form an essential bridge from paradox to coherent thought: God could become man, the infinite could become finite, precisely by God being stripped of the divine self/infinity in order thereby to become finite.

---

[1] ' "The symbol gives rise to thought." That sentence, which enchants me, says two things: the symbol gives; but what it gives is occasion for thought, something to think about. The symbol gives: a philosophy instructed by myths arises at a certain moment in reflection, and, beyond philosophical reflection it wishes to answer to a certain situation of modern culture' (Paul Ricoeur, trans. by Emerson Buchanan *The Symbolism of Evil* (Boston: Beacon Press, 1969), p. 348).

[2] From *Religious Lyrics of the Fifteenth Century*, edited by Carleton Brown (Oxford: Oxford University Press, 1939), p. 187 (spelling modernized).

Now whether such a strategy of invoking the concept of kenosis has proved successful in the long run is precisely the burden of the essays of this volume to examine, if not to resolve. The burden of this chapter, however, is slightly different. For whether the concept of kenosis works on its own terms to resolve, or at least to illuminate, the essential paradoxes of the Christian message, it has at least succeeded to *this* extent: by and large, Christians no longer notice how *inherently* paradoxical is the faith they hold. Perhaps because Christians repeat the Creed too often, perhaps because stray verses of the Bible have become background noise from overuse and excessive repetition, perhaps because nowadays habitual reciters of the Creed are closet materialists in any event, Christians seem not to notice how strange is the creed they proclaim.

Yet such seems not to be the case, at least, of *this* line from the oft-repeated Creed: the teaching that after his death Jesus descended into hell. For even granted Christianity's inherently paradoxical essence, different elements in the Christian proclamation have from time to time proved to be particularly provocative, provoking not so much thought as outrage—or polite neglect. And no assertion inside the Christian Creed has proved more disconcerting for believers than the phrase, 'he descended into hell, and on the third day rose again from the dead.' To be sure, for secular scoffers the *whole* of the Creed is quite literally (as the expression goes) 'beyond belief', no doubt mostly because of the believer's high tolerance for paradox and the unbeliever's refusal to follow along. Take, for example, atheism. Does not most atheism reject the possible existence of God because of the intolerable paradox of asserting an all-powerful, benevolent God over against the created world so filled with evils?

But even assuming the philosopher of religion can overcome his scruples here and admit the existence of an all-powerful, all-munificent God, he will eventually have to face even more flagrant paradoxes in the Christian creed itself, in those doctrines that make Christianity specifically Christian. Perhaps such secular incredulity can alert believers to a feature of their faith too little noticed among them. For whatever else one can say about the Christian faith, its creeds certainly present the unbelieving world with a set of utterly enigmatic statements: faith in one God who is yet, somehow, three; faith that one of those three divine Persons, fully divine ('God from

God, light from light, true God from true God'), was born of a Virgin
and thus became fully human; and finally faith in the ultimate resurrection of all human bodies at the end of time—even though 'we
all know' that at death the atoms composing the body disintegrate
and are recirculated into the cosmos whence they came. Nonetheless,
if Christians have become so familiar with the doctrines of the Trinity,
Incarnation, and resurrection that they have forgotten how enigmatic
they are, that certainly cannot be said of this disconcerting line
from the Apostles' Creed, 'he descended into hell.' Of at least *this*
phrase one cannot say, as one can perhaps of the other doctrines,
that familiarity breeds credibility (or even credulity), if only because,
tellingly, the more solemn (and certainly the more liturgically
familiar) Nicene Creed makes no mention at all of Christ's descent
into hell.

Seen on the face of things, and certainly in light of the popularity
of kenotic theology, such a development would seem odd, for here
paradox reaches its most intense moment. Yet given the discomfort
that the doctrine of Christ's descent into hell seems to have elicited
throughout the history of Christian thought, perhaps that merely
indicates either an implied rejection of kenotic theology *tout court*
or maybe even a rejection of *the* ultimate paradox of the Christian
message: that God, the all-holy and the all-good, emptied himself not
only to take on human form but also in that human form came to
know everything that rejects God, everything that is unholy, evil, and
foul. Here above all, God contradicts God. No wonder, then, that the
history of Christian thought betrays such discomfort with this teaching, not only in its general outlines but also within specific isolable
eras in that history.

For example, something like this general decline in a full-throated
belief in Christ's descent into hell can be traced as well in classical
Protestant thought, which seems to repeat over the course of three
centuries the same 'arc of discontent' that has marked the whole
history of Christian thought. Martin Luther begins the arc near its
apogee by taking the rather spare and ambiguous assertion of the
Apostles' Creed (ambiguous primarily because the clause does not
specify exactly what is meant by the 'hell' into which Jesus descended) and openly avers a very concrete hell of God-abandonment
that Jesus experienced: 'He descended into the deepest of *all* depths',

says Luther, 'under the law, under the devil, death, sin and *hell*; and that, I think, is verily the last and lowest depth.'[3] Then John Calvin begins the mitigating process by attributing to Christ these experiences of godforsakenness only *as death approached*—on earth, that is, and not in any locatable, post-mortem 'hell'. Even so, at least the Geneva theologian insists that the descent into hell does refer to Christ's spiritual sufferings in his relation to God his Father, sufferings that go far beyond those of bodily death, for in approaching death Jesus had to 'grapple hand to hand with the armies of hell and the dread of everlasting death'.[4] Nonetheless, these were for Calvin clearly sufferings that Jesus underwent *in the course of* his passion and death, not after death: 'He paid a greater and more excellent price in suffering in his soul the terrible torments of a condemned and forsaken man.'[5] And finally decline in belief in the *descensus ad inferos* reaches its nadir when the founder of Methodism, John Wesley, simply dropped the line altogether from the Apostles' Creed.[6]

---

[3] Martin Luther, *Sermon* on Ephesians 4:8–10 (emphasis added).

[4] John Calvin, *Institutes of the Christian Religion*, ed. J. T. McNeill, trans. F. L. Battles (Philadelphia: Westminster Press, 1960) II, xvi, no. 10, p. 515.

[5] Ibid., p. 516: 'No wonder, then, if he is said to have descended into hell, for he suffered the death that God in his wrath had inflicted upon the wicked!' We know that this passage clearly refers to Jesus' experience of suffering before and in death because Calvin addresses an objection here that the descent is mentioned as occurring after the burial of Jesus: 'Those who—on the ground that it is absurd to put after his burial what preceded it—say that the order is reversed in this way are making a very trifling and ridiculous objection' (ibid.). Perhaps, but Calvin is arguing entirely *ipse dixit* here. For his insouciant dismissal of this objection does seem to beg a big question: *why* does Scripture 'put after [Christ's] burial what preceded it' if the only soteriologically significant sufferings of Jesus were those he underwent in and at death?

[6] The issue in Methodism is actually rather complicated. See Karen Westerfield Tucker, *American Methodist Worship* (New York: Oxford University Press, 2001), pp. 39–41: 'Another clause from the Apostles' Creed, not found in the oldest forms of the symbol of faith but understood by later Christians to be part of the received text, was short-lived in Methodist usage. It appeared in the 1784 *Sunday Service*, but was deleted at one of the creed's three appearances in the 1786 edition, an omission that some scholars contend did not originate with Wesley. In the 1786 formulation, "he went down into hell" disappeared from the adult baptismal rite while "he descended into hell" was retained in the orders for morning and evening prayer. The discrepancy may be explained as an oversight, but by 1792 it made no practical difference since, with the dropping of morning and evening prayer, the baptismal formulation was the only version to remain. The omission of the phrase may be explained as an effort to remove a theologically volatile subject: the thirty-ninth

A similar arc of decline can be traced in the Church at large: in other words, at least in some respects what happened over the course of three centuries in classical Protestantism might be said to be but a smaller sub-plot in a wider declension of belief in Christ's descent into hell over the past two thousand years. But this declension should *not* be detected in the almost accidental presence of the clause 'and he descended into hell' in the Apostles' Creed over against its absence in the Nicene-Constantinopolitan Creed. For despite its name, the present form of the Apostles' Creed comes *after* the present form of the Nicene Creed; and indeed the earliest forms of the Apostles' Creed make no mention of the *descensus*.[7] As J. A. MacCulloch usefully points out:

Though belief in our Lord's Descent to Hades existed in the Church from the apostolic age, it did not expressly appear in the Baptismal creeds at an early date. Rufinus (c.400) says that *descendit ad inferna* existed in the creed used at Aquileia, [but] adds that the Roman creed did not contain the words, and that they were not found in the Eastern Churches. This is true of the

Anglican Article affirming Christ's descent into hell had prompted debate within the Puritan wing and also among the founders of the Protestant Episcopal Church in America; *it had not been included in Wesley's revision of the Articles.* Only in the late twentieth century would United Methodists reintroduce the phrase, and then as part of the stated "ecumenical" version of the creed produced by the English Language Liturgical Consultation' (p. 40; emphasis added). My thanks to the renowned Methodist theologian Geoffrey Wainwright for alerting me to this passage. See also John Wesley's own remarks on 1 Peter 3:19 in his *Explanatory Notes on the New Testament* (London: Epworth Press, 1976), p. 882: '*To the spirits in prison*—[this verse refers to] the unholy men before the Flood, who were then reserved by the justice of God, as in a prison, till He executed the sentences upon them all; and are now also reserved to the judgement of the great day.' This gloss by Wesley seems to imply that for him the salvific effects of Christ's descent into hell will have no ultimate bearing on the verdict delivered at the Last Judgement. Similarly, when St. Paul says 'he descended to the lowest parts of the earth' (Eph. 4:9), Wesley interprets that as meaning the Virgin's womb (ibid., p. 713).

[7] The so-called 'Old Roman Creed' was first cited by Marcellus, Bishop of Ancyra, and delivered to Julius, Bishop of Rome, around 340. This Creed is nearly identical to the one cited by Rufinus in his *Expositio in Symbolum*, composed around 400. Neither mentions the *descensus*. The Gallican version of the Creed, around the sixth century, is the first to mention the Descent into Hell. The version of the Creed now known as the Nicene Creed comes from the year 374. For further details, as well as the complete text of all these versions, see *Documents of the Christian Church*, edited by Henry Bettenson, third edition edited by Chris Maunder (Oxford: Oxford University Press, 1999), pp. 25–9.

Baptismal creeds, for the earliest approximation to the formula occurs in the allied creeds of the Synods [of 359 A.D.] and of Constantinople in 360 A.D.[8]

Nor does the omission of the *descensus* formula from the Nicene-Constantinopolitan Creed adopted in 374 mean that belief in the Descent was dying out. For an anathema of that same Council condemned those who denied that the Logos in His 'reasonable soul' had descended into Hades,[9] so that the assertion of the belief may be taken as granted even in those creeds that do not explicitly mention it.

Nor should it be forgotten how deeply embedded a doctrine of the Descent is in the New Testament, especially, but not exclusively, in its Petrine strands. Since we will have occasion to refer to these texts throughout the course of this essay, it might serve the convenience of the reader to have them all assembled here in a *catena* for later reference, with the most significant parts of the verses italicized for emphasis:

Men of Israel, listen to this: Jesus of Nazareth was a man commended to you by God by virtue of the miracles, wonders and signs which God did among you through him, as you yourselves know. This man was handed over to you by God's set purpose and foreknowledge, and you—with the help of wicked men—put him to death by nailing him to the cross. But God raised him from the dead, *freeing him from the pangs of Hades, because it was impossible for death to keep its hold on him.* (Acts 2:22–4)[10]

For Christ died for sins once for all, the righteous for the unrighteous, to bring you to God. He was put to death in the body but made alive by the Spirit, through whom he also *went and preached to the spirits in prison who disobeyed God long ago.* (1 Pet. 3:18–19)

But they [sinners] will have to give account to him who is ready to judge the living and the dead. For this is the reason the gospel was preached *even to*

---

[8] J. A. MacCulloch, D.D., *The Harrowing of Hell: A Comparative Study of an Early Christian Doctrine* (Edinburgh: T. & T. Clark, 1930), p. 67.

[9] MacCulloch, p. 71.

[10] Be it noted that the italicized portion of this passage comes from the Western textual tradition. Acts of the Apostles has the most divergent textual variants of all of the books of the New Testament; and most of these variants share enough similarities and come from the western half of the Roman Empire to have been given their own name. I use this textual variant not to make any statement one way or the other on which tradition might embody the 'inspired' (or canonical) text, but simply to highlight that the prevalence of this textual variant points to a similar prevalence of belief in Christ's descent into Hades.

those who are now dead, so that they might be judged according to men in regard to the body, but live according to God in regard to the spirit. (1 Pet. 4:5–6)

So then, whether we live or whether we die, we are the Lord's. For to this end Christ died and lived again, *that he might be the Lord both of the dead and of the living.* (Rom. 14:8–9)

But to each one of us grace has been given as Christ apportioned it. This is why it says: 'When he ascended on high, he led captives in his train and gave gifts to men' [Ps. 68:18]. But what does 'he ascended' mean except that *he also descended to the depths of the earth?* He who is descended is the very one who ascended higher than all the heavens, *in order to fill the whole universe.* (Eph. 4:7–10)

Therefore God exalted him to the highest place and gave him the name that is above every name, so that at the name of Jesus every knee should bend, in heaven and on earth and *under the earth* and every tongue confess that Jesus Christ is Lord, to the glory of God the Father. (Phil. 2:9–11)

But of course *what* is being asserted here by professing that Christ descended into the realm of the dead remains the central issue. Who gets redeemed here? Only the 'just ones' of the Old Testament (Adam, the patriarchs, David, etc.), or select Gentiles too (such as the 'pre-evangelists' to the Greeks like Socrates and Plato), or everyone? In this regard the quite bizarre, even anti-Semitic, views of the heretic Marcion are instructive here, for his heretical spin on the doctrine of the Descent proves, by its weird variation on the theme, just how pervasive was the belief in the Descent in the earliest centuries of the Christian Church. According to Marcion the righteous 'just ones' of the Old Testament are just about the only ones *not* being saved by Christ's descent into Hades! For they are, after all, righteous only in the eyes of Marcion's evil Demiurge-Creator of the material world, a counter-God who opposes everything that flows from Marcion's own 'good God' of the spirit. By Marcion's weird (albeit consistent) logic, all those who disobeyed this *other* God of the Old Testament are thereby faithful, by definition, to the Supreme God. Hence Marcion's fleshless Christ went down to Hades only to deliver *them.* According to Irenaeus (from whom we glean these Marcionite heresies), Marcion taught that Cain and all like him—the Sodomites and Egyptians—and all the heathen who had walked in wickedness of every kind, were saved by Christ's descent. But Abel, Enoch, Noah, all the patriarchs in the bosom of Abraham, and all the prophets who did the bidding of the God of the Old Testament had no share in this salvation.

So odd, even *recherché*, are these views that chances are not inconsiderable that Irenaeus (our only source for these views) is distorting Marcion here (although, based on what our biased sources indicate, Marcion seems to have been a most consistent heretic, and his views on the Descent are certainly consistent with his opening axiom). But for our purposes the issue of the historical Marcion is irrelevant here, for what is crucial is that aspect of Marcion's teaching that Irenaeus does *not* dispute: that Christ descended into Hades for redemptive purposes, and specifically to redeem those whose position in history before the birth of Christ otherwise made soteriological contact with him on earth impossible. For what Marcion, at least in Irenaeus' eyes, has done is to distort only the identity of the *recipients* of Christ's salvific descent, not the descent itself. And that presupposition Marcion shares with all the sub-Apostolic Fathers: Ignatius of Antioch,[11] Justin Martyr,[12] and Irenaeus himself.[13]

[11] 'In view of this, how can it be possible for us to give Him no place in our lives when even the prophets of old were themselves pupils of His in spirit, and looked forward to Him as their Teacher? Indeed, that was the very reason why He, whom they were rightly awaiting, *came to visit them,* and raised them from the dead' (Ignatius of Antioch, *Epistle to the Magnesians,* chapter 9, in *Early Christian Writings,* trans. by Maxwell Staniforth, revised translation, introductions and new editorial material by Andrew Louth (New York: Penguin Books. 1987), p. 73; emphasis added).

[12] In his famous *Dialogue with Rabbi Trypho* (chapter 72) Justin cites an apocryphal verse from the book of Jeremiah which he claimed was still being read in some synagogues but which, he claims, the Jews had begun to suppress to avoid acknowledging Christ's descent to Sheol: 'And the Lord God of Israel', goes this apocryphal verse, 'remembered His dead ones, who slept in the earth of dust, and He descended to preach to them His salvation.' Moreover, Justin also refers to the Jews' mistaken idea that Christ, being put to death, would remain in Hades like some common man, which clearly points to Justin's prior belief in the Descent (not to mention Justin's own agreement with Peter's first sermon on Pentecost that 'Hades had no power over him [Christ]' (Acts 2:24, Western text)).

[13] Not only does Irenaeus make clear his own belief in the Descent in his refutation of Marcion's *interpretation* of that Descent, but he also cites an otherwise unnamed 'Elder' (perhaps Pothinus, his predecessor in the see of Lyons? perhaps Polycarp?) who taught that it was quite sufficient for the Bible to rebuke David and Solomon for their sins and that it would be unseemly for Christians to 'gang up' on them as well, since Christ by his descent had remitted their sins just as he has done for ours by his death.

In all of these men, be it noted, the focus centres on the waiting just ones of Israel (including, of course, Adam and Eve). The great innovation from the pen of Clement of Alexandria holds that, just as God has no favourites—as St. Paul holds (Rom. 2:11) and contrary to the appearances of salvation history—so too Christ's saving intent in his descent into Hades shows no partiality. Other writers had indeed agreed with St. Paul that Gentiles were as acceptable to God as the Jews, at least subsequent to the coming of Christ. But Clement was the first to claim that God's impartiality applied also to the Gentiles who had died before the birth of Christ; and so in the *Miscellanies* he asserts of the Gentiles that, being as worthy of God's favour as Jews, 'the Lord preached to them [as well] in Hades'.[14]

But that very implication in the doctrine proved to be the catalyst for calling it into question, or at least mitigating its soteriological force. For to the very extent that theologians wanted to insist on the limited number of the saved and on the eternity of a populated Hell, to that same extent the doctrine of Christ's descent into Hades had perforce to be limited. For our purposes, Augustine and Aquinas may be taken as the most significant representatives of this approach.

First of all, to Augustine we owe the great boon of distinguishing— and he was really the first to do so—between Hades and Hell, between, that is, the underworld where *all* the dead dwelt and that realm of eternal perdition strictly for the non-elect, where all hope of release or rescue is foreclosed, where all its denizens are forlorn and eternally lost, where all who enter its vast realms first had to abandon hope. As he seems to have been the first to notice among the Latin Fathers, the word *inferus* or its variants did not seem to be used for hell as distinct from the generalized 'underworld' where all the dead dwelled.[15] Despite that linguistic ambiguity, however, he was able to countenance, in a famous passage in *The City of God*, the possibility

---

[14] Clement of Alexandria, *Stromateis* 2, 9.

[15] Augustine, *De Genesis ad litteram* 12, 33. Nonetheless, ambiguities permeate all of Augustine's treatment of eschatology. On the one hand, 'Throughout his life, Augustine remained convinced that the souls of some of the dead, who are condemned to punishment immediately after death because of their sins, will be released from that punishment before God's sentence of judgement is passed.... Augustine frequently insists, however, that not all the dead are capable of receiving God's mercy through the prayers and meritorious actions of the Church done in their name' (Brian E. Daley, S.J., *The Hope of the Early Church: A Handbook of Patristic Eschatology*

that the *inferus* could be the abode of both good and bad souls before Christ's descent there on Holy Saturday.[16] The letter to Evodius (written in AD 414) is particularly relevant here, for it was Evodius who first wrote inquiring about how to interpret the passage in 1 Peter 3:19 that speaks of Christ's descent and preaching to the disobedient souls 'long ago'. By virtue of Augustine's reply[17] we know that it must have been a common interpretation that Christ had preached to all the disobedient souls and that Hades had thereby been completely emptied in the wake of Christ's presence there. Augustine replied that he would like to concede that all were rescued, but what authority, he asks rhetorically, is there for this?[18] His way of interpreting this obscure passage in 1 Peter is to claim that Christ's preaching among the dead refers only to the metaphorically dead: '[Peter] does not oblige us to think that this refers to hell. For this cause was the Gospel preached also to the dead in this life, that is, unbelievers and evil-doers.'[19] As J. A. MacCulloch says of Augustine's conclusion, 'He would like to think that noble and worthy Pagans were rescued, but the verdict of human feeling differs from that of Divine justice. Augustine's predestinarian theories blocked the way to such a belief.'[20]

(Cambridge: Cambridge University Press, 1991), pp. 138, 139. Yet Augustine will also seem to indicate that 'hell is not a permanent state ... until the common passage of all creatures from time into eternity' (ibid., p. 139).

[16] *De civitate Dei* 20, 15: 'For if there seems no absurdity in the belief that the holy men of old, who held a faith in the Christ who was still to come, dwelt in regions far removed from the torments of the ungodly, *but still in the nether world*, until Christ's blood and his descent to those regions should rescue them from that place, then surely from that time onwards the good believers, now redeemed by the shedding of his blood as their ransom, have no experience at all of Hades, as they wait to receive back their bodies and to receive the good things they deserve' (St. Augustine, *Concerning the City of God against the Pagans*, trans. by Henry Bettenson, introduction by John O'Meara (New York: Penguin Books, 1972), p. 926 (emphasis added).

[17] In *The Fathers of the Church: A New Translation*, vol. 20, *St. Augustine, Letters*, vol. III (containing Letters nos. 131–64), trans. by Sister Wilfred Parsons, S.N.D. (New York: Fathers of the Church, Inc., 1953), letter to Evodius (Letter no. 164), pp. 382–98.

[18] 'For if we say that all of those who were found there [in Hades] were set free without exception, it would be a cause of gratification.... Even so, some of these [souls in hell] rouse such an attraction in us that we could wish to have them freed from the sufferings of hell—whether we are singular in that or like others—but human feeling is not the same as the justice of the Creator' (St. Augustine, Letter to Evodius (no. 164), ibid., pp. 383, 384.

[19] Augustine, ibid., p. 397.   [20] MacCulloch, *Harrowing*, p. 123.

These views strongly influenced medieval theologians, especially Thomas Aquinas, who very much took Augustine's views to heart and systematized them in a *questio* devoted to this theme in the larger of his two *Summae* and which heavily relies on Augustine's letter to Evodius. In the second article devoted to this *questio*, he explicitly denies that Christ went down to the hell of the lost, and in the sixth article he denies that Christ delivered any of the lost from hell or even, in the seventh article, that children who died only in original sin were delivered by Christ.[21]

This view about unbaptized infants, needless to say, caused considerable uneasiness, for which the positing of a *limbus patrum*, a kind of forecourt to hell, became essential. But the positing of this Limbo then came to serve not just to mitigate punishment of unbaptized infants, but also mitigated the doctrine of the full extent of Christ's descent into hell, so much so that manuals of theology in the nineteenth century explicitly confined Christ's preaching in Hades to this *limbus patrum*. One manual even says that while the effects of Christ's preaching could be felt on the lost, bringing to them an added sense of shame and confusion, nonetheless Christ never really descended to hell.[22]

As we will see in the next section, such views have undergone a remarkable reversal. Perhaps because the history of the twentieth century was so conspicuously hellish, the feeling has grown that if God cannot be proclaimed as present in hell, can his presence be felt on earth either? But unanimity on that issue hardly reigns, and one

---

[21] Thomas Aquinas, *Summa Theologiae* III, q. 52, aa. 2, 6, 7: 'Christ descended into each of the hells, but in different manner. For in going down into the hell of the lost, He wrought this effect, that by descending thither He put them to shame for their unbelief and wickedness; but to them who were detained in Purgatory, He gave hope of attaining to glory' (*ST* III, q. 52 a. 2, *Respondeo*); 'When Christ descended into hell, all who were in any part of hell were visited in some respect: some to their consolation and deliverance, others, namely, the lost, to their shame and confusion' (*ST* III, q. 52, a. 6 *ad* 1); 'But children who had died in original sin were in no way united to Christ's Passion by faith and love; for, not having the use of free will, they could have no faith of their own; nor were they cleansed from original sin either by their parents' faith or by any sacrament of faith. Consequently, Christ's descent into hell did not deliver the children from thence' (*ST* III, q. 52, a. 7, *Respondeo*). Augustine's letter to Evodius is especially heavily cited in the second article.

[22] T. H. Simar, *Lehrbuch der Dogmatik* (Freiburg im Breisgau: Herder, 1899), vol. I, pp. 539f.

occasionally finds strongly worded dissent regarding this new attempt to revitalize a doctrine of Christ's descent into hell. Although such dissent mostly takes the form of a reaction to views we have yet to set out, nonetheless this criticism of the Descent fits into the same pattern we have seen already as set forth in this section; and so perhaps we can conclude this section with a glance at this criticism.

Perhaps the most vigorous of all these critics is Gerald O'Collins, who quite explicitly aligns himself against what he calls the Calvin–Barth tradition, which he says fails on two counts: '*their monstrous view of God and their misinterpretation of the New Testament*'.[23] The author can work himself up into a high dudgeon here. But precisely because the twentieth century saw so remarkable a resurgence of interest in a doctrine of Christ's descent into hell, O'Collins voice must be heard out, for he sees the descent into hell—defined as *the* realm of godforsakenness and punishment for sin—as entailing a notion that God had to punish Jesus in our stead, and this for him is directly linked to God as punisher of sin:

Certain human causes lurk behind the image of God as an angry punisher. A punishing God has helped to justify and protect authority in families, society and religion. This is not necessarily to allege that parents, rulers and religious leaders have consciously fostered such an image of God as a prop for their position. The image resulted naturally enough from the way they (and those under them) experienced and interpreted human authority. Fear of God has been mobilized to support human subjection. Furthermore, at a personal level the notion of a punishing God corresponds somewhat to self-destructive tendencies within human beings. Drives to self-punishment, the anxiety to propitiate forces within oneself and crippling worries about possible evil consequences of one's actions—all of these elements can coalesce to project a God made in their image and likeness.[24]

We will take up these objects in later sections of this essay after setting forth the revolution in theology of the past century where discomfort changed into a much more full-throated reappropriation.

---

[23] Gerald O'Collins, S.J., *Interpreting Jesus* (London: Geoffrey Chapman, 1983), p. 152; emphasis in the original.
[24] Ibid.

2

In almost every regard, theology after the Second World War, both Protestant and Catholic, has seen a remarkable shift of views in its encounter with this enigmatic *theologoumenon*. On the Protestant side, one need only consider the late Presbyterian Alan E. Lewis's remarkable reappropriation on the theme of Christ's descent in his recent, posthumously published monograph *Between Cross and Resurrection: A Theology of Holy Saturday*.[25] And of course on the Roman Catholic side there are the efforts of the Swiss Hans Urs von Balthasar, who among theologians has pretty much single-handedly brought this theme to the centre of the Christian message.

As is well known, Balthasar came to his views on Christ's descent into hell—which differ quite noticeably not only from the Augustine–Aquinas axis of interpretation but also from the common interpretations of the patristic period—because of his encounter with the erstwhile Protestant physician Adrienne von Speyr, who not only converted to the Catholic Church under Balthasar's aegis but also became the recipient, by his account, of a cataract of mystical graces not seen since the days of St. Teresa of Ávila. Moreover, by far the most intense of those graces related to her experience of what the human soul of Christ must have undergone on Holy Saturday:

Immediately after her conversion, a veritable cataract of graces poured over Adrienne in a seemingly chaotic storm that whirled her in all directions at once.... And so began the first of those 'Passions', ending with the remarkable experience of Holy Saturday, which was to become so characteristic of Adrienne. They were repeated from then on, year after year, revealing in ever new ways a variety of theological relationships. These passions were not so much a vision of the historical scenes of the suffering that had taken place in Jerusalem—there were only occasional glimpses of these, as if for clarification—rather, they were an experience of the interior sufferings of Jesus in all their fullness and diversity—whose maps of suffering were filled in precisely where no more than a blank space or a vague idea seemed to exist.[26]

[25] Alan E. Lewis, *Between Cross and Resurrection: A Theology of Holy Saturday*, foreword by John Alsup (Grand Rapids, MI: Eerdmans, 2001).
[26] Hans Urs von Balthasar, *First Glance at Adrienne von Speyr*, trans. by Antje Lawry and Sister Sergia Englund, O.C.D. (San Francisco: Ignatius Press, 1981), pp. 33, 35.

But such passages as these, and indeed the influence of Adrienne von Speyr's mysticism on Balthasar's theology of Holy Saturday generally, should not obscure other influences, above all theological ones stemming from certain antinomies in the tradition that Balthasar feels can only be resolved by adopting a much more robust theology of the event of Holy Saturday. Contemporary theology is characterized by deep rifts over a number of issues, and Balthasar holds that only a new understanding of Christ's descent into hell will resolve them. Readers of other essays in this volume will notice both a similar need and a similar strategy in Balthasar's treatment of Holy Saturday as can be found in other kenotic theologians treated elsewhere in this volume.[27] Just as Christology has always faced, even in the days of the ministry of St. Paul, certain antinomies and paradoxes for which only the assertion of God's self-emptying could serve as the explanation, so too for Balthasar other antinomies and paradoxes besides those purely Christological ones have compelled him to look at the ultimate moment of God's self-emptying: when the Second Person of the Blessed Trinity descended into hell for the sake of the damned. In that way, hell becomes for Balthasar not just a Christological place but above all a moment in the life of the Trinity.

It shall be the burden of the rest of this essay to examine these primarily *theological* motives for Balthasar's theology of Holy Saturday, as opposed to examining, for example, the biographical reasons, especially his encounter with Adrienne von Speyr. Thus, rather than interrogating the authenticity of her experiences (a task perhaps best left for later generations), this chapter will look at certain issues inherent in the proclamation of the Christian message that have forced this issue of Christ's descent into hell into the foreground, despite the trajectory of the past history of theology (which trajectory, we saw in Section 1, more or less relegated that theme to the background or mitigated its implications). For purposes of this chapter I shall concentrate on two of these *theological* antinomies: the so-called 'scandal of particularity' (meaning the issue of how one man, indeed one event, can save the whole cosmos, together with the related question of how one religion can claim to be true in relation

---

[27] See especially Thomas Thompson's essay on nineteenth-century kenoticists above.

to all the others), and the issue of God's changelessness vis-à-vis the events of the drama of salvation.

3

For Balthasar *the* central issue in Christology—more determinative than issues such as the divinity and humanity subsisting in the one person of Jesus, or the difference between the work and the person of Christ—revolves around the statement of Jesus in the Gospel of John to be 'the Way, the Truth and the Life' (John 14:6). Rather than concentrate on the knotty issues of historical criticism entailed by the famous 'I am' statements in the Fourth Gospel, Balthasar focuses on what such a statement might mean.[28] For even at the purely textual level, this claim raises the issue of the scandal of particularity to an unprecedented pitch, so that if it can be resolved here, all other issues pertaining to Christology and pluralism will find their own resolution there as well. Moreover, precisely because this issue of the 'scandal of particularity' lies deeper in the bedrock of all other Christological issues, Balthasar's use of the concept of kenosis will

---

[28] A note on historical criticism, however, would not be amiss here: Balthasar freely admits that this claim struck Jesus' contemporaries more in his behaviour and demeanour than in his words as such. His *recorded* words, especially those in the Fourth Gospel, were, so to speak, 'precipitated' in the text only after a process of reflection and refinement in the early Church's preaching, a preaching which itself always took as its starting point the totality of the Christ event in the light of the resurrection. As we shall see later when dealing with the whole 'pattern' of Jesus' life—especially the pattern of Claim, Execution, and Validation (of the Claim in the Resurrection)—the dilemmas posed by historical criticism can be met by the same retrospective view of Jesus in light of the Resurrection that all four evangelists also adopt in their narrative technique. Alan Lewis is quite insightful on this issue: 'Humble, bent on obedience and service, prepared to suffer, and unassertive when challenged and provoked, he [Jesus] nevertheless thrusts the word "I" into the centre of deadly controversy, making his own person the critical test of the credibility of his message.... His own message, subject to conflict and controversy, and seemingly quite discredited and defeated from the perspective of his tomb, is now [in the light of the Resurrection] drastically, triumphantly reassessed' (Lewis, *Between Cross and Resurrection*, pp. 51, 63). And precisely because the Gospels are written in the retrospective light of the Resurrection (indeed are written solely to convey its implications), the identity of the Risen Jesus shines through in the very narrative presentation of his earthly ministry.

differ from those theologians who first invoked the concept to resolve issues like Jesus' consciousness or the relation between his human and divine nature. As we shall see, this radicalizes the notion of kenosis in ways that, in my opinion, are unique among kenoticists. But first we must see why the claim of Jesus to be *the* Truth requires a kenotic understanding. In effect, this claim means the following: one product of the universe also claims to be its substrate, or in Balthasar's image, the wave *is* the sea, a claim that is on the face of it not just paradoxical, but absurd; and the response to that claim is bound to result in outrage and rejection. For whatever else Jesus is, he is a human being 'born of woman' (Gal. 4:4), and thus the product of the universe out of which he came and to which he is destined to return at death. But for one product to claim that he is not just a pointer *to* the Truth, *a* way, but is *the* Truth, well that, for Balthasar, is the Claim that could not be tolerated in the Judaism of Jesus' day or in the Greek philosophical outlook of a Hellenized Roman Empire, nor can it be tolerated inside today's evolutionary framework:

The Greek mind found it ridiculous that one of the products of the all-pervasive *physis* should equate itself with the generative matrix. Jewish thought found it even more incredible that a created man should predicate of himself the attributes proper to the Creator of the world and the Covenant-Lord of Israel. It is still nonsense, but now to a modern evolutionary world-view of any persuasion, to assert that one wave in the river that has flowed on for millions of years and will continue to flow on unthinkably for yet more millions once the wave is no more, can be identified with the river. Nonsense, too, to assert that this wave has already comprehended all of that future and enclosed within itself the fullness of time and the end of time. On attempting to estimate the degree of provocation in such fantastic claims, we see clearly that any school of religious or philosophic thought must be surprised and deeply shocked by another statement in the same context: 'They hated me without cause' (John 15:25).[29]

This passage explains both Balthasar's interpretation of the nature of the claim made by Jesus in his life and preaching and the reasons why such a claim would provoke a reaction that would bring about his execution, which represents in a sense the refutation of that claim by

---

[29] Hans Urs von Balthasar, 'Why I am Still a Christian', in *Two Say Why*, trans. by John Griffiths (Chicago: Franciscan Herald Press, 1973), p. 18.

the human race, a refutation that can itself only be counter-refuted by God in the resurrection. Thus the triad of Claim–Crucifixion–Resurrection (or in another formulation, Provocation–Execution–Validation) represents the central *Gestalt* of the Christ event, so that no part of the triad can be omitted without distorting the overall saving pattern that the Christ event means as a whole.

But if the Resurrection means God's own validation of the claim made by Jesus in his earthly life, *what* exactly is being validated? Or in other words, what did Peter mean in his first sermon preached on Pentecost that 'God raised him [Christ] to life, freeing him from the pangs of Hades, for it was impossible for him to be held in its power' (Acts 2:24; Western text)? Why could not Hades 'hold' Christ in its power?

To answer this question Balthasar varies the image of wave and sea slightly by now comparing Jesus to a stone dropped into the sea and whose ripple effects radiate outward. Now with all other human beings, one's ripple effects radiate only forward along time's future-bound direction, and even there one's effects eventually fade, to be overwhelmed by the effects of subsequent history. Perhaps no one's influence and impact entirely die out (history still feels the effects, for example, of Sennacherib's failure to conquer the city of Jerusalem in 701 BC even if that impact was later muted by Nebuchadnezzar's successful siege in 586 BC).[30] But if the saving effects of Jesus are to reach to the whole cosmos (Col. 1:19–20), then his effects must not only be able to move backwards in time, but also there must be something about the radiating power of the stone that prevents it from being swamped by later history. And that can only happen if somehow the claim is already true by virtue of the pre-existence of the Logos and the reality of the Incarnation, so that Christ's descent into hell is an event within the Godhead, by which the entirety of the evil of the world has been fully plumbed:

---

[30] On this point see William H. McNeill, 'The Greatest Might-Have-Been of All', *New York Review of Books*, vol. XLVI, no. 14 (23 September 1999): 62–4: 'This may be an odd thing to say about an engagement that never took place; yet Jerusalem's preservation from attack by Sennacherib's army shaped the subsequent history of the world far more profoundly than any other military action I know of' (p. 62).

If the claim stands, the whole truth must also possess a ballast, an absolute counterweight [*Schwergewicht*] that can be counterbalanced by nothing else; and because it is a question of truth, it must be able to show that it is so. The stone in the one pan of the scales must be so heavy that one can place in the other pan all the truth there is in the world, every religion, every philosophy, every complaint against God *without counterbalancing it.* Only if that is true, is it worthwhile remaining a Christian today.[31]

The stone thus must land on the seabed with such a thud, indeed with such a continually reverberating thud, that it will continue to radiate outwards *in both directions, past and future,* so that its effects can be fully appropriated by each conscious being of the cosmos as a fully contemporary event. And this for Balthasar is the meaning of the otherwise enigmatic line in 1 Peter 3:19 that Christ in his descent came to preach to spirits in prison 'who disobeyed God *long ago*'. Nor can the effects of the Christ event be allowed to fade in the future but it must have a power to make itself fully contemporaneous in the life of the Church through her preaching and sacraments:

The claim to be the overpowering weight on the scales—for all time and in all places, along with the whole scandal it contains—must be powerful enough (and this power is the Holy Spirit) to make itself intelligible 'always, even until the end of the world' and 'to all nations.' This is not to deny the part played by hermeneutics ('you will be my witnesses' and 'teach them to observe all things,' which presumably includes teaching them to under-stand). But the claim, if justifiably upheld, is not dependent upon hermen-eutical acuity.[32]

But precisely here Balthasar radicalizes the tradition and makes his Christology fully kenotic in ways that in my opinion are unpreced-ented in the history of theology. For unlike earlier presentations of the Descent in both East and West that simply assumed that Christ was active in hell (and naturally enough, for that seems to be the implication of 1 Peter 3:18 that Christ 'also went and *preached* to the spirits in prison'), Balthasar insists on Christ's total passivity in hell:

Jesus was truly dead, because he really became a man as we are, a son of Adam, and therefore, despite what one can sometimes read in certain theological works, he did not use the so-called 'brief' time of his death for

---

[31] Balthasar, *Two Say Why,* p. 29.   [32] Ibid., pp. 37–8.

all manner of 'activities' in the world beyond. In the same way that, upon earth, he was in solidarity with the living, so, in the tomb, he is in solidarity with the dead.... Each human being lies in his own tomb. And with this condition Jesus is in complete solidarity.[33]

Once again, no element that makes up the *Gestalt* of this event can be removed without destroying the entire pattern that makes it precisely a saving event. And for Balthasar perhaps the most essential component of this *Gestalt* is the depth of God's self-emptying love in letting the Son taste fully the depths of divine reprobation (it is this implication of Balthasar's theology that we saw had provoked the criticism from Gerald O'Collins). Perhaps no one has seen this more clearly or expressed it more concisely than Aidan Nichols, who manages to bring all these elements together in one paragraph of admirable lapidary insight:

Balthasar stresses Christ's solidarity with the dead, his passivity, his finding himself in a situation of total self-estrangement and alienation from the Father. For Balthasar, the Descent 'solves' the problem of theodicy, by showing us the condition on which God accepted our foreknown abuse of freedom: namely, his own plan to take to himself our self-damnation in Hell. It also demonstrates the costliness of our redemption: the divine Son underwent the experience of godlessness. Finally, it shows that the God revealed by the Redeemer is a Trinity. Only if the Spirit, as the *vinculum amoris* between Father and Son, can re-relate Father and Son in their estrangement in the Descent, can the unity of Revealed and Revealer be maintained. In this final humiliation of the *forma servi*, the glorious *forma Dei* shines forth via its lowest pitch of self-giving love.[34]

Thus the reason Balthasar's Christology fully deserves the label 'kenotic' is because for him that kenosis reaches its fullest expression and its most salvific efficacy in Christ's descent among the dead. As Balthasar himself puts it, here is the realm where self-emptying can go no further:

In Sheol, in the Pit, all that reigns is the darkness of perfect loneliness. But to be without contact with God *means* to be without the inner light of faith, hope, love.... If Jesus has suffered through on the Cross the sin of the world

---

[33] Balthasar, *Mysterium Paschale: The Mystery of Easter*, trans. with an introduction by Aidan Nichols, O.P. (Grand Rapids, MI: Eerdmans, 1990), pp. 148–9.

[34] Nichols, ibid., p. 7.

to the very last truth of this sin (to be forsaken by God), then he must experience, in the solidarity with the sinners who have gone to the underworld, their (ultimately hopeless) separation from God, otherwise he would not have known all the phases and conditions of what it means for man to be unredeemed yet awaiting redemption.[35]

Thus, for Balthasar, kenosis and redemption are not just correlative concepts but terms of identity. Here too we find the answer to the issue that so exercises Gerald O'Collins: that Jesus' experience of godforsakenness bespeaks a destructive image of God. Quite the contrary, precisely because humans have misinterpreted the true nature of God and have not only suffered under that image but sinned in its name, for that very reason Jesus must take upon himself that suffering and that sin (2 Cor. 5:21).

Moreover, O'Collins has not attended sufficiently, in my opinion, to the transformation *inside the Godhead itself* that occurred when the Son of God descended as a dead man to be among the dead. Two issues are at work here: one, what it means for Jesus to be *buried*, that is, to be truly dead among the dead; and two, what it means for God to save us in just this way, by sending His Son to die on the cross 'for us and for our salvation'. The first issue pertains to the anthropology of death, and the second to the meaning we must ascribe to God not based on 'imagery' or sentiment but on the revelation of the cross.

As to the first issue, Balthasar begins by invoking the patristic axiom that what has not been assumed by the human nature of the Son has not been redeemed by him either. And then he points to the interesting silence of Jesus after his resurrection regarding what is 'down there' in the underworld. Then the axiom and the silence combine to this fascinating insight:

But is he, we must ask, really alive? *Is* he active? Or is he not actually distinguished from all the other pilgrims into Hades, from Orpheus and Odysseus to Enoch, Jonah, Aeneas and Dante, precisely in this: that he is truly *dead*? Dead, in order to be able to be truly in the 'place' and in the condition of the dead. For this is precisely the issue: being-with, being in solidarity with the dead. This solidarity does not place him, in contrast to the Orphic and apocalyptic heroes, in any kind of position to observe or

[35] Balthasar, 'Descent into Hell', in *Explorations in Theology*, vol. IV: *Spirit and Institution*, trans. Edward T. Oakes, S. J. (San Francisco: Ignatius Press, 1995), p. 395.

recognize the dead. That is why, as the Risen One, he will not provide any report about what he has seen or done there. . . . In Sheol, in the Pit, all that reigns is the darkness of perfect loneliness. But to be without contact with God *means* to be without the inner light of faith, hope and love.[36]

Now once this has been granted, that the Son must have taken on the same submission to death and all that death entails for the rest of the human race, then it becomes clear why Jesus had to undergo punishment for sin. For far from turning God into an ogre of vengeance and totalitarian violence, the Cross reveals something much different of God:

God cannot love moral evil, he can only hate it. Of its very nature, it stands in complete opposition to God's essence. It is the counter-image of his holy love. There is no right love without wrath, for wrath is the reverse side of love. God could not truly love the good unless he hated evil and shunned it. . . . Therefore God does not forgive unexpiated sin. A mere amnesty is an ignoring of evil, which takes sin lightly or even recognizes in it an existence as of right.[37]

But once that point is conceded, only then does Balthasar's Christology reach the depths of its kenotic logic, for by virtue of the Incarnation Jesus has assumed in his human nature godforsakenness and has incorporated it, by his descent into hell, into the nature of the Godhead itself. This point comes out especially strongly in the last two volumes of his *Theo-Drama*, as in this passage:

Insofar as sin has finally and ultimately been concentrated in the crucified Son, God's final judgment on this sin also proceeds from the Cross. . . . This reversal [from judgment to mercy] is no extrinsicist decision of God: it is made possible *by the incorporation of godforsakenness into the trinitarian relation of love.*[38]

Thus we see that Balthasar's Christology not only merits the name 'kenotic' but is perhaps the most radically kenotic Christology of all, for that kenosis has now become an event within the Trinity itself:

Here we are faced with a bottomless mystery, for in fact there is an immense difference between the generating womb in God the Father and the generated

---

[36] Balthasar, 'Descent', ibid., pp. 407–8.
[37] Balthasar, *Mysterium Paschale*, pp. 138–9.
[38] Balthasar, *Theo-Drama*, vol. IV, pp. 233; emphasis added.

fruit, the Son, although both are one God in the Holy Spirit. Nowadays many theologians say, quite rightly, that it is precisely at the Cross that the difference becomes manifest, at this precise point the mystery of the divine Trinity is fully proclaimed. The distance is so great—for in God everything is infinite—that there is room in it for all the alienation and sin of the world; the Son can draw all this into his relationship with the Father without any danger of it harming or altering the mutual eternal love between Father and Son in the Holy Spirit. Sin is burnt up, as it were, in the fire of this love, for *God*, as Scripture says, *is a consuming fire* that will not tolerate anything impure but must burn it away.[39]

No doubt this 'image of God' can be intimidating, even terrifying, as the great mystics all have recognized. But this too Jesus experienced to the full ('what he has not assumed he has not redeemed'), and *his* experience we can only glance at from the other side of the bridge, *after* God's validation of Jesus in the resurrection, which is our bridge from the abyss of despair to the hope of new life:

And now there *is* something like a bridge over this rift: on the basis of the grace of the Resurrection there is the Church's faith, the faith of Mary; there is the prayer at the grave, the faithful watching and waiting. It is a lightly built bridge, and yet it suffices to carry us. What it spans, however, is not some different medium but the void of everlasting death. Nor can we compare the two sides as if from some higher vantage point; we cannot bring the two together in some rational, logical context by using some method, some process of thought, some logic: for the one side is that of death in God-forsakenness, and the other is that of eternal life. So we have no alternative but to trust in him, knowing, as we walk across the bridge, that he built it. Because of his grace we have been spared the absolute abyss, and yet, as we proceed across the bridge, we are actually walking alongside it, this most momentous of all transformations; we do not observe it, but can only be seized and pulled into it, to be transformed from dead people into resurrected people.[40]

---

[39] Hans Urs von Balthasar, 'The Scapegoat and the Trinity', in *You Crown the Year with Your Goodness: Radio Sermons through the Liturgical Year*, trans. by Graham Harrison (San Francisco: Ignatius Press, 1989), pp. 84–5; emphasis in the original.

[40] Ibid., pp. 91–2.

4

Thus far we have seen how Jesus cannot make the legitimate claim in either word or behaviour to be the Way, the Truth, and the Life—to be, in other words, the sea as well as the white-capped wave—unless that claim be validated by God in the resurrection. But God validates that claim not as a mere matter of verdict, but as an intra-trinitarian *event* in which all that Jesus is and suffered is subsumed into the triune Godhead to be transformed there. Thus, as we saw, the doctrine of kenosis explains (without explaining away) the validity of Jesus' claim to be the absolutely singular. But such a solution then brings us up against what kenosis further means for the notion of event, especially the event of self-emptying, in the Godhead itself. For the doctrine of kenosis ultimately means, as Balthasar puts it, that 'one must allow an "event" into the God who is beyond the world and beyond change.'[41] As one of Balthasar's most acute commentators, G. F. O'Hanlon, puts it in his monograph devoted to this theme:

The Incarnation has as its presupposition what may be called an event in God, and so it reveals to us that God is not rigidly immutable. Moreover the Incarnation itself does affect God: its reality is present and effective within the divine event. In both of these senses it may be said that the Incarnation does change God. Accordingly a philosophical concept of divine immutability deriving from an anti-heretical context and [now become] usual in theology is not longer admissible. This conclusion Balthasar bases on the evidence of Scripture, Fathers, such as Origen and Hilary, and his own trinitarian clarifications.[42]

This, however, does not mean that Balthasar has capitulated to the axiom of process theology that affirms the primacy of becoming over being. Rather, for him God is neither mythically mutable nor philosophically immutable in this sense: Incarnation posits a God who remains truly God and yet is intimately involved in our world. Thus the Incarnation really does betoken a kind of change in God but not in a temporal, mythological kind of way.

---

[41] *Mysterium Paschale*, p. 24.
[42] Gerard O'Hanlon, S.J., *The Immutability of God in the Theology of Hans Urs von Balthasar* (Cambridge: Cambridge University Press, 1990), p. 24.

So what way, then, can God be said to change? The short answer runs: God can be described in the categories of change only by virtue of being a triune God. If God were simply one, he would have become ensnared in the world-process through the Incarnation and cross. But only trinity allows the possibility for that kind of change in the Godhead that we denote by the term Incarnation. Again O'Hanlon gets the issue exactly:

Because God is triune, with both poles of difference and unity guaranteed by the Holy Spirit, the difference between Father and Son can accommodate all created differences including that extreme distance shown on the cross which becomes a revelation of the closest togetherness of Father and Son. In this way the ever-greater trinitarian love of God is the presupposition of the cross. . . . The eternal give and take of trinitarian love . . . can contain the most extreme and various modalities within it, so that the eternal circulation of life that this implies is not adequately conveyed by the traditional axiom of divine immutability.[43]

In that regard, there can be no question that Balthasar has moved beyond the tradition of immutability as classically understood in Augustine and Aquinas and as subsequently adopted by the Reformed theologians who posited what later became known, from Lutheran polemics, as the *extra-calvinisticum*, that is, the doctrine that the Logos of God was not entirely and succinctly present in the Person of Jesus during his earthly life (otherwise, so it was argued, how could the universe continue to be sustained by the Logos, through whom all things had their being?).[44] This Balthasar rejects:

---

[43] O'Hanlon, *The Immutability of God*, p. 27.

[44] Because of the technicality of the term a concise definition might be helpful: '*the Calvinistic extra*, a term used by the Lutherans to refer to the Reformed insistence on the utter transcendence of the human nature of Christ by the Second Person of the Trinity in and during the Incarnation. The Reformed argued that the Word is fully united to but never totally contained within the human nature, and, therefore, even in Incarnation is to be conceived as beyond or outside of (*extra*) the human nature. . . . It is clear that the so-called *extra calvinisticum* is not the invention of Calvinists but is a christological concept, safeguarding both the transcendence of Christ's divinity and the integrity of Christ's humanity, known to and used by the fathers of the first five centuries, including Athanasius and Augustine. . . . Against the Lutherans, the Reformed interpreted the *extra calvinisticum* in terms of the maxim *Finitum non capax infiniti*, the finite is incapable of the infinite. In other words, the finite humanity of Christ is incapable of receiving or grasping infinite attributes such as omnipresence, omnipotence, or omniscience' (Richard A. Muller, *Dictionary of Latin and Greek Theological Terms: Drawn Principally from Protestant Scholastic Theology* (Grand Rapids, MI: Baker Books, 1985), p. 111).

According to this [Reformed doctrine] the Logos, *extra carnem* [outside the flesh], did not abandon his governance of the world during Jesus's earthly sojourn and death, but rather carried out the Incarnation and the death as, so to say, one occupation alongside others. This must also have been the belief of Augustine and Thomas Aquinas to judge from the character of their premises.[45]

In a move of remarkable boldness, at least for a Roman Catholic, Balthasar will reject these premisses with this startling line: precisely because the entirety of the Logos is located in the Person of Jesus, 'the event of the Incarnation of the second divine Person does not leave the inter-relationship of those Persons unaffected.'[46]

Yet Balthasar, it must be stressed once more, does not thereby cave in to a philosophically fashionable subscription to the process theology and philosophy of Alfred North Whitehead or Charles Hartshorne. On the contrary, his respect for Chalcedon and for the generally held patristic axiom of God's immutability leads him to a most carefully nuanced stance regarding the 'philosophical' immutability of God, and to that extent Balthasar would hold to a *limited* concept of kenosis, one that would seem to draw back from more radical versions among 'creation kenoticists' (who hold that creation also entails an act of self-emptying by God) or among the death-of-God theologians who claim that God truly died on Good Friday (or did the death of God occur only in the nineteenth century, when Friedrich Nietzsche published *Thus Spake Zarathustra*?). As O'Hanlon explains, Balthasar's use of the term kenosis is quite nuanced:

However, the Incarnation is a free act of God and is consonant with the nature of God as self-giving trinitarian love. Moreover its effect on God is not to be measured in temporal, spatial or other univocally created categories which would imply some kind of mythological change. Kenosis is a proper theological term to describe the reality of the Incarnation, but it is only used properly if one recognises that it has a decidedly anthropomorphic aspect. This resides in the attribution of temporal and spatial change to God. In fact God remains eternal and united throughout whatever change is due

---

[45] Balthasar, *Mysterium Paschale*, p. 31.
[46] Ibid., p. 30. O'Hanlon rightly sees the import of this sentence in this commentary: 'Balthasar feels compelled to revise the tradition and to posit some real kenosis within God which has ontological status and is not merely functional, soteriological, or a simple addition which does not affect God' (*The Immutability of God*, p. 16).

to the Incarnation. And in the light of these clarifications it may be said that the Incarnation does not change God. Accordingly a concept of mythological, temporary mutability, involving theopaschism or some kind of self-alienation in God, is rejected.[47]

In other words, Balthasar must negotiate the usual set of Christian paradoxes and antinomies with great care: on the surface, it sounds openly contradictory to say that God is both changeable and unchangeable, but something like that position is required of him, indeed he would argue, of all theologians—provided of course the paradox is explained as both necessary and as the only explanation for the reality of change in this world coming from the free decision of a trinitarian God to create and redeem this world of Becoming by becoming man:

> It is vital to be aware of the fact that Balthasar can in this way legitimately answer 'yes' and 'no' to the question about change in God.... Ultimately both sets of statements derive their validity from different meanings of the term change or mutability. So is change something that is due to external cause or internal deficiency, and is it measured in temporal and spatial categories; or is it something that may, in God, be seen as a perfection which allows for life and variety, and even for an immersion in time without itself becoming temporal?[48]

[47] O'Hanlon, p. 24.

[48] Ibid. O'Hanlon makes clear why such subtlety of distinctions is crucial: both Paul's Letter to the Philippians *and* Chalcedon itself demand it! '[On the basis of Philippians 2:5–11 Balthasar] arrives at the necessity of positing a real kenosis in God, and from his repeated emphasis on the ontological, personal identity of the Logos as the subject who unites the two distinct natures in Christ, he will refuse to limit the change and suffering which Christ experiences [to] his human nature alone. This is the advance on Chalcedon and its traditional interpretation which Balthasar proposes. The tendency to consider the human nature of Christ as an *instrumentum conjunctum* which does not affect the divine person he sees as Nestorian in character. And so he is anxious to insist on a more than merely logical *communicatio idiomatum*, to accept that the formula "one of the Trinity has suffered" does indeed mean that God has "suffered", albeit mysteriously. But why "mysteriously": why not say univocally that God suffers? Because—and here we find Balthasar's respect for Chalcedon—there *is* an enduring and incommensurable difference between God and the world, between the divine and human "unmixed" natures of Christ. Any facile attribution of change and suffering to God, based on the fact that the person of Christ is affected by his human nature, represents a failure to maintain the distinction between the natures; it is a relapse into monophysitism and results in a mythical notion of God' (p. 43).

Non-believers have always had a field day mocking these interminable distinctions, for what to Christians is a paradox opening the believing soul to the ultimate mystery of God's redeeming love is to them the hopeless contradiction of faith in an all-powerful, all-loving God who created a world with evil in it and then 'healed' that evil by delivering up His Son to a gruesome death. There can be no doubt that the concept of kenosis does not solve that apologetic difficulty, but is meant to serve the confessional needs of Christians to illuminate the paradoxical ways of their God (this is shown by the context of the liturgical hymn quoted by Paul in Philippians. 2:6–11, for in verse 5 Paul introduces the quote by saying 'put on the mind of Christ Jesus who...humbled himself,' etc.). As far as apologetics is concerned, I think it best to leave the paradox as stark as possible, as Blaise Pascal did so well in his *Pensées*, whose insight here will serve as a fitting conclusion to these reflections:

Pride tells us we can know God without Jesus Christ, in effect that we can communicate with God without a mediator. But this only means that we are communicating with a God who is the prideful result that comes from being known without a mediator. Whereas those who have known God through a mediator know their own wretchedness. Not only is it impossible to know God without Jesus Christ, it is also useless.... For knowing God without knowing our wretchedness leads to pride. Knowing our wretchedness without knowing God leads to despair. Knowing Jesus Christ is the middle course, because in Him we find both God and our wretchedness.[49]

---

[49] Blaise Pascal, *Penseés*, trans. Honor Levi (Oxford: Oxford University Press, 1995), 63–4.

10

Does Kenosis Rest on a Mistake? Three Kenotic Models in Patristic Exegesis

Sarah Coakley

1. INTRODUCTION AND OUTLINE OF THESIS

It is a feature of contemporary philosophical analysis of 'kenotic' Christology (as witnessed by the contributions of C. Stephen Evans and Stephen Davis to this volume), to emphasize the particular problems of *coherence* caused by the notion of divine 'self-emptying'. 'Orthodox' or 'Chalcedonian' Incarnationalism is taken (not unreasonably, given the normative interpretation of Chalcedon from the time of Constantinople II[1]) to imply an assumption that the subject of such 'Incarnation' simply *is* the divine, pre-existent Logos, who had an existence in some sense 'prior' to the taking of humanity, but who, in becoming human must—according to this reading of *kenosis*—have undergone some modification, or 'retraction', of divine characteristics such as impassibility, omniscience, and omnipotence.

---

[1] In the Chalcedonian Definition itself it is not clear that the *hypostasis* is to be straightforwardly identified with the pre-existent Logos, since it (the *hypostasis*) is mentioned only in the context of its being the point of 'concurrence' of the humanity and the divinity. (It might be said that the identification is *implied* by the placement of the 'Definition' in the context, in the *Acta*, of a recapitulation of the earlier conciliar creeds; but the strands are not actually drawn together here in 451). The explicit identification of the *hypostasis* with the Logos is made only later, at the second Council of Constantinople (553). On this point, see my 'What Does Chalcedon Solve and What Does it Not? Some Reflections on the Status and Meaning of the Chalcedonian "Definition"', in eds. Stephen T. Davis, Daniel Kendall, S.J., and Gerald O'Collins, S.J., *The Incarnation* (Oxford: O.U.P., 2002), 143–63.

The question whether, and how, such a modification can be seen as philosophically and religiously coherent then moves from this base of assumptions. And much then hangs, of course, on whether philosophically grounded notions of the divine perfections are allowed to triumph over the biblical witness to the characteristics of Jesus' life, or vice versa.

When we turn to the patristic witness to the possible meanings of Philippians 2:5–11, however, we must immediately be struck by a different set of assumptions. For a start, as is often pointed out (sometimes as a slightly supercilious dig), our patristic authors— for all their bewildering creative difference in the exegesis of this passage—rarely *consider* the possibility of the questioning of divine impassibility or other cognate characteristics in the light of the Incarnation. The fact is that they have other, and complex, strategies for dealing philosophically and doctrinally with the issue of 'divine' self-emptying in Philippians 2, and it will be the purpose of this chapter to compare and contrast three such (well-developed) strategies from the fourth and fifth centuries. In so doing, I aim to play devil's advocate (or is it Socratic gadfly?), and urge that the sophisticated—and different—readings of the *communicatio idiomatum*[2] that we find in these three authors are highly instructive for our contemporary philosophical debate. For what we see first, in the light

---

[2] The doctrine of the 'communication of idioms' (i.e. the account of the precise relationship of the 'distinctive characteristics' of the human and the divine in Christ) has a complex history on which—unfortunately—even now there is no one definitive scholarly monograph (although Richard Cross has recently begun to attempt this task: see, e.g. his 'Perichoresis, Deification, and Christological Predication in John of Damascus', *Medieval Studies* 62, 2000, 69–124). Pre-Chalcedonian authors whom we treat in this essay will often talk—somewhat loosely—of *linguistic* 'attribution', or 'appropriation', of the characteristics of one nature to the other, without clarifying precisely the implied *ontological* relation of the two. And Chalcedon itself does not pronounce, normatively, on the way this matter should be construed. There is a certain anachronism, then, in speaking in this way that suggests that the *communicatio idiomatum* already had, in the period we are considering, a clearly defined status as point of theological decision (with various analytically distinguished options to be weighed and considered). Part of what is offered here, then, is a 'back-formation' attempt at such clarification *re* the relevant patristic material; the much later intra-Reformation debates on the same topic produced, at last, a set of clearly distinguished options: see, for a brief introductory account, Wolfhart Pannenberg, *Jesus—God and Man* (London: S.C.M. Press, 1968), 296–307.

of them, is that the contemporary philosophical analysis has largely ignored the technical issue of the relation of the two natures (and possible variations thereon) in its setting up of the *kenotic* problem. Yet a failure to consider the complexifications afforded by these readings of the *communicatio* causes the contestants in the debate to overlook potentially sophisticated ways of avoiding a modification of the divine nature as a result of the Incarnation. In short, this discussion has in large part overlooked the importance of the doctrine of the 'communication of idioms' altogether.

More particularly, and secondly, one of our chosen authors, Gregory of Nyssa (whose Christology has been unduly neglected until recently on account of its apparent failure to conform to later, Chalcedonian standards), presents us—I believe—with a peculiarly cogent understanding of Philippians 2 which seems anticipatorily to satisfy all the requirements of 'modern' historical consciousness whilst also avoiding divine modification. This is what causes me to title my essay as I have: could it be that the philosophical contortions required to make the notion of divine 'retraction' plausible are unnecessary, and thus 'rest on a mistake'?[3] Finally, we shall also remark briefly in closing on how even the philosophical interpretation of these arcane patristic issues may be subliminally affected by gender associations, given an assumption made by most contemporary philosophical interlocutors about the normative nature of freedom (both human and divine) and thus about their proposed form of intersection. This will be held up for new critical reflection in the light of the patristic material that we reflect upon, and at the same time forge a connection with Ruth Groenhout's contribution to this volume.

Such is enough by way of introduction.

---

[3] I do intend a (slightly ironic) allusion to M. F. Wiles's now classic paper, 'Does Christology Rest on Mistake?' in eds. Sykes and Clayton, *Christ, Faith and History* (Cambridge: C.U.P., 1973), 3–12. In my case the 'mistake' I am attempting to expose is the presumption made by modern philosophical analyses of *kenosis* that there is a necessity to bring 'divine' and 'human' characteristics into the *same plane* and make them into a 'coherent' package. I draw these critical conclusions at the end of this essay.

2. PHILIPPIANS 2 IN PATRISTIC EXEGESIS

A quick perusal of the relevant sections in the first seven volumes of the *Biblia Patristica*[4] should be enough to convince the patristic neophyte of the immense significance for patristic exegesis of Philippians 2. The material is of overwhelming complexity and density; in Origen alone, for instance (to whom a whole volume of *Biblia Patristica* is devoted) there are 219 discussions of the 'hymn' (Phil. 2:5–11), or verses within it. Any pert generalizations about patristic interpretation of this matter would therefore be foolhardy, although more confident scholars of an earlier generation did attempt them. In a now-classic article for the first edition of *The Encyclopedia of Religion and Ethics*,[5] for instance, Friedrich Loofs suggested that patristic exegesis of 'kenosis' could conveniently be tidied into three categories: (a) that which straightforwardly identified the subject of the 'emptying' as the *logos asarkos*; (b) that which adopted a 'Pelagian' reading (pre-eminently, of course, Pelagius himself), and saw the 'historical Jesus' as *earning* his name above every other name by a human act of obedience; and (c) a third, median category (which Loofs slightly confusingly terms 'Antiochene/Occidental'), which brought together elements of the first two categories by seeing the 'decisive' act of 'emptying' as the Logos's Incarnation, the implications then being wrought out in the 'historical Jesus Christ', such that there was a '*co-existence*' of the '*forma Dei*' and the '*forma servi*'.

Now this three-fold typology obviously has its pedagogical uses: Pelagius has a nicely unambiguous position in it as official 'heretic' (b); and Cyril and Nestorius, the great fifth-century Christologians vying for hegemony in the preamble to Chalcedon, can be conveniently ascribed, dialectically, to (a) and (c). But whether it is clear that the distinction between (a) and (c) can always be unambiguously maintained (granted that Tertullian is positioned by Loofs, with

---

[4] *Biblia Patristica: index des citations et allusions bibliques dans la littérature patristique* (Paris: Editions du Centre national de la recherche scientifique, 1975–).

[5] Friedrich Loofs, art. 'Kenosis', in ed. James Hastings, *Encyclopedia of Religion and Ethics* (Edinburgh: T & T Clark, 1914), VII, 680b–87b. Also worth comparing is P. Henry, 'Kénose', in the *Dictionnaire de la Bible Supplément* (Paris: Librairie Letouzey et Ané, 1957), V, 7–162.

Origen, in (a), and Hilary and Augustine, with Ambrosiaster, in (c))
seems to me a moot point. Moreover, we note that Gregory of Nyssa
(and indeed the other 'Cappadocian' fathers of the late fourth century) get virtually no mention at all in Loofs' account; and this is an
extraordinary omission which can only be explained as part of the
selective principle of an earlier *Dogmengeschichte* bent primarily on
clarifying 'false-starts and approximations' *en route* to normative
'Chalcedonianism'. Yet—as I shall shortly argue—Gregory of Nyssa
seems to me to represent a distinct (other) type of exegesis of
Philippians 2 which cuts through many of the difficulties left by
Loofs's categories (a) and (c), especially for those of 'modern' and
'postmodern' historical consciousness. Accordingly I shall adopt the
slightly anachronistic procedure of discussing Cyril and Nestorius's
exegesis of Philippians 2 first; then I shall cut back a generation to the
neglected Gregory of Nyssa, in order to highlight his distinctiveness
and originality. Note, however (as Loofs does after his long and
learned exposition of his three 'types'), that in *all* this patristic material, and for all its extraordinary variety and ingenuity, there is rarely a
whiff of actual modification of divine characteristics: 'The truth is',
remarks Loofs, 'that no theologian of any standing in the early Church
ever adopted such a theory of *kenosis* of the Logos as would involve an
actual supersession of His divine form of existence by the human—a
real "*becoming*-man", i.e., a transformation on the part of the Logos'.[6]

Was this a prejudicial weakness, a failure of philosophical nerve, an
unwillingness to take as fully authoritative the givenness of Scripture?
Or was it an insight of greater wisdom than that evidenced by what
Loofs calls 'popular' exegesis and the tug of Arianism? This matter we
shall now consider through the comparison, first, of the accounts of
Philippians 2 in Cyril and Nestorius. These figures will well exemplify
the two dominant types of patristic *kenotic* theory ((a) and (c))
adumbrated by Loofs.

(a) Cyril (d. 444)

It has been well said that Cyril's entire Christological undertaking
could be ranged under the heading of an extended exegesis of

---

[6] Loofs, art. 'Kenosis', 683a.

Philippians 2.[7] The force of his Logos Christology lies largely in its intense stress on the integrity and mysterious unity of the Logos's act of soteriological condescension in taking on human nature: the personal identity of Christ lies squarely in the pre-existent Logos, and what is 'assumed' (all the characteristics of human nature, including—*contra* Apollinarius—a human mind) involves no change to that identity, but merely an *extension* of its range for the sake of the salvific process. There is an ostensible loss of stature in this act of condescension, to be sure, but no actual ontological transformation of the Logos itself. *Kenosis* here, then, is really *assumption* ('addition' would suggest a false duality for Cyril); for there is no question here of any actual, ontological 'emptying' of divine characteristics, but rather the Logos's act of complete soteriological integrity in his taking on of the human condition. The exegesis of Philippians 2 thus proceeds accordingly:

> What sort of *emptying* is this? To assume the flesh, even in the form of a slave, a likeness to ourselves while not being like us in his own nature but superior to the whole creation. Thus he humbled himself, descending by his economy into mortal bounds.[8]

Or again:

> Since... the divine Logos who came down from above and from heaven 'emptied himself and took the form of a slave' [Phil. 2:7] and was also called 'Son of Man' while remaining what he was (that is, God; for he is unchangeable and unalterable by nature), he is said to have come down because he is now conceived to be one with his own flesh, and so he is called 'the human being from heaven', the same one being complete in his deity and complete in his humanity and understood to exist in one person. There is one Lord Jesus Christ, even though we do not ignore the difference of the natures out of which we say the inexpressible union has been made.[9]

---

[7] See esp. Frances Young, *From Nicaea to Chalcedon* (London: S.C.M., 1983), 260–3, drawing also on R. A. Norris, 'Christological Models in Cyril of Alexandria', *Studia Patristica* 13, 1975, 255–68.

[8] 'On the Unity of Christ', cited and translated in ed. Mark J. Edwards, *Ancient Christian Commentary on Scripture*, VIII, *Galatians, Ephesians, Philippians* (Downers Grove, Illinois: Inter-Varsity Press, 1999), 243; Greek text in Migne PG 75: 1301B [742].

[9] 'Letter to John of Antioch', in R. A. Norris, *The Christological Controversy* (Philadelphia: Fortress Press, 1980), 143; Greek text in eds. Josepho Alberigo et al., *Conciliorum Oecumenicorum Decreta* (Bologna: Istituto per le Scienze Religiose, 1972), 72, lines 11–28.

This being so, how then is the so-called *communicatio idiomatum* construed in Cyril? The matter is a little complex. On the one hand, as is well explicated by Grillmeier,[10] there is no real doubt that—in the Alexandrian tradition of Athanasius—Cyril is assuming a (one-way) *ontological* communication of divine *energeia* from the divine nature to the human; were this not so, the human nature assumed in the Incarnation would not be *changed*, and the salvific point of the whole exercise undermined. But on the other hand, Cyril is extraordinarily anxious that this exchange not be seen as a 'mixture' or 'blending' (a technical and semantic point that will prove an instructive axis of comparison with Gregory of Nyssa[11]); for this could lead, according to Cyril, to the false conclusion that the divine nature has somehow been contaminated by the human. Where 'appropriation' of the human characteristics to the divine are concerned, then (and this is Cyril's way of talking about the *communicatio*) this is emphatically *not* a matter of ontological leakage, but a mysterious 'attribution' for the sake of salvation:

we all confess that the divine Logos is impassible, even though, since he himself carries out the mystery [of salvation], he is seen to attribute to himself the passions that occur in his own flesh. ... In order that he may be believed to be Savior of the universe, Christ refers the passions of his own flesh—as I have said—to himself by means of an appropriation which occurs for the sake of our salvation.[12]

Now so far the picture looks consistent, if a little *mysterious*. *Kenosis* involves no change in the divine nature, but a means of transference of divine 'energy' into the human nature. However, the 'mysterious' dimension *re* the 'attribution' of human characteristics to the divine Logos (never fully explained) becomes conceptually strained when Cyril is forced to confront some of the issues of Christ's suffering in the passion narratives; and it is here (I am going to argue) that his predecessor Gregory had a more convincing and effective approach that Cyril does not consider. For Cyril there seem to be two basic ploys

---

[10] Aloys Grillmeier, *Christ in Christian Tradition*, I, 2nd edn. (Atlanta: John Knox Press, 1975), 476.

[11] By the time of Cyril the language of 'mingling' has become suspect of the overtones of 'confusion': see further, below.

[12] 'Letter to John of Antioch', in Norris, *The Christological Controversy*, 144; Greek text in eds. Alberigo et al., 72, lines 42–4, and 73, lines 1–11.

for 'explaining' the displays of human suffering, nescience, and even despair that we find in the story of Christ's death. One is to play the paradox card hard: to underscore the utter 'ineffability' of the *hypostatic* union, and thus to declare that 'he suffered unsufferingly'. This has the force of rhetorical fiat, and doggedly defends the personal unity, but it can scarcely count as an *explanation*. The other ploy is actually to admit the separation-out of suffering into the human side (an admission in some tension with the maintenance of *absolute* personal unity):

> We assert that this is the way in which he suffered and rose from the dead. It is not that the Logos of God suffered in his own nature, being overcome by stripes or nail-piercing or any of the other injuries; for the divine, since it is incorporeal, is impassible. Since, however, the body that had become his own underwent suffering, he is—once again—said to have suffered these things for our sakes, for the impassible One was within the suffering body.[13]

We must conclude, then, from this brief account of *kenotic* themes in Cyril, that the magisterial avoidance of divine passibility is not effected without some remaining element of strain attending the discussion of Christ's human weakness. For here are precisely those elements of the biblical narrative that modern kenoticists have fastened onto as in need of clearer and more unembarrassed metaphysical explanation. In Cyril, the divine *unity* of Christ's person is the supposedly greatest strength: it guarantees the salvific efficacy of the Incarnation *tout court*; it rejects the possibility of disjunct duality in the person. But can it do so without ultimately 'supervening' over those elements of humanity most in need of salvation? The weakness seems to lie finally in the working out of the details of the *communicatio*.

These potential weaknesses were also of course in the mind of Nestorius, Cyril's notorious Christological rival, and one of the more maligned thinkers of the patristic era. Let us see whether, and how, he might be said to improve on the matter.

(b) Nestorius (d. *c.*451)

Since Nestorius's Christological starting-point is notably different from Cyril's, we should not be surprised to find a different reading

---

[13] 'Second Letter to Nestorius', in Norris, *The Christological Controversy*, 133; Greek text in eds. Alberigo et al., 42, lines 20–9.

of the significance of Philippians 2. In Nestorius we have what has been called an 'additive'[14] view of Christ's person: rather than starting from a (Cyrilline) straightforward *identification* of the person of Christ with the pre-existent Logos, it is in the 'conjunction' or 'union' of the Logos with a 'human being' that we locate the person of 'Christ'. 'Christ' therefore 'signifies the two natures', at once God *and* man. Yet Nestorius is no less passionately committed than Cyril to the main-tenance of divine impassibility (indeed, he fears Cyril's 'solution' to the Christological paradox precisely endangers it); hence, in his exe-gesis of Philippians 2 he is exceedingly careful to underscore how the 'natures' remain distinct. A lengthy quotation from him is here in order:

A creature [i.e. the Virgin] did not produce the Creator, rather she gave birth to the human being, the instrument of the Godhead. The Holy Spirit did not create God the Logos... Rather, he formed out of the Virgin a temple for God the Logos, a temple in which he dwelt.... Paul... recounts all at once everything which happened, that the [divine] being has become incarnate and that the immutability of the incarnate deity is always maintained after the union. That is why... he writes... 'Let this mind be in you which was also in Christ Jesus, who being in the form of God... emptied himself, taking the form of a slave' [Phil. 2:5–7]. He did not say, 'Let this mind be in you which was in God the Logos, who being in the form of God, took the form of a slave'. Rather, he takes the term *Christ* to be an expression which signifies the two natures, and without risk he applies to him both the style 'form of a slave', which he took, and that of God. The descriptions are different from each other by reason of the mysterious fact that the natures are two in number.

Furthermore, it is not only this—that Christ as God is unaffected by change—which must be proclaimed to Christians but also that he is ben-evolent, that he takes the 'form of a slave' while existing as he was, in order that you may know not only that he was not altered after the union but that he has been revealed as both benevolent and just.[15]

Nestorius goes on from here to recount how, in his earthly life, Christ systematically undoes all the wrongs of Adam; throughout, it is his

[14] This is Grilllmeier's appellation: see *Christ in Christian Tradition*, I, 453.
[15] 'First Sermon Against the *Theotokos*', in Norris, *The Christological Controversy*, 124–6; Greek text in ed. Friedrich Loofs, *Nestoriana: die Fragmente des Nestorius* (Halle: Niemayer, 1905), 252, lines 10–15.

historical 'obedience' in *forma servi* (conjoined with his equal status in *forma dei*) which effects salvation: 'Because of his disobedience in the case of a tree, Adam was under sentence of punishment; Christ made up for this debt, too, "having become obedient" [Phil. 2:8] on a tree.'[16]

From this we can judge how apt is Loofs' explication of Nestorius's reading of Philippians 2 as a 'mixed type' between the 'Alexandrian' and the 'Pelagian'.[17] The 'emptying' is *both* the metaphysical act of Incarnation, construed now as a *conjunction* of natures (rather than Cyril's *assumption* by the divine Logos), and *also* Christ's human/ historical undoing of the effects of Adam's sin, his radical outworking of 'obedience'. The possibility of the double-reading is of course precisely the outcome of Nestorius's distinctive construal of the 'two natures' doctrine.

But what, then, of Nestorius's understanding of the *communicatio*? Here, again, unfortunately, things get a little murky. Much depends on how much evidence for Nestorius's position we may deduce from the enigmatic *Bazaar of Hericleides* (only preserved in Syriac, and exceedingly hard to evaluate); but if we take this following passage to be authentic to Nestorius, we arrive at a distinctive understanding of the *communicatio* that was later—in an admittedly clearer form—to have a long and honourable history:

There must be two natures, that of the divinity and that of the humanity. The divinity has emptied itself into the likeness of a servant. The humanity, in the likeness of a servant, has been raised into *the name which is above all names.* . . . This is in fact what summarizes the chief greatness of the nature of humanity. It is he who accepts *a name that is more excellent than all names.* He does this neither in consequence of moral progress nor in consequence of knowledge and faith. Rather he accepts that it has come about that humanity should be transformed in his image and person. In this way humanity becomes by exaltation what God is, the name which is above all names.[18]

---

[16] Ibid, in Norris, *The Christological Controversy*, 127; Greek text in ed. Loofs, *Nestoriana*, 256, lines 13–14.

[17] 'Pelagian' is actually misleading, if it assumes a need to 'earn' divine status.

[18] *The Bazaar of Heracleides*, 58, 61, in Edwards, *Ancient Christian Commentary on Scripture*, VIII, 253, using the translation from the Syriac of G.R. Driver and L. Hodgson, *The Bazaar of Heracleides* (Oxford: Clarendon, 1925).

If this is rightly understood, then Nestorius is insisting that each nature, maintaining its distinctiveness, is nonetheless referred to the person of Christ, such that *in him* there may be a transformative and salvific exchange without detrimental effects for the integrity of either: neither the divinity is besmirched, nor the humanity magicked into a form which denies or represses its natural and embodied frailty. But it might be objected that this (a) reads Nestorius over-charitably (a moot point); and/or (b) glosses the difficulties of this apparent metaphysical fiat. For if Cyril was problematic over the final integrity and significance of Christ's human sufferings, Nestorius remains equally elusive about the precise ontological significance of the *communicatio*. At times he can suggest that the attribution of divine and human characteristics to the 'person' is merely *linguistic*;[19] yet if that were so what would be changed, ontologically, by the event of Incarnation, a change that he clearly wishes to endorse vis-à-vis the humanity? At other times, he tries to effect a compromise by suggesting a real exchange at the level of the *prosopon* (a sort of outer, 'crust' interaction) which somehow does not finally affect the integrity of the separable natures at a deeper level.[20] The matter is made the more obscure by trying to interpret Nestorius through the veil of Syriac terms; but the result is neither clear nor obviously coherent. So again, as with Cyril, we confront a paradox: there is seemingly the *potential* for a philosophically coherent position here, and one as animated as is Cyril's (if not more so) by the desire to protect the divine characteristics from change; yet the outcome vis-à-vis the technical outworkings of the *communicatio* is far from fully satisfactory or consistent.

With these remaining problems in mind, let us now turn back a generation to Gregory of Nyssa. Can we find in him a more satisfactory or coherent position?

(c) Gregory of Nyssa (d. *c.*395)

We have dubbed Cyril's reading of Philippians 2 under the metaphor of *assumption*, and Nestorius's under that of *conjunction*; it might be

[19] See Norris, *The Christological Controversy*, 130, 139, for passages that suggest this approach.

[20] Grillmeier discusses this theme in the *Bazaar* at length, and highly critically: see *Christ in Christian Tradition*, I, 510–19.

apt in contrast to term Gregory's exegesis that of a *progressive trans-fusion.* Let me explain.

From the perspective of later Chalcedonianism, Gregory's position (and his concomitant exegesis of Philippians 2) hovers somewhat ambiguously, it might seem, between the poles of 'Alexandrian' and 'Antiochene' readings. This may be one of the reasons he has been found hard to categorize by the old-style proponents of nineteenth-century *Dogmengeschichte*; some see him as covertly Apollinarian (though Gregory is actually *countering* Apollinarius), and others as nascently 'Nestorian': Tixeront, in his *Histoire des dogmes* (1912) points out that both patterns are present.[21] The reason for this assessment, as we shall see, is that Gregory simultaneously accepts the 'Alexandrian' tradition of the Incarnation involving an actual, ontological transformation of the human in virtue of the Logos's *kenosis*, but also insists on the integrity of *a* (particular) human being, Jesus, as being the 'tabernacle' where this transformation occurs.[22] The crucial difference from both the (later) models of Cyril and Nestorius, however (and this also constitutes the *novum* that may be attractive from a modern, 'historical-critical' perspective), is that, in Gregory's understanding of the transformation of the human in Jesus, the process is not *immediate.* Rather, it is throughout the lifetime of Jesus' ministry, life, and death—and supremely and decisively in the resurrection—that this purification and transform-ation occurs; not that there is *sin* to be removed in Jesus himself, but merely a plumbing of every weakness and *pathos* that is characteristic of the genuinely human: the move from immaturity to maturity, from uncertainty to triumph, from fear to certitude, from grief to confi-dence is effected in this purification of the human. The 'personhood' of Christ is thus not, as in Cyril, already pre-identified (*qua* Logos),

---

[21] See Joseph Tixeront, *Histoire des dogmes dans l'antiquité chrétienne,* II (Paris: J. Gabalda,1912), 128; cited and discussed by Brian E. Daley, S.J. in 'Divine Tran-scendence and Human Transformation: Gregory of Nyssa's Anti-Apollinarian Christ-ology', *Studia Patristica* 32, 1997, 87–95; at 87. (This article by Daley is now reprinted in ed. Sarah Coakley, *Re-thinking Gregory of Nyssa* (Oxford: Blackwell, 2003), 67–76; but page references are given here from the original *Studia Patristica* version of the essay.)

[22] See, for instance, GNO II/2, 126; quoted by Daley, 'Divine Transcendence', 87. Gregory of Nyssa's works are cited by reference to the critical edition, *Gregorii Nysseni Opera* (GNO) (Leiden, 1958–).

such that the danger of the reading of the *kenosis* is that the
'assumption' of human characteristics looks like a mere takeover
bid that instantly trumps weakness—or else rhetorically declares
the Logos the subject of it without further explanation. But nor is
the dualism in Christ so uncomfortable as we tend to find Nestorius's
'solution', with its understandable attempts to 'stop' the characteristics of humanity and divinity from direct mutual exchange in the
'person', yet with its own apparent uncertainties about whether this is
finally soteriologically convincing. Rather, what Gregory proposes is
a *real*, but gradual, transfusion of divinity into the human, until, as
he memorably puts it, the humanity is 'absorbed by the omnipotent
divinity like a drop of vinegar mingled in the boundless sea'.[23] Thus
the seemingly unguarded language of 'mingling' or 'mixture' (later to
become a negative *shibboleth* to Cyril, and indeed explicitly deflected
by the Chalcedonian Definition[24]) is here fully advised: the divine
characteristics are progressively absorbed by the human, but not
without every dimension of authentic humanity being held up to
transformative interaction, until, in the resurrection, the process is
found complete.

What reading of Philippians 2 attends and supports this view?
Whilst Gregory's Christology is scattered throughout many of his
writings, three passages from the *Antirrheticus Against Apollinarius*
are especially revealing here: 'He *emptied himself*, as the Scripture
says, so that as much as nature could hold it might receive.'[25] And
again:

And even the word *emptied* clearly affirms that he was not always as he
appeared to us in history.... He *emptied himself*, as the apostle says, by

---

[23] GNO VIII/1: 126–7; Gregory uses this metaphor in various places: see also GNO
II/2, 132–3, and GNO III/1, 201. For a more detailed account of the interpretative
problems and interest of Gregory's metaphor of 'mingling', see J.-R. Bouchet, 'Le
vocabulaire de l'union et du rapport des natures chez saint Grégoire de Nysse', *Revue
Thomiste* 68, 1968, 533–82; and also my 'Power, gender and "mingling" in Gregory of
Nyssa's theory of christological *kenosis*', unpublished paper given at the Oxford
Patristics Conference, August 2003.

[24] Consider the requirements of the Chalcedonian Definition: 'without confusion,
without change'.

[25] GNO III/1, 123; in Edwards, *Ancient Christian Commentary on Scripture*,
VIII, 24

contracting the ineffable glory of his Godhead within our small compass. In this way *what he was* remained great and perfect and incomprehensible, but *what he assumed* was commensurate with the measure of our own nature.[26]

This is further explained:

Since the human is changeable, while the divine is unchangeable, the divinity is unmovable with respect to change, neither varying for the better nor for the worse (for it cannot take into itself what is worse, and there is nothing better); but human nature, in Christ, undergoes change towards the better, being altered from corruption to incorruption, from the perishable to the imperishable, from the short-lived to the eternal, from the bodily and the formed to what is without either body or form.[27]

Now we note from this particular exegesis that the 'mingling' of which Gregory regularly speaks obviously does not mean a *two-way* ontological exchange (Cyril's major worry). It is more like a glass being filled from an (incomprehensibly larger, indeed qualitatively and 'incomprehensibly' different) container, till everything divine has been taken in *that can be*. Not—says Gregory—that the characteristics of divinity and humanity are *compatible*; but nor are they meant to be: one (the divine) is infusing the other (the human) until it is fully restored to its proper perfection in the resurrection.[28] This, then, is Gregory's distinctive, and original, contribution to the exegesis of Philippians 2, and thus also to the store of possible renditions of the *communicatio*. We turn now to essay a brief contemporary assessment of these various alternative readings.

[26] GNO III/1, 159; in Edwards, *Ancient Christian Commentary on Scripture*, VIII, 242.

[27] GNO III/1, 223; this translation from Brian E. Daley, S.J., ' "Heavenly Man" and "Eternal Christ": Apollinarius and Gregory of Nyssa on the Personal Identity of the Savior', *Journal of Early Christian Studies* 10, 2002, 469–88, at 480–1.

[28] See esp. GNO III/1, 156–7, 158–9; in the excerpted translation from the *Antirrheticus* in Anthony Meredith, *Gregory of Nyssa* (London: Routledge, 1999), the relevant passages are at 54, 56–7. A more recent account of Gregory's Christology that fills out these themes with exactitude is to be found in John Behr, *The Nicene Faith: The Formation of Christian Theology* II/2 (New York: St. Vladimir's Seminary Press, 2004), 435–58.

3. CONTEMPORARY PHILOSOPHICAL IMPLICATIONS

When moving back from the patristic thought-world to that of contemporary philosophy of religion, we may be struck, first, by two (I believe debatable) assumptions made by those current 'kenoticists' who feel compelled to propound a 'substantive change' in the divine characteristics as a result of the Incarnation. These assumptions seem to be suggested by Evans and Davis, when they write as follows:

It seems safe to say that a conception of God as timeless and immutable would not be the most natural view of God if one took seriously the idea that the Incarnation itself is our primary window into God's being. For the Incarnation seems to shout to us that God is intimately involved in the temporal world and capable of change that is radical and even shocking in character. What is missing, in my view, if we think of the Incarnation merely as the temporal outcome of a timeless divine intention, is any sense that God himself enters the human condition, takes on human flesh, and experiences reality as a human does. A real Incarnation must not merely be an addition to God; it must make some difference to God as God.[29]

And:

The basic idea [of a kenotic theory] is that Christ was indeed simultaneously truly divine and truly human, possessing as he did all properties essential to divinity and humanity, and this was made possible by the Logos emptying itself, during the period of Jesus' earthly life, of those properties that normally characterize divinity but are inconsistent with humanity.... [For] *it is logically impossible for any being simultaneously to have all the members of both properties* [i.e. human and divine] (my emphasis).[30]

It is precisely in these kinds of statements, I suggest, that we see the effects of not considering the implications of some form of the doctrine of *communicatio idiomatum* seriously at the outset. For on the one hand (see Evans's remarks, first) we have the suggestion that

---

[29] See Evans, 'Kenotic Christology and the Nature of God', Ch. 8, p. 197 above.
[30] See Davis, 'Is Kenosis Orthodox', Ch. 5, p. 115 above.

'God' (*tout court?*) becomes human in the Incarnation, and thus that this must thereby imply 'change' to Godself. But this stops neither to consider the Trinitarian base of Incarnation theory (i.e. to locate the Incarnation as a specific undertaking of the *Second Person*), nor does it distinguish between 'Incarnation' and *metamorphosis* or *transmogrification.* Yet the doctrine of the *communicatio* is, as I hope to have illustrated, precisely intended to guard this crucial distinction. What happens in the Incarnation is *not* a simple turning of God into a human (this spectre was already headed off in the Sabellian controversy); but rather the coming into 'union' (however construed) of the divine Logos and humanity. The issue is thus not how divine characteristics can *be* human characteristics, but rather how one will affect and change the other (if at all) by their 'concurrence' (to use the language of Chalcedon). And this it is that the discussion of the *communicatio* specifically addresses, in all its various possible forms. So the first misunderstanding that needs to be allayed is the suggestion that Incarnation involves 'God' *turning into* 'man'.

Davis's remarks here are initially much more explicit about the necessary duality of the Incarnation than are Evans's; but he too, it seems to me, makes a further (and second) questionable assumption that the categories of 'divinity' and 'humanity' must somehow be *merged* so as to effect 'coherence' (just as, in an earlier piece of writing on the subject, he gave the analogy for the Incarnation of a tennis player (God) operating with one hand tied behind his back (the *kenotic* effects of *becoming* man)[31]). What is lost here is precisely, again, what the *communicatio* is striving to convey—that 'divinity' and 'humanity' *are* indeed radically distinct and qualitatively different categories, which cannot thus be collapsed into one flat package without seriously deleterious effects for the whole understanding of the salvific process.

In her excellent recent book, *Jesus, Humanity and the Trinity,* Kathryn Tanner has exposed precisely these sorts of 'modern' assumptions to critical gaze. Her central point—in which she evidences influence from Karl Rahner[32]—is that Christology that intends to be

---

[31] S. T. Davis, *Logic and the Nature of God* (Grand Rapids: Eerdmans, 1983), 125; discussed in my *Powers and Submissions: Spirituality, Philosophy and Gender* (Oxford: Blackwell, 2002), 23–5.

[32] See, e.g., Karl Rahner, *Theological Investigations,* I (Baltimore: Helikon Press, 1961).

'orthodox' radically loses its way if it starts from the assumption that the humanity and divinity of Christ are like two vying (but potentially well-matched?) contestants striving to inhabit the same space. As she well puts it, '[human] relations with God are utterly noncompetitive because God, from beyond this created plane of reality, brings about the *whole* plane of creaturely being and activity in its goodness.'[33] And the same principle applies, *mutatis mutandis*, to human–divine relations in Christ; thus, as Richard Norris has also argued (with the use of a similarly memorable metaphor) we must give up the 'two baskets' image of humanity and divinity if we wish to be true to the intentions of classical (and especially Chalcedonian) Christology.[34] We are not trying to squeeze together, or coalesce, two sets of features which (annoyingly?) present us with logical opposites; rather, we are attempting to conceive of a unique intersection precisely *of* opposites, in which the divine—that which is *in se* unimaginably greater and indeed creator and sustainer of the human—is 'united', *hypostatically*, with that 'human', forming one concrete subject.

If this is so (and of course, it may be debated or disbelieved), then where does it leave us in regard to the coherence of 'kenotic' Christologies? Let me end with some enumerated lessons and questions which may accrue from our visit to the exotic world of fourth- and fifth-century exegesis of Philippians 2. I do not pretend to provide definitive answers to all the issues I raise here in closing; my main goal has been to attempt to shift the focus of the philosophical discussion of *kenosis* in some potentially creative new directions.

1. The lessons of our constellating 'heroes' from the patristic thought-world may be seen to be mixed. I have tried to suggest that both Cyril's and Nestorius's alternative readings of the *communicatio* are worthy of consideration, and—whilst enshrining remaining internal difficulties of their own which I have highlighted—both are capable, in principle, of being refined and improved in ways

---

[33] Kathryn Tanner, *Jesus, Humanity and the Trinity* (Minneapolis: Fortress Press, 2001), 4.

[34] See R. A. Norris, 'Chalcedon Revisited: A Historical and Theological Reflection', in ed. B. Nassif, *New Perspectives on Historical Theology* (Grand Rapids: Eerdmans, 1996), 140–58.

compatible with 'Chalcedonianism', broadly understood.[35] However both, for reasons we have explored above, present us with difficulties relating to the areas of Jesus' humanity that have evinced most interest in 'modern' 'historical-critical' readings of the Gospels (and indeed therefore amongst modern 'kenoticists'): his apparent occasional nescience, his need for growth and psychological development, his frailty and fear in the face of suffering and death. Whilst these difficulties may not be entirely insuperable,[36] they tend to involve what I have termed a heavy playing of the 'paradox card'; and it is always an interesting question when, and to what degree, a theologian/philosopher is willing so to play.

2. Thus, it has been my particular interest in this chapter to place in the forefront an alternative (but only *questionably* 'proto-Chalcedonian'[37]) Christological alternative, that represented by Gregory of Nyssa; for it seems to me that his distinctive reading of Philippians 2 avoids many of the paradoxical difficulties of the other two renditions of the *communicatio* considered, whilst also providing a plausible and cogent account of the features of Jesus' humanity (just mentioned) that have so exercised modern 'kenoticists'. If, as I have suggested, his alternative could indeed be found to be finally coherent,[38] we might be able to declare that modern kenoticism 'rests on a mistake'.

---

[35] I think of Thomas Weinandy's recent defence of Cyriline/Chalcedonian impassibility on the one hand (see Thomas G. Weinandy, *Does God Suffer?* (Edinburgh: T & T Clark, 2000), esp. 172–213), or of Herbert McCabe's defence of an Antiochene/Chalcedonian version of the *communicatio* on the other (see Herbert McCabe, *God Matters* (London: G. Chapman, 1987), esp. 39–51).

[36] See the thorough philosophical account of the remaining problems—as perceived through the lens of medieval Christology—in Richard Cross, *The Metaphysics of the Incarnation* (Oxford: O.U.P., 2002).

[37] I say this because of the difficulties of reconciling Gregory's reading of Phil. 2 with the Chalcedonian requirement 'without change'. Yet Cyril's understanding is also problematic on that score.

[38] In this essay I have concentrated on the way in which Gregory's rendition of the human nature in Christ allows for genuine change and transformation in ways coincident with the Gospel texts and 'modern' historical approaches to them. It would be a larger task to attempt a full defence of the coherence of Gregory's Christology, and certain prima facie problems do remain, e.g. how to understand the relation of the Logos and the 'man' Jesus without fear of 'two Christs'.

3. The final concluding point is one I have raised in earlier essays on *kenosis* and which Stephen Evans graciously takes up at the end of his essay for this volume. It is that (in my view) the 'competitive' reading of the human–divine relations in Christ has gender overtones that need to be faced, and—if necessary—exorcised in any contemporary philosophical attempt to give credibility to 'Chalcedonian orthodoxy', whether *kenotically* conceived or otherwise. Here I can only repeat what I have suggested elsewhere at greater length,[39] namely, that the strong commitment to an 'incompatibilist' view of freedom in much analytic philosophy of religion today, combined with the 'competitive' view of divine–human relations just described, has unacknowledged overtones of a valorized 'masculinism'[40] (freedom from constraint, relationship, dependence) which leads to a *false choice* Christologically: *either* a ceding of certain divine characteristics in a *kenotic* understanding of the Incarnation based subliminally on competition (Davis, Evans); *or* a 'two minds' dualism infected by thought-experiments which vividly reconfirm the dominance of the dependence–control anxiety (variously, Morris, Swinburne, Brown[41]). This chapter has been devoted to suggesting that we need to get beyond these alternatives, and to re-embrace alternative readings of *kenosis* that take the *communicatio* tradition seriously, along with its understanding of the radical difference of status of the 'divine' and the 'human'. Such a view need not think of human 'freedom' as involving divine 'self-restraint' at all, I suggest, but rather as being enabled precisely *by* the sustaining and continuing matrix of divine creative power. It is not for nothing that it is Gregory of Nyssa who memorably insists that the *kenosis* of the Incarnation is the sign *of* supreme divine power, not of the loss of it.[42]

---

[39] In *Powers and Submissions*, esp. 3–39 and 98–105; and in 'Kenosis: Theological Meanings and Gender Connotations', in ed. John Polkinghorne, *The Work of Love: Creation as Kenosis* (Grand Rapids: Eerdmans, 2001), 192–210.

[40] I do not intend by the use of this term any suggestion of physiological or psychological essentialism.

[41] These authors and their views are discussed in some detail in my *Powers and Submissions*, 26–30.

[42] See GNO III/4, 59–61; the English can be found in 'Address on Religious Instruction', in ed. E. R. Hardy, *Christology of the Later Fathers* (Philadelphia: Westminster Press, 1954), 300–1.

11

The Logic of Assumption

Edwin Chr. van Driel

1. INTRODUCTION: CLASSICAL AND KENOTIC CHRISTOLOGY

Most chapters of this volume are concerned with a constructive discussion of kenotic Christology. Most of them, however, also include a polemic twist, the object of which is what I call classical Christology: the post-Chalcedonian Christology of the Middle Ages, the Reformers, and Roman-Catholic, Lutheran, and Reformed scholastic theology. Both classical and kenotic theologians are influenced by the language of Chalcedon:

> at once complete in Godhead and complete in manhood, truly God and truly man, ... one and the same Christ, Son, Lord, Only begotten, recognized in two natures, without confusion, without change, without division, without separation; the difference between the two natures being in no way annulled by the union, but rather the properties of each nature being preserved and concurring into one person and supposit.

But classical and kenotic theologians differ in their interpretation of the notion *one person, two natures*.

The classical theologian thinks about the Incarnation in terms of an *addition*. Before the Incarnation the Word, the second person of the Trinity, had one nature, divinity. In the Incarnation a second nature is added: humanity. In this context, a nature is best understood as a set of properties and powers by which the person can operate. In this chapter, I am going to refer to such a set of properties and powers as a 'power-pack'.[1] Before the Incarnation, the Word had only the divine power-pack. The divine power-pack includes properties and powers like omnipotence, omniscience, omnipresence, living in eternity, et cetera. In the Incarnation the Word gains an additional power-pack, the human power-pack. The Word can now act through both power-packs: no longer has he only divine properties and powers, but with the human power-pack he gains human powers like physical action, growth in knowledge, and locomotion.

The kenotic theologian, by contrast, understands the Incarnation in terms of a *divestment*. The kenoticist believes that Scripture saying that the Incarnate 'came down from heaven' (John 3) and 'emptied himself' (Phil. 2) cannot be explicated by the notion of an assumption of a temporal, limited, and suffering human life, but needs to be explained by a theory of real abandonment.[2] The kenoticists in this volume suggest that the Word gave up properties like omnipotence, omniscience, and omnipresence in order to take up their human antipodes. They do not suggest that in giving up these properties and powers the Word gives up the divine nature itself. Here they all follow Stephen Davis's suggestion that the properties given up by the Word are not essential to being divine, but rather accidental. In the Incarnation, the Word holds on to his divinity, but divests from his accidental properties insofar as they are incompatible with humanity.[3] Although Davis does not further specify what the essence of 'being divine' amounts to on this view, Stephen Evans says that 'What is retained will chiefly be the self-giving love that is regarded as lying at the heart of divinity and which is exhibited precisely in God's willingness to empty himself for the sake of his creatures.'[4]

[1] A metaphor introduced into the philosophical jargon by Marilyn McCord Adams.
[2] See, for instance, Charles Gore, *Dissertations on Subjects Connected with the Incarnation*, 2nd edn. (London: John Murray, 1907), 203–4.
[3] See Stephen T. Davis, *Logic and the Nature of God* (Grand Rapids: William B. Eerdmans Publishing Co., 1983), 124. Davis repeats the same suggestion in 'Jesus Christ: Savior or Guru', in Stephen T. Davis (ed.), *Encountering Jesus: A Debate on Christology* (Atlanta: John Knox Press, 1988), 51–2 [39–59]; and in 'Is Kenosis Orthodox?', Ch. 5 of this volume, pp. 115–16 above.
[4] C. Stephen Evans, 'The Self-Emptying of Love: Some Thoughts on Kenotic Christology', in Stephen T. Davis, Daniel Kendall, SJ, and Gerald O'Collins, SJ

From the beginning of the kenotic movement right through to the chapters of this book, kenotic theologians have levelled two major arguments against the classical theory. The first is that the kenotic theory is better able to account for the New Testament picture of Jesus as sharing the normal limitations of human experience: of growing in wisdom and being ignorant at times, and of being hungry, tired, and sometimes frustrated.[5] The second argument is that the kenotic theory most naturally gives us a portrait of a unified Christ,

(eds.), *The Incarnation: An Interdisciplinary Symposium on the Incarnation of the Son of God* (Oxford/New York: Oxford University Press, 2002), 249 [246–72].

There is at least one very important difference between the kenoticists writing in this book and nineteenth-century kenotic writers like the bishops H. L. Martensen, Charles Gore, or Frank Weston. The latter are all concerned to spell out how the divine Word in his kenosis still exercises his divine functions as upholding the universe, while the former have given up on this. Martensen argues that the divine Word lives 'a twofold existence; that He lives a double life in His world-creating and in his world-completing activity'. (H. L. Martensen, *Christian Dogmatics: A Compendium of the Doctrines of Christianity* (Edinburgh: T. & T. Clark, 1898), 267). Gore states that the apostolic writers 'contemplated the continuance of the divine and cosmic functions through the Incarnation', and suggests that 'the personal life of the Word should have been lived as it were from more than one center—that He who knows and does all things in the Father and in the universe should (reverently be it said) have begun to live from a new center when he assumed manhood, and under new and restricted conditions of power and knowledge' (Charles Gore, *Dissertations*, 206, 215). Weston argues that even while the Incarnate Word's self-awareness is always mediated by his human nature, his Incarnation does not imply an interruption of his relationship as Creator to his creation, so that 'the Person who is Mary's Babe is at the same moment Ruler of the Universe through His divine relations therewith' (Frank Weston, *The One Christ: An Enquiry into the Manner of The Incarnation*, rev. edn. (London: Longmans, Green and Co., 1914), 162).

On the other hand, Davis's approach is to say that the divine Word could have 'planned ahead, made arrangements, settled matters ahead of time' (Stephen T. Davis, 'Jesus Christ: Savior or Guru?', 54), while Evans makes use of a strong social trinitarian notion in suggesting that, while the divine Word was incarnate, his sustaining work was 'carried on by the other Persons' (C. Stephen Evans, 'The Self-Emptying of Love', 259.

Clearly, R. Swinburne (*The Christian God* (Oxford: Clarendon Press, 1994), 230, n. 32) and Sarah Coakley (*Powers and Submissions: Spirituality, Philosophy and Gender* (Oxford/Malden Mass.: Blackwell Publishers, 2002), 21) are correct when they suggest that Gore—and one might add, Martensen—make use of what now is called the two-minds model. In that sense these nineteenth-century kenoticists might have more in common with the twentieth-century defenders of classical Christology than with contemporary kenoticists.

[5] See, just for the writers in this volume, C. Stephen Evans, 'Kenotic Christology and the Nature of God', Ch. 8, p.199 and earlier in 'The Self-Emptying of Love', 250–1;

whereas the classical theory gives us a person divided by two minds, two centres of consciousness.[6]

The first argument suggests that the imperfections of Jesus' life as described in Scripture must embarrass the classical theologian. Classical theologians 'vigorously affirm the humanity of [Christ's] bodily functions, but often just as vigorously deny humanity to his thought processes', observes Gordon Fee.[7] Fee seems to speak here from experience in personal encounters; but, as other kenoticists, he could have pointed to medieval theologians like Aquinas. The latter ascribes to Jesus' human nature the divine gifts of beatific vision and maximal grace. Through the beatific vision Jesus' human nature would have had an immediate and continuous knowledge of God and of all things that are known by God; through maximal grace Jesus' natural and supernatural capacities would have been actualized to the fullest degree. These gifts exclude such imperfections as having to grow in knowledge and having moments of ignorance.[8]

The second argument suggests that on the classical view, Christ has something of a split personality. Kenotic theologians can point to recent work in analytic philosophy of religion that resorts to the analogy of the Freudian divided mind to explain the classical view.[9]

One might read these two arguments as contradictory: whereas the first argument says that the classical theory tends to mix up the two natures of Christ, the second holds that the classical theory tends to separate the two natures too much. The two natures are united without being properly divided; they are also divided without being

Ronald J. Feenstra, A Kenotic Christological method for understanding the Divine Attributes', Ch. 6, p. 139, and earlier in 'Reconsidering Kenotic Christology', in R. J. Feenstra and Cornelius Plantinga, Jr. (eds.), *Trinity, Incarnation, and Atonement* (Notre Dame: University of Notre Dame Press, 1989), 129 [128–52].

[6] See, again just for the writers in this volume, C. Stephen Evans, 'Kenotic Christology and the Nature of God', Ch. 8, p. 199, and earlier in 'The Self-Emptying of Love', 251; Ronald J. Feenstra, 'Reconsidering Kenotic Christology', 129.

[7] Gordon D. Fee, 'The New Testament and Kenosis Christology', Ch. 2 of this volume, p. 25 n.1 above.

[8] Aquinas and the medieval tradition are for instance targeted by Charles Gore in the *Dissertations*, 166–79. The goal of the whole essay on 'The Consciousness of Our Lord' is to bring 'under the eye of the reader the inadequacy *in one respect* of much of the patristic and all the mediaeval literature' (ix).

[9] See, for instance, Thomas V. Morris, *The Logic of God Incarnate* (Ithaca/London: Cornell University Press, 1986), 105–6.

properly united. A more charitable reading will see them as advancing a constructive dilemma: either one does not take seriously that Christ had two full, complete natures, in which case Christ's human consciousness is too godlike to fit the Gospel narratives; or one does take it seriously, in which case you make Christ schizophrenic.

In this chapter, I will focus on the first argument levelled by the kenoticists. In the following two sections I argue that, contrary to what the kenoticists think, within the classical Christological framework assumption by the divine Word does not imply distribution of maximal grace and the beatific vision. In the fourth section, I strengthen my argument by showing that those classical theologians who did say that Christ's human nature received these exceptional gifts, said so based on arguments independent of the classical Christological theory. Finally, in the fifth section I turn briefly to the second argument levelled by the kenoticists against the classical theory, the argument about the unity of mind of the Incarnate. As I will demonstrate, some parts of my response to the first argument will have a bearing on how we should conceive of the mind of Christ.

The purpose of my chapter is rather modest. Although my sympathies lie with the classical theory, I do not aim to give a full-blown defence of classical Christology, nor a complete rebuke of kenotic Christology. All I intend to do is to point out a misunderstanding of classical Christology on the part of some kenoticists. In doing so, I also hope to correct my fellow classical theologians who share in this misunderstanding; classical theologians such as Gordon Fee's students who 'hold a kind of naive docetism, where Jesus appeared as a real person, but who was God in such a way that it superseded anything truly human about him except for the accidents of his humanity—basically his bodily functions: eating, talking, sleeping, and so on'.[10] Against these theologians I side with the kenoticists who point out that such a picture is hardly tenable if we take the New Testament stories about Jesus seriously. Against the kenoticists I hold that such a picture is not implied by the classical theory. Thus, I want to contribute to the conversation between classical and kenotic theologians.

---

[10] Gordon Fee, 'The New Testament and Kenosis Christology', Ch. 2, p. 25 above.

2. PERSONS AND NATURES

In this section I want to sharpen our understanding of the nature and goals of the classical discussions about the hypostatic union. As Sarah Coakley has rightly pointed out, Chalcedon did not provide the theologians of the Church with a Christological theory, but only with a set of boundaries delimiting what can be said and what cannot be said about the event of the Incarnation. Chalcedon provided the formula 'one person recognized in two natures, without confusion, without change, without division, without separation'. It did not, however, define 'person' or 'nature', nor did it account for the relationship between the two. It also left open the question how two 'non-confused' but 'non-separated' natures relate to one another.[11] Therefore, it was up to later generations of theologians to work out an account of the metaphysics of the Incarnation that most naturally fit with the Chalcedonian standards. In my discussion of classical Christology I will concentrate on what I take to be its most fruitful period, the time of the medieval scholastics. I will pay special attention to Thomas Aquinas, whose work is so often used as a starting point for reflections on the classical theory, and to Duns Scotus, whose proposals I believe to contain a more fruitful approach for further Christological thinking.

After Chalcedon, one of the main issues in need of clarification was the relationship between persons and natures. Aristotelian metaphysics distinguishes primary and secondary substances. A secondary substance is a general nature, for example, 'humanity'. A first substance is an individual substance nature, for example, 'Paul'. It seemed common sense to think of an individual human nature as a person.[12] A person was taken to be a special case of a supposit. A supposit is the independently existing, ultimate subject of a set of

---

[11] Sarah Coakley, 'What Does Chalcedon Solve and What Does It Not', in Stephen T. Davis, Daniel Kendall S.J., and Gerald O'Collins S.J. (eds.), *The Incarnation*, 161 [143–63].

[12] The medieval theologians all interpret Christ's human nature as an individual human nature, often referring to John of Damascus: 'The Word of God did not assume human nature in general but in particular'; *De Fide Orthodoxa* III.11. Cf. Aquinas, *Summa Theologiae*, 3a, q.2, a.2, ad 3.

properties. A person is a supposit of a rational nature.[13] Therefore
Paul, who is an individual with a rational substance nature, humanity,
is a person. But if every individual human nature is its own supposit,
its own person, this would mean that, by assuming a human nature,
the divine Word also assumed a human person: a violation of
Chalcedon's standard. Therefore, Chalcedonian theologians face two
issues: how to reconceptualize the difference between persons and
natures, and how to conceive of the relationship between a person
and its nature—or, in the case of Christ, between a person and his
natures.

2.1. The Difference between Persons and Natures

The medievals developed a rich variety of models and theories to
answer these questions.[14] For present purposes it is enough to distinguish two major strategies. The first strategy, unique to Aquinas
and his followers, proposes that we think about the relationship

The problem with the differentiation between natures and persons is often illustrated with a reference to Boethius' definition of a person: 'A person is an individual
substance of a rational nature.' (*De Duabus Naturis* 3). Cf. Aquinas, *Summa Theologiae*, 3a, q.2, a.2 obj.3.

It is interesting that in the generation immediately preceding the great British
kenoticists, the influential English New Testament scholar and theologian B. F.
Westcott rejected the particularity of Christ's nature and taught its generality.
Among many places: 'The Lord's humanity was universal and not individual, as
including all that belongs to the essence of man, without regard to sex or race or time'
(*The Gospel According to St. John: The Authorised Version With Introduction and Notes*,
re-issued with a new introduction by A. Fox (London: James Clarke & Co., 1958
(1882)), 11). It would merit some research to see how widespread this view was and
whether there is a connection between Westcott's influence and the popularity of the
kenotic view. After all, Westcott's position suggests that all interest in the historical
Jesus and the particularity of his humanity is of null and void; and many theologians
who for theological and historical reasons were interested in the particularity of Jesus'
humanity might mistakenly have taken Westcott's position as the implication of
classical Christology and embraced the kenotic alternative.

[13] 'Person adds to supposit only one qualification, that of being a determinately
rational nature.' Aquinas, *Summa Theologiae*, 3a, q.2, a.3, responsio.

[14] See for extensive discussion of these models and theories: Marilyn McCord
Adams, 'The Metaphysics of the Incarnation in some Fourteenth-Century Franciscans', in *Essays Honoring Allan B. Wolter* (New York: The Franciscan Institute, 1985),
21–57; and Richard Cross, *The Metaphysics of the Incarnation: Thomas Aquinas to
Duns Scotus* (Oxford/New York: Oxford University Press, 2002).

between a person and its nature as a relation between a whole and one of its parts. The second strategy, defended by Scotus and others, recommends that we think about this relationship as analogous to the relation between a subject and one of its accidental properties.

For Aquinas, we may start with his distinction between the way parts and accidents participate in the larger entity to which they relate. Parts share in the original *esse* (existence) of the composite, but accidents do not.[15] Persons are such composites in which all the parts share in one *esse*: persons are composites of a rational nature, its individuating qualities, and its accidental properties.[16] When new parts are added to the composite, they come to share in the original *esse* of the composite. To illustrate, Aquinas gives the example of a man who is born blind and receives new eyes,[17] and the example of the resurrected body that will be brought into communion with the *esse* of the pre-existing soul.[18] Neither the eyes from the first example nor the body from the second example has *esse* on its own, Aquinas believes, but it receives *esse* from the composite of which it becomes a part.

Working with these metaphysical principles, Aquinas has a theological reason to prefer as a model for the hypostatic union the part–whole model over the accident–substance model. Since accidents have their own *esse*, the substance–accident model will hold that in Christ there is the *esse* of the human nature, and the *esse* of the original divine person with which the human nature is united. Aquinas believes that this results in the Nestorian heresy.[19] He prefers therefore a model on which the human nature becomes part of the larger whole of the person of the divine Word. Christ is a composite person containing both the human and the divine power-pack,[20] and for which the Word's original eternal *esse* becomes the *esse* of the human nature.[21]

---

[15] Aquinas, *Summa Theologiae*, 3a, q.2, a.6, ad 2.

[16] Ibid. 3a, q.2, a.2, responsio.

[17] Ibid. 3a, q.17, a.2, responsio.

[18] Ibid. 3a, q.2, a.6, ad 2.

[19] Ibid. 3a, q.2, a.6, responsio.

[20] Ibid. 3a, q.2, a.4. Aquinas has to confess some incoherence here since he also wants to uphold that the person of the divine Word is completely simple, given the simplicity of its divine nature.

[21] Ibid. 3a, q.17, a.2, ad 2.

Defenders of the accident–substance model have criticized Aquinas from two directions. They have rejected Aquinas's examples of parts that come to share in the *esse* of the whole. Scotus argues that the nature of change shows that every constituent of a composite has its own *esse*. Only thus can we explain how substances can go through the coming and going of their parts and accidents, and parts and accidents can sustain after they are no longer united with their original substances.[22] Furthermore, on Aquinas's model the human nature is informed by the divine nature, in whose *esse* it comes to share. This however validates the Chalcedonian rule of two natures without confusion. By trying to avoid Nestorianism, Aquinas runs the risk of being driven into the arms of Monophysitism.[23]

An alternative strategy is therefore needed. The proposal is to start with the individual substance nature and formulate the conditions under which it is personified. One approach is to conceive of the personifier as a positive property added to the individual substance nature. Underlying this approach is the idea that an individual nature is constituted by two positive entities: a common nature and an individuating property. The individual substance nature of Socrates is a combination of the common nature 'humanity' and the individuating property 'Socrateity'. The recommendation is to think of the property that personifies an individual substance nature as analogous to the individuating property. Combined with an individual substance nature, the personifier yields a person. In the case of Christ we have an individual human nature that does not have its own personifier, but is personified by the person of the divine Word. The relation between the person of the divine Word and its human nature is analogous to the relation between a subject and an accident.[24]

Although this approach fits with his own theory of individuation, Duns Scotus pointed out that the notion of a personifier as a positive

---

[22] Cf. for this argument Marilyn McCord Adams, 'The Metaphysics of the Incarnation', 29–30.

[23] Cf. for this argument Richard Cross, *The Metaphysics of the Incarnation*, 58, 70.

[24] Scotus registers this approach in *Quodlibet* q.19, sec. 19.56–19.59 (see: John Duns Scotus, *The Quodlibetal Questions*, trans. Felix Alluntis O.F.M. and Allan B. Wolter O.F.M., (Washington D.C.: The Catholic University of America Press, 1975), 432–3), but Scotus does not identify its defenders.

entity is also marred by theological and metaphysical problems. His most important argument, and the one that inspired his own approach, is that on this theory the divine Word can only assume those individual substance natures that are not yet personified. As we will see below, it is a key notion for classical theologians that every individual substance nature can be assumed.[25]

Scotus therefore proceeds differently. First he distinguishes between divine and created personhood, the latter of which we will concentrate on. According to Scotus, we should not think of created personified natures as individual substance natures combined with other positive entities, but as individual substance natures instantiating a number of metaphysical conditions. To spell out these conditions, Scotus distinguishes three forms of dependence: actual dependence, possible dependence, and dispositional dependence. A nature is actually dependent if an extrinsic personifier sustains it. A nature is possibly dependent if it is possible that an extrinsic personifier sustains it. A nature is dispositionally dependent if it has the tendency to depend on an extrinsic personifier, that is, if it would depend on an extrinsic personifier unless prevented from such by the interference of some causal agent. Scotus argues that a created nature is personified if it is neither actually dependent nor dispositionally dependent. Every created nature is possibly dependent, because every created nature is in obediential potency to be assumed by a divine person. No created nature has a natural tendency to be dependent on an extrinsic personifier, not even Christ's human nature. In all cases except Christ's human nature, the nature was actually independent and personified. In Christ's case alone, the human nature was made to depend on an extrinsic personifier.[26] So, this is Scotus's picture: for every individual human substance

---

[25] Duns Scotus, *Quodlibet* q.19, sec. 19.61–19.62 (*Quodlibetal Questions*, 433). Scotus levels as a metaphysical argument against the view described above that one could say that just as a common nature is naturally prior to its combination with the individuating property, the individuated nature is natural prior to the addition of its personifier. But God can make what is naturally prior without making what is naturally posterior, so according to this strategy God could make an individuated nature that is not personified. This violates the Aristotelian principle that a nature cannot exist without a personifier. Cf. for this argument Marilyn McCord Adams, 'The Metaphysics of the Incarnation', 31.

[26] *Quodlibet* q.19, sec. 19.63–19.68 (*Quodlibetal Questions*, 434–5).

nature there are two options. Either the nature is elected to be hypostatically united with a divine person, in which case it is brought in a relation of ontological dependence to this nature, or it is left by itself, in which case it will count as its own personifier.[27]

For Scotus, the heart of the hypostatic union is a relationship of ontological dependence of the human nature on the divine Word. Scotus likens this relationship to an aspect of the relationship between an accident and the substance in which it inheres. He believes that in such a relationship we can make a distinction between at least two aspects. An accident informs the substance in which it inheres; but ontologically prior to that, the accident is ontologically dependent on the substance in which it inheres. Of course, Christ's human nature is not an accident, but a substance, and can therefore not be seen as an accident of the divine Word. And since classical theology denies that a created entity can trigger a change in a divine subject, the relationship between Christ's human nature and the divine Word cannot be likened to the relationship of informing that exists between an accident and its substance. But, suggests Scotus, the relationship of ontological dependence between this human nature and the divine Word is analogous to the relationship of ontological dependence between an accident and its substance.[28]

2.2. The *Communicatio Idiomatum*

A second major issue for the classical theory is the doctrine of *communicatio idiomatum*. More important than the internal medieval discussions is the major change in content of this doctrine between the pre-Chalcedonian discussions among the *patres* and the post-Chalcedonian medieval discussions. As is documented in Sarah Coakley's contribution to this book, the *patres* understand the *communicatio idiomatum* as the communication of the powers of one

---

[27] As will be clear, Scotus has to give a different account of divine personality, since a divine person is not in obediential potency to be assumed by another person. Scotus ends up giving a characterization of divine persons as positive entities. See for a short overview Richard Cross, *Duns Scotus* (New York/Oxford: Oxford University Press, 1999), 62–7.

[28] *Quodlibet* q.19, sec. 19.83, 84 (*Quodlibetal Questions*, 439–40).

nature to the other nature. For example, Gregory of Nyssa, Coakley's favourite, teaches that the humanity 'is absorbed by the omnipotent divinity like a drop of vinegar mingled in the boundless sea'.[29] Divinity itself is not changed, but is progressively transfused into the human nature. The same holds for Cyril of Alexandria, who suggests that human characteristics are appropriated to the divine, but that the divine *energeia* are ontologically communicated to the human nature.[30]

For the medievals the Chalcedonian 'two natures, without confusion, without change' makes these notions of absorption of the divine by the human nature suspect. For the medievals *communicatio idiomatum* is not an issue of communication of the powers of one nature to the other, but the communication of both natures to the one person in which they concur. The doctrine of the *communicatio idiomatum* is the doctrine of the correct ascription of divine and human properties to the person of the divine Word, and of the correct proposition formulations thereof. This position is consistent with the classical intuitions about the Incarnation as an event in which the divine Word adds another human power-pack to his earlier divine power-pack. The goal of the act of assumption is not change, but addition: the divine Word becomes the subject of a whole new range of acts and passions. Both power-packs are held without confusion or change. This 'dual power-pack position' is seen most clearly in the medieval theologians' understanding of the humanity's ability to sin: almost all of them hold that Christ's human nature can sin, even if his divine nature and person cannot.[31]

2.3. Distinguishing the Issues

On the basis of these observations we can draw two conclusions about the nature of the discussions concerning the hypostatic

[29] Quoted in Sarah Coakley, 'Does Kenosis Rest on a Mistake? Three Kenotic Models in Patristic Exegesis', Ch. 10, p. 258 above.

[30] Ibid. p. 252.

[31] Cf, for instance, for Scotus: *Ordinatio* III, dist. 12, q. unica (translated in Damian McElrath, ed., *Franciscan Christology* (New York: The Franciscan Institute, 1980), 182).

union in classical theology. First, for the classical theologian the doctrine of the hypostatic union is a theory about ontological dependence. It is not a theory about communication of power from the personifier or its original nature to the assumed nature. The doctrine gives an account of how this particular human nature does not terminate in its own person, but is ontologically dependent on another person. It is not an account of cognitive or voluntary influence of one nature on the other.

In fact—and this is our second conclusion—the theory says nothing about the make-up of these two power-packs at all. It contends that the divine Word assumed a human nature like ours. The theory does not, however, imply anything about what it is to be human, or divine. The first defenders of the hypostatic union were probably Platonic dualists; many of its medieval defenders were proponents of Aristotelian hylomorphism. Some of its modern adherents may be physicalists of some sort. The doctrine of hypostatic union is not wedded to any of these theories. Whatever human nature is, that is what the divine Word assumed. Further, whatever is divine, that is the essential nature of the assuming Word. *Patres* and medieval scholastics alike were adherents of the classical doctrine of God, propagating an immutable, impassible, and simple divinity. But some of the doctrine's modern defenders reject these as characteristics of the divine nature.[32] Therefore, while Stephen Evans is correct when he argues that a kenoticist has to reject the classical doctrine of God for divine mutability and so on,[33] classical Christology can accommodate both.

3. ASSUMABILITY

The classical notion of the hypostatic union gives us a theory about the ontological dependence of an assumed individual nature on an external personifier. In this section I will show that any distribution

---

[32] For example, Marilyn McCord Adams, *Horrendous Evils and the Goodness of God* (Ithaca/London: Cornell University Press, 1999), especially 164 v.v.

[33] C. Stephen Evans, 'Kenotic Christology and the Nature of God', Ch. 8, p. 197 above.

of beatific vision or maximal grace to the assumed nature has to be independent of the act of assumption itself.

As we saw in the previous section, Scotus holds that an individual human nature is personified not because a positive entity is added to the nature, but because the individual nature fulfils a number of conditions. Scotus prefers this account of personhood because

any nature whatsoever is simply in obediential potency to depend upon a divine person. Therefore, if there were some positive entity which made the nature a person in its own right, then this entity would have been assumed by the Word and thus Christ's human nature would be invested with a dual personality, which is impossible. For if it were personalized by something created, this would render it formally incommunicable to another person....

Besides, if human nature formally became a person by reason of some positive entity, the Word could not put off the nature he had assumed without either letting it remain depersonalized (which seems incongruous) or else giving it some new entity by which it would have created personality. But this too is impossible.[34]

Scotus goes on arguing why the latter option is impossible, namely because this new entity would not fit in the ontological make-up of the existing nature.

Scotus propagates a radical idea in this passage. Whether or not an individual human nature fulfils the conditions of personhood is accidental to that nature, since every human nature is in obediential potency to depend on the divine Word. Not only Christ's human nature, but every human nature can be assumed by the Word, and a once assumed nature can also be put off by the Word. In other words: instead of assuming the human nature of Mary's babe, the Word could have assumed your human nature. The nature born out of your parents, living in this time and hour, and currently personified by you, could also have been the human nature of the divine Word. Similarly, the human nature that actually was assumed by the Word could also have lived an unassuming life as Jesus, son of a carpenter from Nazareth. The Word could even have assumed both natures, and many more in addition![35]

[34] *Quodlibet* q.19, sec. 19.61, 19.62 (*Quodlibetal Questions*, 433).
[35] *Ordinatio* III, d.1, q.3 (John Duns Scotus, *Opera Omnia*, ed. Luke Wadding (Lyons, 1639), VII.1, 44–50.

While this position might sound radical, it is not born out of Scotian subtlety. It is the standard view found in medieval Christological textbooks.[36] For example, Aquinas writes:

> For if the human nature were not assumed by a divine person, then the human nature would have its own personhood. . . . By this union the divine person prevents the human nature from having its own proper personhood.[37]

Suppose, however, that the humanity were to be separated from the divinity. Then the humanity would have its own *esse*, distinct from the divine *esse*. For nothing prevented it from having its own proper *esse* except for the fact that it did not subsist on its own (*per se*).[38]

This view is a direct consequence of the medieval theories about natures and persons. But the medievals had two strong theological motives to work out this consequence. Both motives concern the freedom of the Creator vis-à-vis the creation. First, creation cannot be such that the Creator is not free to come near or to withdraw, to

[36] Recently, this view was also defended in Thomas P. Flint, 'The Possibilities of Incarnation: Some Radical Molinist Suggestions', *Religious Studies*, 37 (2001), 307–20.

[37] Aquinas, *Summa Theologiae*, 3a, q.4, a.2, ad 3.

[38] *Questiones Quodlibetales* IX, q.2, a.3, responsio; quoted in Alfred J. Freddoso, 'Human Nature, Potency and the Incarnation', *Faith and Philosophy*, 3 (1986), 46 [27–53]. Freddoso thinks that these passages should not be read as if Aquinas agreed with Scotus, but he does not give us any other argument for this view than his own objection against Scotus (Cf. also Thomas P. Flint, 'The possibilities of Incarnation: some radical Molinist suggestions', 317–18).

Freddoso's own position is that every individual substance nature has its personifier necessary, and thus that Christ's human nature is necessarily assumed by the divine Word (28). The opposite position violates Leibniz's law of identity (36). To show this, Freddoso states that for every personifier P and individual substance nature N,

(i) N is identical with P.
(ii) N has the property of being necessarily such that it exists when and only when N exists.
Therefore
(iii) P has the property of being necessarily such that it exists when and only when N exists.

Freddoso believes that the medievals would accept (i). However, with Leibniz's Law, it follows that (iii), which is Freddoso's position. Freddoso's argument fails, though. Scotus at least would not accept (i), for on his account of personhood N is not identical with P, but N is identical with P if and only if N has two accidental properties, namely the properties of being not actually dependent and of being not dispositionally dependent.

assume or to put off. If Christ's human nature were the only nature God could assume, this would unacceptably restrict God's abilities. Secondly, the act of assumption is an unmerited and free act of grace. If the assumed human nature were not accidentally, but essentially hypostatically united with the divine Word, assumption would no longer be such an unmerited and free act. This second motive is embedded in the Augustinian notion that the assumption of this particular human nature should be seen as a special case of God's predestination. As God predestines some human persons to eternal glory, so God predestines this human nature to the glory of being hypostatically united with the divine Word.[39] Every human nature is dependent on God's will either to be hypostatically united with the divine Word or to be its own personifier.

I suggest that we view these notions of the assumability of every human nature and the accidentality of personhood as part of a larger picture. As we noted in an earlier section, a person is the supposit of a rational nature. Every individual substance necessarily has or is a supposit; the supposit that a human nature has or is distinguishes itself only by its rationality. Rationality, however, does not play a role in the act of assumption by the divine Word. The only thing established in the assumption is a dependence-relation of an individual substance nature to divine Word. Whether something can be brought into such a relationship depends on it being an individual substance nature, not on it being an individual substance nature of a rational or other kind. Therefore, every individual substance nature, with or without rational capacities, is assumable; and every individual substance nature has its supposit accidentally.

While this claim about the general assumability of all individual substance natures might sound even more outrageous than the earlier claim about the assumability of all human natures, it is again a claim recognized by almost all medieval theologians as a

[39] As Augustine writes, 'The most illustrious light of predestination and grace is the Savior himself,—the mediator himself between God and men, the man Christ Jesus. And, pray, by what preceding merits of his own, whether of works or of faith, did the human nature which is in him procure for itself that it should be this? Let this have an answer, I beg. That man, whence did he deserve this,—to be assumed by the Word co-eternal with the Father into unity of person, and be the only-begotten Son of God?' (*De praedestinatione sanctorum liber ad Prosperum et Hilarium primus,* 30.xv).

claim logically implied by classical Christology.[40] Aquinas, for example, points out: 'To the first question [about whether human nature is more assumable than other natures] it has to be said that, according to his absolute power, God can assume an irrational nature. It also does not matter that irrational natures are not persons.'[41] It is in this notion of the general assumability of all individual substances that we find the basis for our thesis. The gifts of maximal grace and beatific vision presuppose receivers with rational capacities—will and intellect. Irrational substance natures can therefore not receive these gifts. If every individual substance nature is assumable, including irrational substance natures, the act of assumption does not imply the gifts of maximal grace and beatific vision. According to the classical account of assumability, every individual substance nature is assumable, and thus the act of assumption does not imply the distribution of maximal grace and beatific vision.

[40] Ockham takes it even one step further. He claims that not only can every created substance nature be assumed by a divine person, but that 'God can bring it about that one created nature depends on another as on a nature that sustains it; for example, the soul can be the term of a relation of union to a body or a stone, since no contradiction is involved.' (*Rep.* III, q. 1 Y; quoted in Marilyn McCord Adams, 'Relations, Inherence and Subsistence: or, Was Ockham a Nestorian in Christology,' *Nous*, 16 (1982), 69 [62–75]. I doubt whether Ockham is right. The difference between assumption by a divine and a created person is that the divine person is a positive entity, but the created person is an individual substance nature fulfilling a number of conditions (see note 27). That means that in the case of assumption by a created person, there is no personifier that can serve as the ultimate ontological subject of the assumed nature. My intuition is that this hampers the act of assumption.

[41] *Scriptum super Libros Sentiarum* III, d.2, q.1, a.1, ad 1. It is true that Aquinas continues that according to God's ordered power it is not fitting for non-rational natures to be assumed, since the assumed nature is destined for maximal beatification, and this involves a rational mental capacity which non-rational creatures do not share. One will note, however, that the goal whereto God uses the act of assumption is conceptually distinct from the act of assumption itself. If God decides to endow the assumed nature with maximal beatification, God should not assume a nature that cannot receive this gift. Nonetheless, this is independent of the inherent assumability of these natures.

In the *Summa Theologiae* Aquinas interprets 'assumability' exclusively as a 'fittingness for hypostatic union', and on the basis of fittingness, dignity, and need concludes that only human natures are capable of being assumed (*Summa Theologiae*, 3a, q.4, a.1, responsio). I do not read this as rejection of the earlier position in the *Scriptum*, only as an incomplete summary. Aquinas's treatment of Christological issues in the *Scriptum* is usually more complete and nuanced than the discussion in the *Summa Theologiae*.

4. MAXIMAL GRACE AND BEATIFIC VISION

Nonetheless, there are scores of classical theologians who *do* hold that the assumed nature in Christ received these gifts and properties, from those documented in Ronald Feenstra's essay to the evangelical students of Gordon Fee who were appalled by the idea that Christ could be beaten in a one-to-one game of basketball.[42] However, their arguments are logically independent of the classical theory of assumption.

To support this claim, let us concentrate on Thomas Aquinas. Aquinas's account of the human nature of Christ is guided by a principle of perfection: 'It would not be right for the Son of God to assume an imperfect human nature. It had to be perfect, because through it the whole race was to be brought back to perfection.'[43] Given this principle, Christ embodies, with one category of exception, every perfection of which a human nature is capable.

With respect to Christ's cognitive life, the principle of perfection results in a threefold knowledge. Human nature has a potential for beatific vision, in which it sees God and all other things in God. Christ's human nature received this knowledge from conception[44] until the cross,[45] knowledge through which he throughout his life had a direct vision of God and knew all things past, present, and future.[46] Furthermore, human nature has a capacity to receive knowledge by way of intellectual enlightenment. Therefore, Christ received in this way the complete amount of knowledge an intellect is able to receive either by its own working or by revelation.[47] Of course, this kind of knowledge overlaps completely with the beatific vision, in which Christ's human nature sees all these things directly in God. Nonetheless, Christ's human nature received this knowledge a third time when all his natural capacities for knowledge acquisition

---

[42] Gordon D. Fee, 'The New Testament and Kenosis Christology', Ch. 2, p. 26 above.

[43] Aquinas, *Summa Theologiae*, 3a, q.9, a.1, responsio.

[44] Ibid. 3a, q.7, a.4, responsio.

[45] Ibid. 3a, q.46, a.7, 8.

[46] Ibid. 3a, q.10, a.2, responsio.

[47] Ibid. 3a, q.11.

by way of experience were completely actualized, so that Christ knew everything that possibly can be known by way of the working of intellect and experience.[48]

As we might expect, these extravagant claims give Aquinas little space to account for the Biblical notions of Christ's growth in knowledge (Luke 2:57) or unawareness of the day of the Son of Man (Mark 13:32). Aquinas explains the first by saying that, while there was no growth in Christ's beatific vision or the infused intellectual knowledge, there was growth in Christ's experiential knowledge, since experience implies knowledge acquisition;[49] and he explains the latter by arguing that Christ did know of this day through the beatific vision (through which he knows all future events), but that the texts mean that he did not make that day known.[50]

The same principle of perfection pervades Aquinas's treatment of Christ's voluntary and emotional life. As Christ received the beatific vision so he also received maximal grace.[51] As the notion of beatific vision hampers Aquinas in his explanation of Jesus' growth in knowledge, so does the notion of maximal grace hamper his explanation of Jesus' increasing in grace (Luke 2:57). Aquinas suggests that we should take the text to mean that as Jesus became older, he had more opportunity to show his wisdom.[52] Finally, there is only one exception to the principle of perfection: since for soteriological reasons Christ has to suffer, the gifts of grace do not carry through to Christ's body.[53]

Aquinas's perfection principle is motivated by two interconnected arguments, one soteriological and the other metaphysical. The soteriological argument says that, since Christ is the source of our eschatological perfection, Christ has to be perfect in the highest

---

[48] Ibid. 3a, q.12. Even while he did not experience everything there is to experience, his perfect reasoning skills makes him a scientist *per excellence*. 'For example, when he saw the heavenly bodies he could understand their power and the effects they have on things here below, although these did not, in fact, fall within his sense experience' (*Summa Theologiae*, 3a, q.12, a.1, contra 2).

[49] Ibid. 3a, q.12, a.2, responsio and ad 2.

[50] Ibid. 3a, q.10, a.2, ad 1.

[51] Ibid. 3a, q.7, a.9.

[52] Ibid. 3a, q.7, a.12 ad 3.

[53] Ibid. 3a, q.14.

degree. For instance, since we receive the beatific vision through Christ, the beatific vision 'must be found in the supreme degree in Christ, since the cause must always be superior to what it causes'.[54] Aquinas illustrates this by pointing to fire: what makes things hot, is itself the hottest thing.[55] The metaphysical argument is based on the causal principle that 'the closer anything draws to a cause which is acting upon it the more will it be affected by it.'[56] Aquinas transfers this principle to the ontological order and argues that because 'the soul of Christ, which is united to the Word in person, is more closely joined to this Word than any other creature ... it is influenced more fully by that light, in which God is seen by the Word himself, than any other creatures.'[57] The proximity of the divine essence to the human nature produces in it the fullness of knowledge and grace, just as the light of the sun lightens up the light of the air.[58]

The soteriological and the metaphysical arguments are interconnected because Aquinas conceives of the relationship between God, Christ's human nature, and the elect as a descending hierarchy in which God is the source of all; Christ's human nature receives a maximal degree due to its nearness to the divine, and the elect receive from Christ by being members of the body of which he is the head.

Both arguments are disputable. The soteriological argument is disputable because Christ did not need to be perfect throughout his life in order to be the source of our eschatological perfection. If Christ's death and resurrection is the primal source of our bliss, only the resurrected and glorified Christ has to enjoy beatific vision and maximal grace. The metaphysical argument is disputable since, as William of Ware and Scotus point out,[59] the Word making a created nature for its personhood ontologically dependent on himself is quite a different matter from the Word deciding to communicate

[54] Ibid. 3a, q.9, a.2, responsio. Cf. 3a, q.7, a.1, responsio; 3a, q.7, a.9, responsio; 3a, q.8, a.5, responsio; 3a, q.9, a.1, responsio.

[55] Ibid. 3a, q.7, a.9, responsio.

[56] Ibid. 3a, q.7, a.1, responsio.

[57] Ibid. 3a, q.10, a.4, responsio.

[58] Ibid. 3a, q.9, a.2, ad 2. Cf. 3a, q.8, a.1, responsio; 3a, q.9, a.4, ad 1; 3a, q.10, a.4, responsio.

[59] While responding to an argument of Henry of Ghent similar to Aquinas's, see Richard Cross, 'Incarnation, Indwelling, and the Vision of God: Henry of Ghent and some Franciscans', *Franciscan Studies*, 57 (1999), 119–20 [79–130].

something of himself to the cognitive and voluntary powers of this nature. Whether or not a creature receives the beatific vision and maximal grace is a free decision of God; God veils and unveils God according to God's own discretion.

Most importantly, both arguments and the perfection principle are not logically implied by the classical theory of assumption. The classical theory is independent of any soteriological theory; and one can hold the classical theory but reject Aquinas's move to apply causal notions to the ontological realm, as William of Ware and Scotus show.

The same can be said about other arguments to attribute the beatific vision and maximal grace to Christ's human nature. Scotus, for example, while rejecting Aquinas's arguments, still attributes these gifts to Christ, guided by the hermeneutical principle that 'in extolling Christ, I prefer to praise him too much than to fail by defect, if through ignorance I must fall into either excess.'[60] Peter Lombard, whose *Sententiae* guided the thoughts of many generations of medieval theologians, used the distinction of the four states of human being: before sin, after sin but before grace, under grace, and in glory. Maintaining the soteriological rule that Christ took something from each state of human being he came to save, Lombard holds that Christ took immunity from sin from the first phase, punishment and other defects from the second, maximal grace from the third, and the beatific vision from the last phase.[61] Anselm of Canterbury argues that Christ needed to be omniscient, in order to recognize the good and teach his people, and that he had complete happiness, because only he who involuntarily suffers discomfort is unhappy.[62]

Many more examples could be given, since all the medievals tend to elevate Christ's human nature and maximize its perfection. What is illustrated by all the given examples is that the soteriological and metaphysical reasons to do so are independent of the classical theory of assumption and hypostatic union itself.

---

[60] In *Ordinatio* III, d.13, qq.1–4; see: Damian McElrath (ed.), *Franciscan Christ-ology*, 163 [158–67].
[61] Lombard, *Sententiae* III, xvi, 2.
[62] St. Anselm, *Cur Deus Homo* II.13 and II.12.

5. THE ASSUMER AND THE ASSUMED

The kenotic theologian is mistaken if she thinks that her classical colleague stands embarrassed when the New Testament tells us about a Jesus who grows in knowledge and grace, who is at times ignorant, hungry, tired, or frustrated. This is the kind of Jesus the classical theory calls for: one with a complete human nature, neither confused with nor changed by the divine nature with which it is hypostatically united. The classical theory does not imply the gifts of maximal grace or the beatific vision; nor would, I believe, the classical theologian be wise to teach the distribution of these gifts on other grounds.

Where would the discussion between the kenotic and the classical theologians go from here? Maybe the kenoticist would press the point of the *communicatio idiomatum* and wonder whether it is logically possible that one person has such mutually exclusive properties as omniscience and ignorance, omnipotence and being limited in power, living in eternity and dying on the cross. Here the kenoticist and the classical theologian are in the same boat. However many divine properties the kenoticist might want to declare contingent, at some point the kenoticist will have to admit that the Incarnate has properties that are mutually exclusive—let it just be the properties of being the creator of heaven and earth and not being the creator of heaven and earth—and she will have to take refuge in a form of the doctrine of *communicatio idiomatum* to save the consistency of her doctrine.[63]

It might also be that the kenoticist accepts the answer to her first objection against the classical theory, and moves on to her second point: the argument that the classical theology ends up with a person divided by two minds, and cannot give an account of the psychological unity of Christ. Refuting that argument calls for another essay. Nonetheless I want to make a few comments on this topic; but I will strictly limit myself to stating how the insights we gained above might help the classical theologian in meeting this second challenge.

The classical theory characterizes the relationship between the human nature and its divine person as one of ontological dependence.

---

[63] See Stephen T. Davis, 'Is Kenosis Orthodox?', Ch. 5, pp. 119–21 above.

Christ's human nature is not, like all other human natures, its own, independent personifier, but terminates in the person of the Word. In the preceding sections I have not done much in explaining what such a relationship of dependence implies, frankly because the sources do not spell out such implications. What does it mean for a nature not to be ontologically independent, but to depend completely on an external personifier? What ontological consequences does it have? And does it have more than ontological consequences? For example, in the case of rational natures, does it also have psychological consequences? Does it affect the self-consciousness of a human nature to be ontologically dependent on a divine person? I think here we encounter a lacuna in the classical theory, a lacuna that in fact has called for the development of kenotic Christology.

However, in one respect the strategies of both theories are remarkably alike. Both theories are much more focused on the relationship between the two natures than on the consequences of the assumption for them separately. Aquinas and his medieval colleagues, fusing the classical theory with the notions of beatific vision and maximal grace, end up with the divinization of the human nature. On their approach, the human nature is made as godlike as is possible. The human nature is adapted to the divine nature. In reaction, the kenoticists have developed a doctrine of the humanization of the divine nature. The divine nature gives up as many divine attributes as is possible; it is adapted to the human nature. My suggestion is that the Chalcedon's language of 'two natures, without confusion, without change', calls for an approach that differs from both of these. What we should do is to unpack the dependence relationship between the human nature and its divine personifier. We should ask what it means for this individual human nature, complete and unchanged, to be made totally dependent on the Word. What does this mean, ontologically, but also psychologically?

My intuition is that there are psychological consequences for this nature. Not in the sense of a divinization of this human nature—that would be a change of the nature—but in the sense of a different psychological self-awareness on the part of this nature. The assumed nature has a human 'I'. But this human 'I' is not independent, but dependent. It is ontologically dependent on the divine Word. My intuition is that this changes the content of the self-awareness of this 'I'.

It will probably be impossible to give an a priori account of this change. What would it mean if God, of whom we always think as the 'Thou', as the Other, were really the same as the 'I'? However, we don't have to give an a priori account of this consequence. We can read the stories about the one human for whom, as we believe, all of this was reality.

The New Testament tells us the stories of a human life for whom God was the other as well as the same (John 14), of one who came from below (Luke 2) as well as from above (John 8), who came from Nazareth but spoke with an authority as no other human (Matt. 7). Here is a human who 'takes no thought for the ordinary personal interests that dominate most human lives. He has no wife or home, no career or interest in the accumulation of possessions. Instead he gives himself wholly to the proclamation of the kingdom of God and the nurture of his followers. He finally gives his very life as "a ransom for many", not shirking a painful and shameful death for the sake of the redemption of human beings.'[64] Stephen Evans takes this portrait to be an affirmation of the kenotic view, but is it not as much what we could expect from a life that is made completely ontologically dependent on the divine Word?

I would like to illustrate my point with a reference to a discussion in New Testament studies. Recently, the New Testament scholar N. T. Wright has, in the context of wider theories, devoted several chapters and papers to the self-understanding of Jesus.[65] Following earlier work by Ed Sanders and Marcus Borg, Wright's focus is on Jesus' relationship with the Temple. Jesus, Wright argues, 'believed himself called to do and to be in relation to Israel what, in Scripture and Jewish belief, the Temple was and did'.[66] For Israel, the Temple was the place where God dwelt in her midst, where fellowship with God and forgiveness by God were assured by the daily sacrifices. Now

---

[64] C. Stephen Evans, 'Kenotic Christology and the Nature of God', Ch. 8, p. 196 above.

[65] N. T. Wright, *Jesus and the Victory of God* (London: SPCK, 1996), 612–53; 'Jesus and God', in *The Challenge of Jesus* (Downers Grove, Ill.: Inter-Varsity Press, 1999), 96–125; 'The Divinity of Jesus', in Marcus J. Borg and N. T. Wright (eds.), *The Meaning of Jesus: Two Visions* (San Francisco: HarperSanFrancisco, 1999), 157–68; and 'Jesus' Self-Understanding', in Stephen T. Davis, Daniel Kendall S.J. Gerald O'Collins S.J. (eds.), *The Incarnation*, 47–61.

[66] N. T. Wright, *The Challenge of Jesus*, 111.

Jesus offered welcome and forgiveness to sinners, as was normally obtained by going to the Temple. Jesus criticized the Temple and announced her destruction; he likens his own body to it and predicts his resurrection. Jesus enters Jerusalem and enacted the long awaited coming of God to his Temple. In all of these and many more actions, Wright argues, Jesus was acting as a one-man Temple-substitute. 'Jesus was claiming, at least implicitly, to be the place where and the means by which Israel's God, YHWH, was at last personally present to and with his people. Jesus was taking the huge risk of acting as if he were the Shekinah in person, the presence of YHWH tabernacling with his people.'[67] This, Wright suggests, betrays Jesus' self-understanding: 'Jesus believed himself called to do and be things which, in the tradition to which he fell heir, only Israel's God, was to do and be.'[68] Jesus believed himself to be the embodiment of God's presence. In him, God tabernacled in our midst.

Interestingly, Wright never goes further than this. He never claims that Jesus believed or knew himself to be God. This occasioned some critique from evangelicals who thought that Wright should have been more forthright in his conclusions.[69] Yet it seems to me that Wright is correct here. For orthodox Christians, the challenge of the Gospels has always been that Jesus never directly affirms that he is God. Doing things that God is supposed to do, yes. Acting as the embodiment of God's presence, yes. Nowhere, however, is there direct confirmation from Jesus himself about his divine nature.

For classical theologians of the medieval kind, this is a challenge. If Jesus had the beatific vision, he knew all things; he also knew that he was God. Why did he not confirm this? For kenotic theologians, it is a challenge as well. This Jesus is after all the divine Word, who literally came down from heaven. But on the classical view as I have laid it out in this essay, this is exactly the picture that we can expect. Jesus is the embodiment of God. His human being is completely consumed by the divine Word, and he is aware of that. He understands himself as the one in whom God is in the midst of his people. Nevertheless, his self-awareness is the awareness of this human nature. It is not the

[67] Ibid. 114.   [68] Ibid. 59.   [69] Ibid. 47.

kenotic self-awareness of the Word's divine nature. The divine mind knows itself to be divine; the human mind knows itself to be totally absorbed by the divine.

This is, I submit, the direction in which the classical theologian has to go in answering the second kenotic challenge. Whether it will satisfy the kenoticist, I am not sure. If the kenoticist wants a Christ 'having two natures but constituting a single person with a single mind and body', as Stephen Evans suggests,[70] the kenoticist and her classical colleague will not reach an understanding. As Chalcedon says, the Incarnate has two complete natures, which, as the third Council of Constantinople (553) stipulated, includes having *two* wills and *two* minds. But if classical and kenotic theologians could agree on accepting this stipulation, I submit my suggestion for further exploration.[71]

[70] C. Stephen Evans, 'Kenotic Christology and the Nature of God', Ch. 8, p. 199 above.

[71] I am grateful to Rowan Greer, Maurice Lee, Kimberly Miller van Driel, Jared Witt, and especially Marilyn McCord Adams for very helpful comments on earlier versions of this chapter. I want to thank Kimberly Miller van Driel for translating my many Dutchisms into proper English sentences.

12

Kenosis and Feminist Theory

Ruth Groenhout

The concept of kenosis is that of a self-emptying, a self-giving, a self-sacrificing. It has become commonplace in feminist thought to argue that women are socialized to be inordinately self-sacrificing, and that this socialization is a very bad thing. So can a feminist endorse a kenotic theology? Wouldn't a theology that makes an act of self-sacrifice theologically central to an understanding of Christianity be necessarily opposed to a feminism that advocates the empowerment and self-ownership of women? Feminist theory is developed out of a concern for the rights of women to live full, flourishing lives. Kenosis holds up for us the example of a self-sacrificing saviour whom we are to emulate by giving up our claims to power and authority, and by sacrificing our selves for the sake of others. The contradiction seems clear and incontrovertible, and the notion of a kenotic feminist theology seems to be, at least on the face of it, an oxymoron.

But to get clear on these issues, it is important to make sure that one's terms are well defined—sometimes an apparent contradiction dissolves when one is careful about the way various concepts are defined and terms utilized. This is the case, I want to argue, with feminism and self-sacrifice. The apparent contradiction between feminist concerns and kenotic theology that appears on first glance loses its contradictory nature on more careful examination. Further, I want to argue, feminists may find that they need to endorse certain forms of self-sacrifice in order to be consistent in their feminism.

This chapter begins with the apparent contradiction. I will briefly summarize the claims of some of the feminists who have argued that women's besetting sin is that of self-denial rather than pride, and consider why that might lead one to reject a kenotic theology. After developing the case for the incompatibility of kenotic theology and feminist thought, however, I will then go on to argue that a better understanding of self-sacrifice dissolves the contradiction. A proper understanding of both feminist ideals and kenotic theology leads to far more overlap between these two streams of thought than one might expect. In fact, I will argue, a properly understood notion of self-sacrifice is essential to an adequate feminist theory, and feminism offers important considerations for determining what the proper meaning of kenotic self-sacrifice is. We get a better understanding of both concepts when we think of them in tandem.

1. FEMINIST THEORY AND WOMEN'S SELF-SACRIFICE

Valerie Saiving's 1960 article on women and self-sacrifice is the *locus classicus* for much of the feminist rejection of the notion of self-sacrifice, particularly in theological circles.[1] In that article Saiving argues that men and women are prone to different types of sin—men to pride, women to lack of self—and that the preaching of the gospel must take those differences into account in order for it really to constitute good news rather than an oppressive burden. Men, with their tendency to pride and self-glorification need to hear a gospel of emptying of self, of servanthood and humility. Squelching their sense of self opens them up to receive the needed grace of God. Women, Saiving argued, are prone to have no sense of self at all, however. The feminine situation, as Saiving defines it (drawing heavily on an object-relations theory[2] account of gender and on Simone de

[1] Valerie (Goldstein) Saiving, 'The Human Situation: A Feminine View', *Journal of Religion* 40 (April, 1960): 100–12.

[2] Object-relations theory is psychological theory of how identity, particularly gender identity, is formed through relationships with others during infancy and childhood. One classic development of object-relations theory can be found in Nancy Chodorow's *The Reproduction of Mothering* (Berkeley: University of California Press, 1978). Chodorow argues that feminine and masculine identities are formed

Beauvoir's analysis of the social construction of the feminine[3]) is one of experiencing a deep need 'to surrender self-identity and be included in another's "power of being"'.[4] Given this fundamental 'feminine' psychological construction, women's fundamental temptation to sin comes not from pride or will to power, but from 'triviality, distractability, and diffuseness; lack of an organizing center or focus; dependence on others for one's own self-definition; tolerance at the expense of standards of excellence;... in short, underdevelopment or negation of the self'.[5] A more adequate theological account of sin, Saiving concludes, would result in a rejection of self-sacrifice as the paradigm of love for women.

Saiving's argument was, and is, a powerful one, and it generated quite a bit of subsequent scholarship in feminist and theological circles.[6] A more recent version of Saiving's thesis, developed from a distinctly Reformed perspective, can be found in the work of Serene Jones. Jones argues that a feminist perspective on traditional Reformed doctrines such as sin, grace, and the church requires a revision of those basic doctrines in much the same way as Saiving's article revised the sin of pride. Particularly in cases of women who are in abusive relationships, are poor or marginalized, or in other ways disempowered, Jones argues, the message of the gospel ought not to be one of giving up the self, but rather one of gently gathering the

primarily through the infant's and young child's interactions with a female primary care-giver and an absent male parent figure. The result is that the young girl's gender identity is formed by identification and closeness to the mother, while the young boy's gender identity is formed by rejection of and separation from the mother. Women, then, lack a clear sense of boundaries between self and other, while men's sense of identity is constructed in a largely negative fashion by excluding anything seen as feminine, nurturant, or maternal. Both gender identities, Chodorow argues, are less than healthy, and she advocates shared parenting as a way of creating healthier gender identities.

[3] Saiving does not directly cite Beauvoir, but her account of women's condition reflects *The Second Sex* in many ways.

[4] 'The Human Situation', p. 108.

[5] 'The Human Situation', p. 109.

[6] For a contemporary debate on issues of autonomy, vulnerability, and self-sacrifice see Daphne Hampson's 'On Autonomy and Heteronomy' and Sarah Coakley's '*Kenosis* and Subversion: On the Repression of "Vulnerability" in Christian Feminist Writing', as well as both authors' responses in *Swallowing a Fishbone? Feminist Theologians Debate Christianity*, ed. Daphne Hampson (London: Society for Promoting Christian Knowledge, 1996), 1–16, 82–111.

wounded, scattered elements of the self back together, breathing life
and self-worth into them. Such a gospel is necessary for providing a
sufficiently robust sense of self for women to take action against
abuse, and value themselves sufficiently to struggle against addiction,
oppression, and disempowerment. Jones's discussion of Luther's
conception of justification is representative:

> What happens if feminist theology places this woman in the position of the
> sinner before God in Luther's courtroom drama? First, feminist theory helps
> us realize that this woman suffers from an illness different from Luther's
> classical sinner. Her sin is not one of overly rigid self-containment; her
> brokenness lies in her lack of containment, in her cultural definition in
> relation to others.... She lacks the structuring boundaries that allow her to
> be an other in relationship to God in faith.... She comes before God not as a
> defendant caught in the bondage of the will; she comes as one whose will has
> been diluted in her many relations. In an ironic twist, one might say her will
> could benefit from bondage, for in its present state, her agency has dissolved
> into the fluid motions of her relations.[7]

For the individual in such a situation, Jones continues, the doctrine
of justification can only be a saving message if we begin the story of
justification with sanctification, rather than starting the other way
round as Luther does. That is, for women, the doctrine of sanctification, of being called by God toward wholeness and holiness can lead
to a recognition of sinfulness and the need for God's forgiveness and
healing.[8] But the message of sanctification needs to come first to
restore to women a sufficiently robust notion of self and self-worth to
make the recognition of sinfulness an opportunity to rejoice in
forgiveness. Starting with justification is likely to destroy an already
tenuous sense of identity, Jones thinks, and produce despair rather
than hope.

There is much that is worthwhile in both Saiving's and Jones's
work, and their arguments are both timely and valuable. Both
authors attempt to distance themselves from a simplistic gender
dualism at some level. Saiving frames her argument in terms of
'feminine psychological types', and argues that groups of men

---

[7] Serene Jones, *Feminist Theory and Christian Theology: Cartographies of Grace*
(Minneapolis: Fortress Press, 2000), 62–3.

[8] *Feminist Theory and Christian Theology*, pp. 63–4.

might evince such psychological types. Jones at various points does acknowledge the power that women can wield in society. At the same time, there is more than a hint of strong gender dualism, particularly in Saiving's article. Since her account of the origin of 'the feminine' is based on childhood development and different experiences of sexuality, it is difficult to see how it could be an accurate description of men's lives.

If these accounts of sin and sacrifice are read in the context of pop psychology books of the Mars–Venus sort, they can easily lead to the claim that men need to hear a message of self-sacrifice, but women should not. Men's besetting sin is pride, women's is diffusion, and Christ's call in the New Testament that Christians 'take up their cross' and follow applies to men in a way that it does not apply to women. So goes a certain feminist rejection of self-sacrifice.

The picture painted so far contains more than a grain of truth, and hence can be a powerful picture. But it is also problematic when it is taken as the whole truth. While it may be true that certain women in particular cultural/social/historical contexts need to hear a message of empowerment rather than self-sacrifice, this does not entail that feminism and self-sacrifice are incompatible, or that self-sacrifice can never be an appropriate moral choice for women. It is important to be clear about what I am claiming here. I am fully aware of how important Saiving's and Jones's work is, of the extent to which theology and various biblical texts have been used to justify and sometimes worsen abuse, and of the social dynamics that make women objects of abuse in many cultures. At the same time I also want to emphasize that abuse and oppression are not the whole story when it comes to women's lives and identities. Women throughout history have been capable of strength and purposiveness, and if we define women's nature in terms of oppression we lose sight of the accomplishments women have achieved in the past as well as the accomplishments they may be capable of achieving in the future.

So I am not in any way trying to deny or diminish the abuse and oppression many women have suffered. But I am resisting a simplistic gender-dualism that defines the very nature of all women's experience in terms of abuse and oppression. Such a gender-dualism is neither true to our experience nor an adequate foundation for women's struggle against the evils of abuse and oppression.

And one particular reason we need to reject such a simplistic gender-dualism is that self-sacrifice is an important part of feminist theory in general. I will argue below that any feminism worth its salt will have to incorporate some notion of self-sacrifice into its theoretical apparatus. If that is the case, then for feminist theology to eschew self-sacrifice will be to eschew one of the crucial components of good feminist theory. Further, the eschewal of women's self-sacrifice rests on a false and pernicious idea of women's nature, as well as a misunderstanding of self-sacrifice. To defend these claims, however, I will have to develop what is meant by the notion of self-sacrifice, and what assumptions about women's nature underlie the conviction that women should not be called to self-sacrifice. I will start with self-sacrifice, and then consider the ways in which feminist theory necessarily assumes a picture of women's nature and agency that precludes the rejection of a self-sacrificial ideal.

2. WHAT IS THE MEANING OF SELF-SACRIFICE?

A. Taxonomy

Self-sacrifice can mean a number of different things, particularly when one moves from the (moderately) more straightforward notion of a sacrifice of the self to the theological notion of kenosis, or a kenotic theology. We could perhaps begin with the various interpretations of kenosis that theologians have offered. Sarah Coakley offers a very brief typology of meanings that she describes as occupying 'a sliding-scale of meaning from "risk" to "self-limitation" to "sacrifice" to "self-giving" to "self-emptying"—and even to "annihilation"'.[9] To this list, I would add the notion of giving up prerogatives to which one's nature entitles one, which falls between self-limitation and sacrifice. Two things are worth noting about this list. The first is that the two ends, which occupy positions that are relatively easy to define, are both problematic from a theological

---

[9] Sarah Coakley, 'Kenosis: Theological Meanings and Gender Connotations' in John Polkinghorne, ed., *The Work of Love: Creation as Kenosis* (Grand Rapids: William B. Eerdmans Publishing Co., 2001), 203.

standpoint. The first, risk, offers an insufficient meaning for kenosis, while the last, annihilation, is incompatible with Christian doctrine. I'll argue for that last claim shortly, but a word is in order about the first.

Is 'risk' sufficient to capture the notion of kenosis portrayed in the scriptural narrative? It seems relatively clear that it is not. Regardless of whether one thinks of God's foreknowledge as absolute (on an Augustinian model) or as probabilistic, it is difficult to interpret Christ's Incarnation as merely risky. Becoming flesh, foreseeing or knowing of death on the cross is not really captured well by the phrase 'risk'.

The remainder of Coakley's list does seem to progress from a (slightly) weaker set of concepts through much more robust notions, though the spectrum is complicated by the fact that any of the concepts can be defined broadly enough to include all the others. That is, 'self-limitation' is a fairly minimal notion of kenosis, but broadly defined it can include self-imposed limitations that involve substantive self-sacrifice, as when a prisoner in a concentration camp gives up food to another so that the second can live. With that qualification, however, there are interesting differences among the concepts that I would like to briefly mention.

Self-limitation: This conception of kenosis is fairly minimal because, although it could involve (as mentioned above) fairly substantive sacrifices, it nonetheless carries with it a basic sense of self-determination and continuity of selfhood. The limitations imposed are imposed by the self, implying that the self retains some sense of robust identity. Further, although the limitation can be for the sake of another, the concept itself does not require this—I can limit myself for my own sake or for the sake of another.

Giving up prerogatives: I add this concept to Coakley's list because I think it adds a slightly different set of concepts to a notion of kenosis. If we think of kenosis as giving up prerogatives that are due one on the basis of one's nature, we can hold on to a sense of a core self or identity that remains, though what is due that self is set aside, with the implication that it is set aside temporarily. Fairy tales are full of stories of royalty who dress as peasants for a time, but who always eventually return to their throne by the end of the story. This way of thinking about kenosis differs from self-limitation in that the self is thought of not as limiting its own powers, but as giving up its due. Giving up prerogatives, unlike self-limitations, does have an unavoidably other-directed connotation, as the prerogatives due one are generally due one from others.

Sacrifice: The simplest (and vaguest) term is sacrifice. Sacrifices can range from trivial sacrifices made for an individual's own long-term good, to giving up one's life. I don't think this term has a sufficiently determined content to help in analysis here; it is probably best thought of as the general category under which all the other terms fall.

Self-giving: With self-giving we move to a term that implies a measure of loss of self. Self-limitation implies that the self continues to determine itself—after all, it is the self that is doing the limiting. But self-giving implies some measure of giving up self-determination, though it leaves open the degree to which the self is given up. Further, the notion of self-giving is also necessarily other-directed. To give of one's self is not possible unless there is a recipient. Self-giving, however, leaves open the possibility of fairly minimal gifts, along with the potential for complete self-sacrifice.

Self-sacrifice: Self-sacrifice is the strongest term because it implies that in some significant way the self is actually lost. At a minimum it involves some sort of denial of the self, though this can be the denial of one part of the self for the sake of another part. At the maximum it involves what the phrase literally means—the sacrifice of the self, or of life. Further, in order for this to be a sacrifice (rather than, say, mere destruction) it also must involve giving up the self for some other person, or some other good. Self-sacrifice is the term I have focused on in this chapter because it has connotations of giving more than just some aspect of the self—it suggests a giving up of the self itself, of giving up parts of one's identity. When the parts of one's identity given up are central to one's sense of self, it may involve a loss of identity at some level.

Annihilation: The category of annihilation is stronger than that of self-sacrifice, since it implies the complete loss of self. To be annihilated is to cease to exist. Annihilation, I would argue, is too strong a notion of self-sacrifice to be appropriate as an account of kenosis. The argument for this is clearest if we have examples of theorists who do advocate an annihilationist notion of self-sacrifice.

B. Annihilation and Critique

Because self-sacrifice does have connotations of giving up the self, of losing the self altogether, it can shade into annihilation. We can see this move toward annihilation, I think, and also what is problematic about it, at two levels: the level of social institutions and the level of the individual. To illustrate the first, I would like to consider a book that directly addresses the issue of kenotic theology and feminist thought. In *Kenosis and Feminist Theology: The Challenge of Gianni Vattimo*, Marta Frascati-Lochhead defends Vattimo's view that the true meaning of kenosis in Christian thought is the overcoming of the violence of metaphysics. What is meant by metaphysics, here? Why is it thought to be violent? And why should it be overcome?

Metaphysical claims, particularly when made about other individuals, seem to define the whole reality of another, leaving no room for that other to self-define. This imposition of identity is understood by Vattimo (following Heidegger) to be a kind of violence, a brutal imposition of unchosen identity on someone who should be free to determine his or her own being. Because this violence is assumed to be inherent in all metaphysical theorizing, it can only be overcome by giving up all metaphysical claims.

The violence of metaphysics that occurs in a religious context, Frascati-Lochhead contends, can only be overcome by the secularization of the western church, a secularization heralded in the philosophy of Heidegger and Nietzsche as interpreted by Gianni Vattimo.[10] There is a certain level at which these claims make sense. After all, kenosis is a self-emptying. Kenotic theology, then, would indicate a self-emptying theology, an a-theology if you will. In the context of an institutional church that is called to be the body of Christ in the world, but that has too frequently acted as a force of political domination and oppression, perhaps there is some need to call the institutional church to repent and to turn to a self-image that involves servanthood rather than consolidation of power and wealth. Presumably such a line of reasoning leads to Frascati-Lochhead's conclusions, with a few detours through Nietzsche and Heidegger

---

[10] Marta Frascati-Lochhead, *Kenosis and Feminist Theology: The Challenge of Gianni Vattimo* (Albany: State University of New York Press, 1998), 150–1.

along the way. Read through the philosophy of Gianni Vattimo, Frascati-Lochhead argues, Nietzsche and Heidegger provide the impetus for rejecting any totalizing metaphysics, and with that rejection overcoming the violence that can be done to others in the name of metaphysical claims. And the conclusions reached are that the church should give up any metaphysical claims, and thus secularize, and that this is the true meaning of kenosis.

I would like to resist this understanding of kenosis, of kenotic theology, and of self-sacrifice, however. There are several reasons why I think that Frascati-Lochhead's account provides a wrong-headed account of kenosis. First, while metaphysical claims can provide the impetus for violence and oppression, they are not necessary conditions for such evil. Violence and oppression can arise from any number of conditions, including anomie, a loss of meaning, and the absence of a metaphysics that makes sense of life. Further, metaphysical claims can also provide the impetus for alleviating suffering and fighting against oppression. History is at least as full of examples of those who fought oppression on the basis of a particular metaphysics as of those who caused oppression on the basis of metaphysical claims. So the attempt to re-interpret kenosis as 'a self-overcoming of metaphysics' seems to me to be wrong-headed: it makes it too easy to ignore the real violence and terror that exists in the world in favour of academic posturing about the violence of metaphysics. We don't reach out to another person in love by abjuring metaphysical claims; we do so by providing food when they are hungry, care when they are sick.

Secondly, interpreting kenotic self-sacrifice as the destruction of the self (in this case, the auto-destruction of a church with any recognizable identity) is misguided. For Frascati-Lochhead, a kenotic church must necessarily move toward secularization, because, she argues (following Vattimo interpreting Heidegger), any metaphysical claims represent a violence toward difference and otherness. She is, of course, right to recognize that without metaphysical claims the church is likely to become secularized, but wrong to see this secularization as appropriate kenotic self-sacrifice. If the church becomes secularized, it no longer exists as a church. But if it no longer exists as a church, it cannot do the very things it is made to do, that is, to act as the body of Christ in the world by feeding the hungry, clothing the naked, and calling people into a right relationship with their Creator. A secularized church cannot do any of these tasks, because it is no longer a church at all.

Finally, the paradoxical nature of Frascati-Lochhead's proposal becomes even clearer when one turns to the topic of feminism. The book examines a number of contemporary feminist theologians and in each case takes the theologian to task for having too robust a notion of the metaphysics of the person.[11] In each case, any hint that a theorist thinks that people are individual subjects, that there is some*thing* that they are, is held up for criticism, since a true kenosis involves the continual hunt for and destruction of any claims that might suggest an incipient metaphysics. The attempt becomes ridiculous at some point. All the author's energy is devoted toward ferreting out some whiff of metaphysics, and the notion that both theology and feminism might have some actual role to play in changing the world is completely lost. This conception of kenosis has slid into annihilation. In so doing it has lost sight of, and lost the ability to call others to, service of the Kingdom of God.

Sliding from self-sacrifice to annihilation can occur at the individual level as well. The paradox of kenotic self-emptying arises because the self that is emptied must continue to exist as a self to be emptied. If emptying is understood as complete destruction, as absolute emptying of all identity and even existence, then the self-emptying results in pure emptiness. But that is nihilism, not self-emptying. We find an example of this in some of the thought of Simone Weil.[12] She seems to advocate, in places, an absolute nihilism of the self, and tried to live out such annihilation in her life, resulting in her death by starvation. In *Gravity and Grace* she writes:

I cannot conceive of the necessity for God to love me, when I feel so clearly that even with human beings affection for me can only be a mistake. But I can easily imagine that he loves that perspective of creation which can only

---

[11] This is the substance of the criticism of Rebecca Chopp on pp. 178–80, Sallie McFague on p. 195, and Rosemary Ruether on p. 208.

[12] There is another side of Weil. That other side tends to appear when she is focusing on others rather than herself. The aspect of Weil that I identify here, however, is what one of her most ardent supporters calls a 'perverse version of sacrifice' in some of her writings. (See Eric Springsted's *Simone Weil and the Suffering of Love* (Cambridge, MA: Cowley Publications, 1986), 79.

be seen from the point where I am. But I act as a screen. I must withdraw so that he may see it. I must withdraw so that God may make contact with the beings whom chance places in my path and whom he loves. It is tactless for me to be there. It is as though I were placed between two lovers or two friends. I am not the maiden who awaits her betrothed, but the unwelcome third who is with two betrothed lovers and ought to go away so that they can really be together.[13]

Weil's rather poignant image of the unwanted third party seems a perfect reflection of the woman with no sense of self Serene Jones is concerned about in the passage I quoted earlier. We are confronted here with a woman who understands herself as deeply unlovable. The only thing she has to offer is to disappear, to go away, and thus to leave the Creator alone with the Creation. Weil follows up this comment with the following prayer: 'May I disappear in order that those things that I see may become perfect in their beauty from the very fact that they are no longer things that I see.'[14] A more poignant expression of Weil's rejection of self is hard to imagine.

As in the case of Frascati-Lochhead, Weil takes the notion of self-sacrifice too far in the direction of annihilation. Weil seems incapable of recognizing that she is a part of the beloved creation that she herself wants to return to God. Her own self-giving love is predicated on a denigration of the self she has—it is fit *only* to be given up. But proper self-sacrifice *must* emphasize the worth of the self that is emptied out. This is not to say that one must think one's self truly great before being worthy of service in the Kingdom—Jesus' claim that the last shall be first makes that untenable. But the self-emptying Jesus models for us originates in a recognition that, since the self is precious, emptying it really is a sacrifice. Weil's words suggest that the self is such a nothingness that its sacrifice is really no big deal at all. Jesus' own sacrifice on the Cross is astonishing and hard to grasp precisely because the self that was sacrificed is God. The self that is called to self-sacrifice must be a self that has a value, not necessarily a value from its own efforts, of course, but a value nonetheless. The sacrifice, in fact, would hardly be a sacrifice if what was given up was worthless.

[13] Simone Weil, *Gravity and Grace* (Lincoln: University of Nebraska Press, 1952), 88–9.
[14] *Gravity and Grace*, p. 89.

Weil's words, then, suggest annihilation rather than an acceptable self-sacrifice. They denigrate the self that God has created, has created good, and now loves with a deep and abiding love. Such a self should not be conceptualized as an unwanted third. Self-sacrifice, properly understood, requires that one have a robust sense of the value of the self that is to be emptied. One might object at this point that Weil had a robust sense of self, such a strong sense of self, in fact, that she was able to push herself to make precisely the sacrifices she made.[15] I think this gets at an important distinction. Weil certainly had a very strong will. But a strong will is not the same thing as a strong sense of self. We can see the difference if we ask whether we see in Weil a real delight in her own existence, a sense that it is good for her to have been created and alive. And such a sense of joy of existence is not a strong theme in Weil's writing.

So a robust sense of self is not identical with a strong will, though the two can and frequently do co-exist. The sense of self I am arguing for here is a sense that one is loved for one's own sake, that one's existence is a good thing, and that one can properly love the fact that one is alive and able to do things that are worth doing. As with any character trait, an excess of these beliefs clearly becomes a vice, but the absence of these beliefs is also a character flaw. Feminist theory at its best advocates the appropriateness of such an identity for women, and the work of both Saiving and Jones is valuable just to the extent that it alerts us to the ways in which some women are made incapable of this joy by forces of oppression.

Such a robust sense of self places limits on what sorts of sacrifices are called for; it requires us to use a teleological framework for evaluating self-sacrifice. Self-sacrifice is of no value, and may be sinful, when it occurs for the sake of something that is not worthwhile. An individual with a robust sense of being a loved child of God should not squander that loved self on trivial and inconsequential things. (And here Saiving's article is a valuable reminder that some people are tempted in precisely this way. We ought not, however, to assume that all such people are women nor that all women face only this temptation.)

---

[15] My thanks to Sarah Coakley for raising this point during the Kenotic Christology Workshop.

But there are things that are of more worth than the individual life as well. In particular, bringing about the Kingdom of God is something to which all Christians are called, and for which we are called to give up claims of self-interest. Giving up the self because it is easier to do what others want than to fight for one's own rights is inappropriate self-sacrifice. Giving up the self in the service of God is not. Self-sacrifice, then, is a good, but never the whole good to which one looks forward. There is nothing in Christian theology that supports the claim that annihilation of the self ought to be one's final goal.

One further aspect of proper self-sacrifice is worth noting here. Self-sacrifice can be legitimate when it aims at goals that fit the sacrifice that are made. This allows for one important distinction with respect to self-sacrifice that is fully in line with the feminist concerns I mentioned earlier. The sort of sacrifice of the self that feminist critics rightly reject is a sacrifice that leads to a loss of self for the agent. But it also is a sacrifice that allows others to continue to act in ways that are evil or oppressive or destructive. When women are abused, they lose a sense of self, and thus experience a sort of self-sacrifice (though not, I have argued, proper self-sacrifice). Great damage is done to them. But their abuser is also damaged in being allowed to continue to act in this way. It is a self-inflicted damage, and a very different kind of damage from that done to the abused, but a damage nonetheless. Proper self-sacrifice is proper precisely when it aims to stop or limit the destruction of other people or of healthy social relations. When oppressive social structures are challenged, oppressors are offered the opportunity to be healed of their own brokenness, though they are unlikely to recognize this as a valuable opportunity.

So one further teleological aspect of self-sacrifice should be emphasized here. When sacrifice leads to a worsening of oppression or a complicity with abuse it can never be termed proper. When, on the other hand, sacrifice aims at stopping abuse, and at healing social relationships, it operates for the ultimate benefit of all involved. Such a sacrifice is justified. One aspect that distinguishes proper from improper self-sacrifice is the question whether the sacrifice aims at the true good of all concerned or whether it instead leads to further destruction of the moral character of both parties involved.

I should also emphasize here that I am not advocating a sort of pop-psychology notion that self-sacrifice always leads to a better life. Sometimes self-sacrifice does lead to the development of a richer sense of self and an ability to be more truly who one is and ought to be. And in the ultimate sense I have faith that proper self-sacrifice does look forward to a time when all things will be made new. But we don't, here and now, live in the ultimate sense. Self-sacrifice is just that, many times, and it has a tragic edge to it in our current existence that we should not gloss over. It will not necessarily lead to a long, happy, fulfilled life. It is more likely to lead to ulcers, stress-induced health problems, and the breakdown of close personal relationships. It is important to recognize that self-sacrifice results in real loss. Recognition that it will result in such a loss does not mean sacrifice is not what one is called to, but it does mean that what one sacrifices for had better be worth it.

Because proper self-sacrifice is thus situated in the context of such a robust sense of self, it is also important to note that ultimately the individual must be the one to determine what is or is not proper self-sacrifice. To have a notion of one's identity before God involves seeing oneself as uniquely called to a particular vocation, a vocation that will undoubtedly involve various sacrifices. Which particular sacrifices are appropriate to one's particular calling, however, cannot always be judged by others. There are clearly lives that are easily recognized as appropriate cases of self-sacrifice, and lives that are recognizable as self-centred. But most human lives are found somewhere in between these two extremes, and we are rarely in a position to decide for another what an appropriate sacrifice might be, or, when someone is called to make sacrifices, what will lead to real and substantial losses.

Both of these points follow from the notion that proper self-sacrifice occurs in the context of a robust sense of the worth of the self. The tragic dimension of self-sacrifice arises precisely because the self sacrifices real and worthwhile goods. In a world unbroken by sin, perhaps many of these sacrifices would not need to be made, though there might still be mutual self-giving. In the world in which we live, they are sacrifices worth making, but still genuine sacrifices. And which sacrifices are the ones a particular person is called to make is something the individual needs to work out in the context of the life she is called to live. Though we may be called to self-sacrifice, we are not called to desire the annihilation of the self.

Both of these notions—that self-sacrifice is a real sacrifice, and that it should not be equated with a call to annihilation—are defended by Oliver O'Donovan. He argues that there have been two wrong responses to the notion that loving self-sacrifice occurs properly in the context of the expectation of future reward.[16] The first involves seeing self-sacrificial love as, in some way, not a real sacrifice because it simply requires the rejection of what is not truly a part of one's proper self. On this view, the reward of self-sacrifice is not really a future reward because it is completely internal to the lived self's current experience. O'Donovan rejects this view because, as he points out, 'If the life of love is not in itself a burden, it does, nevertheless, involve us in burdens. No account of the Christian moral life can be adequate unless it is allowed to point forward to the resurrection.'[17] Too strong an emphasis on the fittingness or benefits of (current) self-sacrifice obscures the extent to which we live in the not-yet time when creation still groans in anticipation of full restoration.

This echoes the point I made above. Sacrifices can be real. When we look at the lives of the great civil rights leaders, especially someone like Fanny Lou Hamer, we see the extent to which they did make great sacrifices, and we see that their lives did not always culminate in happiness and satisfaction because of it.[18] There is a moral heroism involved in such sacrifices, but also a tragic edge.

But there is an opposite danger, one that appears, as I have noted, on occasion in Weil's thought. This is the annihilationist view that labels desiring one's own good as sinful. O'Donovan describes the view thus: 'Desire, it is argued, introduces an element of self-interest which compromises the true loss-of-self-in-other which is the essence of love. In desiring, the subject loves himself. The good of God's final reign implies *his* welfare. ... Love is thus corrupted into self-seeking.'[19] O'Donovan argues that such a view discloses, first, an

---

[16] Oliver O'Donovan, *Resurrection and Moral Order: An Outline for Evangelical Ethics*, 2nd edn. (Grand Rapids: William B. Eerdmans Publishing Co., 1994), 248–9.

[17] *Resurrection and Moral Order*, p. 249.

[18] See, for example, Chana Kai Lee's *For Freedom's Sake: The Life of Fanny Lou Hamer* (Urbana: University of Illinois Press, 1999).

[19] *Resurrection and Moral Order*, p. 249.

inherent rejection of all teleological ethics (and it is interesting to note that one biographer of Weil notes that she hated Aristotle[20]), and an accompanying confusion over the nature of what it means for something to be objectively good.

That which is objectively good, O'Donovan argues, is that which is properly responded to with love and desire. An improper ordering of desire occurs when I make something that is not truly good the object of my desire. But when the object of my love is truly good, then desire is the objectively correct response. So, O'Donovan concludes, 'When the object of love is God himself, the author of all love and of all subjects who love, there need be no more anxious enquiry about right and wrong love, selfish and unselfish love.... These questions have all been resolved when the question about the object of love has been resolved.'[21] This general picture of the nature of self-sacrificial love captures the sense both that self-sacrifice must be oriented correctly, and that it involves real sacrifice, that it is undertaken in the hope of a future in which all things will be made new, and properly involves loving one's own good in the context of loving God above all else.

3. REVISITING BOTH FEMINISM AND KENOTIC THEOLOGY

There are many structural similarities between Christianity and feminism. Both operate within eschatological frameworks, and both criticize the world as it is found in favour of an ideal vision of some sort or another. (Whether these basic structural similarities are contingent, or whether they arise because feminism appeared in the context of a generally Christianized West is a question I will leave for the historians to argue over.) This basic similarity converges on a concern for the suffering, oppression, and marginalization of various groups. In each case the world-view rejects complacent acceptance of the status quo and calls believers to fight for change. But neither can

---

[20] *Gravity and Grace,* Introduction by Gustave Thibon, p. 7.
[21] *Resurrection and Moral Order,* p. 250.

promise that change will occur in the believer's lifetime. Christians have been waiting for all things to be made right for many centuries now, and feminists have the historical record of women like the suffragettes who often fought for reforms that would not occur until after their own death. Susan B. Anthony never voted, Jane Addams never saw the elimination of the Chicago slums, and contemporary feminist legal theorists are unlikely to see the end of sexual harassment. The history of the feminist movement is full of women who sacrificed their own happiness in order to fight for a cause they saw as just.

If political action will not bring me any benefit, if I could devote myself to fighting for basic rights such as the right to vote, but never see the day when women actually could vote, then why should I bother? Feminism has always accepted the presence of values that require the sacrifice of self-interest for the sake of justice. And this attitude is expressed in the structure of feminist institutions that require inclusion of various standpoints in leadership, and in the constant reference in feminist literature to non-gender based oppression as a feminist issue.

The question then becomes what is worth the sacrifice, not whether sacrifice is sometimes the proper response. Here there will, of course, be disagreement between some versions of feminism and some aspects of Christian theology. I'd prefer to set aside the question of compatibility, however, and focus on what feminist theory may have to offer theological thinking on the issue of self-sacrifice. Feminist thought on the issue of self-sacrifice is most valuable for theology in terms of its analysis of the ways in which the rhetoric of self-sacrifice has been used to deny women opportunities to serve God, and in terms of its analysis of the ways in which women's self-sacrifice for inappropriate ends has been advocated by thinkers speaking from a Christian standpoint.

Examples are helpful here. When women's fight to enter the ministry is criticized as a case of women being self-seeking and power-hungry, the rhetoric of self-sacrifice is being misused. Men's work as ministers and pastors is not essentially a case of power-hungry lust for control, but rather a matter of answering a sacrificial call to Christian service. Women's attempt to enter the ministry, then, is the same. When the rhetoric of self-sacrifice is used to prevent women from devoting their lives to service of the Kingdom, the concept is misused.

Alternatively, we sometimes see inappropriate goals held up for women. My local newspaper recently ran an article on a church in this area that has developed a mentorship programme that pairs younger women in the church with older ones for the purpose of mentoring the younger women in the Christian life. The main activities in which the group is involved are flower arranging, setting a beautiful table, and interior decorating tips. The assumptions behind this mentoring seem to be that women exist for the sake of particular others, namely their spouse and children (and, it is further assumed, all good Christian women have both). Their Christian duties involve making life aesthetically pleasant for those others. This is a strange perversion of the gospel message. Attractive table settings may have their place, but they cannot be the focus of a true Christian life.

Finally, feminist notions of women's agency require an endorsement of certain types of self-sacrifice in certain cases. Most feminists would be embarrassed to offer a view of women's natures that assumes women to be helpless, weak, irresponsible, and incapable of self-direction. Unfortunately, the picture of women's nature assumed by some feminist critiques of self-sacrifice do strike me as coming perilously close to that view. If, on the contrary, we begin with a respect for women's strength and agency, and with a willingness to recognize women's moral decisions as arising out of both reason and responsibility, then we must recognize the possibility that some women have been called to self-sacrifice, that their sacrifice was a morally justifiable, perhaps praiseworthy choice, and that they fought for a worthwhile cause.

To recognize people, male or female, as moral agents, requires that we credit them with the strength and will needed to make decisions for which they can be held accountable, and for which they can be praised or criticized. If one denies that the call to self-sacrifice can be appropriate for women, one is pre-judging the moral agency available to them. The range of moral decisions they can make is limited in advance, without input from them, in ways that reflect a less-than-fully-human picture of women's nature. On feminist principles, rejecting the notion that women should be called to self-sacrifice is evidence of the assumption that women are weaker and less capable moral agents. This hardly seems an appropriate basis for feminist theorizing.

As mentioned earlier, theorists such as Saiving and Jones offer an important warning here as to how calls to self-sacrifice can be misused, and the ways in which such calls can function to increase rather than mitigate injustice. These are important and valuable warnings. But they should not lead us to throw out the notion of self-sacrifice altogether. Instead, paradoxically, they should lead us to a clearer awareness of the evils of oppressive social systems that make proper self-sacrifice impossible.

4. CONCLUSION

Self-sacrifice is something we are called to. But if we stop there we may say both too little and too much. Self-sacrifice is appropriate only when what is given up is proportionate to the value of the final goal. Self-sacrifice for the purpose of keeping a clean house, for example, is a squandering of the value of a human life. (Clean houses may be an important means to some further good, of course, but they are not, for their own sake, worthy of single-hearted devotion.) Even the choice so many women are lauded for, devoting one's life to one's children, may be a form of idolatry.

I don't mean to deny that caring for children can be a high calling, for both men and women, and a central part of one's vocational identity. The church has, in recent years, come to recognize and try to rectify the tendency for some men to neglect their families while serving as pastors or missionaries, and I am not advocating that women now begin to participate in that same neglect. But as Augustine reminds us in his *Confessions*, the things that tempt us to turn away from God are often the good things God has given us.[22] While children and family rightfully play an important part in many people's lives, we also need to be aware of how attending to those

---

[22] St. Augustine, *Confessions*, Book II v., trans. Henry Chadwick (Oxford: Oxford University Press,1998)

(important and vital) things can be used as an excuse for failing to perform other tasks, tasks that can often be carried out in addition to parenting. If we choose to have children, we should fulfil our obligations to them, but we should not use parental obligations to evade other obligations.

Further, self-sacrifice should not be understood as a matter of spineless submission to whatever anyone else requests or demands of the agent. Saiving is correct to alert us to the ways in which we can sin by failing to become someone who is capable of doing great things. Just as Moses tried to evade the call of God by claiming he was incapable of speaking clearly, and Saul hid among the baggage to avoid his calling to be King, we are tempted to evade the service we may be called to. For many women, this evasion is made far too easy by societal expectations. But Jesus' actions in the case of Mary and Martha, affirming Mary's choice to sit at his feet rather than busy herself in household duties, should be an important challenge to these societal expectations. We need a robust notion of self-worth, for both women and men, that can lead to bold calls for justice, prophetic voices, and a refusal to accept a status quo marred by oppressive hierarchies. Such a notion provides the context from within which it is possible accurately to recognize that one might be called to self-sacrifice, to recognize what sorts of sacrifices are legitimate, and to accept that call in a responsible way.

Such a conception of self-sacrifice is not foreign to feminist thought. It is just such a picture of women's worth and moral agency that has been assumed in much of the feminist literature. So a feminist kenotic theology is not, ultimately, an oxymoron. One can be a feminist and advocate that women sacrifice themselves for an appropriate cause. Put more strongly, unless one thinks that women's choices to sacrifice themselves for something appropriately important are justified, one runs the risk of denying women their own moral agency. When placed in the context of a robust notion of self worth, and when oriented toward service to the Kingdom rather than purposeless self-abnegation, self-sacrifice is an appropriate call for all who call themselves followers of Christ.

There is one final concern that I should briefly touch on. In some feminist theological circles this claim that women can and should identify with Jesus' sacrifice is seen as inherently problematic, both because of the claim that women should not sacrifice, and because Jesus was male, and therefore not someone with whom women can identify. I've argued already that recognizing women's full moral agency requires acknowledging that they can be called to self-sacrifice. But the question whether women can find an exemplar in a male figure remains to be considered. And again it seems that a recognition of the full humanity of both men and women forces us to answer in the affirmative. Jesus, the creeds affirm, is fully human and fully God. He was also male, since one cannot be human without bodily, sexed existence. His life, death, and resurrection, however, are not intrinsically tied to his masculinity, but to his humanity.

Further, unless these theorists are willing to argue for the opposite claim—that women can never serve as exemplars or ideals for men—they ought not to argue that men cannot play that role for women. If our participation in the life of Christ is a participation made possible by God's Incarnation, and if women can fully participate in that life with Christ, then women can also model Christ to men. I fear that any other view is likely to lead to the view that there must be two separate religions, a religion of Christ and self-sacrifice for men and a religion of Christa and self-affirmation for women. (I think Mary Daly has, in fact, reached this conclusion.) And such a simplistic gender essentialism is untrue to our experience, untrue to Scripture, and ultimately destructive of both men's and women's lives. It illegitimately truncates what we can understand our calling to be, and so limits who we can become in the service of God.

If we begin where Scripture itself does, with the affirmation that all that exists is created to be good by a loving Creator, and that humans, in particular, are created as the very image of the living God, we begin from the right perspective for thinking about self-sacrifice. The existence each of us enjoys is a beautiful gift, to be treasured and enjoyed and protected when necessary. But our ability to image God does not stop with enjoying the good life we've been given. Being an image, rather than the original source, implies that there is something greater than our own existence, something that provides meaning and context for our own worth. It implies, therefore, that our own existence is not the be-all and end-all of value, and that it must sometimes be given up for a higher cause.

13

Conclusion: The Promise of Kenosis

Stephen T. Davis and C. Stephen Evans

1

For Christians, that branch of theology called Christology is perennially important. In every generation, Christians must rethink and restate their understanding of Jesus Christ. They must be able to explain in contemporary terms, both to themselves and to the unbelieving world, who Christ is. Such explanations are especially necessary in times (like ours) of Christological ferment and confusion. That rethinking must always be done, so the two of us believe, consistently with scripture and in serious conversation with the theological tradition. But it must be done: Christology is *the* crucial Christian doctrine.

The Christological theory, or family of theories, called kenosis is an attempt to get clear on the person of Jesus Christ, especially in the light of the teachings and activities of Jesus as described in the four gospels. We believe the theory can also be used to answer certain criticisms of Christological orthodoxy. We hold that kenosis is a valid theological option for Christians, and the majority of the writers in this volume wish to commend it to the Christian community, both scholars and ordinary believers, for serious consideration. (Though we note that some of our authors are ultimately critics of a kenotic theory.)

Indeed, we are personally convinced that some sort of kenosis is inevitable for orthodox or Chalcedonian Christians who have fully grasped the implications of the Incarnation. That fact will emerge, we believe, almost as soon as any sort of description is given of the Logos's transition from an exclusively divine mode of being to an incarnate mode of being. As Edward Oakes argues at the outset of his essay in the present volume, orthodox Christology holds that in the Incarnation the infinite became finite.[1] To us it seems that the only way for an infinite thing to become a finite thing is by giving up or emptying itself or divesting itself, in some sense, of some infinite properties. Non-kenotic theories resist this conclusion in a number of ways. Traditionally, it has been urged that the Incarnation involves only the adding of properties and not the loss or modification of any properties. But if an infinite divine being begins to exist in a finite mode, must this not involve some change in that being itself? We do not claim that intuitions here settle the matter, and the essays by Sarah Coakley and Edwin Chr. van Driel show that traditional Christologies have resources for dealing with these issues. However, we think that kenotic views have real strengths that have not been fully appreciated.

As Davis argues in his essay, virtually every sensible reader of Philippians 2 allows that the Logos divested itself in the Incarnation at least of such properties as its non-servant status and its status of not having been born. (We might simplify the first point by saying that in the Incarnation the Logos divested itself of the divine glory, as seems a clear implication of John 17:5.) And any attempt to argue that the divine glory is not one of God's attributes seems hopeless (see Psalm 19:1; Luke 2:9; John 17:5). That God is immeasurably glorious—which entails that God does not, apart from the Incarnation, exist 'in the form of a servant'—is a divine attribute right alongside omniscience and omnipotence. Accordingly, in our view, every Christologist who affirms Philippians 2:6–11 is a kenoticist in at least a limited sense. The opponents of kenosis need to take this

---

[1] See Edward T. Oakes, S.J., ' "He descended into hell": The Depths of God's Self-Emptying Love on Holy Saturday in the Thought of Hans Urs von Balthasar', p. 218 above.

point fully into account and develop a view that does justice to this self-emptying.

In John 13:1–20, a kind of mini-kenosis is described. During supper with the disciples, Jesus 'got up from the table, took off his outer robe, and tied a towel around himself. Then he poured water into a basin and began to wash the disciples' feet and to wipe them with the towel that was tied around him.' In first-century Palestine, foot washing was a servant's job. So strongly did Peter feel this point that he objected to what Jesus was doing. 'You will never wash my feet,' he said. But Jesus persisted. He pointed out that the disciples did not understand the meaning of what he was doing, and would only do so afterwards, which of course meant after his crucifixion and resurrection. But Peter only agreed to allow Jesus to wash his feet when Jesus strongly said to him: 'Unless I wash you, you have no share with me.'

This act on the part of Jesus doubtless has many levels of meaning. Jesus' washing of their feet was surely meant to be symbolic of his imminent death on the cross, at which point—so Christians believe—our sins were atoned for and we were made clean. But after the foot washing, Jesus supplied a second explanation: he was setting an example for the disciples. He said: 'Do you know what I have done to you? You call me teacher and Lord—and you are right, for that is what I am. So if I, your Lord and Teacher, have washed your feet, you also ought to wash one another's feet.... Servants are not greater than their master, nor are messengers greater than the one who sent them. If you know these things, you are blessed if you do them.'

We call this act of foot washing a mini-kenosis because Jesus, so to speak, temporarily emptied himself of his Lord-like and Master-like prerogatives and dignity. He dressed like a servant and then did a servant's job. Of course we do not see here the kind of ontological kenosis that is discussed in this book, namely, the Logos divesting itself of certain divine properties in order to become a human being. What we see in John 13 is a kind of moral kenosis, namely, a master voluntarily taking on the role of a slave. Still, centuries of Christians have been gripped by this simple story. The religious power inherent in this act of love and humility is precisely one of the points that makes kenosis so compelling to those who defend it.

2

Those who reject kenosis do so for a great variety of reasons. But perhaps the most important of them is the idea that kenosis is inconsistent with the most exalted notions of God or with our deepest philosophical intuitions about God. Usually the debate revolves around such traditional divine properties as immutability, impassibility, and greatness. We agree with Sarah Coakley, in her fine contribution to this book, that there is little hint of kenosis in the Church Fathers, and especially in Cyril and the Cappadocians. The obvious reason, as she points out, is that those thinkers were strongly wedded to divine impassibility and immutability. But most Christians today think that the Logos did suffer in the Incarnation (although not because of any deficiency in God), and that God is subject to a least certain sorts of change.

Does kenosis conflict with our deepest convictions about God? At this point, it seems, we quickly reach an impasse. Who is more exalted, more God-like, more worthy of worship—a God who can or a God who cannot undergo change? Or—a God who can or a God who cannot undergo self-limitation? Or, to ask the question in Anselmian terms, which God is *greater*? Opinions will obviously differ here.

Virtually all theologically orthodox Christians, whether they defend kenosis or not, work with a largely similar view of God. They hold that God is the absolutely unique, necessary, and eternal creator of the heavens and the earth, and is, at least apart from the Incarnation, omnipotent, omniscient, perfectly good, and loving. At other points, however, there are differences. Let us use the term 'God1' to refer to a divine being who has all the common properties listed above plus the properties of being *impassible* (is not able to suffer) and *immutable* (is not capable of any kind of genuine change). And let us use the term 'God2' to refer to a divine being who has all the common properties listed above and is neither impassible nor immutable. (God2 may still of course be immutable in the weaker sense of never changing his basic nature, always keeping his promises, not being fickle or capricious like the gods of the pagans, etc.; indeed, those who believe in God2 typically insist on this point.)

We do not expect to be able definitively to break the impasse between believers in God1 and believers in God2. But perhaps something helpful can be said. Let's use the term *G-property* to refer to any property or attribute of a person that makes the person who has it *greater* than that person would be without it. Obviously, whether a property is or is not a G-property may vary from context to context. Normally, the property of *being red-headed* is not a G-property; normally, the properties of being *wise* and of being *all-powerful* are G-properties.

There are several complex difficulties in the neighbourhood here. We only want to point out that in both *Monologion* II and *Proslogion* V, Anselm said of God: 'Therefore, thou art just, truthful, blessed, and *whatever it is better to be than not to be*' (italics added). We can call this point 'Anselm's criterion'. Now what it is 'better to be' surely in part varies from one type of entity to another. It is better for a human being to be courageous than not to be courageous, for example. But that would hardly be true for God—not at least for an omnipotent and omniscient God who knows how everything turns out and can even determine how things turn out. 'Courage' is not a property that such a God can possibly have, at least not in any normal sense of the word 'courage'.

Still, Anselm's criterion, rough as it is, allows us to ask: Which is it better for God to be—capable or incapable of change? Or: which is it better for God to be—capable of self-limitation or incapable of self-limitation? We think it is better for God to be capable of self-limitation than not. That is, we think a God who is capable of change and self-limitation is greater, *mutatis mutandis*, than a God who is not. We wish to make several points in support of this claim. (We also hold that it is better for God to be passible than impassible; but since the notion that God suffers due to human sinfulness and pain is a virtual commonplace among most Christians today, we will not argue the point.)

First, we are convinced that biblical teaching ought to trump disputed a priori theological intuitions, as Ronald Feenstra argues in this volume.[2] Whether God1 is greater than God2 can certainly be

---

[2] See Ronald Feenstra, 'A Kenotic Christological Method for Understanding the Divine Attributes', Ch. 6 of this volume, esp. pp. 154–64.

disputed; we concede that Christians in good conscience can disagree about that. Moreover, we are aware that biblical teachings about what Jesus said and did are capable of interpretation, and that believers in God1 can find ways of interpreting texts about Jesus growing in wisdom and stature, not knowing the date of the parousia, and so on. Still, since we believe that kenosis fits more naturally with the picture of Jesus that the four evangelists paint, and also that what scripture teaches is theologically normative, we opt for God2. Our philosophical intuitions are not certain enough that we can rely on them to trump what seems to be biblical teaching.

Some will object to this as Richard Swinburne does, who in effect argues that (what we are calling) God1 is metaphysically simpler than God2, and is thus more likely to be a truer description of God.[3] We have two problems with this picture. (1) We are not sure what notion of 'simplicity' Swinburne is deploying here. (2) The principle of parsimony says that if two theories are equal in explanatory power, one should accept the simpler theory. But we do not accept that simplicity has important relevance to the current issue, since we deny that God1 and God2 are equal in explanatory power. We hold that God2 is far more explanatorily powerful. Witness the abstruse intellectual handsprings that defenders of God1 have to turn when it comes to explaining the apparent changes that God undergoes in scripture or the apparent cases of real suffering and even anguish experienced by Christ in the Bible. Swinburne himself is driven to postulate that the Incarnate God has a 'divided mind', really two minds, one human and one divine, which surely threatens the unity of Christ as a person, and leads to a very strained picture of Jesus as having powers and knowledge that he does not know he possesses.[4]

Finally, we believe that God2 is actually *greater* than God1 because, as Evans previously argued, there are far more options open to God2.[5] A God who lacks the power to limit itself seems to us to be less powerful, and thus less great, than a God who has the power to limit himself. We doubt that a God who is incapable of self-limitation

[3] See Richard Swinburne, *The Christian God* (Oxford: Oxford University Press, 1994), pp. 230–3.

[4] Swinburne, pp. 200–9.

[5] See C. Stephen Evans, 'Kenotic Christology and the Nature of God', Ch. 8 of this volume, esp. pp. 205–14.

can enter into covenants or make promises to his creatures, and worry that a God who cannot bind himself is simply too different from the biblical God, who always identifies himself by his relationships: 'the God of Abraham, Isaac, and Jacob'.

3

We believe that some resist a kenotic understanding of the Incarnate Christ because of a fear that such a view will erode his divinity. It might be conceded by opponents of a kenotic theory that such an account of the Incarnation does a better job of accounting for the fully human portrait of Jesus in the gospels. However, does a kenotic view undermine the full divinity of Christ?

Davis gives a clear argument that the answer is no in his earlier essay.[6] However, it is worth paying a little more attention to what one might call the supernatural dimension of the portrait of Jesus given in the gospels. It is true, as kenoticists wish to stress, that Jesus sometimes appears finite in his knowledge and power. However, it is also true that in the gospels Jesus frequently performs miracles and possesses knowledge that an ordinary human would not possess. An excellent example would be the story in John 4, in which Jesus tells a Samaritan woman, whom he has apparently never met before, that the man she has referred to as her husband is not really her husband, though she has had five different husbands (John 4:17). If Jesus has put aside such properties as omniscience and omnipotence, how can he have such knowledge and perform such miracles as calming the storm in Luke 8:19–25?

Kenoticists are in no way uncomfortable with the supernatural dimension that Jesus exhibits here and in many other places, but they explain this dimension by pointing to another fundamental characteristic of the biblical portrait: Jesus lived his life in complete dependence upon and in complete union with the Father and the Spirit. When Jesus performs a miracle, on a kenotic view of the Incarnation, he does not suddenly draw upon a hidden 'power-pack' of divine

---

[6] See Stephen Davis, 'Is Kenosis Orthodox?' Ch. 5 of this volume, pp. 112–38.

properties that he has been holding in reserve all along, to be pulled out on special occasions. Rather, he draws upon the power of the Father through a life lived in the Spirit. We believe that it is crucially important to notice, in the context of a discussion of kenosis, an obvious but often overlooked fact, namely, that Jesus lived his life in complete and continuous dependence on the Holy Spirit and that he lived a life of perfect submission to the Father.[7]

Interestingly, it is in John's gospel, the book that gives the clearest portrait of Jesus as divine, that this dependence on the Father and Spirit is emphasized most strongly. For example, in John 6:38 Jesus says that he has come not to do his own will but 'to do the will of him who sent me'. In John 7:16 Jesus says that 'my teaching is not my own. It comes from him who sent me.' In John 10:18 Jesus says that he intends to lay down his life because of the 'command I received from my Father'. Jesus performs the mighty miracle of the raising of Lazarus in John 11, but does so by first praying to the Father, thanking the Father that he always hears Jesus. In John 14:10 Jesus tells us that the Father lives in him and that the work Jesus does is really the work the Father is doing through him. And in John 17:5, Jesus shows his dependence upon the Father by his prayer that the Father would glorify him with the glory that Jesus had with the Father 'before the world began', the glory that Jesus has willingly given up to become incarnate as a human being.

So there is no contradiction at all between the supernatural dimension of Jesus' earthly life and a kenotic account of the Incarnation. In fact, the kenotic account highlights the deep unity between Father, Son, and Spirit that endures throughout the Incarnation, and emphasizes the way a truly human Jesus as the Son of God provides a model for us of how human life is to be lived. For we too can live our lives in dependence upon the Father and in union with the Spirit, and thus be united to Christ as well. Even the miracles Jesus performs do not separate him from humanity; in fact, he explicitly tells his disciples that if they have faith they will have access to the same miraculous power he himself has shown: 'I tell you the truth, anyone who has faith in me will do what I have been doing. He will do even

---

[7] See the discussion of 'Spirit-Christology' in Thomas Thompson's 'Nineteenth-Century Kenotic Christology', ch. 4 this volume, p. 106 above.

greater things than these, because I am going to the Father' (John 14:12).

4

There is obviously much more to be said about the Christological issues raised by kenotic theories of the Incarnation. We believe that the challenge of kenotic theory will be helpful even to those who eventually reject a full kenotic theory. For a kenotic account will stimulate those who reject it to think more deeply about the meaning of the Incarnation and do more justice to the full humanity of Jesus.

However, we think that a full-fledged kenotic account offers the best hope of an account of the Incarnation that is genuinely orthodox and yet does complete justice to the biblical portraits of Jesus. No theory of Christology can or should try to dispel the mystery of God's Incarnation, least of all a kenotic account. To the contrary, a kenotic account should increase our wonder and sense of awe that God's love and power could stoop so low for our salvation. A love that so recklessly throws away the privileges and prerogatives of divinity appeals not merely to our intellects but also to our hearts. It offers us a God who is truly Emmanuel—God with us, suffering with us, fully embracing the human condition. All for love.

Bibliography

Achilles Tatius, *The Adventures of Leucippe and Clitophon*, trans. S. Gaselee, Loeb Classical Library (Cambridge, Mass.: Harvard University Press, 1947).

Adams, Marilyn McCord, 'Relations, Inherence and Subsistence: or, Was Ockham a Nestorian in Christology', *Nous*, 16 (1982), 62–75.

—— 'The Metaphysics of the Incarnation in some Fourteenth-Century Franciscans', in *Essays Honoring Allan B. Wolter* (New York: The Franciscan Institute, 1985).

—— *Horrendous Evils and the Goodness of God* (Ithaca, NY: Cornell University Press, 1999).

Adams, Robert, *Finite and Infinite Goods* (Oxford: Oxford University Press, 1999).

Alberigo, Josepho et al. (eds.), *Conciliorum Oecumenicorum Decreta* (Bologna: Istituto per le Scienze Religiose, 1972).

Alston, William, 'Divine–Human Dialogue and the Nature of God', in *Divine Nature and Human Language: Essays in Philosophical Theology* (Ithaca, NY: Cornell University Press, 1989).

—— 'Some Suggestions for Divine Command Theorists', in *Divine Nature and Human Language* (Ithaca, NY: Cornell University Press, 1989).

Anselm of Canterbury, 'Proslogion', in Brian Davies and G. R. Evans (eds.), *The Major Works* (Oxford: Oxford University Press, 1998).

Aquinas, Thomas, *Summa Theologica*, rev. ed., trans. Fathers of the English Dominican Province (New York: Benziger, 1948; rpt. Westminster, MD: Christian Classics, 1981).

Athanasius of Alexandria, 'Four Discourses against the Arians', in Philip Schaff and Henry Wace (eds.), *A Select Library of Nicene and Post-Nicene Fathers of the Christian Church*, 2nd series, 4 (Edinburgh: T. & T. Clark and Grand Rapids, Mich.: Wm. B. Eerdmans, n.d.).

Athanasius, *On the Incarnation*, trans. and ed. by a religious of C.S.M.V. (Crestwood, New York: St. Vladimir's Seminary Press).

Augustine, *St. Augustine, Letters*, iii, trans. Sister Wilfred Parsons, S.N.D., *The Fathers of the Church: A New Translation*, 20 (New York: Fathers of the Church, Inc., 1953).

—— *Concerning the City of God against the Pagans*, trans. Henry Bettenson, intro. John O'Meara (New York: Penguin Books, 1972).

Augustine, St., *Confessions*, trans. Henry Chadwick (Oxford: Oxford University Press, 1998).

Baillie, Donald, *God Was In Christ: An Essay on Incarnation and Atonement* (New York: Charles Scribner's Sons, 1955).

Balthasar, Hans Urs von, 'Why I am Still a Christian', in *Two Say Why*, trans. John Griffiths (Chicago: Franciscan Herald Press, 1973).

—— *First Glance at Adrienne von Speyr*, trans. Antje Lawry and Sister Sergia Englund, O.C.D. (San Francisco: Ignatius Press, 1981).

—— 'The Scapegoat and the Trinity', in *You Crown the Year with Your Goodness: Radio Sermons through the Liturgical Year*, trans. Graham Harrison (San Francisco: Ignatius Press, 1989).

—— *Mysterium Paschale: The Mystery of Easter*, trans. Aidan Nichols, O.P. (Edinburgh: T. & T. Clark; Grand Rapids.: Wm. B. Eerdmans, 1990).

—— *Theo-Drama III: The Dramatis Personae: The Person in Christ*, trans. Graham Harrison (San Francisco: San Francisco Press, 1992).

—— *Theo-Drama IV: The Action*, trans. Graham Harrison (San Francisco: Ignatius Press, 1994).

Barth, Karl, *Church Dogmatics*, eds. G. W. Bromiley and T. F. Torrance, 4 vols. (Edinburgh: T. & T. Clark, 1956–75).

—— *Church Dogmatics*, vol. IV/1: The Doctrine of Reconciliation, eds. G. W. Bromiley and T. F. Torrance, trans. G. W. Bromiley (Edinburgh: T & T Clark, 1956).

Behr, John, *The Nicene Faith: The Formation of Christian Theology*, II/2 (New York: St. Vladimir's Seminary Press, 2004).

Bensow, Oscar, *Die Lehre von der Kenose* (Leipzig: A. Deichert Verlagsbuchhandlung, 1903).

Berkhof, Louis, *Systematic Theology*, 4th edn. (Grand Rapids, Mich.: Wm. B. Eerdmans, 1941).

Bettenson, Henry (ed.), *Documents of the Christian Church* (New York: Oxford University Press, 1960).

—— and Maunder Chris (eds.), *Documents of the Christian Church*, 3rd edn. (Oxford: Oxford University Press, 1999).

Biblia Patristica: index des citations et allusions bibliques dans la littérature patristique (Paris: Editions du Centre national de la recherche scientifique, 1975–).

Bockmuehl, M., ' "The Form of God" (Phil. 2:6): Variations on a Theme of Jewish Mysticism', *Journal of Theological Studies*, 48/1 (1997) 1–23.

Bonhoeffer, Dietrich, *Christ the Center*, trans. John Bowden (New York: Harper & Row, 1966).

Book of Confessions, The (New York: Office of the General Assembly of the Presbyterian Church (USA), 1983).

Bouchet, J.-R., 'Le vocabulaire de l'union et du rapport des natures chez saint Grégoire de Nysse', *Revue Thomiste*, 68 (1968), 533–82.

Bowie, Ewen, 'The Readership of Greek Novels in the Ancient World', in James Tatum (ed.), *The Search for the Ancient Novel* (Baltimore: Johns Hopkins, 1994).

Breidert, Martin, *Die Kenotische Christologie des 19. Jahrhunderts* (Gütersloh: Gütersloher Verlagshaus Mohn, 1977).

Brown, Carleton (ed.), *Religious Lyrics of the Fifteenth Century* (Oxford: Oxford University Press, 1939).

Brown, David, *The Divine Trinity* (London: Duckworth, 1985).

—— 'Trinitarian Personhood and Individuality', in Ronald J. Feenstra and Cornelius Plantinga, Jr. (eds.), *Trinity, Incarnation, and Atonement: Philosophical and Theological Essays*, Library of Religious Philosophy, 1 (Notre Dame, Ind.: University of Notre Dame Press, 1989).

Bruce, A. B., *The Humiliation of Christ*, 5th edn. (Edinburgh: T & T Clark, 1900).

Calvin, John, *Institutes of the Christian Religion*, ed. J. T. McNeill, trans. F. L. Battles, 2 vols. (Philadelphia: Westminster Press, 1960).

Campbell, Joseph, *The Hero with a Thousand Faces* (Princeton: Princeton University Press, 1972).

Carnell, E. J., *The Case for Orthodox Theology* (Philadelphia: Westminster Press, 1959).

Carroll, John T. and Green, Joel B., *The Death of Jesus in Early Christianity* (Peabody, Mass.: Hendrickson, 1995).

Chariton, *Callirhoe*, trans. G. P. Goold, Loeb Classical Library (Cambridge, Mass.: Harvard University Press, 1995).

Chodorow, Nancy, *The Reproduction of Mothering* (Berkeley: University of California Press, 1978).

Coakley, Sarah, '*Kenosis* and Subversion: On the Repression of "Vulnerability" in Christian Feminist Writing', in Daphne Hampson (ed.), *Swallowing a Fishbone? Feminist Theologians Debate Christianity* (London: SPCK, 1996).

—— 'Kenosis: Theological Meanings and Gender Connotations', in John Polkinghorne (ed.), *The Work of Love: Creation as Kenosis* (Grand Rapids, Mich.: Wm. B. Eerdmans, 2001).

—— *Powers and Submissions: Spirituality, Philosophy and Gender* (Oxford: Blackwell Publishers, 2002).

—— 'What Does Chalcedon Solve and What Does it Not? Some Reflections on the Status and Meaning of the Chalcedonian "Definition" ', in Stephen

T. Davis, Daniel Kendall, S.J., and Gerald O'Collins, S.J. (eds.), *The Incarnation: An Interdisciplinary Symposium on the Incarnation of the Son of God* (Oxford: Oxford University Press, 2002).

—— 'Power, gender and "mingling" in Gregory of Nyssa's theory of Christological *kenosis*', unpublished paper given at the Oxford Patristics Conference, August 2003.

—— *Rethinking Gregory of Nyssa* (Oxford: Blackwell, 2003).

Cross, Richard, 'Incarnation, Indwelling, and the Vision of God: Henry of Ghent and some Franciscans', *Franciscan Studies*, 57 (1999) 79–130.

—— *Duns Scotus* (Oxford: Oxford University Press, 1999).

—— 'Perichoresis, Deification, and Christological Predication in John of Damascus', *Medieval Studies*, 62 (2000), 69–124.

—— *The Metaphysics of the Incarnation: Thomas Aquinas to Duns Scotus* (Oxford: Oxford University Press, 2002).

Cyril of Alexandria, 'Cyril of Alexandria's Second Letter to Nestorius', in Richard A. Norris, Jr. (ed. and trans.), *The Christological Controversy* (Philadelphia: Fortress Press, 1980).

—— 'Cyril's Letter to John of Antioch', in Richard A. Norris, Jr. (ed. and trans.), *The Christological Controversy* (Philadelphia: Fortress Press, 1980).

—— 'On the Unity of Christ', in Mark J. Edwards (ed. and trans.), *Ancient Christian Commentary on Scripture, VIII, Galatians, Ephesians, Philippians* (Downers Grove, Ill.: Inter-Varsity Press, 1999).

Daley, S.J., Brian E., *The Hope of the Early Church: A Handbook of Patristic Eschatology* (Cambridge: Cambridge University Press, 1991).

—— 'Divine Transcendence and Human Transformation: Gregory of Nyssa's Anti-Apollinarian Christology', *Studia Patristica*, 32 (1997), 87–95. Reprinted in Sarah Coakley (ed.), *Re-thinking Gregory of Nyssa* (Oxford: Blackwell, 2003).

—— ' "Heavenly Man" and "Eternal Christ": Apollinarius and Gregory of Nyssa on the Personal Identity of the Savior', *Journal of Early Christian Studies*, 10 (2002), 469–88.

Dalmeyda, Georges, *Xénophon d'Éphèse, Les Éphésiaques (ou Le Roman d'Habrocomès et d'Anthia)* (Paris: Société d'Édition 'Les Belles Lettres', 1962).

Davies, W. D., *Paul and Rabbinic Judaism*, 4th edn. (Philadelphia: Fortress Press, 1980).

Davis, Stephen T., *Logic and the Nature of God* (London: Macmillan; Grand Rapids, Mich.: Wm. B. Eerdmans, 1983).

Davis, Stephen T., 'Jesus Christ: Savior or Guru?', in *Encountering Jesus: A Debate on Christology* (Atlanta: John Knox Press, 1988).

—— (ed.), *Encountering Jesus: A Debate on Christology* (Atlanta: John Knox Press, 1988).

—— 'Tradition, Scripture, and Theological Authority', in S. T. Davis (ed.), *Philosophy and Theological Discourse* (London: Macmillan, 1997).

—— *Christain Philosophical Theology* (Oxford: Oxford University Press, 2006).

Dawe, Donald G., *The Form of a Servant: A Historical Analysis of the Kenotic Motif* (Philadelphia: Westminster, 1963).

Driver, G. R. and Hodgson, L., *The Bazaar of Heracleides* (Oxford, Clarendon, 1925).

Dunn, J. D. G., *Christology in the Making* (London: S.C.M. Press, 1980; Philadelphia: Westminster, 1981).

—— *The Theology of Paul the Apostle* (Grand Rapids, Mich.: Wm. B. Eerdmans, 1998).

Edwards, Mark J. (ed. and trans.), *Ancient Christian Commentary on Scripture*, VIII, *Galatians, Ephesians, Philippians* (Downers Grove, Ill.: InterVarsity Press, 1999).

Ellis, George, 'Kenosis as a Unifying Theme for Life and Cosmology', in John Polkinghorne (ed.), *The Work of Love: Creation as Kenosis* (Grand Rapids, Mich.: Wm. B. Eerdmans, 2001).

Engberg-Pedersen, Troels (ed.), *Paul Beyond the Judaism/Hellenism Divide* (Westminster / John Knox Press, 2001).

Evans, C. Stephen, *Kierkegaard's Fragments and Postscript: The Religious Philosophy of Johannes Climacus* (Atlantic Highlands, NJ: Humanities Press, 1983).

—— *Passionate Reason: Making Sense of Kierkegaard's* Philosophical Fragments (Bloomington, Ind.: Indiana University Press, 1992).

—— *The Historical Christ and The Jesus of Faith: The Incarnational Narrative as History* (Oxford: Clarendon Press, 1996).

—— 'The Self-Emptying of Love: Some Thoughts on Kenotic Christology', in Stephen T. Davis, Daniel Kendall, S.J., and Gerald O'Collins, S.J. (eds.), *The Incarnation: An Interdisciplinary Symposium on the Incarnation of the Son of God* (Oxford: Oxford University Press, 2002).

—— 'Tradition, Biblical Interpretation, and Historical Truth', in Craig Bartholomew, C. Stephen Evans, Mary Healy, and Murray Rae (eds.), *'Behind' the Text: History and Biblical Interpretation* (Grand Rapids: Zondervan, 2003; UK: Paternoster, 2004).

Fairbairn, A. M., *The Place of Christ in Modern Theology* (New York: Charles Scribner's Sons, 1916).

Fairweather, Eugene R., 'The "Kenotic" Christology', in F. W. Beare, *A Commentary on the Epistle to the Philippians* (New York: Harper & Row, 1959).

Fee, G. D., 'Philippians 2:5–11: Hymn or Exalted Prose?', *Bulletin for Biblical Research*, 2 (1992), 29–46.

—— *Paul's Letter to the Philippians*, New International Commentary on the New Testament (Grand Rapids, Mich.: Wm. B. Eerdmans, 1995).

Feenstra, Ronald J., 'Pre-existence, Kenosis, and the Incarnation of Jesus Christ', Ph.D thesis (Yale University, 1984).

—— 'Reconsidering Kenotic Christology', in Ronald J. Feenstra and Cornelius Plantinga, Jr. (eds.), *Trinity, Incarnation, and Atonement: Philosophical and Theological Essays*, Library of Religious Philosophy, 1 (Notre Dame, Ind.: University of Notre Dame Press, 1989).

—— and Plantinga, Cornelius, Jr. (eds.), *Trinity, Incarnation, and Atonement: Philosophical and Theological Essays*, Library of Religious Philosophy, 1 (Notre Dame, Ind.: University of Notre Dame Press, 1989).

Fisk, Bruce N., 'Offering Isaac Again and Again: Pseudo-Philo's Use of the Aqedah as Intertext', *Catholic Biblical Quarterly*, 62 (2000) 481–507.

—— 'Do You Not Remember? Scripture, Story and Exegesis in the Rewritten Bible of Pseudo-Philo', *Journal for the Study of the Pseudepigraphia*, Sup. 37 (Sheffield, 2001).

Flint, Thomas P., 'The Possibilities of Incarnation: Some Radical Molinist Suggestions', *Religious Studies*, 37 (2001), 307–20.

Forsyth, P. T., *The Person and Place of Jesus Christ, The Congregational Union Lecture for 1909* (Philadelphia: Westminster Press, 1910).

Fowl, Stephen E., 'The Story of Christ in the Ethics of Paul', *Journal for the Study of the New Testament*, Sup. 36 (Sheffield, 1990).

—— 'What Is A Hymn?', *Journal for the Study of the New Testament*, Sup. 36 (Sheffield, 1990).

Frascati-Lochhead, Marta, *Kenosis and Feminist Theology: The Challenge of Gianni Vattimo* (Albany, NY: State University of New York Press, 1998).

Freddoso, Alfred J., 'Human Nature, Potency and the Incarnation', *Faith and Philosophy*, 3 (1986), 27–53.

Frye, Northop, *The Great Code: The Bible and Literature* (San Diego: Harcourt Brace, 1983).

Geach, Peter T., *Providence and Evil*, The Stanton Lectures, 1971–72 (Cambridge: Cambridge University Press, 1977).

Geiselmann, George R., 'Scripture, Tradition, and the Church: An Ecumenical Problem', in D. Callahan, H. Oberman, and D. O'Hanlon, S.J. (eds.), *Christianity Divided* (New York: Sheed & Ward, 1961).

Gore, Charles, *Dissertations on Subjects Connected with the Incarnation*, 2nd edn. (London: John Murray, 1907).

Gregory of Nyssa, 'Address on Religious Instruction', in E. R. Hardy (ed.), *Christology of the Later Fathers* (Philadelphia, Westminster Press, 1954).

—— *Gregorii Nysseni Opera* (Leiden, 1958–).

Grillmeier, Aloys, *Christ in Christian Tradition, 1: From the Apostolic Age to Chalcedon (451)*, 2nd edn., trans. John Bowden (Atlanta: John Knox, 1975).

Gundry, Robert H., 'Style and Substance in "The Myth of God Incarnate" according to Philippians 2:6–11', in S. E. Porter, P. Joyce, and D. E. Orton (eds.), *Crossing the Boundaries: Essays in Biblical Interpretation in Honour of Michael D. Goulder* (Leiden: Brill, 1994).

Hägg, T., *The Novel in Antiquity* (Berkeley: University of California Press, 1983).

Hall, Francis J., *The Kenotic Theory* (New York: Longmans, Green and Co., 1898).

Hampson, Daphne, 'On Autonomy and Heteronomy', in Daphne Hampson (ed.), *Swallowing a Fishbone? Feminist Theologians Debate Christianity* (London: SPCK, 1996).

Hawthorne, Gerald F., *Philippians*, WBC, 43 (Waco: Word, 1983).

Hebblethwaite, Brian, *The Incarnation: Collected Essays in Christology* (Cambridge: Cambridge University Press, 1987).

Heiserman, C. E. A., *The Novel Before the Novel* (Chicago: University of Chicago Press, 1977).

Hengel, Martin, *Crucifixion* (Philadelphia: Fortress Press, 1977).

Henry, P., 'Kénose', in *Dictionnaire de la Bible Supplément* (Paris: Librairie Letouzey et Ané, 1957).

Heyer, C. J. den, *Paul: A Man of Two Worlds*, trans. J. Bowden (Philadelphia: Trinity Press International, 2000).

Hick, John, 'Jesus and the World Religions', in John Hick (ed.), *The Myth of God Incarnate* (London: S.C.M. Press; Philadelphia: Westminster, 1977).

—— *The Metaphor of God Incarnate: Christology in a Pluralistic Age* (Louisville: Westminster John Knox Press, 1993).

Hock, Ronald F., 'The Greek Novel', in David E. Aune (ed.), *Greco-Roman Literature and the New Testament*, Society of Biblical Literature Sources for Biblical Study, 21 (Atlanta: Scholars Press, 1988).

—— Chance, J. Bradley, and Perkins, Judith (eds.), *Ancient Fiction and Early Christian Narrative* (Atlanta: Scholars Press, 1998).

Hooker, M., 'Philippians 2:6–11', in E. E. Ellis and E. Grässer (eds.), *Jesus und Paulus* (Göttingen: Vandenhoek und Ruprecht, 1975).

Hoover, Roy W., 'The Harpagmos Enigma: A Philological Solution', *Harvard Theological Review*, 64 (1971), 95–119.

Horsley, R. A. and Silberman, N. A., *The Message and the Kingdom* (Minneapolis: Fortress Press, 1997).

Hurst, L., 'Re-enter the Pre-existent Christ in Philippians 2:5–11?', *New Testament Studies*, 32 (1986).

Ignatius of Antioch, *Epistle to the Magnesians*, chapter 9, in Andrew Louth (ed. and rev. trans.), *Early Christian Writings*, trans. by Maxwell Staniforth (New York: Penguin Books, 1987).

James, Graham, 'The Enduring Appeal of a Kenotic Christology', *Theology*, 86 (1983), 7–14.

Jeffers, James S., *The Greco-Roman World of the New Testament Era* (Downers Grove, Ill.: Inter-Varsity Press, 1999).

Jeremias, J., 'Zur Gedankenführung in den paulinischen Briefen', in J. N. Sevenster and W. C. van Unnik (eds.), *Studia Paulina in Honoerem J. de Zwaan* (Haarlem, 1953).

Jones, Serene, *Feminist Theory and Christian Theology: Cartographies of Grace* (Minneapolis: Fortress Press, 2000).

Käsemann, Ernst, *The Testament of Jesus: A Study of the Gospel of John in the Light of Chapter 17*, 2nd edn., trans. Gerhard Krodel (Philadelphia: Fortress Press, 1968).

Kasper, Walter, *The God of Jesus Christ*, trans. Matthew J. O'Connell (New York: Crossroad, 1991).

Kierkegaard, Søren, *Kierkegaard's Journals and Papers*, ii, ed. and trans. Howard V. Hong and Edna H. Hong (Bloomington, Ind.: Indiana University Press, 1970).

—— *Philosophical Fragments*, ed. and trans. Howard V. Hong and Edna H. Hong (Princeton: Princeton University Press, 1985).

La Touche, E. Digges, *The Person of Christ in Modern Thought*, Donnellan Lectures, 1911–12 (London: James Clarke & Co., 1912).

Lee, Chana Kai, *For Freedom's Sake: The Life of Fanny Lou Hamer* (Urbana, Ill.: University of Illinois Press, 1999).

Leftow, Brian 'Anti Social Trinitarianism', in Stephen T. Davis, Daniel Kendall, S.J., and Gerald O'Collins, S.J. (eds.), *The Trinity: An Interdisciplinary Symposium on the Trinity* (Oxford: Oxford University Press, 1999).

Leo I, 'Pope Leo I's Letter to Flavian of Constantinople', in Richard A. Norris, Jr. (ed. and trans.), *The Christological Controversy* (Philadelphia: Fortress Press, 1980).

Lewis, Alan E., *Between Cross and Resurrection: A Theology of Holy Saturday*, foreword by John Alsup (Grand Rapids, Mich.: Wm. B. Eerdmans, 2001).

Lightfoot, J. B., *St. Paul's Epistle to the Philippians* (1868; 1913; repr., Zondervan, 1953).

Lohmeyer, Ernst, *Kyrios Jesus: Eine Untersuchung zu Phil. 2:5–11* (Heidelberg, 1961).

Loofs, Friedrich (ed.), *Nestoriana: die Fragmente des Nestorius* (Halle: Niemayer, 1905).

—— 'Kenosis', in James Hastings (ed.), *Encyclopedia of Religion and Ethics*, vii (Edinburgh: T. & T. Clark, 1914).

McCabe, Herbert, 'The Myth of God Incarnate', in *God Matters* (London: G. Chapman, 1987).

—— *God Matters* (London: G. Chapman, 1987).

McClendon, Jr., J. W., *Systematic Theology: Doctrine* (Nashville: Abingdon, 1994).

MacCulloch, D.D., J. A., *The Harrowing of Hell: A Comparative Study of an Early Christian Doctrine* (Edinburgh: T. & T. Clark, 1930).

MacDonald, Dennis R., *The Homeric Epics and the Gospel of Mark* (New Haven: Yale, 2000).

—— (ed.), *Mimesis and Intertextuality in Antiquity and Christianity* (Harrisburg, Penn.: Trinity Press International, 2001).

McElrath, Damian (ed.), *Franciscan Christology* (New York: The Franciscan Institute, 1980).

Mackie, J. L., 'Evil and Omnipotence', *Mind*, 64 (1955), 200–12. Repr. in William L. Rowe and William J. Wainwright (eds.), *Philosophy of Religion: Selected Readings*, 2nd edn. (New York: Harcourt Brace Jovanovich, 1989).

Mackintosh, H. R., *The Person of Jesus Christ* (London: Student Christian Movement, 1912; rpt. 1925).

—— *The Doctrine of the Person of Jesus Christ*, 2nd edn. (Edinburgh: T & T Clark, 1913; repr. 1978).

McNeill, William H., 'The Greatest Might-Have-Been of All', *New York Review of Books*, 46/14 (23 September 1999), 62–4.

Macquarrie, John, 'The Pre-existence of Jesus Christ', *Expository Times*, 77 (1966), 199–202.

—— 'Kenoticism Reconsidered', *Theology*, 77 (1974), 115–24.

Malina, B. J. and Neyrey, J. H., *Portraits of Paul: An Archaeology of Ancient Personality* (Louisville: Westminster John Knox, 1996).

Martensen, H. L., *Christian Dogmatics: A Compendium of the Doctrines of Christianity* (Edinburgh: T. & T. Clark, 1898).

Martin, Dale, *Slavery as Salvation: The Metaphor of Slavery in Pauline Christianity* (New Haven: Yale University Press, 1990).

Martin, Ralph P., *Carmen Christi: Philippians 2:5–11 in Recent Interpretation and in the Setting of Early Christian Worship* (Grand Rapids, Mich.: Wm. B. Eerdmans, 1983).

—— *A Hymn of Christ: Philippians 2:5–11 in Recent Interpretation & in the Setting of Early Christian Worship* (Downers Grove, Ill.: Inter-Varsity, 1997).

—— and Dodd, Brian (eds.), *Where Christology Began: Essays on Philippians 2* (Louisville: Westminster John Knox Press, 1998).

Meredith, Anthony, *Gregory of Nyssa* (London: Routledge, 1999).

Miller, Patrick D., *Deuteronomy*, Interpretation Series (Louisville: John Knox, 1990).

Moltmann, Jürgen, *The Way of Jesus Christ: Christology in Messianic Dimensions*, trans. Margaret Kohl (New York: HarperCollins, 1990).

—— 'God's Kenosis in the Creation and Consummation of the World', in John Polkinghorne (ed.), *The Work of Love: Creation as Kenosis* (Grand Rapids, Mich.: Wm. B. Eerdmans, 2001).

Morris, Thomas V., 'Divinity, Humanity, and Death', *Religious Studies*, 19 (1983), 457.

—— *The Logic of God Incarnate* (Ithaca, NY: Cornell University Press, 1986).

—— 'The Metaphysics of God Incarnate', in Ronald J. Feenstra and Cornelius Plantinga, Jr. (eds.), *Trinity, Incarnation, and Atonement: Philosophical and Theological Essays*, Library of Religious Philosophy, 1 (Notre Dame, Ind.: University of Notre Dame Press, 1989).

Moule, C. F. D., 'Further Reflections on Philippians 2:5–11', in W. W. Gasque and R. P. Martin (eds.), *Apostolic History and the Gospel* (Grand Rapids, Mich.: Wm. B. Eerdmans, 1970).

—— 'The Manhood of Jesus in the New Testament', in S. W. Sykes and J. P. Clayton (eds.), *Christ, Faith, and History* (Cambridge: Cambridge University Press, 1972), 95–110.

Moule, H. C. G., *Studies in Philippians* (Cambridge: Cambridge University Press, 1899; repr. Kregel, 1977).

Muller, Richard A., *Dictionary of Latin and Greek Theological Terms: Drawn Principally from Protestant Scholastic Theology* (Grand Rapids, Mich.: Baker Books, 1985).

Neill, S. and Wright, N. T., *The Interpretation of the New Testament: 1861–1986*, 2nd edn. (New York: Oxford, 1988).

Nestorius, 'Nestorius's First Sermon Against the *Theotokos*', in Richard A. Norris, Jr. (ed. and trans.), *The Christological Controversy* (Philadelphia: Fortress Press, 1980).

—— 'Nestorius's Second Letter to Cyril', in Richard A. Norris, Jr. (ed. and trans.), *The Christological Controversy* (Philadelphia: Fortress Press, 1980).

Neuner, J. and Dupuis, J. (eds.), *The Christian Faith in the Doctrinal Documents of the Catholic Church* (Dublin: Mercier Press, 1973).

Nietzsche, Friedrich *The Birth of Tragedy*, trans. Francis Golffing (Garden City, New York: Doubleday, 1956).

Norris, R. A., 'Christological Models in Cyril of Alexandria', *Studia Patristica*, 13 (1975), 255–68.

—— 'Chalcedon Revisited: A Historical and Theological Reflection', in B. Nassif (ed.), *New Perspectives on Historical Theology* (Grand Rapids, Mich.: Wm. B. Eerdmans, 1996).

Norris, Jr., Richard A. 'The Council of Chalcedon's "Definition of the Faith" ', in Richard A. Norris, Jr. (ed. and trans.), *The Christological Controversy* (Philadelphia: Fortress Press, 1980).

O'Brien, Peter T., *The Epistle to the Philippians*, New International Greek Testament Commentary (Grand Rapids, Mich.: Eerdmans, 1991).

O'Collins, S.J., Gerald, *Interpreting Jesus* (London: Geoffrey Chapman, 1983).

O'Donovan, Oliver, *Resurrection and Moral Order: An Outline for Evangelical Ethics*, 2nd edn. (Grand Rapids, Mich.: Wm. B. Eerdmans, 1994).

O'Hanlon, S.J., Gerard, *The Immutability of God in the Theology of Hans Urs von Balthasar* (Cambridge: Cambridge University Press, 1990).

Pannenberg, Wolfhart, *Jesus—God and Man*, 2nd edn., trans. Lewis L. Wilkins and Duane A. Priebe (Philadelphia: Westminster Press, 1977).

—— *Systematic Theology*, ii, trans. Geoffrey W. Bromiley (Grand Rapids, Mich.: Wm. B. Eerdmans, 1991).

Pacal, Blaise, *Pensées*, trans. Honor Levi (Oxford: Oxford University Press, 1995).

Peacocke, Arthur, 'The Cost of New Life', in John Polkinghorne (ed.), *The Work of Love: Creation as Kenosis* (Grand Rapids, Mich.: Wm. B. Eerdmans, 2001).

Plantinga, Alvin, 'Advice to Christian Philosophers', *Faith and Philosophy*, 1 (1984), 253–71.

Plantinga, Jr., Cornelius, 'Social Trinity and Tritheism', in Ronald J. Feenstra and Cornelius Plantinga, Jr. (eds.), *Trinity, Incarnation, and Atonement:*

Philosophical and Theological Essays, Library of Religious Philosophy, 1 (Notre Dame, Ind.: University of Notre Dame Press, 1989).

Polkinghorne, John (ed.), *The Work of Love: Creation as Kenosis* (Grand Rapids, Mich.: Wm. B. Eerdmans, 2001).

Rahner, Karl, *Theological Investigations*, I (Baltimore: Helikon Press, 1961).

—— 'Scripture and Tradition', in K. Rahner (ed.), *Encyclopedia of Theology: The Concise Sacramentum Mundi* (New York: The Seabury Press, 1975).

—— *Foundations of Christian Faith* (New York: Crossroads Publishing Co., 1984).

Ramsey, Arthur Michael, *From Gore to Temple: The Development of Anglican Theology between Lux Mundi and the Second World War, 1889–1939* (London: Longmans, 1960).

Reardon, Bryan P. (ed.), *Collected Ancient Greek Novels* (Berkeley: University of California Press, 1989).

Richard, Lucien J., *A Kenotic Christology: in The Humanity of Jesus the Christ, the Compassion of Our God* (Washington, DC: University Press of America, 1982).

—— *Christ: The Self-Emptying of God* (Mahwah, NJ: Paulist Press, 1997).

Ricoeur, Paul, *The Symbolism of Evil*, trans. Emerson Buchanan (Boston: Beacon Press, 1969).

Rolston, III, Holmes, 'Kenosis and Nature', in John Polkinghorne (ed.), *The Work of Love: Creation as Kenosis* (Grand Rapids, Mich.: Wm. B. Eerdmans, 2001).

Rowe, William L., and Wainwright, William J. (eds.), *Philosophy of Religion: Selected Readings*, 2nd edn. (New York: Harcourt Brace Jovanovich, 1989).

Saiving, Valerie (Goldstein), 'The Human Situation: A Feminine View', *Journal of Religion*, 40 (1960), 100–12.

Sanders, John, *The God Who Risks: A Theology of Providence* (Downers Grove, Ill.: Inter-Varsity Press, 1998).

Schmeling, Gareth, *Xenophon of Ephesus* (Boston: Twayne, 1980).

Scotus, John Duns, *Opera Omnia*, ed. Luke Wadding (Lyons, 1639).

—— *The Quodlibetal Questions*, trans. Felix Alluntis, O.F.M., and Allan B. Wolter, O.F.M. (Washington, DC: The Catholic University of America Press, 1975).

Segal, A. F., *Paul the Convert: The Apostolate and Apostasy of Saul the Pharisee* (New Haven: Yale, 1990).

Simar, T. H., *Lehrbuch der Dogmatik*, i (Freiburg im Breisgau: Herder, 1899).

Sloyan, Gerard S., *The Crucifixion of Jesus: History, Myth, Faith* (Minneapolis: Fortress Press, 1995).

Springsted, Eric, *Simone Weil and the Suffering of Love* (Cambridge, Mass.: Cowley Publications, 1986).

Stead, Christopher, *Divine Substance* (Oxford: Oxford University Press, 1977).

—— 'The Concept of Divine Substance' in *Substance and Illusion in the Christian Fathers* (London: Variorum Reprints, 1985).

—— 'The Significance of the Homoousios' in *Substance and Illusion in the Christian Fathers* (London: Variorum Reprints, 1985).

Steenburg, David, 'The Case against the Synonymity of *morphe* and *eikon*', *Journal for the Study of the New Testament*, 34 (1988), 77–86.

Stephens, Susan A., 'Who Read Ancient Novels?', in James Tatum (ed.), *The Search for the Ancient Novel* (Baltimore: Johns Hopkins, 1994).

Strimple, R., 'Philippians 2:5–11 in Recent Studies: Some Exegetical Conclusions' *WTJ* 41 (1978/79).

Swinburne, Richard, *The Coherence of Theism* (Oxford: Oxford University Press, 1977).

—— *The Christian God* (Oxford: Clarendon Press, 1994).

Tanner, Kathryn, *Jesus, Humanity and the Trinity* (Minneapolis: Fortress Press, 2001).

Tavard, George H., *Holy Writ or Holy Church* (New York: Harper, 1959).

Tertullian, 'On the Flesh of Christ', in Alexander Roberts and James Donaldson (eds.), *The Ante-Nicene Fathers*, iii (Edinburgh: T. & T. Clark; Grand Rapids, Mich.: Wm. B. Eerdmans, n.d.).

Thomasius, Gottfried, 'The Person of the Mediator', in Claude Welch (ed. and trans.), *God and Incarnation in Mid-Nineteenth Century German Theology* (New York: Oxford University Press, 1965).

Thompson, Marianne Meye, *The Humanity of Jesus in the Fourth Gospel* (Philadelphia: Fortress Press, 1988).

Tixeront, Joseph, *Histoire des dogmes dans l'antiquité chrétienne*, II (Paris: J. Gabalda, 1912).

Torrance, Thomas F., 'The Goodness and Dignity of Man in the Christian Tradition', *Modern Theology*, 4 (1988), 309–22.

Tucker, Karen Westerfield, *American Methodist Worship* (New York: Oxford University Press, 2001).

Vanstone, W. H., *Love's Endeavour, Love's Expense: The Response of Being to the Love of God* (London: Darton, Longman, & Todd, 1977).

Vincent, M. R., *Epistles to the Philippians and Philemon*, ICC (Edinburgh: T. & T. Clark, 1897).

Vogler, Christopher, *The Writer's Journey: Mythic Structure for Storytellers & Screenwriters* (Studio City, CA: Michael Wiese Productions, 1992).

Weil, Simone, *Gravity and Grace* (Lincoln: University of Nebraska Press, 1952).

Weinandy, Thomas G., *Does God Suffer?* (Edinburgh: T. & T. Clark, 2000).

Welch, Claude (ed. and trans.), *God and Incarnation in Mid-Nineteenth Century German Theology* (New York: Oxford University Press, 1965).

—— *Protestant Thought in the Nineteenth Century*, i (New Haven: Yale University Press, 1972).

Wesley, John, *Explanatory Notes on the New Testament* (London: Epworth Press, 1976).

Westcott, B. F., *The Gospel According to St. John: The Authorised Version With Introduction and Notes*, re-issued with a new introduction by A. Fox (London: James Clarke and Co., 1958 (1882)).

Weston, Frank, *The One Christ: An Enquiry into the Manner of the Incarnation* (London: Longmans Green, 1907; rev. edn. 1914).

Wiles, M. F., 'Does Christology Rest on a Mistake?' in S. W. Sykes and J. P. Clayton (eds.), *Christ, Faith and History* (Cambridge: Cambridge University Press, 1973).

Willis, David, *Calvin's Catholic Christology: The Function of the So-called Extra Calvinisticum in Calvin's Theology* (Leiden: E. J. Brill, 1966).

Wright, N. T., '*Harpagmos* and the Meaning of Philippians 2:5–11' *Journal of Theological Studies*, 37 (1986), 321–352.

—— *The Climax of the Covenant: Christ and the Law in Pauline Theology* (Edinburgh: T. & T. Clark, 1991; Minneapolis: Fortress Press, 1992).

—— *Jesus and the Victory of God* (London: SPCK, 1996).

—— 'Jesus and God' in *The Challenge of Jesus: Rediscovering who Jesus Was and Is* (Downers Grove, Ill.: Inter-Varsity Press, 1999).

—— 'The Divinity of Jesus', in Marcus J. Borg and N. T. Wright, *The Meaning of Jesus: Two Visions* (San Francisco: HarperCollins, 1999).

—— 'The Truth of the Gospel and Christian Living' in Marcus J. Borg and N. T. Wright, *The Meaning of Jesus: Two Visions* (San Francisco: Harper-Collins, 1999).

—— 'Jesus' Self-Understanding', in Stephen T. Davis, Daniel Kendall, S.J., and Gerald O'Collins, S.J. (eds.), *The Incarnation: An Interdisciplinary Symposium on the Incarnation of the Son of God* (Oxford: Oxford University Press, 2002).

Wykstra, Stephen, 'Rowe's Noseeum Argument from Evil', in Daniel Howard-Snyder (ed.), *The Evidential Problem of Evil* (Bloomington, Ind.: Indiana University Press, 1996).

Young, Frances, *From Nicaea to Chalcedon* (London: S.C.M., 1983).

Zizioulas, John, *Being As Communion: Studies in Personhood and the Church* (Crestwood, NY: St. Vladimir's Seminary Press, 1985).

Index

About the Calvin Center for Christian Scholarship

The Calvin Center for Christian Scholarship exists to coordinate and provide leadership for the project of advancing and improving intentional Christian scholarship at Calvin College. "Intentional Christian scholarship" means research and reflection that deliberately bring the resources of the Christian faith to bear upon a subject, whether by scrutinizing the fundamental premises of a theory or a field; by elaborating the ethical consequences of social structures, research methods, or ways of thought; by creating imaginative or artistic works; or by helping Christians understand their world better through the critical appropriation of new work being done in the academy. The Center supports the work of Calvin College faculty as well as cooperative projects that engage the resources of scholars and agencies from many traditions within global Christianity.

For more information about CCCS visit
www.calvin.edu/admin/cccs/

Lightning Source UK Ltd.
Milton Keynes UK
UKOW04f2228220118
316640UK00001B/33/P